FORMULA+FETISH

MARK WOODS

■■■ black dog press

Excerpt from Lieutenant Commander Oscar Smith

THE FETISH OF FORMULAS

United States Naval Institute Proceeding, Vol. 50, no. 261, November 1924

In the Navy of the present day, are we not making a fetish of formulas? We are developing a rule for this and a method for that, reducing everything to a standard so that knowledge is easy to gain, inspections easily made, and administration easily accomplished …

… Read the story of the opposition by the military minds to tanks, smoke screens and every new form of warfare developed by modern science, and the fact that such a mental condition develops is unmistakable. It developed in the British. It controlled the Germans. It almost ruined the French. Fortunately, we were not put to the test.

But it does appear that our service is liable to drift into this condition during these years of peace. Formulas and instructions are devised with the intent and purpose of making things easy for us. It seems proper for us to stop and consider the fact that men do not advance, and nations do not progress, when things are made easy. What we need is an incentive to drive us ahead, with rewards for every success. Let us not stop where we are, nor be content with whatever we have gained in the past; let us not remain bound by methods which may be improved; let us not make a fetish of formulas, but, taking full advantage of our present position, let us have a period of mental development and individual effort. Withdraw the threat that one mistake, no matter how small, will ruin our careers; that he who makes no effort but follows the rules will become an admiral, while he who tries and makes a partial failure, is ruined for life. The Wrights did not conquer the air on a series of successes but by overcoming repeated failures. Langley's failure did more for the success of aviation than had he never tried. We cannot deliver our full abilities nor properly serve our country if we are restricted too closely by rules and methods; therefore, let us have a period of freedom, that our minds may expand and develop to their maximum, for the sake of the service and the glory of our country ….

CONTENTS

MARK WOODS: QUEERING CATEGORIES

Paul Carey-Kent

Mark Woods makes two main bodies of work. We might call them "objects" and "staged self-portraits". When two things come together, one is bound to ask how they relate. Let us consider them in turn and see if we can solve that puzzle.

Woods learned his making in the rare combination of boat-building and jewellery design. Those skills feed into the construction of objects that land somewhere between fashion, fetish and cabinet of curiosity, while remaining readable as sculpture. In short, you are radically unsure of what you are looking at. Take *Lambing Time*, 2019. A baby's bottle comes to mind, but who makes those out of leather? And there's a nipple on both ends – is this just a reorientation of the expected two breasts, or are we inciting competition between twins sucking from the same source? Then there's the addition of silver attachments which one would be tempted to call nipple rings, were they closer to the putative feeding points. They provide a fetishistic element, in tune with how the pink colouration suggests flesh – although none of the pinks are quite the right pink for anybody that I've seen; they are pseudo-flesh colours. Woods calls it "millennial pink", saying it was widely used in late '90s fashion, and adds that he enjoys playing with its gender associations, often contrasting it with black. The curve and scale of *Lambing Time* is closer to a banana, though the title brings in sheep farming, suggesting that it might be lambs that are supplied with the milk. Really, though, the object isn't any more plausible as farm equipment than as a purse or a sex toy. One can imagine a Surrealist dreaming of one of these, then putting it in a painting. As in such paintings, we're drawn in to wondering what's what – but nothing quite adds up.

There's a more directly bodily feel to *Pierced Heart of Broken Nails*, 2014. That is real human hair, in a somewhat pubic disposition, even if the fingernails screech their fakeness. At least it's not the heart that's broken – or is it? Some sort of displacement seems likely. Among the "findings" cited in the list of materials is what looks disturbingly like an isolated tongue. Actually, says Woods, it's "micro crystalline wax impregnated bouclé fabric",[1] which takes us into another dimension of material precision fetish. Bouclé, derived from the French word meaning "curled" or "ringed", is a fabric made from looped fibres of a yarn.

The strangeness is only increased in recent productions by the multiplication of the forms. *Cocktail Strap-on* goes some of the way there, appearing like a single object, but modular. Evidently it's strapped onto a cocktail table, standing in expectation of us mixing a Wet Pussy (peach schnapps, vodka, cranberry juice and a dash of lime juice) and a Slow Comfortable Screw (sloe gin, orange juice, vodka, and Southern Comfort) followed by a Screaming Orgasm (vodka, Irish cream, Kahlúa). All of which fits the title's blatant suggestion, if not of tales of the cock, then those of a cock-substitute.

Lamb shank Bolt-on goes a little further in introducing multiplicity, with the implication of some sort of industrial process. Not only are these things dysfunctional, lots of them are being made. Woods may have surprised himself with this move, given that he recalls – as a jeweller – that he hated making earrings because you need to make "two of the damn things".[2] The multiples in *Bolt-down Fetish* come with elaborate found settings, as much display mechanisms as plinths. Those curved spikes, by the way, are straight until Woods "puts the kink on".[3] Are these organisms reproducing in some way? Evolution throws up some strange items, but it is hard to see what goals would be achieved by these particular mutations. Or are they manufactured? Again, the difficulty of

LAMBING TIME, 2019
Rubber, leather, fabric, metal findings.
200 x 80mm

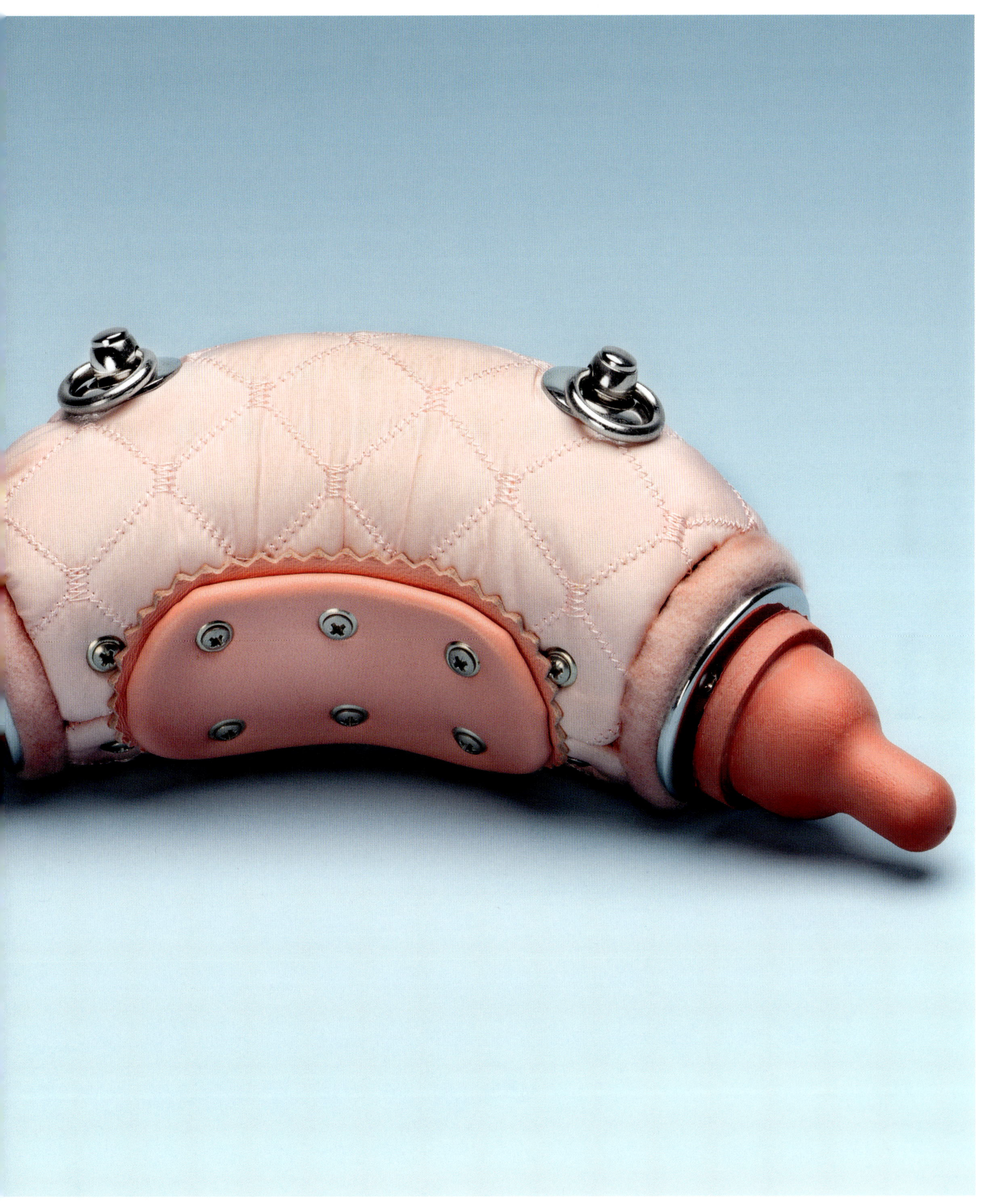

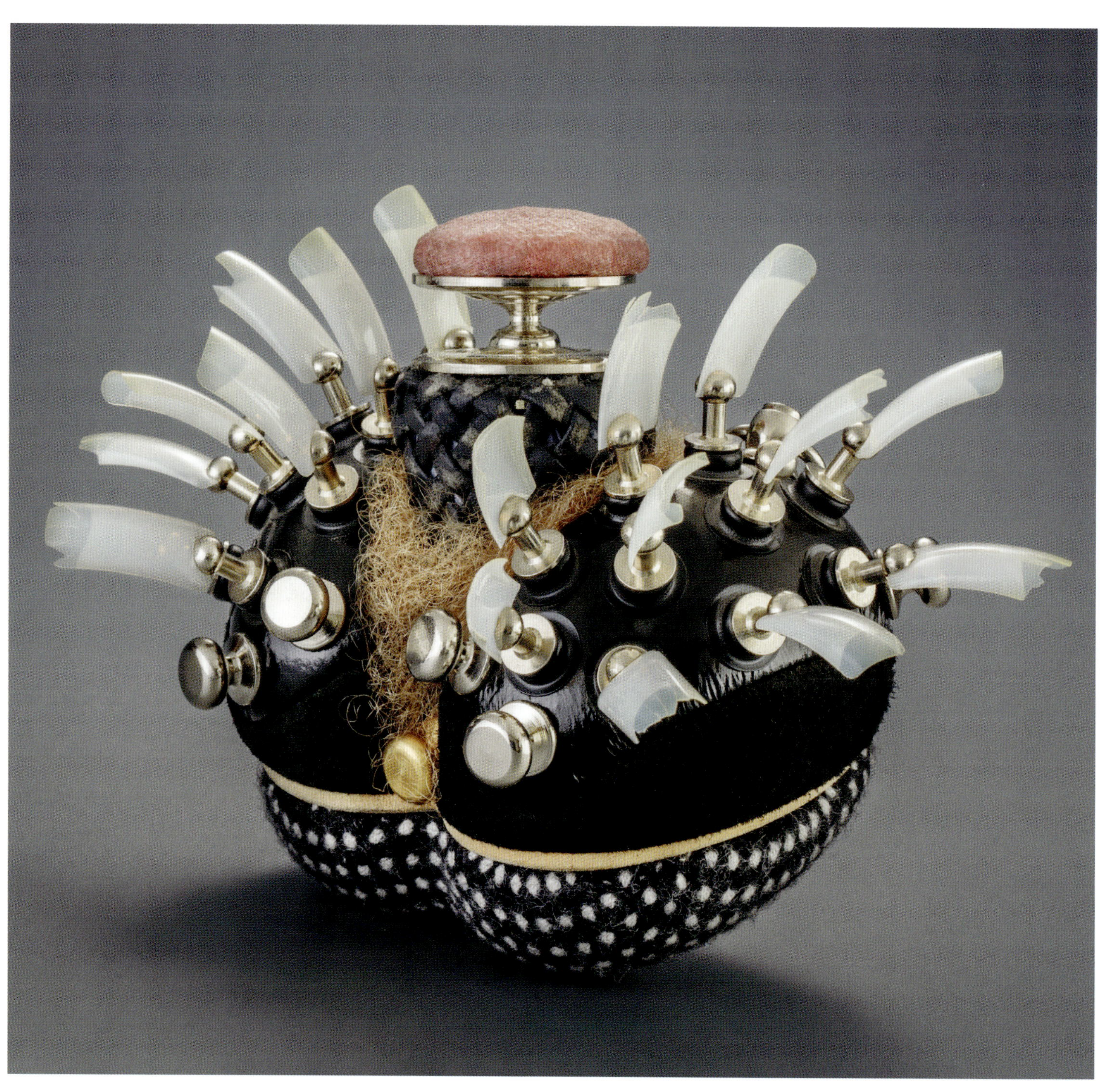

PIERCED HEART OF
BROKEN NAILS, 2014
Leather, fabric, wax
impregnated bouclé,
false fingernails,
human hair.
130 x 120 x 100mm

COCKTAIL STRAP-ON,
2023
Leather, fabric,
wax, metal findings,
cushion.
750 x 350 x 750mm

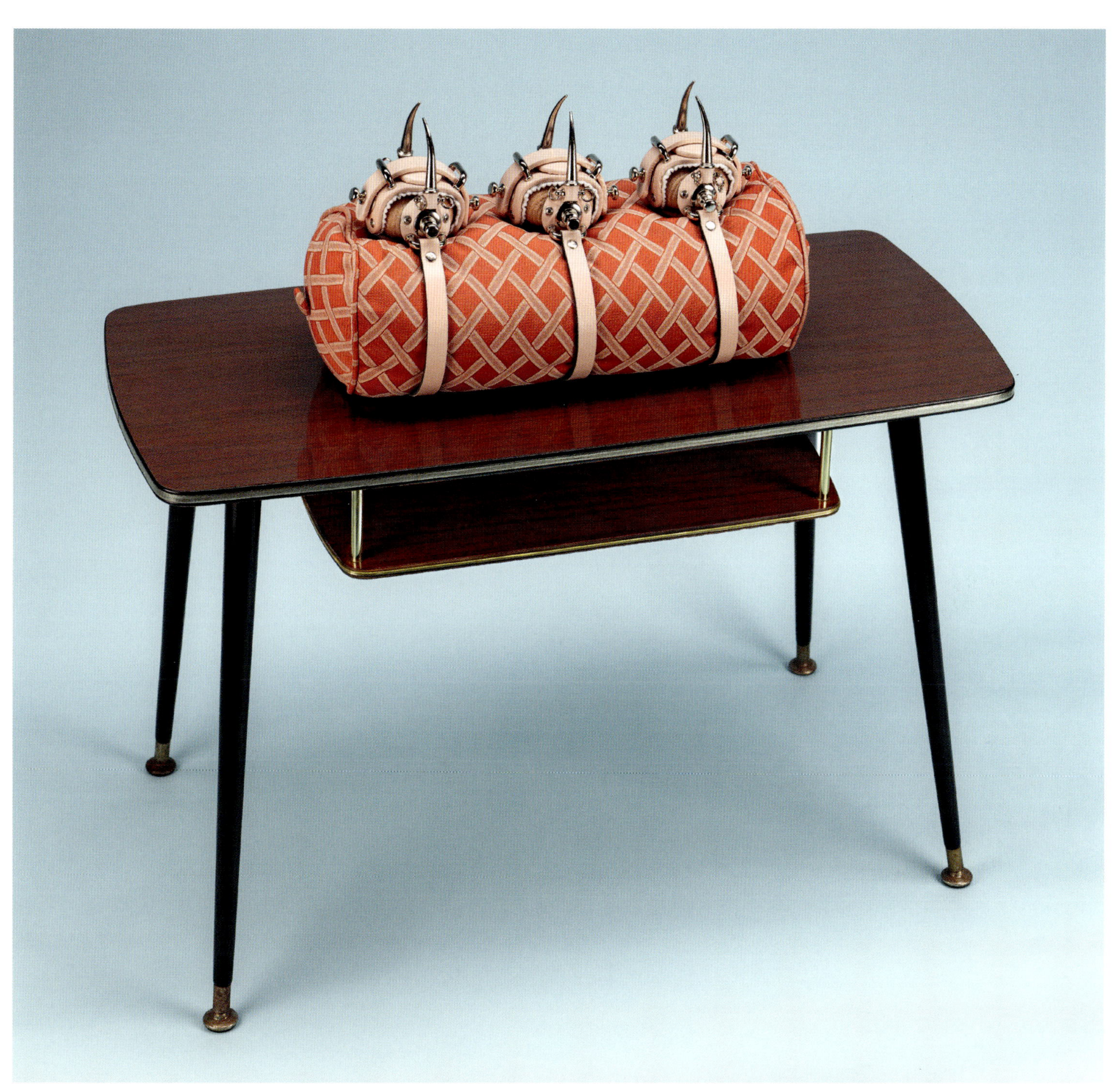

9

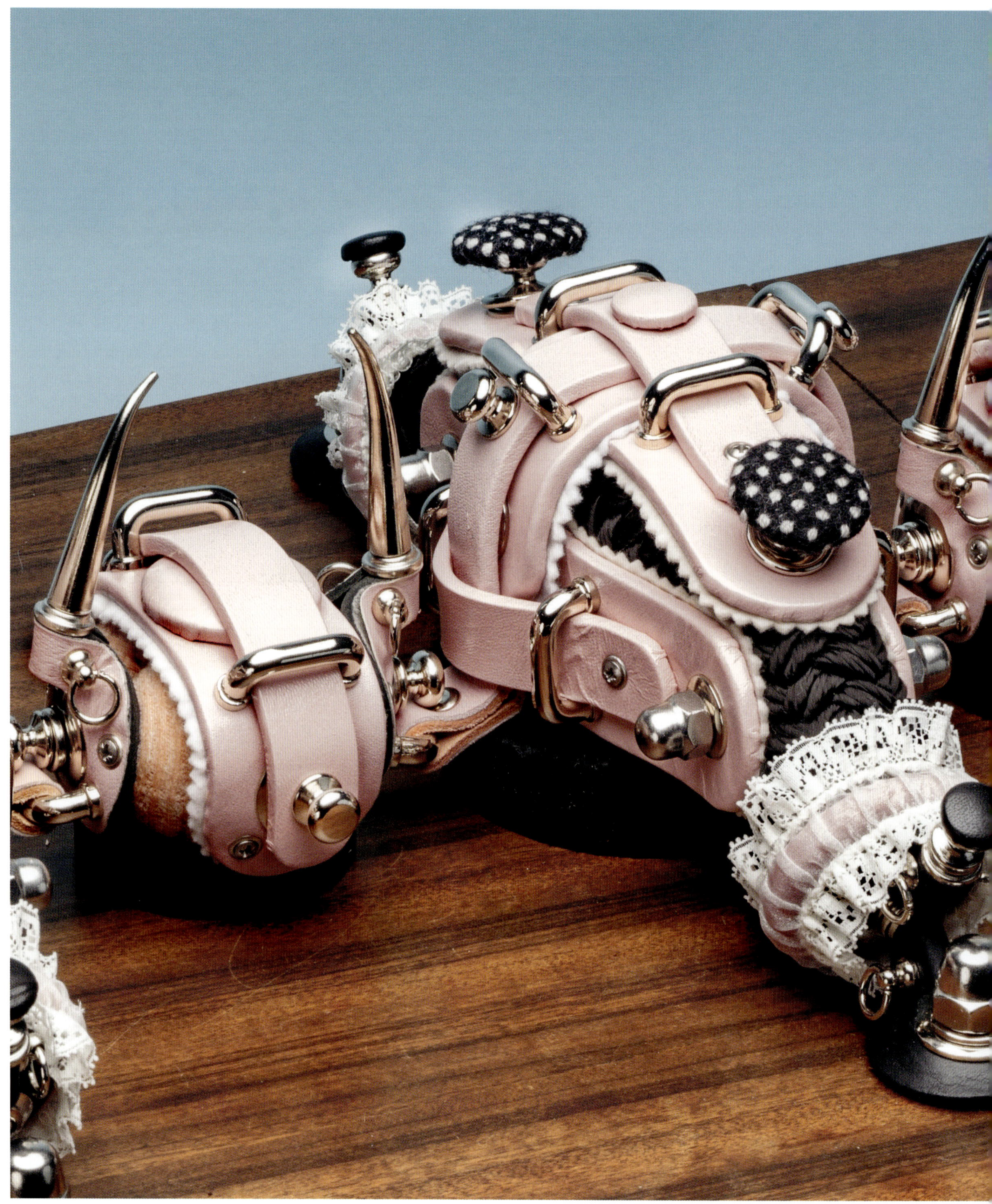

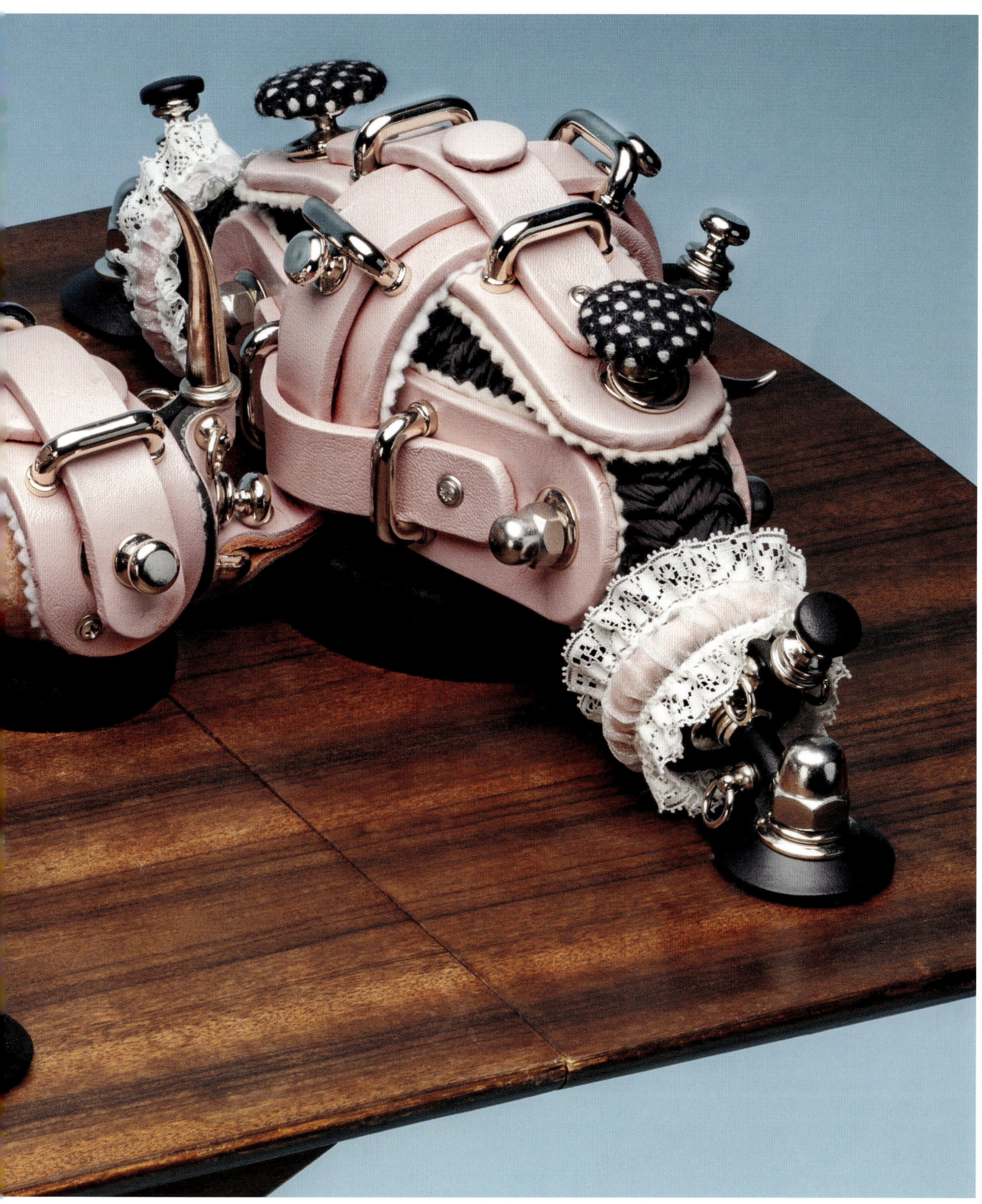

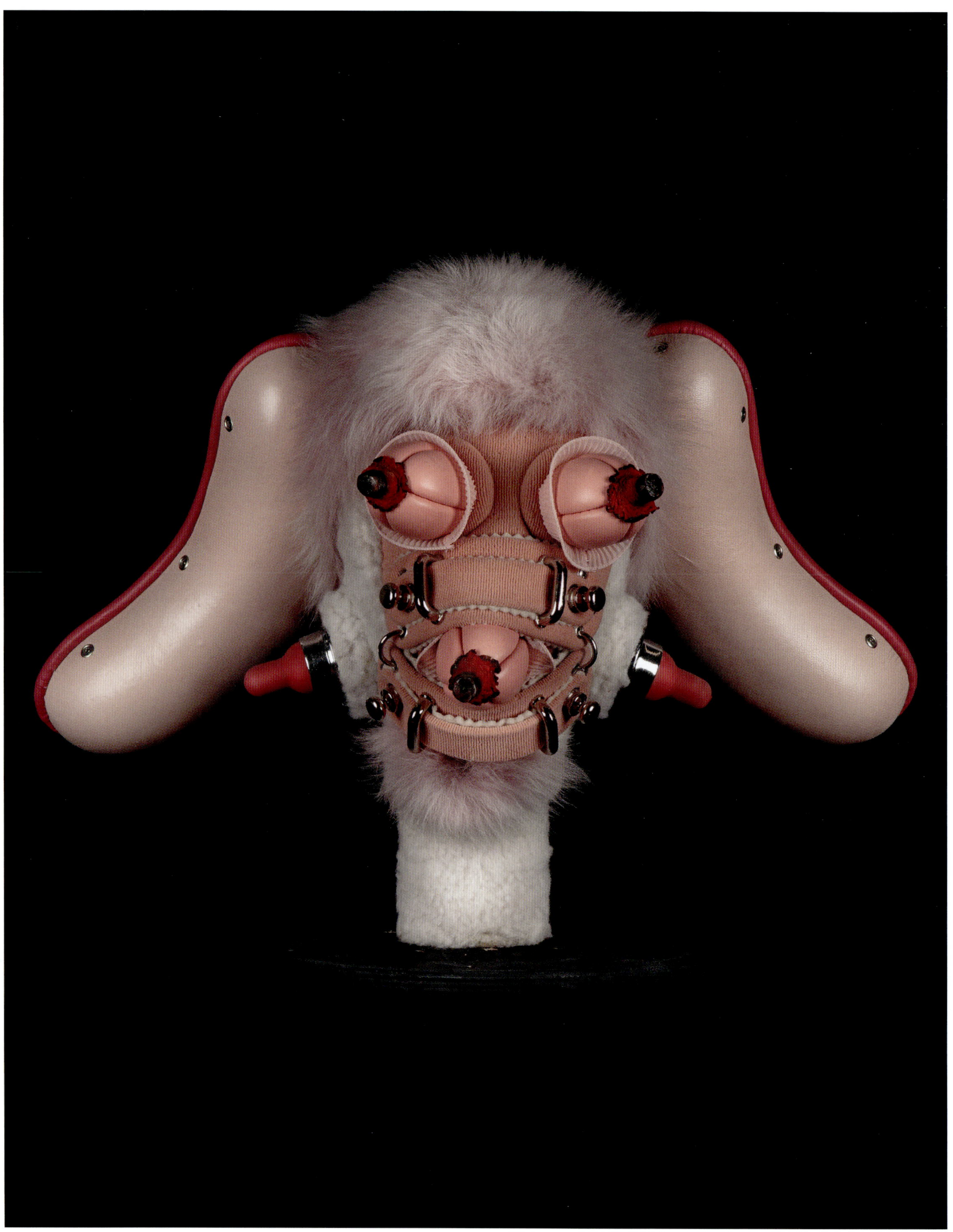

identifying any purpose rather contradicts the idea of industrial production. We're driven back to their context: these must be art, but cunningly tricked up to send us in other directions.

Mannequin Head introduces the object as figure. It might act as a transition point into the self-portrait photographs. Relevant to the fetishistic character of the sculpture, Woods says he's always had a thing for cameras "as objects, as a gear freak thing". Rather than wishing to record the world, it already makes for a nice connection to his wider practice, as well as an unusual starting point for taking photographs. Moreover, he says, "I've always been rather envious of photographers for how they get to control people, for the power of the camera to direct the subject. Here I am object and subject. Maybe I should talk to a psychiatrist?"[4]

He describes his technique in straightforward terms:

> Clicker in my hand, I practise poses in a mirror, ponce around. I sometimes allow the clicker to be seen, happy to show actually this is someone photographing himself. Not a fashion shoot, but all about the self – me at the centre, reflecting what I encounter in my life, childhood to now – confessional ...[5]

The highly theatrical self-portraits that result are just as hard to classify. Clearly they depict Woods, but how much of the self do they capture? They look more like portraits – or caricatures – of others. Many of them challenge the traditional binary of male-female. True, this isn't what it was, but the combination of a beard and a dress remains unusual. Austrian singer and drag queen Conchita Wurst brought the look into mainstream culture, but can hardly be said to have popularised it.

But let's start with a bearded man being a bearded man. *Doctor Fraud* looks, judging by the prominent phallus, to be a poke at then near-homonymic Freud. But the phallus is golden ... is that to value it or to ridicule its supposed value? One suspects the latter, but, after all, Woods has one. He did say he should see a psychiatrist, and Freud would surely have something to say about how Woods accounts for his recurring use of layered leather: "I want to make it look as if it is part of the reins I remember being led by as a child. I was in baby blue. I was a bad boy."

Lolita brandishes a phallus, too, but the effect is rather different. The primary reference isn't to Freud's theory of penis envy, nor to the pretensions of the phallocracy, but to the power of the seductress over the penis. Woods, of course, makes an entertainingly implausible Lolita – not just a woman with a beard, but a pubescent girl with a beard at an age when boys don't yet have them. And the power is inappropriate, an enticement to illegal and immoral activity. The fault in that lies, of course, with the responder, but it might be thought that Woods plays both roles here – the look of the predatory man, the dress of the provoking girl. Yes, Freud would have plenty to do.

Woods' personae tend to blend into each other. The tied top sported by Lolita turns out to be judged suited to the requirements of *Office Dresscode*. This underlines the implicit tease whereby the objectivity implied by a "code" runs up against the subjectivity of judging different people differently for wearing the same clothes. "You can't wear that!" one can imagine Woods being told – "that part of the code is not for men". The typewriter in *Office Dresscode* evokes assumed women's work in the pre-computerised office. It also carries on between images. We can assume that Doctor Fraud won't be doing his own typing. We don't seem, incidentally, to be in the present day. The typewriters, the fashions and the furniture suggest the pre-digital age, which makes the beard that much more disruptive – it belongs to the time when "men were men". In *First Day at Kindergarten*, the primary disruption is of assumptions about age. We don't expect a smartly dressed business person to wear children's shoes and carry a stuffed toy around. It makes sense, though, if the workplace is being equated with the kindergarten, and we all know how childish office politics can be. It's a pink unicorn – back to pink – a fantasy animal suggesting, alternatively, a fantasy version of the worker's life once out of the office.

All of which attempted analysis enacts our instinct to find categories within which things will fit. Woods frustrates that process, and makes the reduction to primary contrasts particularly difficult. It's as if Woods is wilfully setting out to confuse us.

Perhaps we shouldn't categorise things at all, then? Yet there are reasons for the instinct to do so. If we tried to treat every new item as a new type of thing, we'd soon run into the sand of mental overload. We seek to classify – "ah, it's one of those!" – so that we can bring previous knowledge and experience to bear. It may be, though, that our categories are wrong, or that they are of the wrong type. Woods' objects can be seen as addressing the first issue, his

previous pages
*LAMB SHANK BOLT-ON
FETISH* (detail), 2024
Leather, rope, fabric,
metal findings.
1020 x 360 x 560mm

opposite
MANNEQUIN HEAD,
2020
Shop dummy head, fur,
fabric, leather, wax,
metal findings.
740 x 350mm

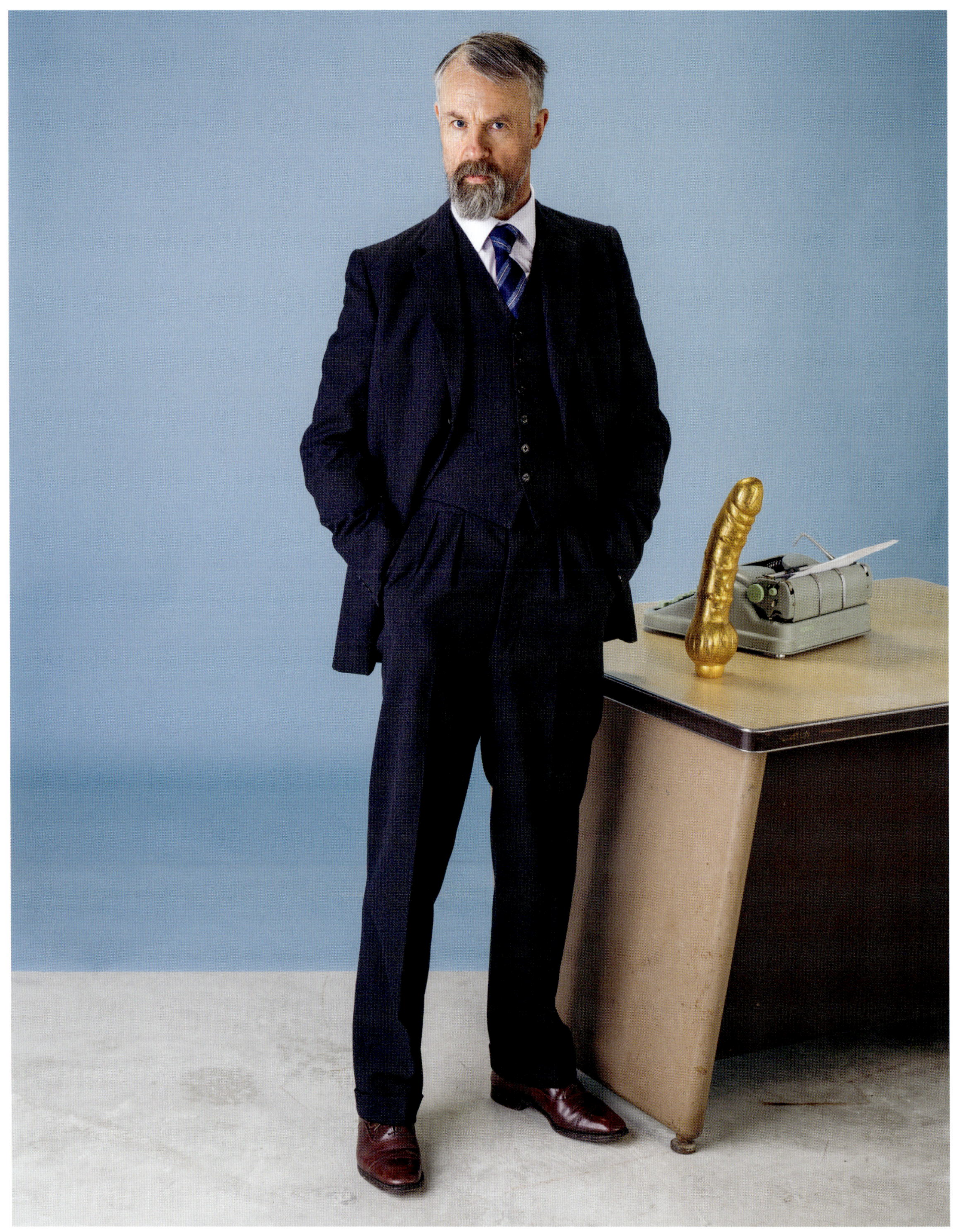

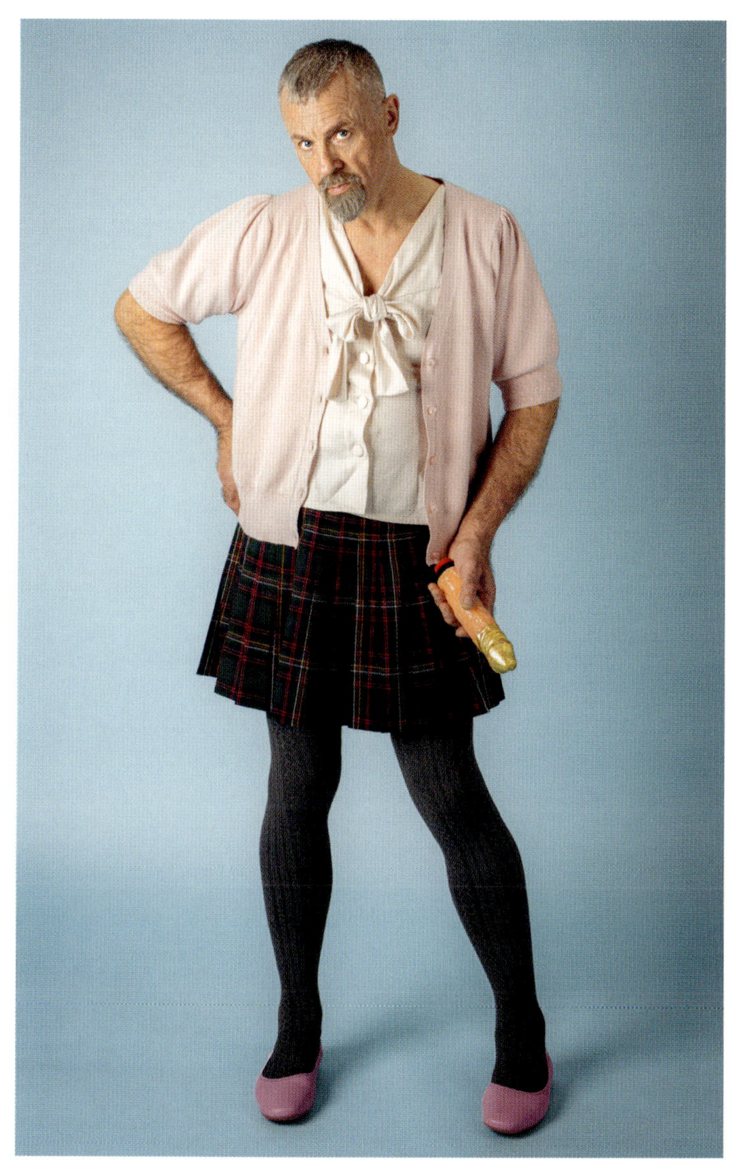 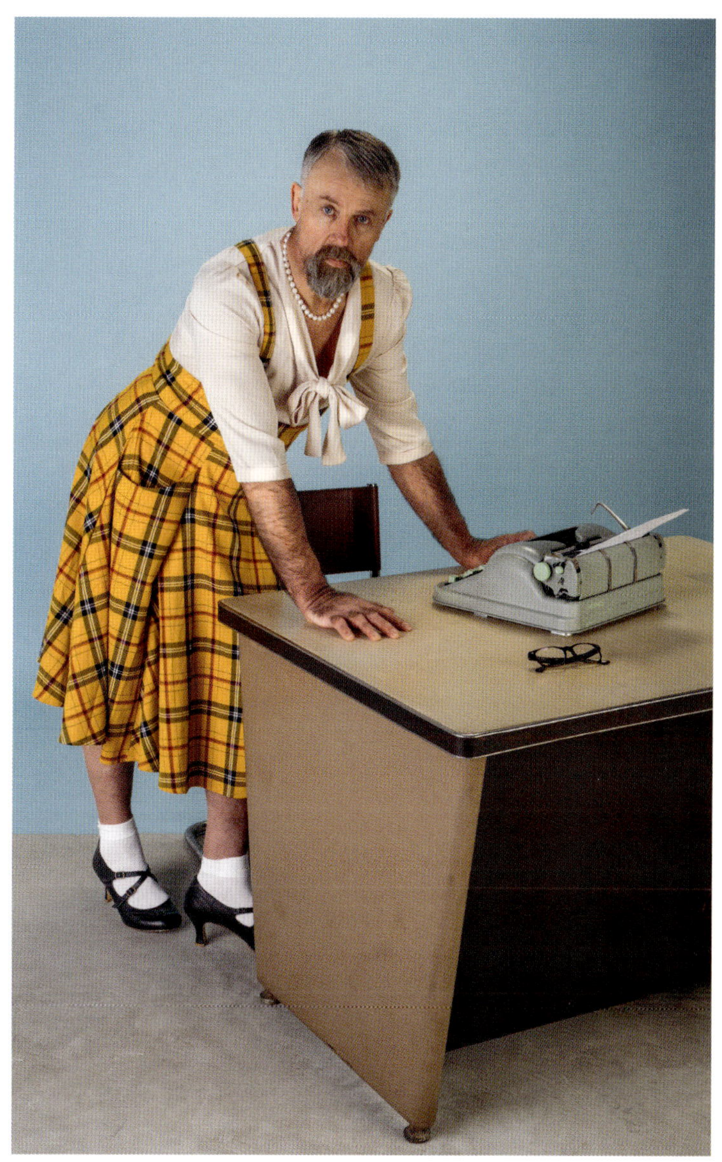

opposite
DOCTOR FRAUD, 2022
Photographic print.
Dimensions variable

above left
LOLITA, 2022
Photographic print.
Dimensions variable

above right
OFFICE DRESS CODE,
2022
Photographic print.
Dimensions variable

self-portraits the second. The philosopher Gilbert Ryle coined the term "category mistake" for when a person talks about something as though it's a different type of thing than the thing it is.[6] "Friday is in bed", for example, or "green is clever". Ryle claimed this was significant because philosophical misunderstandings arise from making such errors. His prime example was that of the idea that the mind works in a similar yet altogether separate way to the body. Just such a "category mistake" causes us to believe we can talk comparably about mental and physical phenomena.

Woods seems to be drawing us into such category mistakes. We find we're talking about his objects as if they might be something other than art, but these are traps, leading us to misrepresent what we see. We might also note that the fetish runs through his work, in two senses that we might term "European" and "African". First is the ascription of sexual qualities to what is not sexual. To focus, for example, on leather, balloons or feet as one's primary triggers of desire is in some way to miscategorise them. Second is the ascription of spiritual properties and powers to objects, which Woods is attracted to for how it "adds to their strangeness". This puts me in mind of another putative category mistake, that of the musicological display of African artefacts. It is often criticised nowadays for how it ignores the practical meaning of objects in everyday life in favour of presenting them as if they were art objects.

As for the type of category, binary categories in particular often get a bad press. This century has seen an increasing reluctance to accept the simple divisions associated with, for example, sex (male versus female), sexual preferences (heterosexual versus homosexual), and consciousness (intelligent versus unintelligent life – can a computer be intelligent? What does the underground communication of trees suggest?). Those old binaries are increasingly seen as being imposed on the world by the historic holders of economic, political, symbolic, and cultural capital. In Legacy Russell's *Glitch Feminism*,[7] the freedoms of the virtual world are used to describe how the restructuring of physical forms towards the goal of remixing identity altogether can constitute a potential alternative to those simplified normative binaries. Woods is enacting just such a move, and Russell would approve of that:

> When we gender a body, we are making assumptions about the body's function, its socio-political condition, its fixity. When the body is determined as a male or female individual, the body performs gender as its score, guided by a set of rules and requirements that validate and verify the humanity of that individual. A body that pushes back at the application of pronouns, or remains indecipherable within binary assignment, is a body that refuses to perform the score. This non-performance is a glitch. The glitch is a form of refusal.

What is the effect of Woods' confusion of categories and challenge to category types? First and foremost, perhaps, it's an aesthetic strategy, a way to generate surprising and visually striking objects and images. But both the objects and the self-portraits also perform those ambiguities and refusals as means of queering power, as a way to challenge the norms implicit in our conceptual and linguistic structures. Is this to suggest that Woods is gay? True, there is a campness to the work that fits with some gay stereotypes. But that would be too straightforward. Woods is heterosexual, or as he puts it (at the age of 63): "If I'm gay, I should have realised it by now".[8] That fits: Woods is queering those expectations as well. We end up, then, in a rather odd place. Yet that may be salutary – and there's plenty to enjoy in how we get there.

Notes

1. Mark Woods in conversation with Paul Carey-Kent.
2. Mark Woods in conversation with Paul Carey-Kent.
3. Mark Woods in conversation with Paul Carey-Kent.
4. Mark Woods in conversation with Paul Carey-Kent.
5. Mark Woods in conversation with Paul Carey-Kent.
6. Gilbert Ryle, *The Concept of Mind*, London, Hutchinson University Library, 1949.
7. Legacy Russell: *Glitch Feminism: A Manifesto*, Brooklyn and London, Verso Books, 2020.
8. Mark Woods in conversation with Paul Carey-Kent.

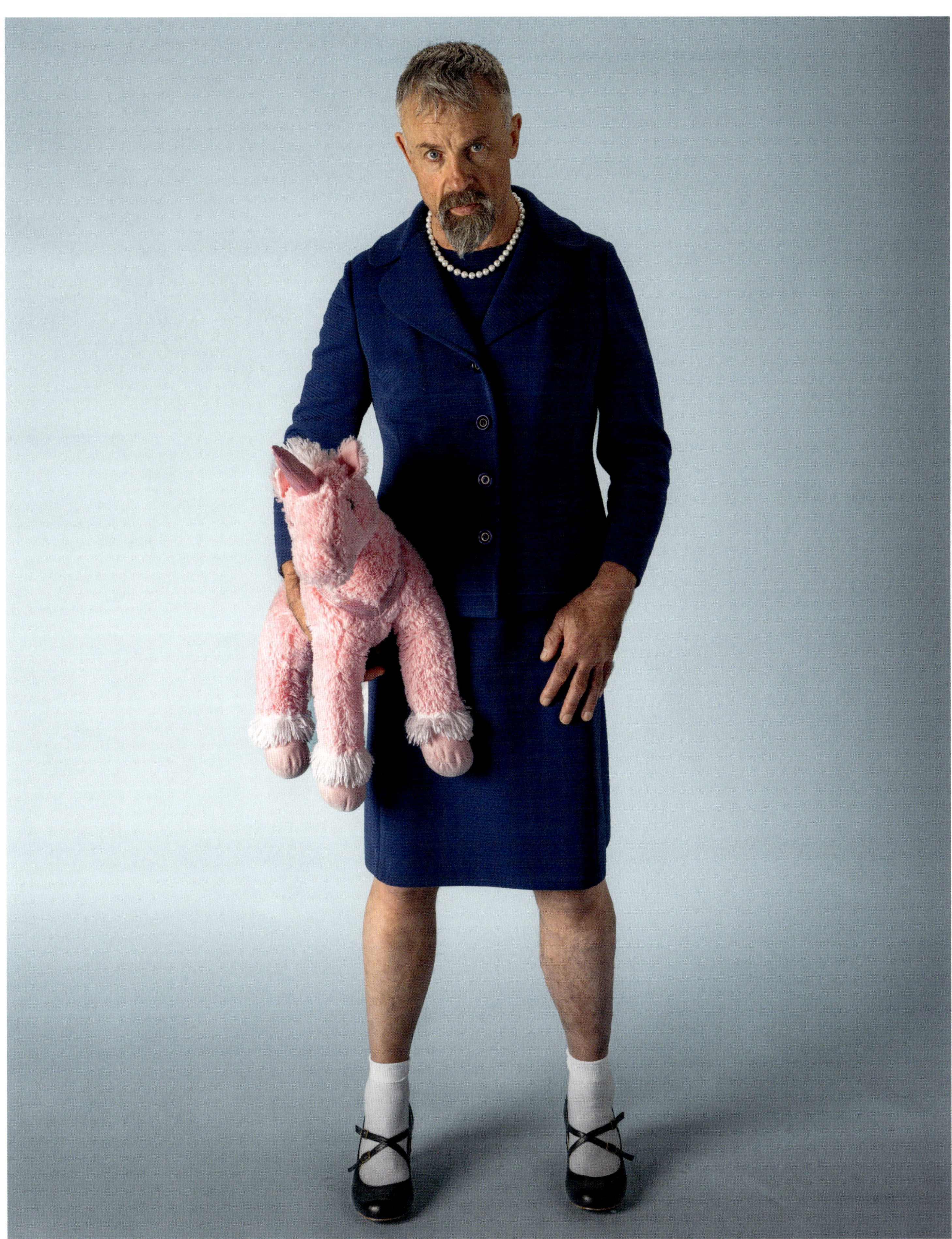

VESSELS OF DISTRACTION, CABINETS OF LIGHT:
Reference and Illusion in the Work of Mark Woods

Peter Suchin

Analysis and understanding, whether exercised by the professional critic or the independent viewer, requires a clear and steady gaze. One needs, as it were, to look the art object in the eye. In the case of Mark Woods' constructions and photographic portraits, such optical attention is immediately returned – or even, perhaps, calmly but insistently blocked. In the artist's installations, too, one may find it difficult to ascertain exactly what it is that one is looking at, since in using multiple (and multiplying) mirrors as key components of these works Woods has ensured that one's gaze is shifted about, disrupted, sharply redirected.

Woods' practice, as something overtly visual and sensually intense, is, at the same time, armed with a kind of "defence system" against the very application of the human gaze.[1] Yet some of the visual devices he employs positively beg for attention, engaging the viewer in a transparently titillating fashion, baiting them with unsubtle sexual imagery and sleek, sensuous surfaces – leather, velvet, polished wood – crafted to an astonishingly high degree. The level of technical skill involved in, for example, the making of Woods' laboriously built boxes is an intrinsic

below left, below right, opposite
THE ONLY LANGUAGE SPOKEN, 2010
Walnut cabinet, replica sewing machine case, cocobolo, MDF, glass mirror, rhodium-plated silver, felt leather, silk.
1200 x 480 x 360mm

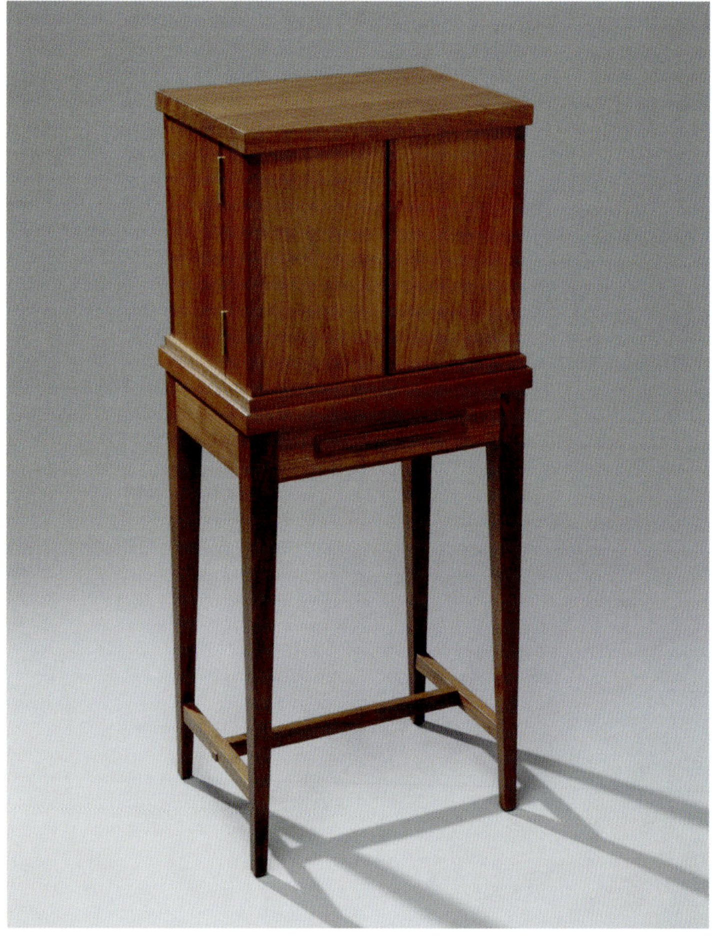

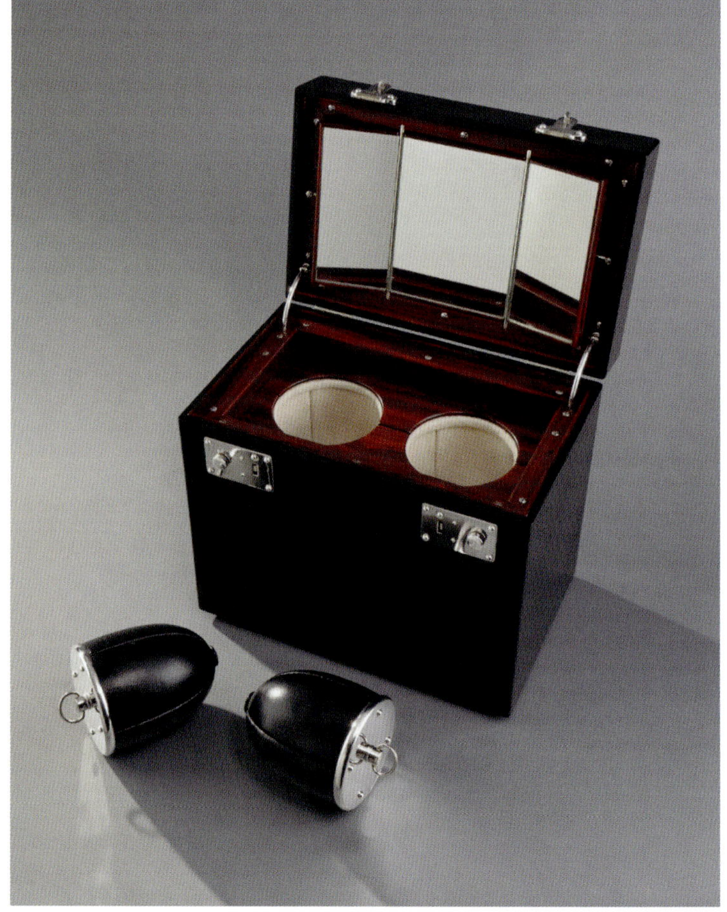

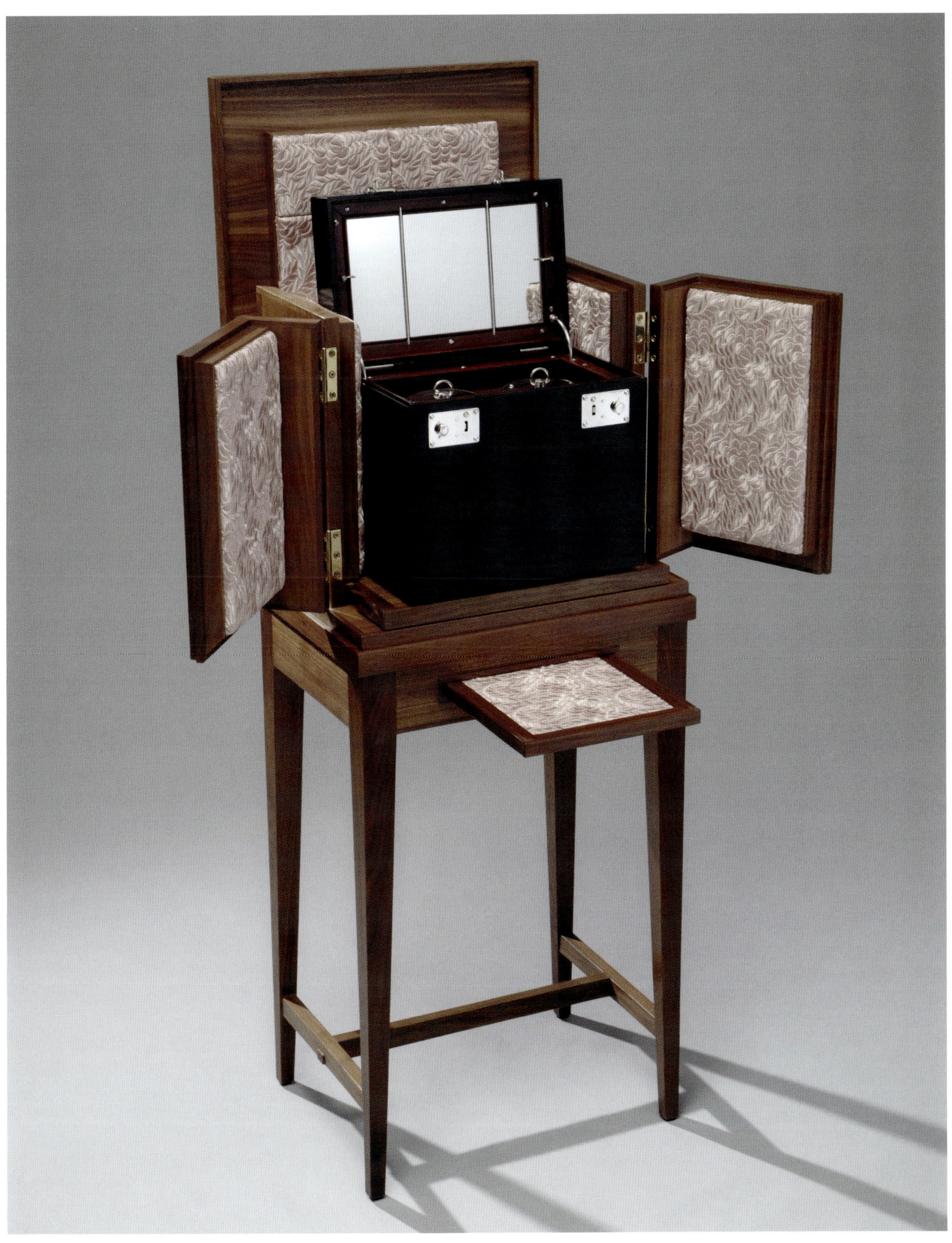

part of the exchange between the artwork and the viewer, since these elaborate constructions both act to attract and yet keep one away from the "inner sanctum" of the work. The seduction has two primary aspects – that of the box, functioning as an entity in its own right, and that which it protects but also obscures. Prior to his becoming an artist Woods was a boat-builder and jewellery designer, activities which both demanded high levels of know-how, concentration and attention to detail. As Richard Sennett notes in his important study *The Craftsman*, the overcoming of difficulties is an implicit part of developing complicated physical skills.[2] This training has been helpful within Woods' practice as an artist as well. He is still making vessels, though of an entirely different kind.

Walter Benjamin famously described what he called the *aura* of a work of art as "the unique phenomena of a distance, however close it may be".[3] Assuming the relation between the boxes' exteriors and interiors is hierarchical, then Benjamin's model is highly apt. The work's exterior would then function as a container or frame, an elaborate shell serving to further heighten the importance of whatever it holds.[4] The structural relation between this contemporary reliquary and what it surrounds is, however, rather ambivalent, since container and contained are technically developed to an equal degree. But if we recognise that the focus of our attention needs to be, at some point, directly upon what is inside the box, then the container is readable as a mere distraction or delay. The artist, having given us such an overwhelmingly seductive frame, has drawn our attention to the precious contents yet continued to obscure them. One can, and with Woods' practice indeed does, "look at [or see] seeing", in the sense that Marcel Duchamp intended that curious term. There are a number of parallels with respect to the work of Duchamp and Woods, notably the use of *delay* as a means of controlling how a given piece is perceived.

A further parallel involves a concern with mirrors and reflections, and both artists have employed the structuring device of limiting access to their work via peepholes or carefully contrived spaces or gaps. In this respect, Duchamp's *Étant donnés* (1946–66) is paradigmatic.[5]

In his 2021 discussion with Vanya Balogh,[6] Woods expressed his deep interest in Surrealism and in related conceptions of the unconscious, both of which may uneasily suggest the existence of an authentic or inviolate "inner-self", a concern echoed in the dialectic of inside and outside to which I refer above. He has also remarked on how, as a boy growing up within the narrow, "machismo" mentality so prevalent within 1970s British culture, "being feminised was something you were frightened of" – "being ridiculed and being disempowered" were central threads of that fear. As he has got older, "being open to the feminine" has become a central strand of his practice, most obviously so in the series of photographs in which he presents himself to the camera in neatly stereotypical female garb. Within this body of work, Woods is consciously in control of the images he makes, his gaze confidently meeting that of the future viewer. It might be claimed that, in the UK at any rate, sexual roles and their supposed expression through particular kinds of clothing, hairstyle, voice and position or stance have remained, well into the twenty-first century, rather narrowly defined. Woods' photographs pose a threat to those cultural quarters still ensconced in the traditionalism of what they may well hold as "certainties" of personal essence and rigid definition, though the force of his images resides not in a simple binary switching around of the received pattern but in, rather, its blank refusal. There is a wry comedy within these "outrageous" self-portraits which is an important part of their parodic intent. Irony and laughter do not suggest the replacement of one fixed model with another, but completely deride the idealised veracity of "true" or "definitive" behavioural modes.

As Julia Kristeva and other Poststructuralist theorists have argued, certain types of signifying practice place "the [human] subject in process" or "on trial".[7] Kristeva asserts "that modern art insists upon the individual as fragmented, wandering, at loose ends, as one who cannot find himself in the mirror of any ideology". This claim may be construed as documenting a disturbing cultural shift, but it in fact alludes to a liberating reinscription of the established behavioural codes. This transformation carries an ethical edge. Kristeva asserts that "a practice is ethical when it dissolves those narcissistic fixations … that are narrowly confined to the subject … the [work] fulfils its ethical function only when it pluralizes, pulverizes, 'musicates' these truths … to the point of laughter." It is not so much the brazenness of Woods' gaze within the self-portraits that embodies this destabilising force, but rather the *inbetweenness* of the images. They strictly refute the notion of a fixed or "authentic" self.

In the exchange with Balogh, Woods calls one of his own sculptures "a cross between a sex toy and an African fetish object". To include within one's practice allusions to sexual fetishism can be risky, it being very easy to accuse Woods of making pornographic work. Certain

below
Duchamp's *ÉTANT DONNÉS* (1946–66)

opposite top
Installation shot of
PEEPHOLE ROOM, A RETURN TO OLD CERTAINTIES, 2017
Mixed media.
4300 x 4300 x 3000mm
Angus Hughes Gallery, London

opposite below
Still of *AUTOMATA PIECE, THE COMPLETION OF THE EROTIC TASK*, 2014
Photographic print.
Dimensions variable

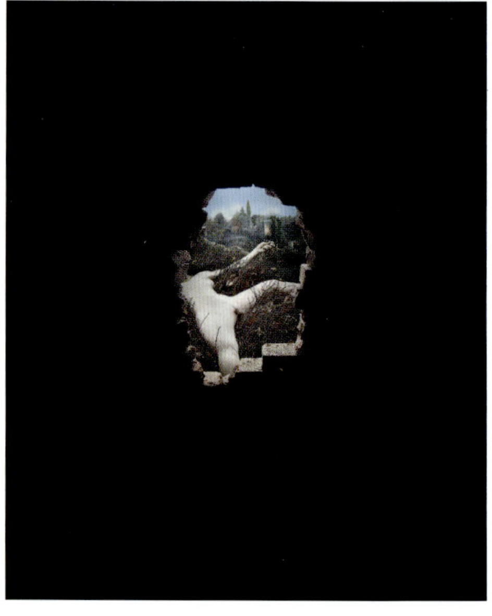

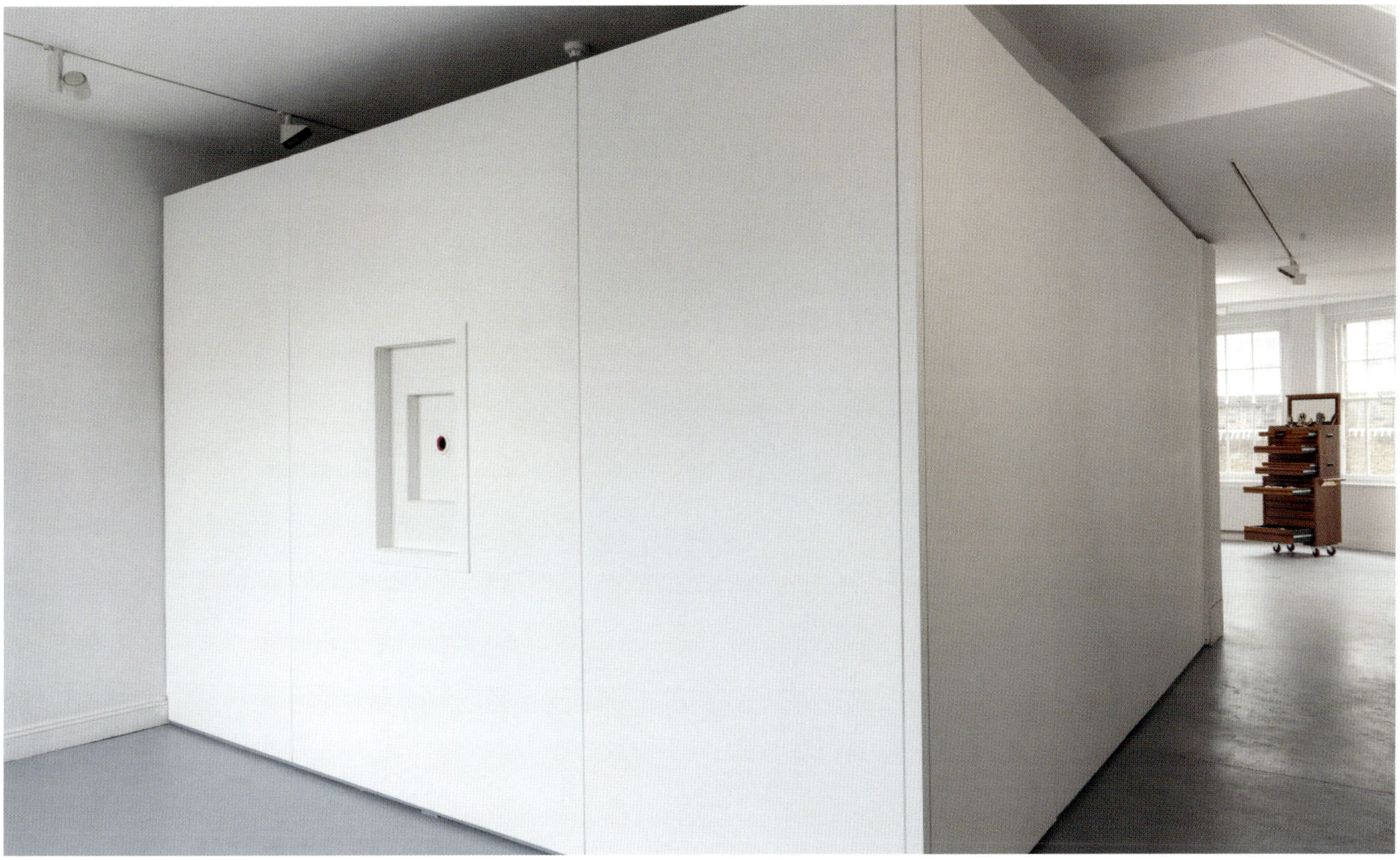

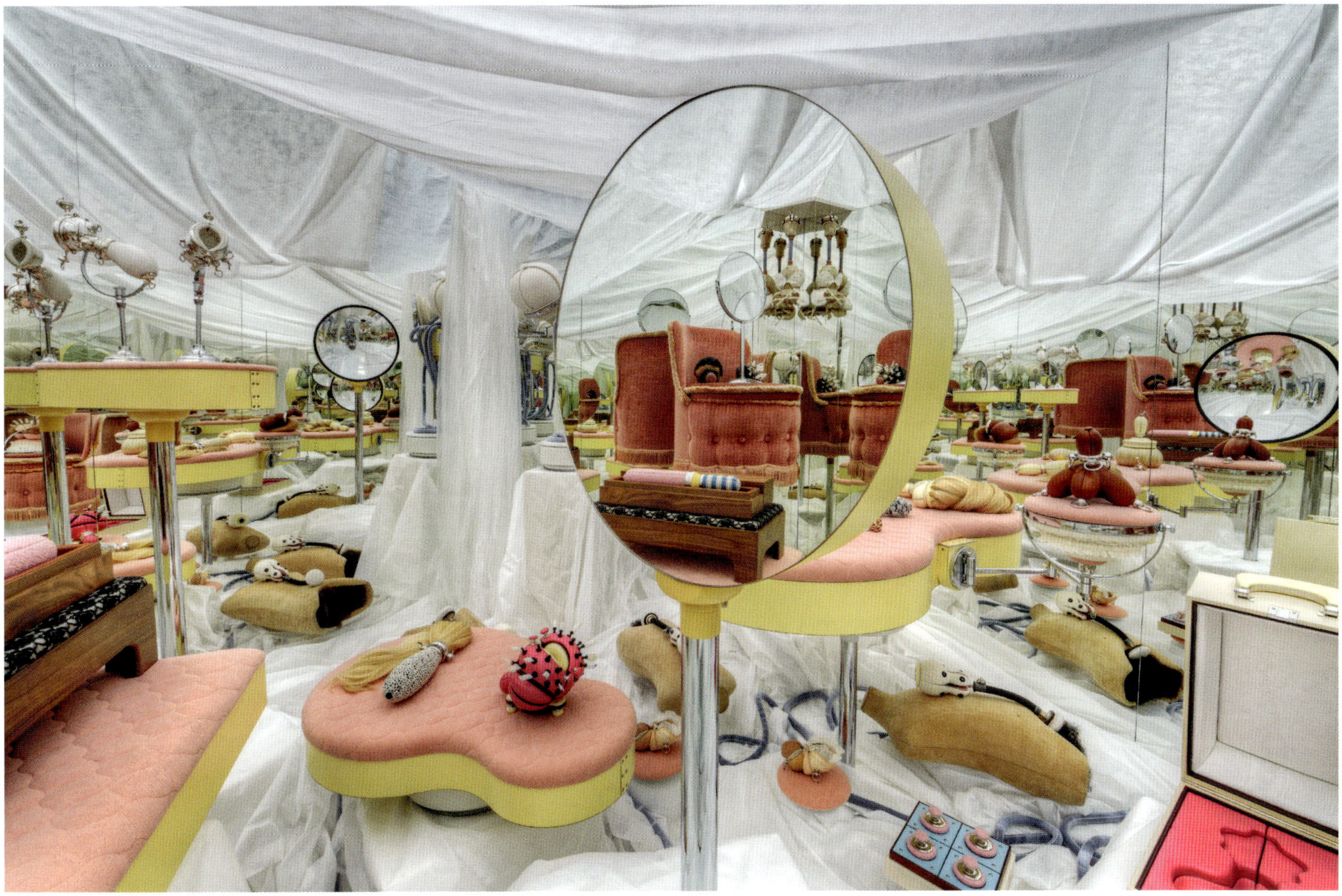

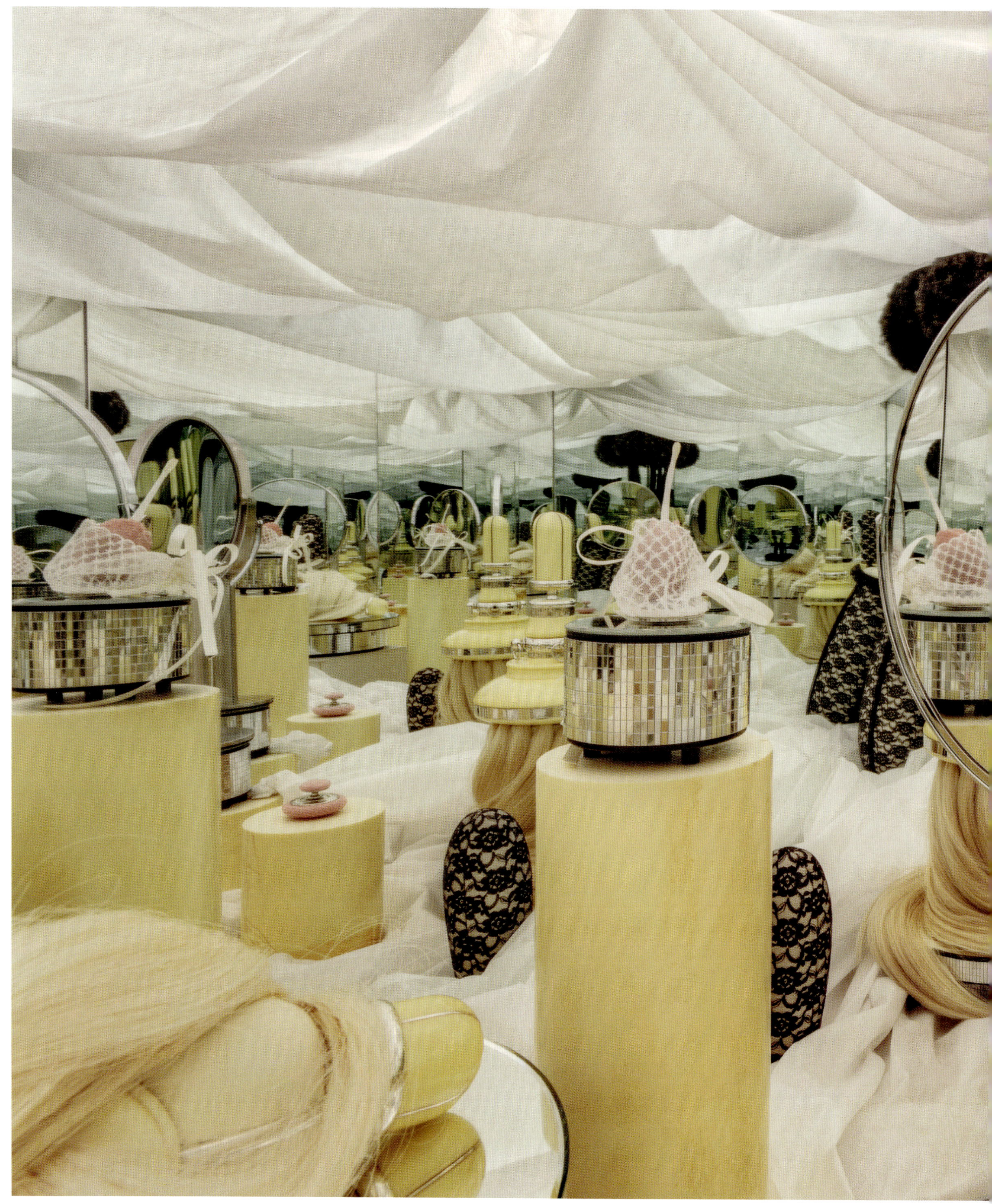

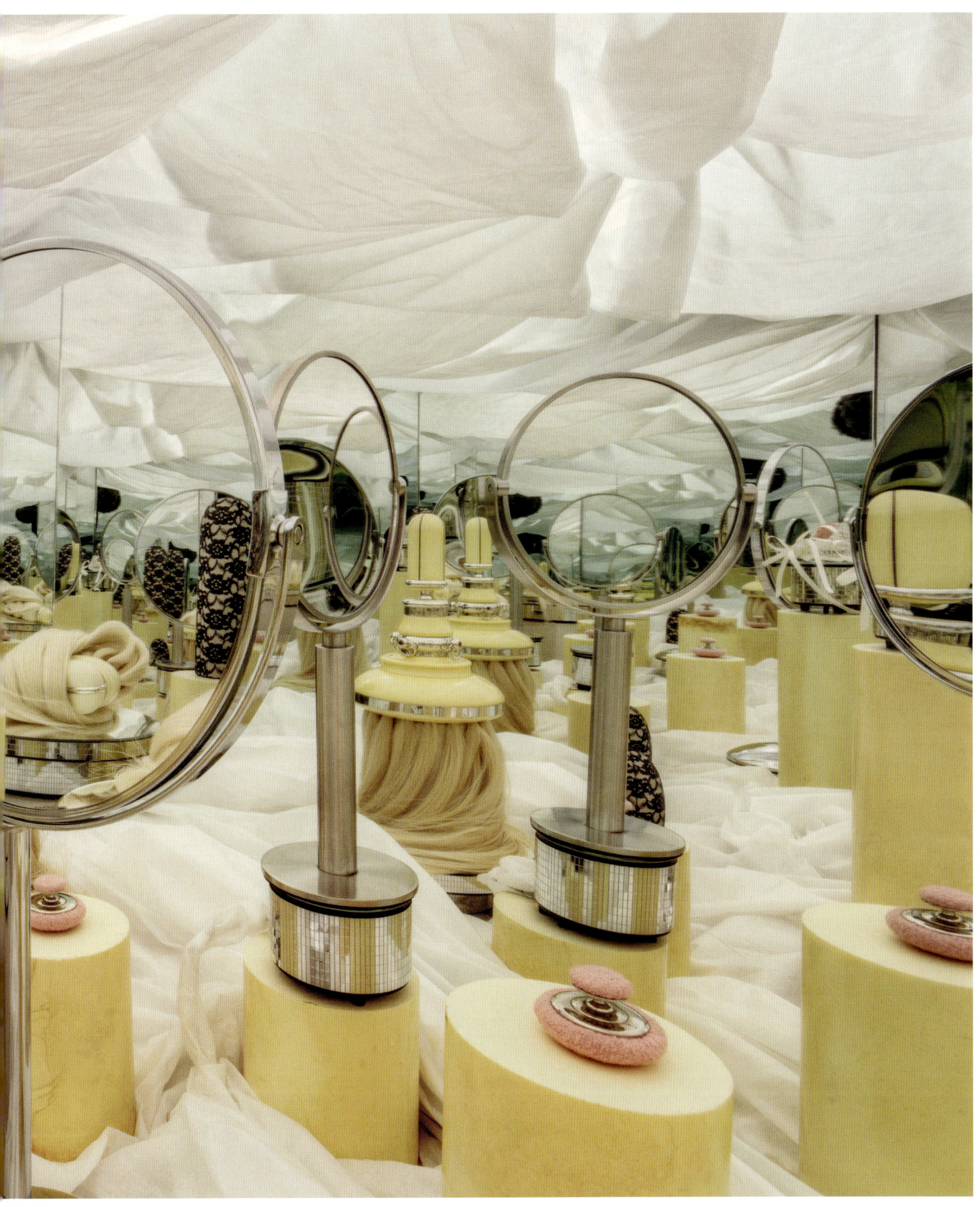

problematic assumptions immediately come into play, but a more nuanced account of the
"pornographic" helps to open out this loaded term, rethinking its relation to established society.
In her 1967 essay "The Pornographic Imagination", Susan Sontag attempted precisely this task:

> The more enlightened architects of moral policy are undoubtedly prepared to
> admit that there is something like a "pornographic imagination," although
> only in the sense that pornographic works are tokens of a radical failure or
> deformation of the imagination. And they may grant … that there also exists a
> "pornographic society": that, indeed, ours is a flourishing example of one, a society
> so hypocritically and repressively constructed that it must inevitably produce an
> effusion of pornography as both its logical expression and its subversive, demotic
> antidote. But nowhere in the Anglo-American community of letters have I seen it
> argued that some pornographic books are interesting and important works of art.
> So long as pornography is treated as only a social and psychological phenomenon
> and a locus for moral concern, how could such an argument ever be made?[8]

Sontag's projected expansion of the category of the pornographic would include an important
task for the artist, and would involve making forays into and taking up positions on the
frontiers of conscious (often very dangerous to the artist as a person) and reporting back
what's there: "[The artist's] job is inventing trophies of his experiences – objects and gestures
that fascinate and enthral, not merely … [to] edify or entertain. His principal means of
fascinating is to advance one step further in the dialectic of outrage."

Yet even in relation to how pornography was positioned within culture at the time of
writing, Sontag realised that this scurrilous framework was a space in which the artist could
carry out serious and important work. "Pornography", she noted, "is one of the branches of
literature – science fiction is another – aiming at disorientation, at psychic dislocation".[9]
Disruption and dislocation are key tropes of modern art and literature, going back at least as
far as Arthur Rimbaud's renowned letter to Paul Demeny, dated 15 May 1851: "I say one must be
a *seer*, make oneself a *seer*", writes Rimbaud; "The Poet makes himself a *seer* by a long, gigantic
and rational *derangement of all the senses*."[10] The artist becomes a shaman, entering into a deep
psychic exploration of the self, partly on behalf of others who cannot or will not go there.
A later example of the artist committed to this deep investigation of "inner experience" (Bataille)
is William Burroughs.[11] "In my writing", suggests Burroughs, "I am acting as a map maker, an
explorer of psychic areas … a cosmonaut of inner space".[12] The "pornographic" elements within
Woods' sculptures draw on stereotypes of gender and desire, unequivocally asserting their
presence yet parodying them through comedic excess. These works enact a clash of meanings,
an unsettling of illusions. Are these difficult objects "kitsch", high art, or something caught
between readily acceptable forms? Partly "primitive" in appearance, they seem, at the same
time, brand new, yet from another time than our own. We are clearly in the territory of the
uncanny, the realm in which, by definition, things are *out of place*.[13]

In conversation with Vanya Balogh, Woods refers to his interest in making the viewer
"feel uneasy", and to the "essential element" of randomness associated with works of art.[14]
The staging of a situation in which the watcher quickly becomes the watched is, even in a time
of selfies and the internet, an act that goes against conventional gallery mores. In juxtaposing
what one might take to be a coarse depiction of female genitalia with "well-mannered"
decorative panels of metal, wood and leather, something akin to a Surrealist shock is indeed
brought about, but this is only one among several evident effects. As Maria Walsh observed
in *Art and Psychoanalysis*, "The subject 'I' only becomes aware of the gaze as an object when
the world refuses to reciprocate our desire to be seen or to see."[15] Wresting control of who
sees what, when, and how is one of Woods' prime strategies for the instigation of unease.

The convoluted notion of *disaffirmative* art is also relevant when considering Woods' images
and constructions. Art conventionally affirms the culture from which it emerges, and art as
celebration is a rather tired trope. Can one generate at the present time a truly critical, non-
affirmative practice? Nietzsche wrote that "art is essentially affirmation, blessing, deification
of existence".[16] The idea of an art that does not celebrate and affirm seemed, to Nietzsche at
least, a nonsense, and today's pluralist paradigm is frequently closer to self-expression than
critique. Terry Atkinson has proposed that "the disaffirming art is bothersome and kind of
enjoyable as such (interesting)"[17] – Mark Woods' awkward and unsettling practice gives us
much food for thought in this regard.

Notes

1 In *The Evil Eye* (John Murray, 1895), Frederick Thomas Elworthy describes ancient amulets whose purpose was to avert the negative, controlling power of the "evil eye":

Anything ... calculated to excite the curiosity, the mirth, or in any way to attract the attention of the beholder was considered to be the most effectual. There were three methods ... These were by exciting laughter or curiosity; by demonstration of good fortune so as to excite envy in the beholder ... and by doing something painfully disagreeable to cause him an unpleasant feeling of dread.

Such devices, concocted to attract in order to distort the trajectory of a negative force, remind one of Woods' paradoxical visual forms. Elworthy also supplies the example of heraldic emblems cunningly assembled so as to dazzle opponents if employed, presumably on a shield or banner, in battle.

A classic example of self-reflexivity with respect to visual representation is Michael Powell's film *Peeping Tom* (1960), in which the central character murders his victims whilst filming them as they view the horror on their own faces in a mirror attached to his camera. Woods' deep concern with the artistic potential inherent in mirrors places him within a long tradition of artists who foreground the complexities of mirroring, doubling and distorting light. The practice of *mise-en-abyme* (into the abyss), in which the image contains a reduced rendition of itself "ad infinitum" goes back at least as far as the imagery of shields within shields in medieval heraldic emblems. Woods is surely familiar with the history of optical toys, as well as with optical illusions as a means of disguising military craft in times of war. For a brief introduction to the former, see Basil Harley, *Optical Toys* (Shire, 1988). The so-called "dazzle ships" are included in the exhibition catalogue *Camouflage* (Scottish Arts Council, 1988). For a technical/philosophical investigation of the properties of mirrors, see Richard Gregory, *Mirrors in Mind* (WH Freeman, 1997).

2 Richard Sennett, *The Craftsman*, Allen Lane, 2008. For a review essay of Sennett's book, see Peter Suchin, "Considering Craft", *Art Monthly*, no 318, July/August, 2008.

3 Walter Benjamin, "The Work of Art in the Age of Mechanical Reproduction" in WB, *Illuminations*, Fontana, 1979, p 224. Benjamin's interests included the nineteenth-century Panorama, a mechanical device through which several viewers simultaneously observed, via peepholes, rapidly moving images of the city. For an image of this device, see Susan Buck-Morss, *The Dialectics of Seeing: Walter Benjamin and the Arcades Project*, MIT, 1989, illustration 4.1, p 82.

4 As Jacques Derrida pointed out, the frame, seemingly a merely subservient part of the artwork's presentation, is in fact a determining feature with respect to establishing what exactly it is that constitutes the work of art. A short but important passage in Derrida's *The Truth in Painting* (University of Chicago Press, 1987) is pertinent with respect to Woods: "Where does the frame take place. Does it take place. Where does it begin. Where does it end. What is its internal limit. Its external limit. And its surface between the two limits." (The implied question marks are missing in the text). See also Paul Druro (ed.), *The Rhetoric of the Frame: Essays on the Boundaries of the Artwork*, Cambridge University Press, 1986.

5 The observation about "seeing seeing" is from Marcel Duchamp's *Box of 1914* (1914), included in Michel Sanouillet and Elmer Peterson (eds.), *The Essential Writings of Marcel Duchamp*, Thames & Hudson, 1975. Note Duchamp's suggestion to "Have a room entirely made of mirrors which one can move – and photograph mirror effects". For this remark see MD, *a l'infinitive/in the infinitive*, the Typosophic Society, 1999, p 14.

See Michael R Taylor's *Marcel Duchamp: Étant donnés*, Philadelphia Museum of Art, 2009. In looking through Duchamp's peephole one is simultaneously engaged in an act of voyeurism while also being the potential subject of someone else's gaze, again an instance of "seeing of seeing". See also Rosalind Krauss, "Where's Poppa?", in Thierry De Duve (ed.), *The Definitively Unfinished Marcel Duchamp*, MIT Press, 1993. Here, in her discussion of Duchamp's fascination with optical phenomena, she draws attention to Jean-Paul Sartre's example of the peeper-through-the-keyhole becoming, in turn, the one who is watched, in *Being and Nothingness* (original French edition by NRF, 1943).

One of the most brazen "coincidences" operating between Duchamp and Woods is that of male artists dressing in women's clothes in order to concoct a playful, at times absurd, interruption of conventional gender roles. Duchamp "practised" his persistent alter ego under the name Rrose Sélavy, whereas Woods makes no attempt to hide beneath a wig or other disguise. So much of Woods' practice involves hiding and deception that seeing him as himself, if dressed incorrectly when judged by current social norms, takes one back to matters of the authentic, the copy, and the fake. Something ridiculous about the highly commodified nature of consumption, and of the strained, implied inviolability of male and female roles, is played out in these photographs. The artist's tongue is in his cheek.

Duchamp was also a pioneer of the "artwork" in a box with his *Box in a Valise* (1935–41), containing reproductions of around 70 of his own pieces. The key study of the history and realisation of this project is Ecke Bonk's *Marcel Duchamp: The Portable Museum*, Thames & Hudson, 1989. Whereas Duchamp's valise was an editioned archive of miniature reproductions, Woods produces unique containers for unique pieces. Each box he makes is an "exoskeleton" for the sculpture it holds. Partly because of their elaborate fabrication, the boxes bear a family resemblance to containers manufactured for general use, though the latter were often made of much cheaper materials than those used by Woods. For a history and reproductions of such popular designs, see Marian Klamkin, *The Collector's Book of Boxes*, David & Charles, 1981. But the convoluted, layered manufacture of Woods' boxes suggests a potential mismatch between the outside and the inside of these structures, which are in this respect reminiscent of games or puzzles with secret compartments, or innocent-looking everyday devices in which maps, compasses and other useful items are secreted for use by spies. The implication is one of decoding the formula allowing access to the box, discovering the secret code or "catch" allowing access to the interior of the interior. The literature on such elaborate devices praises the sophisticated planning and technical know-how of their makers, an intricacy of concept and execution shared by Woods. See Allan Fea, *Secret Chambers and Hiding Places*, Methuen, 1901 (revised edition, 1908), and Charles Connell, *The Hidden Catch*, Elek Books, 1955.

6 "Mark Woods in Conversation with Vanya Balogh", in Mark Woods, *Absorption*, Cross Lane Projects, 2021 (unpaginated).

7 This quotation and those immediately following it are from, respectively: Julia Kristeva, *Revolution in Poetic Language*, Columbia University Press, 1984, p 22; Catherine Francblin, "Interview with Julia Kristeva", *Flash Art*, no. 126, February-March 1986, p 46; *Revolution in Poetic Language*, p 233.

8 This and the following quotation are from Susan Sontag, "The Pornographic Imagination" (1967), included as a supplementary essay in Georges Bataille, *Story of the Eye*, Marion Boyars, 1979, pp 86 and 92.

9 Sontag, "The Pornographic Imagination", p 94.

10 Arthur Rimbaud, included in Wallace Fowlie (ed.), *Rimbaud: Complete Works, Selected Letters*, University of Chicago Press, 1970, p 307.

11 Georges Bataille, *Inner Experience*, State University of New York, 2014.

12 William Burroughs, quoted in Eric Mottram, *William Burroughs: The Algebra of Need*, Marion Boyars, 1977, p 13.

13 Individuals or objects problematically and disturbingly displaced is a central component of what Sigmund Freud and others have theorised as "the uncanny". For a detailed discussion of this multi-layered theme, see Nicholas Royle, *The Uncanny*, Manchester University Press, 2003.

14 "Mark Woods in Conversation with Vanya Balogh", in Mark Woods, *Absorption*, Cross Lane Projects, 2021 (unpaginated).

15 Maria Walsh, *Art and Psychoanalysis*, IB Tauris, 2013, p 57.

16 Friedrich Nietzsche, *The Will to Power*, Vintage, 1968, p 434.

17 Terry Atkinson, "Dissaffirmation and Negation", in TA, *Mute 1*, Galleri Prag, Copenhagen, 1988, p 9. See also Peter Suchin, "Ghosting and Greasing: Terry Atkinson's 'Disaffirmative' Art", in Nigel Whitely (ed.), *De-Traditionalisation and Art*, Middlesex University Press, 2001.

OBJECTS

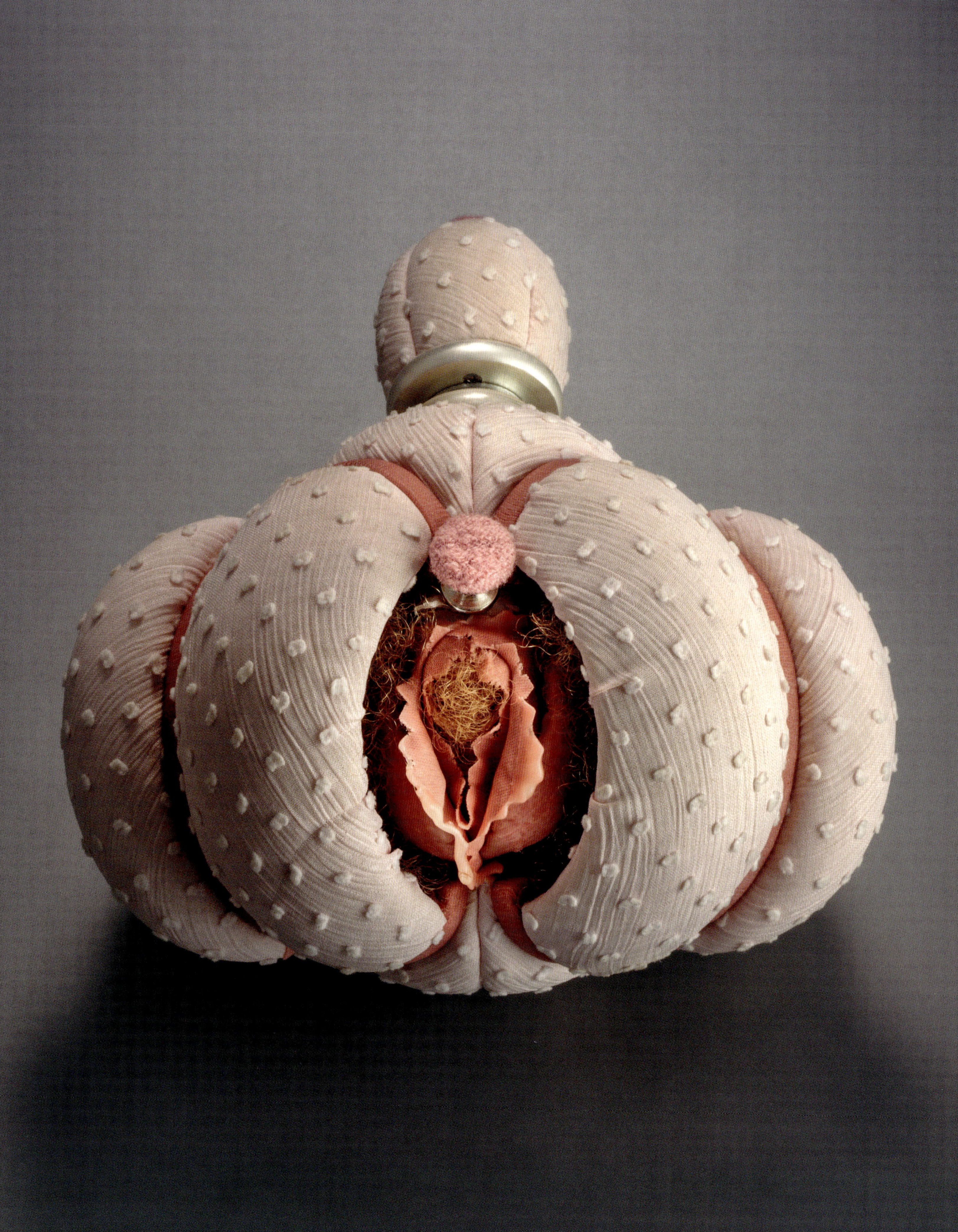

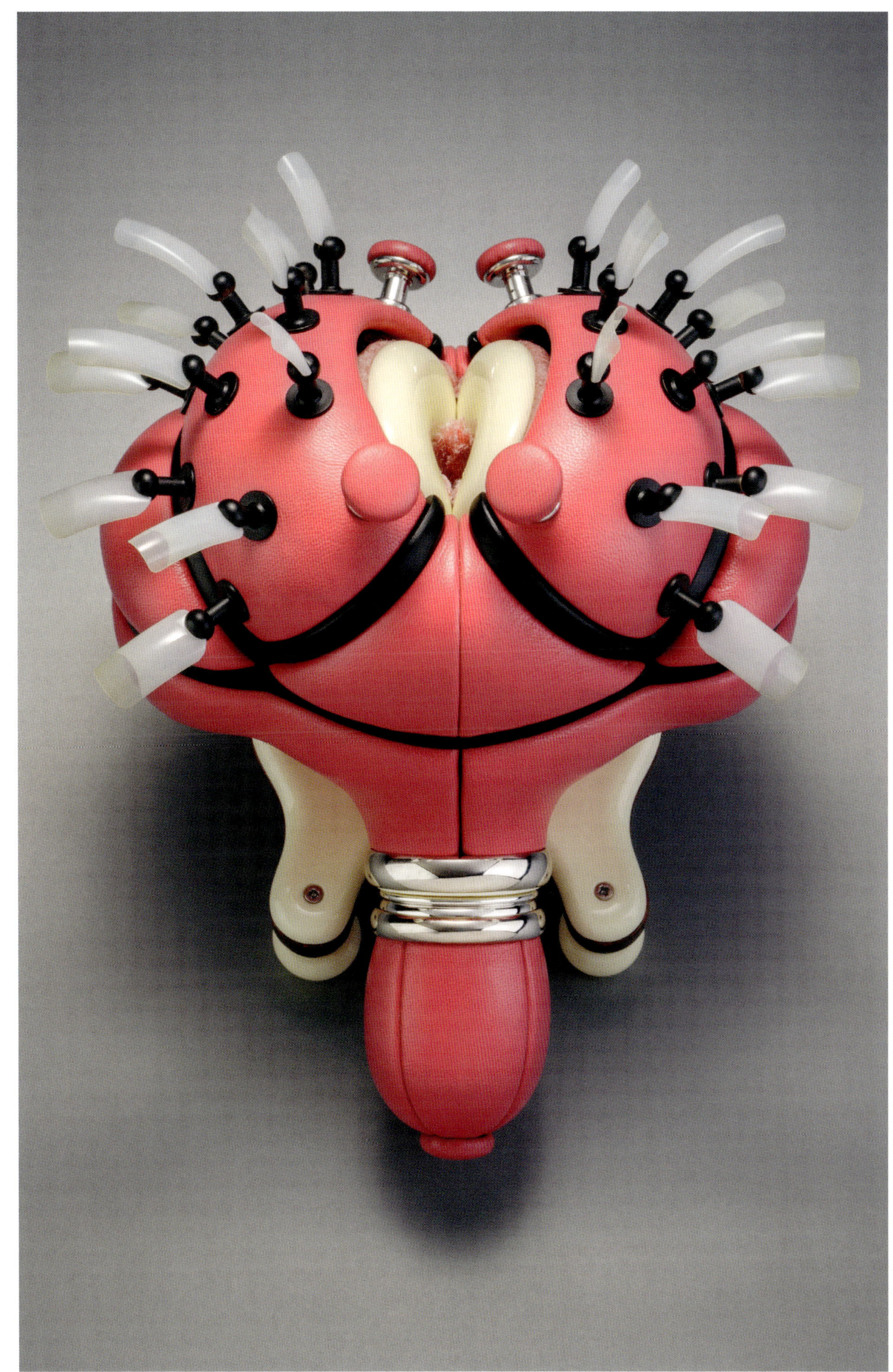

opposite
LITTLE GIRL, PETER PAN, 2013
Fabric, wood, wax, metal findings, human hair.
190 x 190 x 120mm

right
AND IN HER REFLECTION, SHE SAW THE THING THAT SHE WOULD BECOME, 2013
Leather, wood, fabric, plastic, rhodium-plated silver, cocobolo, wax, false fingernails.
190 x 190 x 120mm

*THE TALISMAN OF
FATHER WALSH*, 2019
Leather, fabric, wood,
wax, metal findings,
human hair.
340 x 180 x 200mm

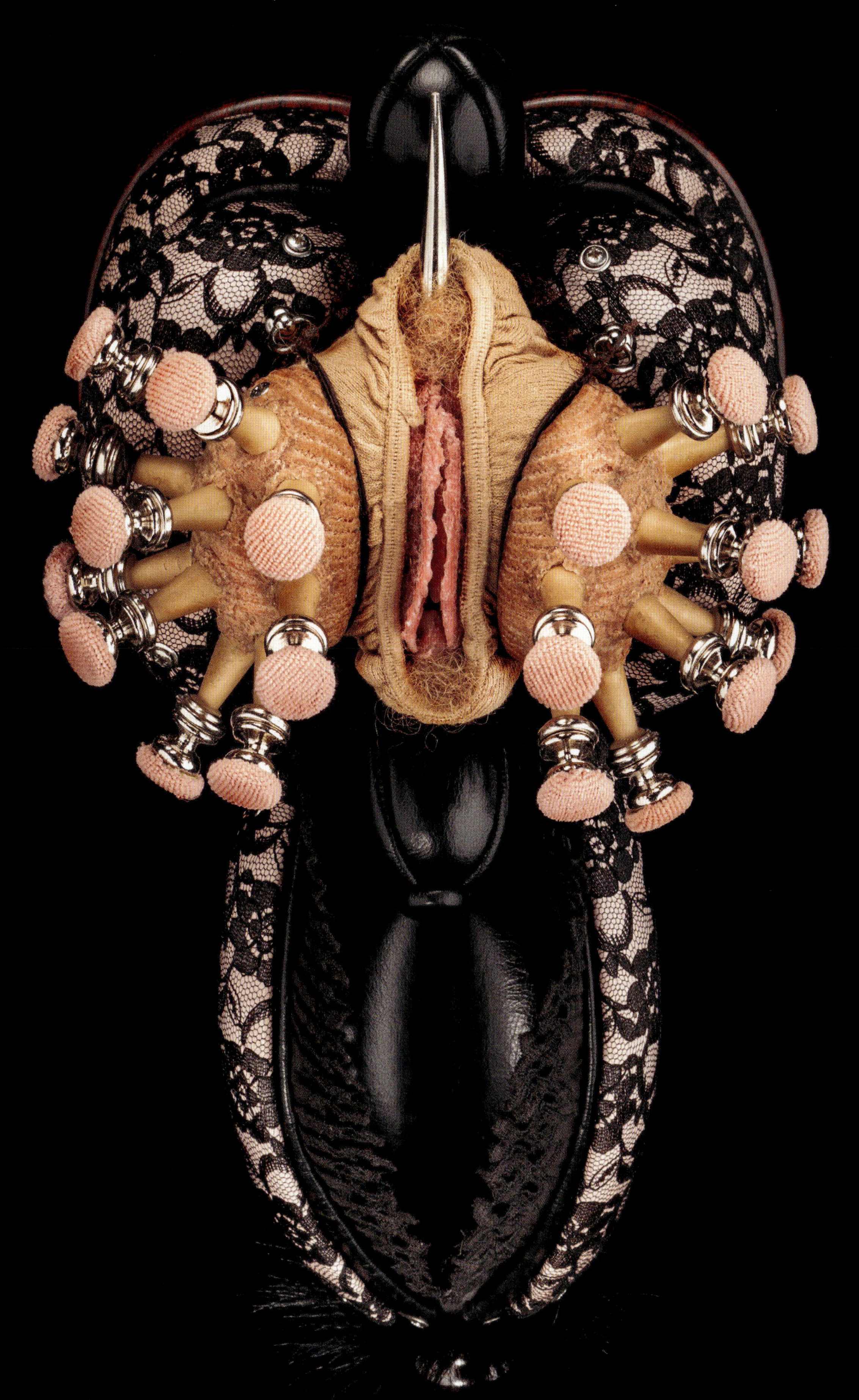

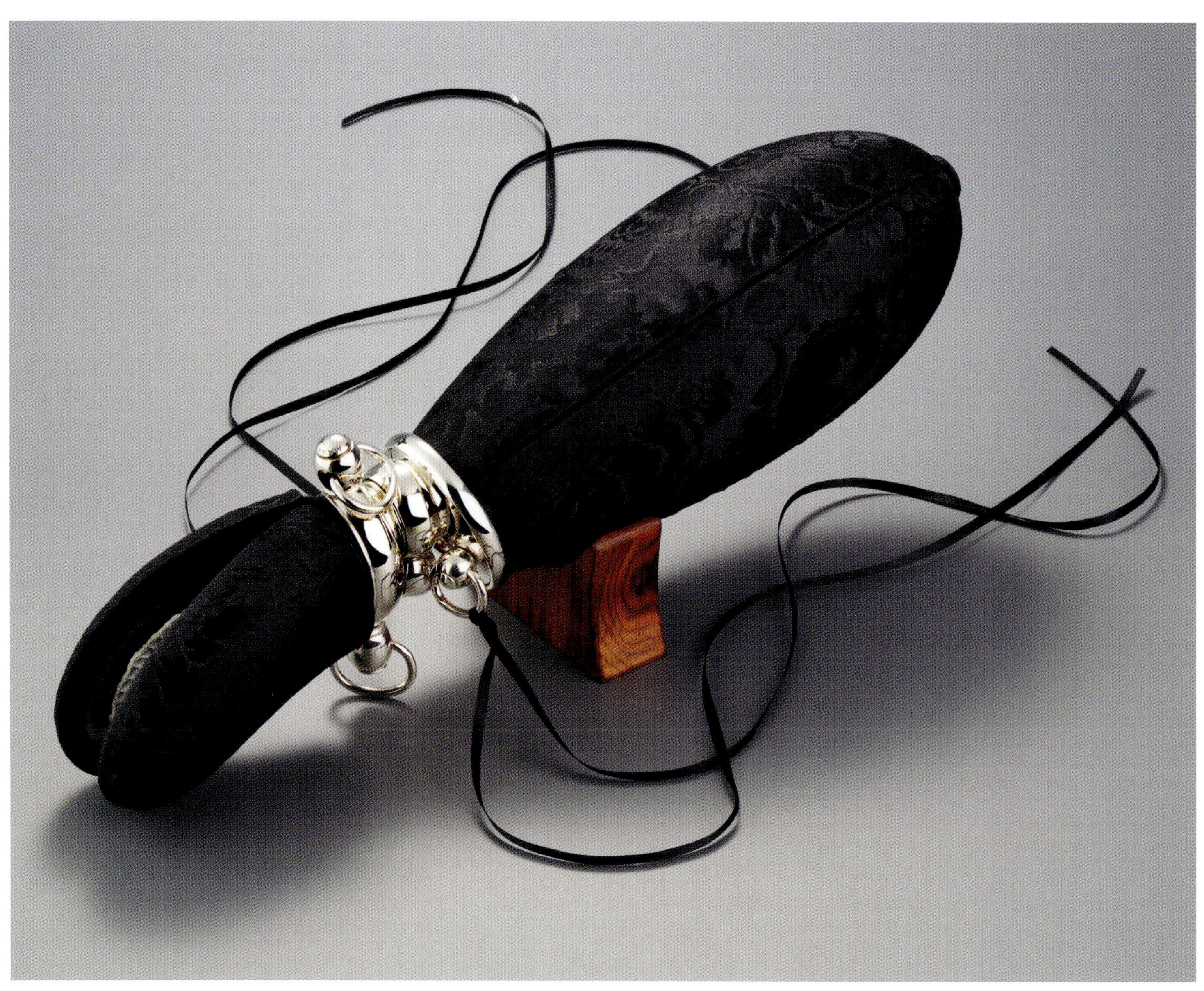

above
PUPAE, 2009
Fabric, wood, rhodium-
plated silver.
320 x 90mm

opposite
*THE DEVIL IN YOUR
MIND BECAME AN
ANGEL IN MINE*, 2015
Resin, plastic, fake
snakeskin, false
fingernails, fur, metal
findings.
440 x 230 x 120mm

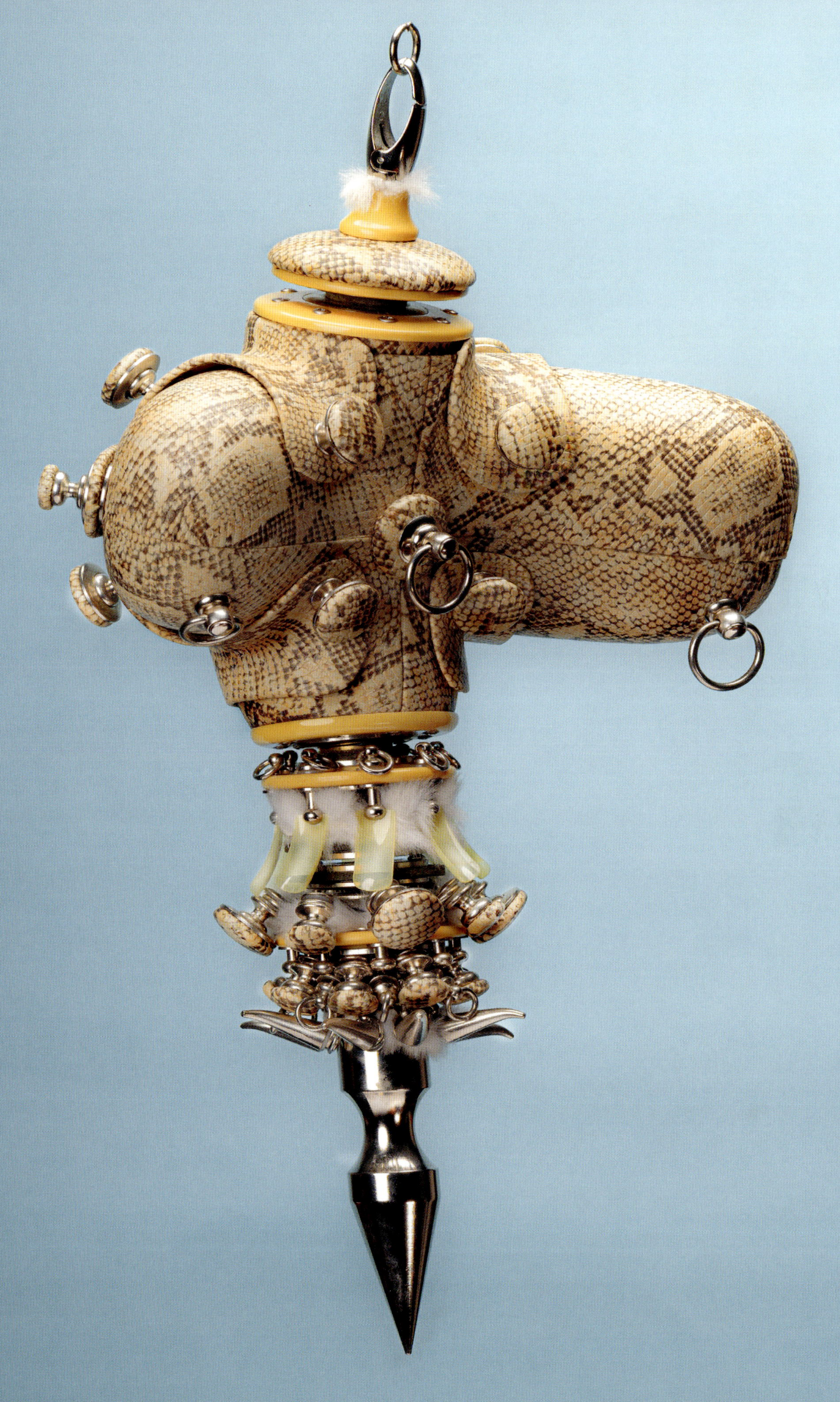

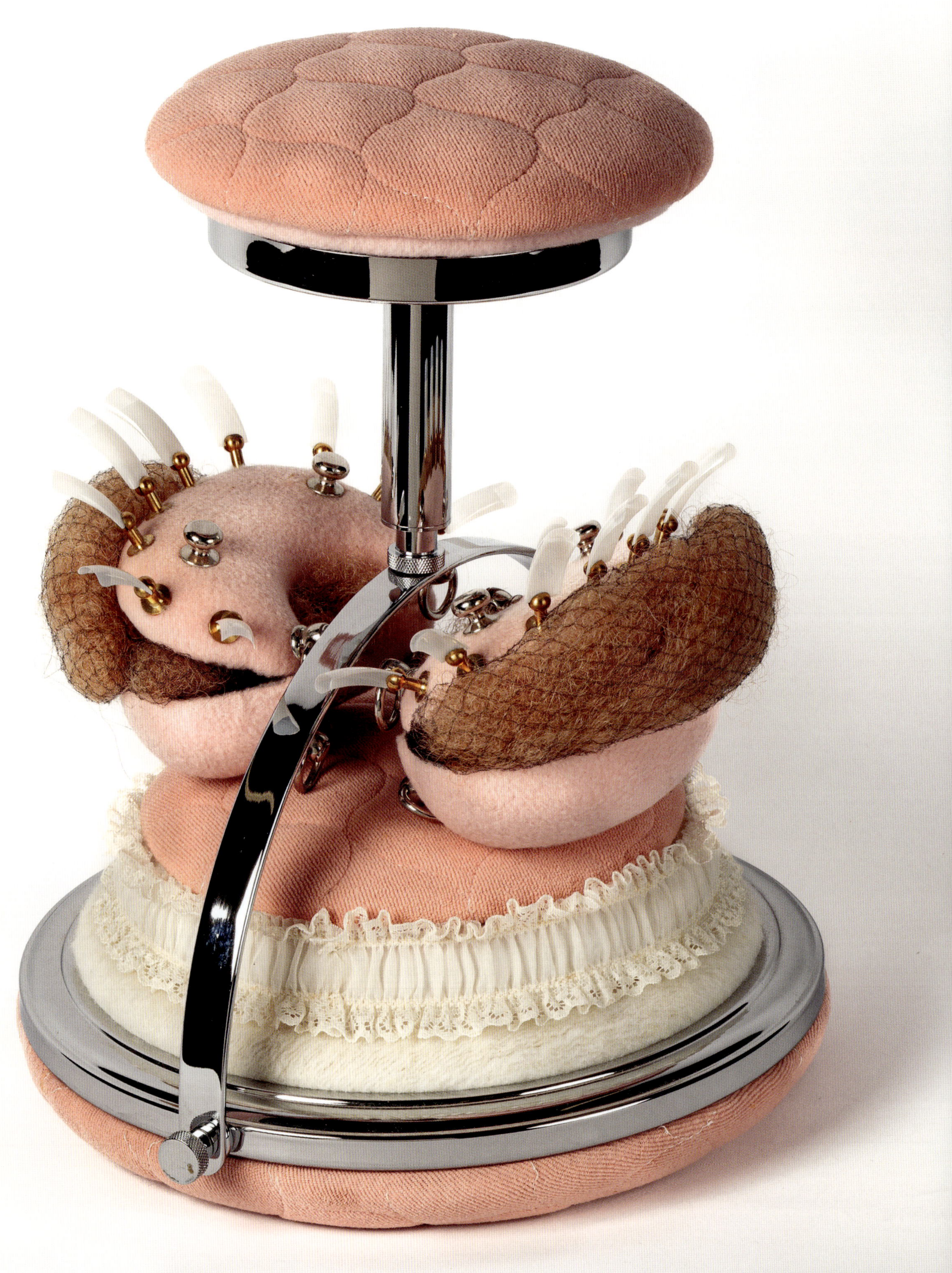

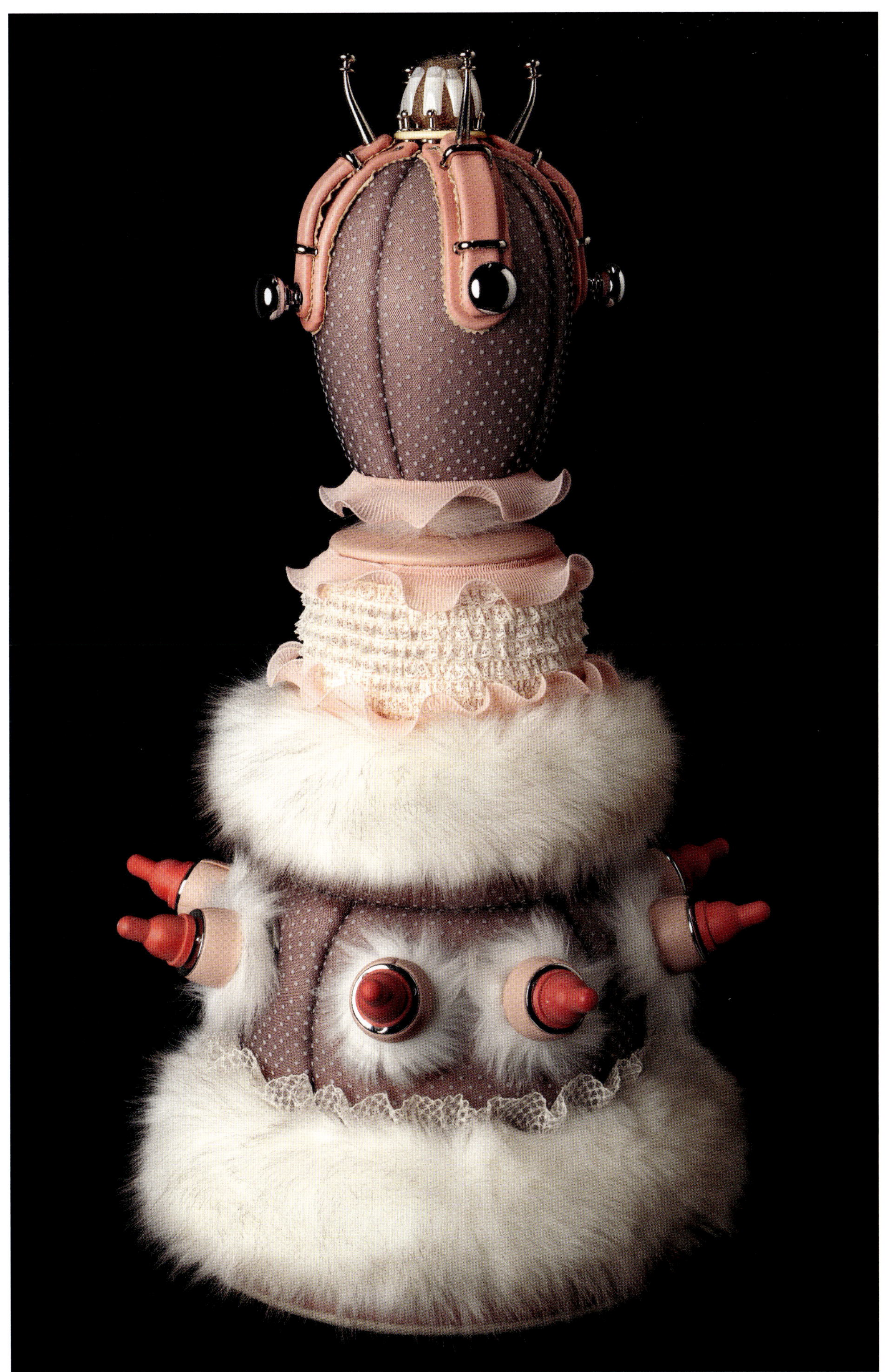

opposite
*THE EFFEMINATE BIG
MAC*, 2013
Chrome shaving mirror
frame, fabric, MDF,
false fingernails, metal
findings.
330 x 280mm

right
*THE CAKE OF EARTHLY
DELIGHTS*, 2019
Wood, fabric, fake
fur, rubber, false
fingernails, leather,
metal findings,
human hair.
1600 x 730 x 600mm

THE ABSORPTION OF
LIGHT & LOVE, 2015
Leather, fabric, plastic,
wood, metal findings,
human hair.
350 x 160 x 140mm

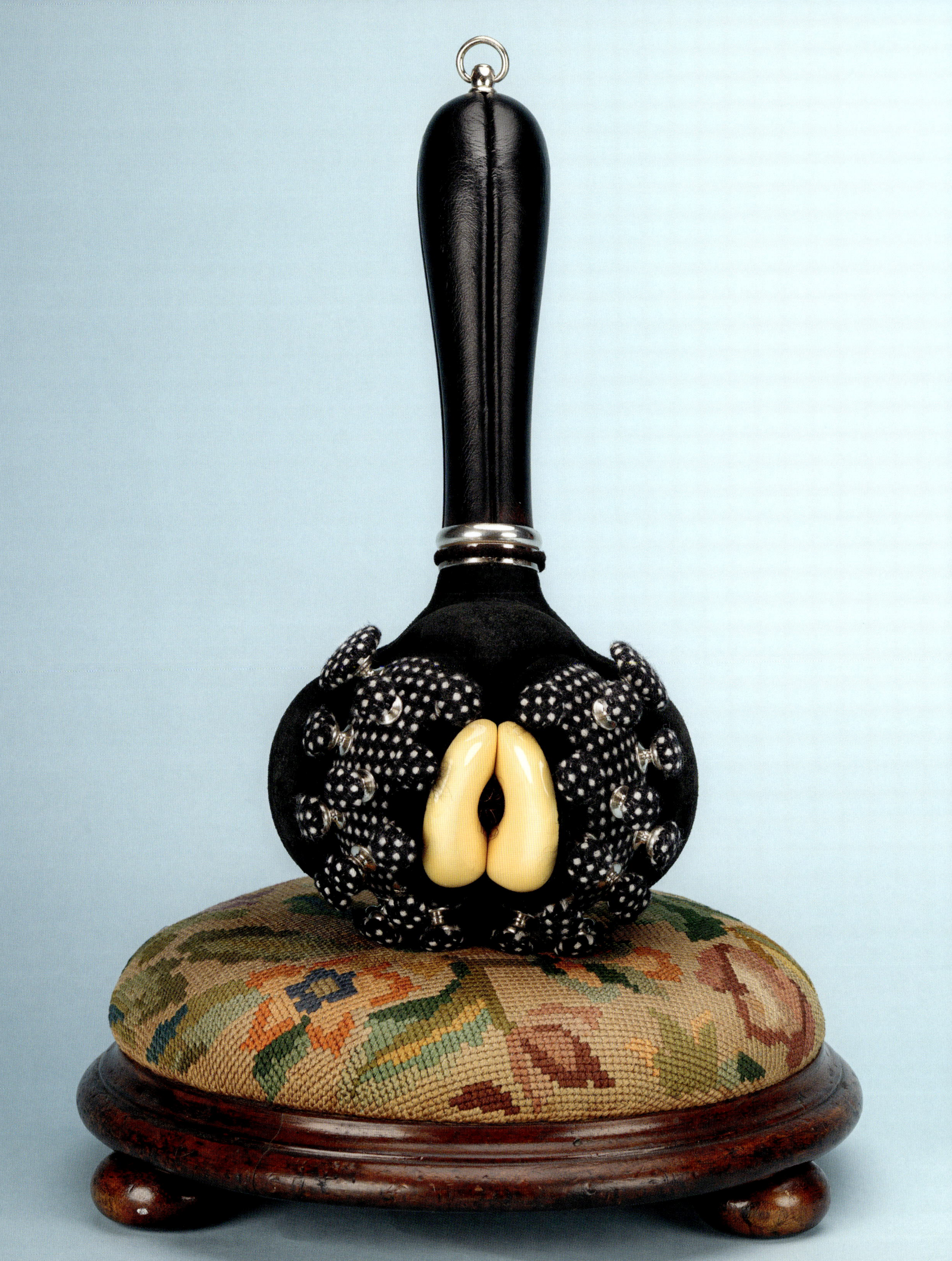

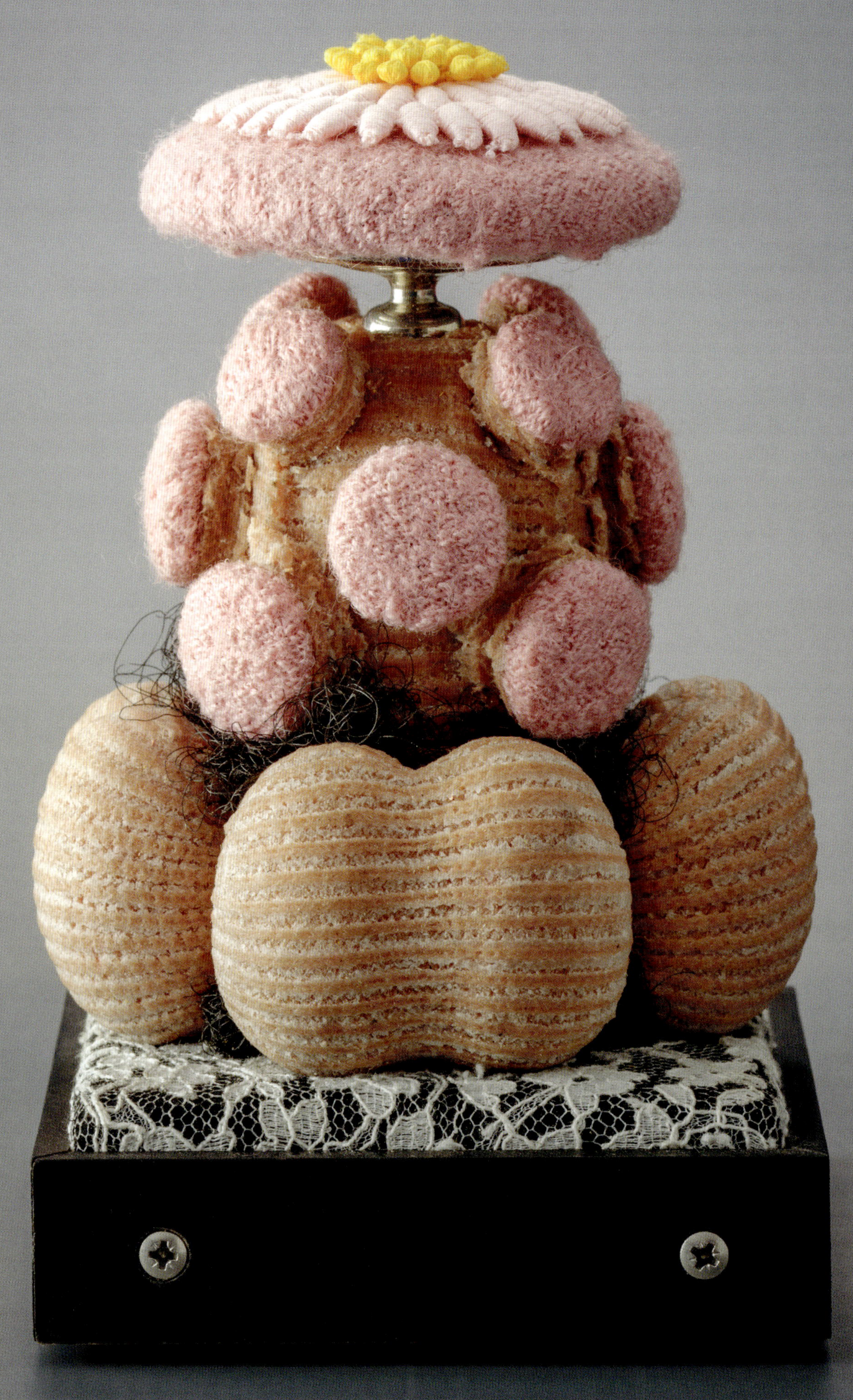

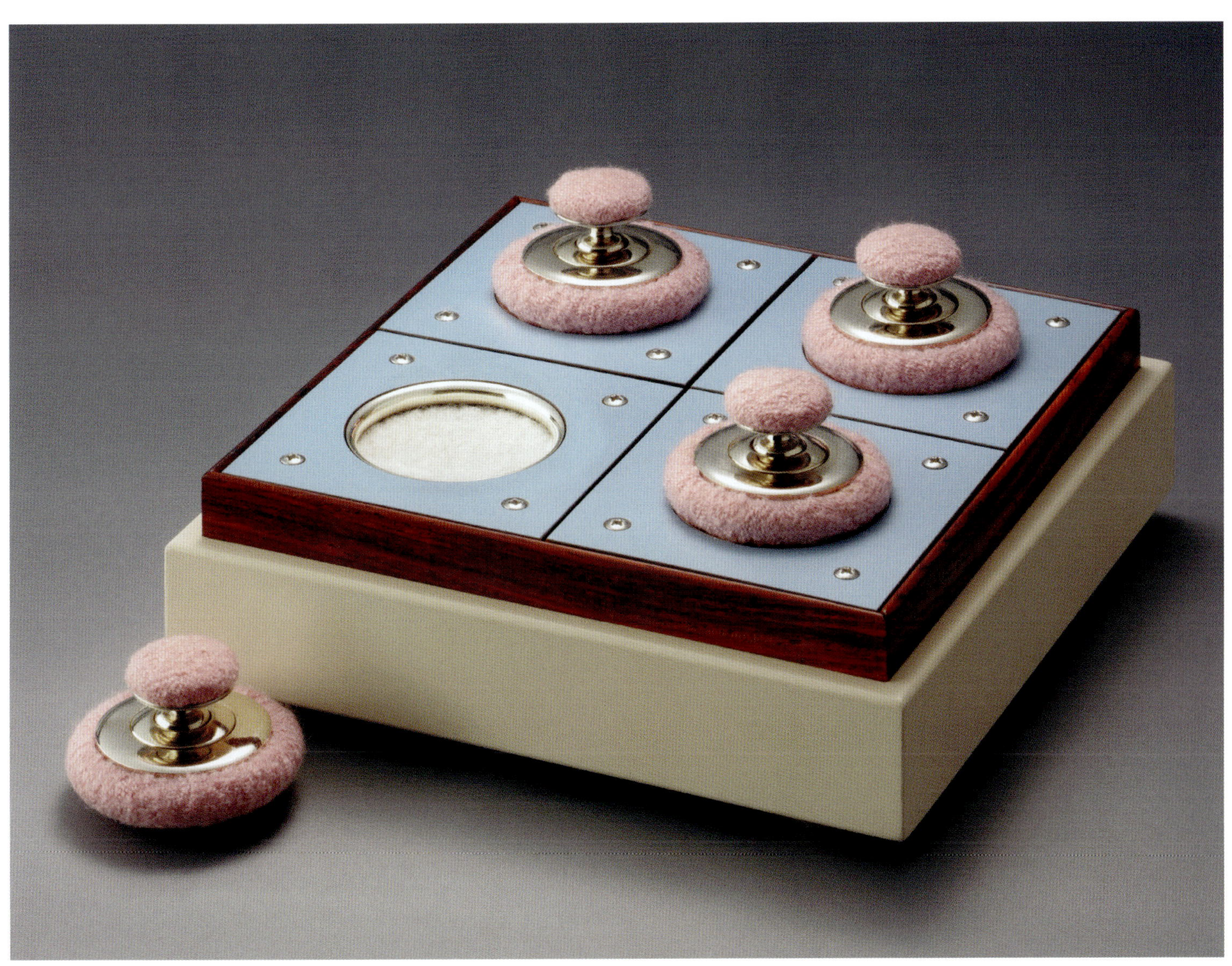

opposite
SOOZ WALL FETISH,
2015
Fabric, wood, wax,
embroidered flower,
human hair.
140 x 95 x 95mm

above
POWDERPUFF GAME,
2013
Fabric, wood, paint,
silver, metal findings,
formica.
80 x 180 x 180mm

overleaf
*TO BE AROUSED IN
HELL, WOULD ONLY
MEAN TORMENT
(BALBONS)*, 2013
Leather, fabric, plastic,
metal findings, silver,
human hair.
330 x 80mm

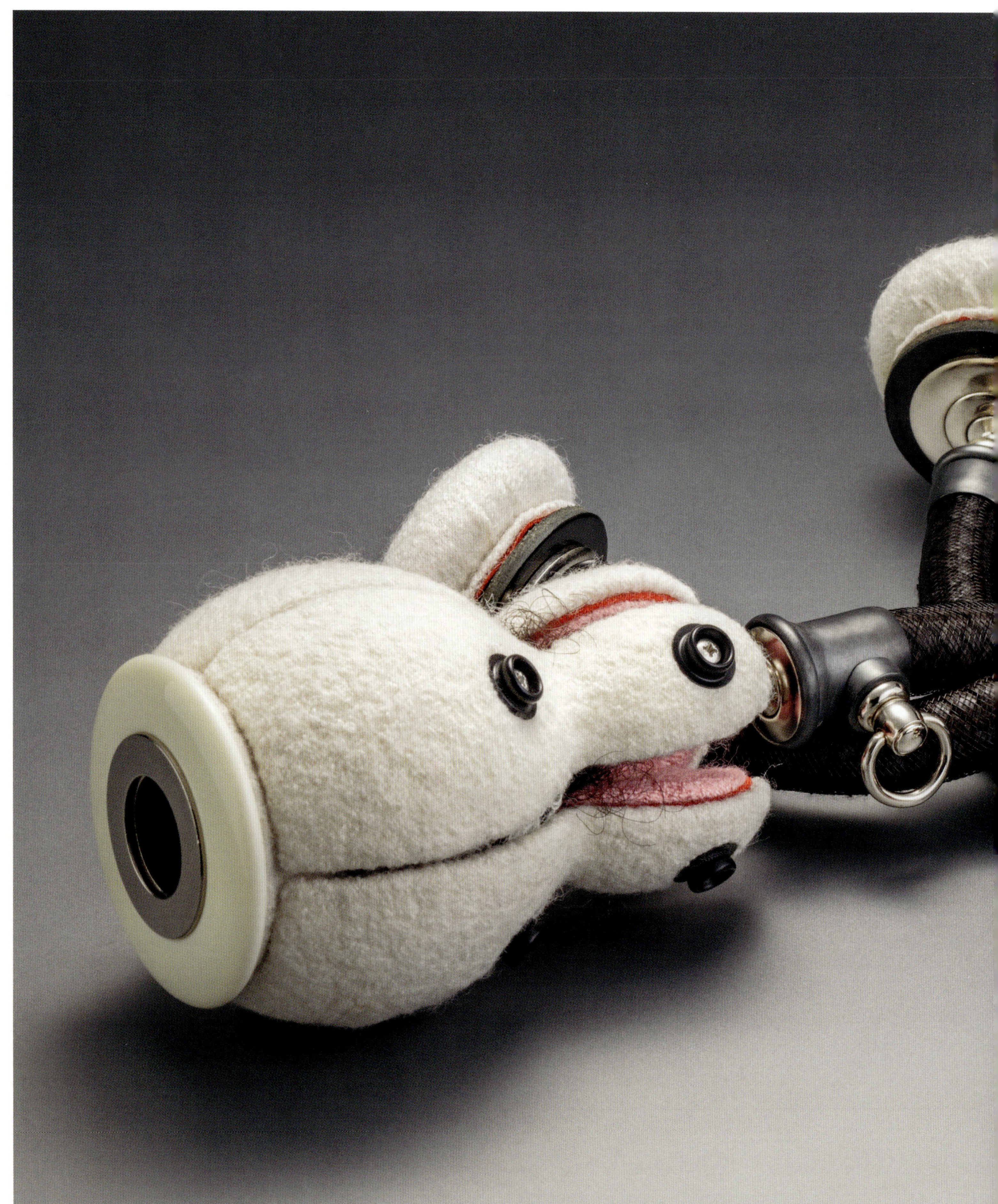

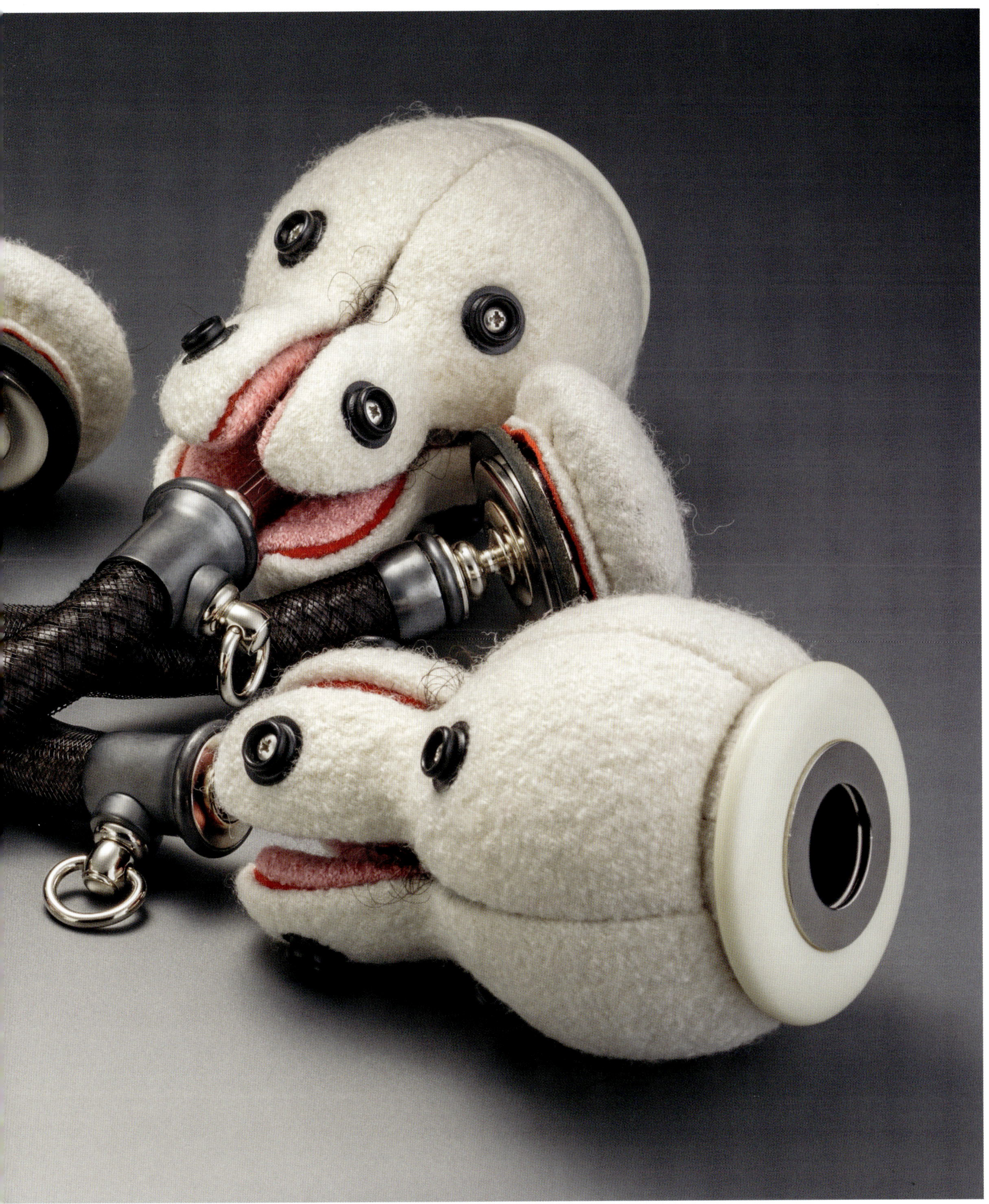

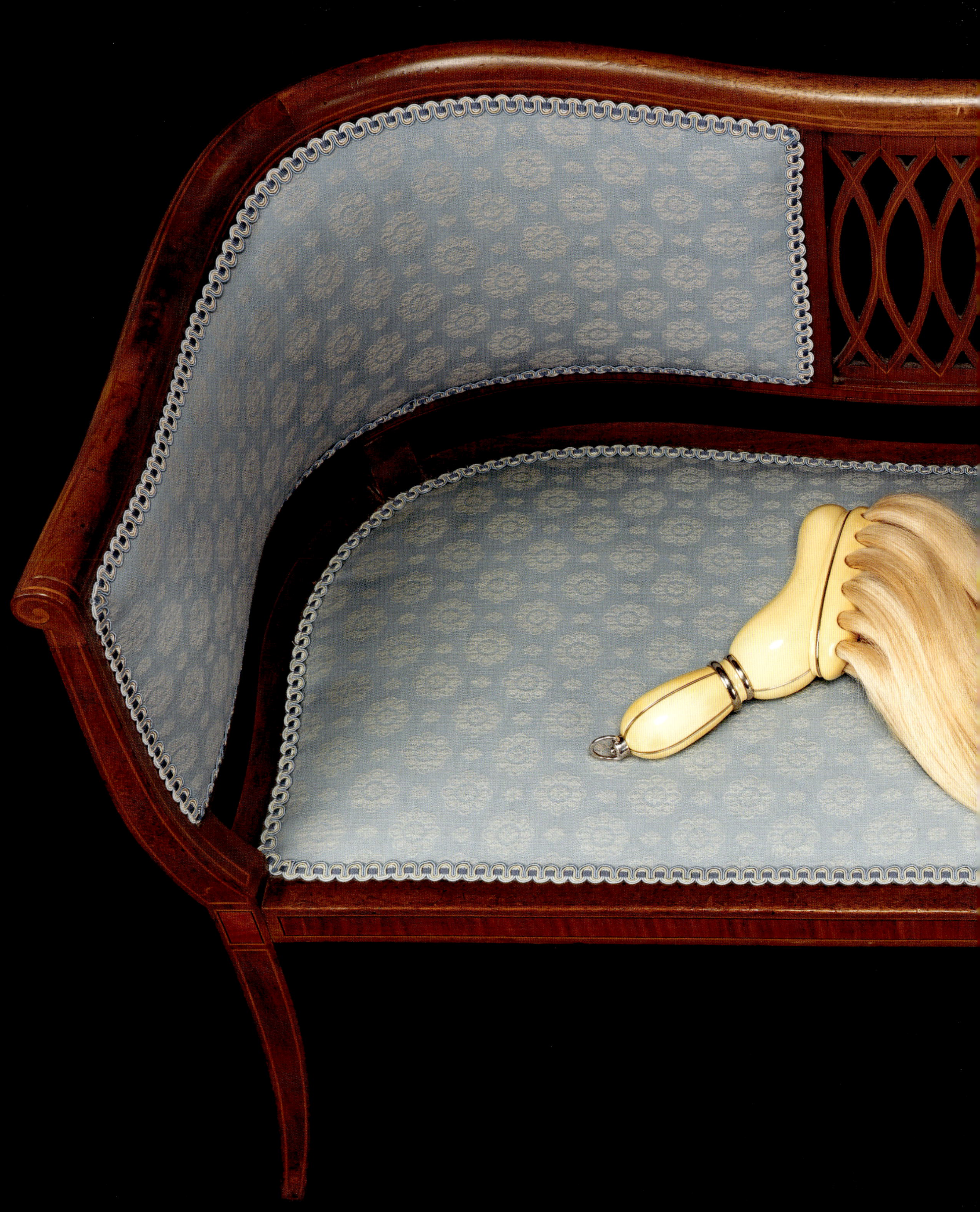

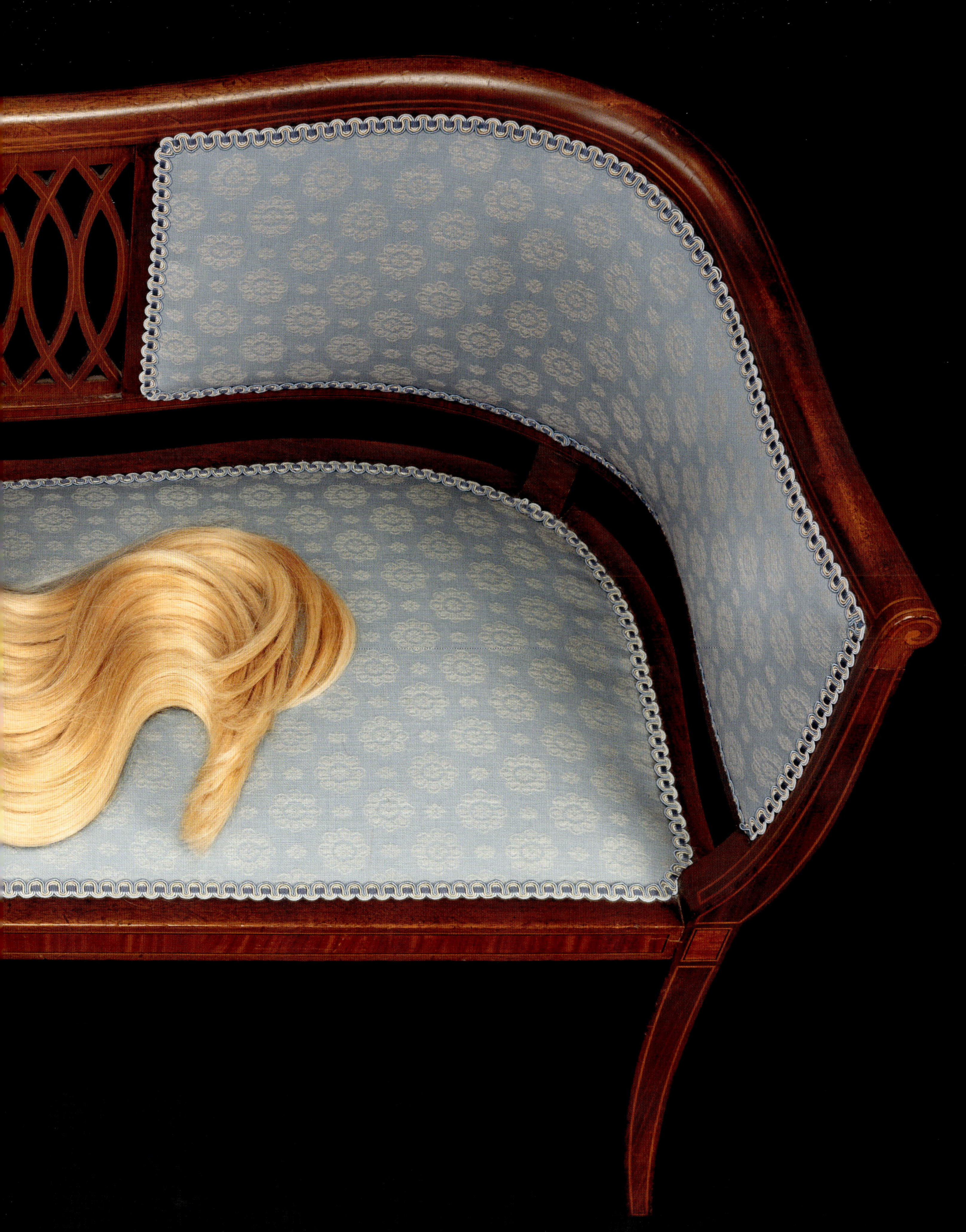

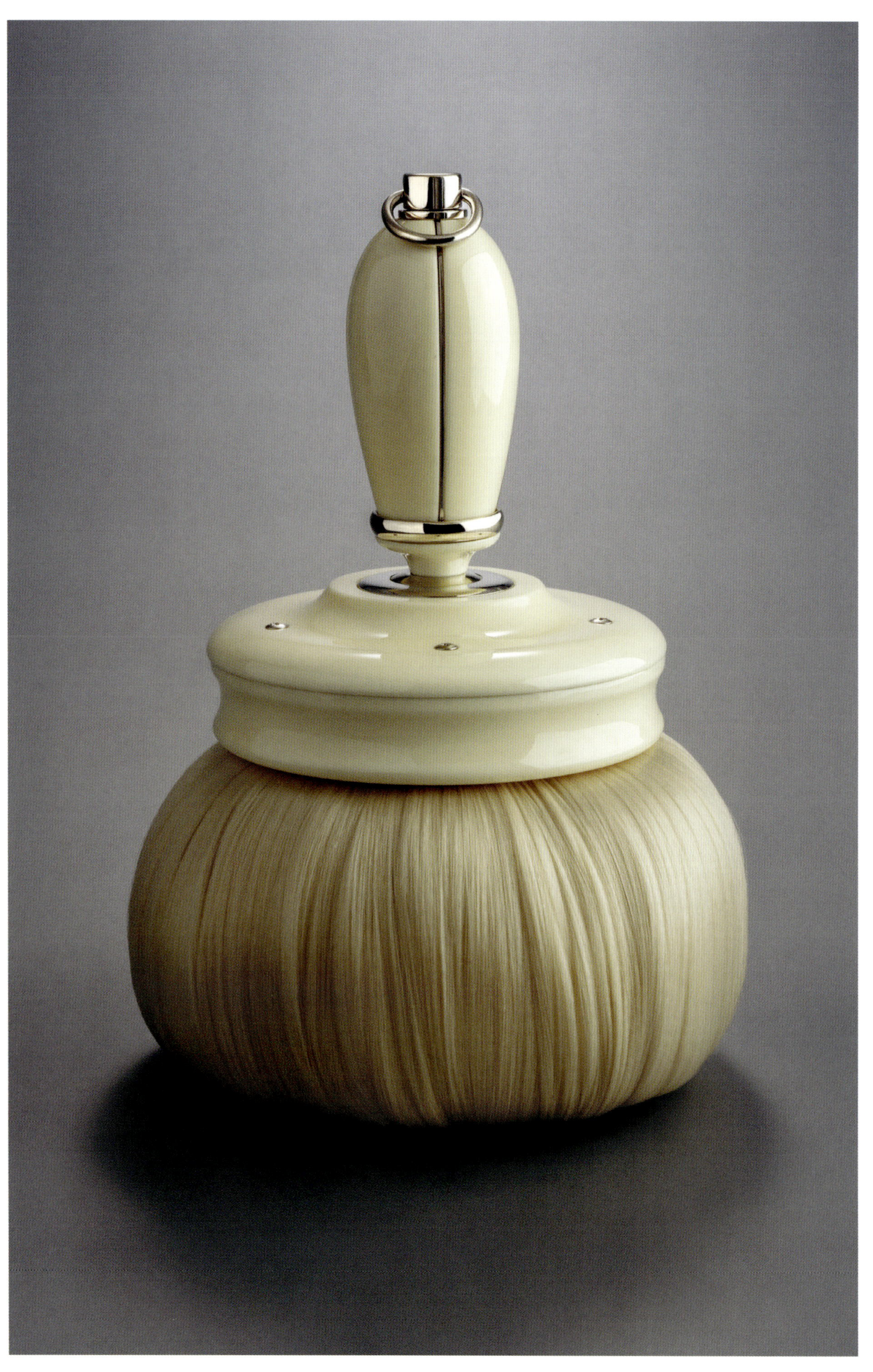

previous pages
BLONDE BOMBSHELL,
2013
Plastic, rhodium-plated
silver, human hair.
220 x 70 x 70mm

left
BLONDE HAIR BUN,
2013
Plastic, synthetic hair,
silver, metal findings.
230 x 150 x 150mm

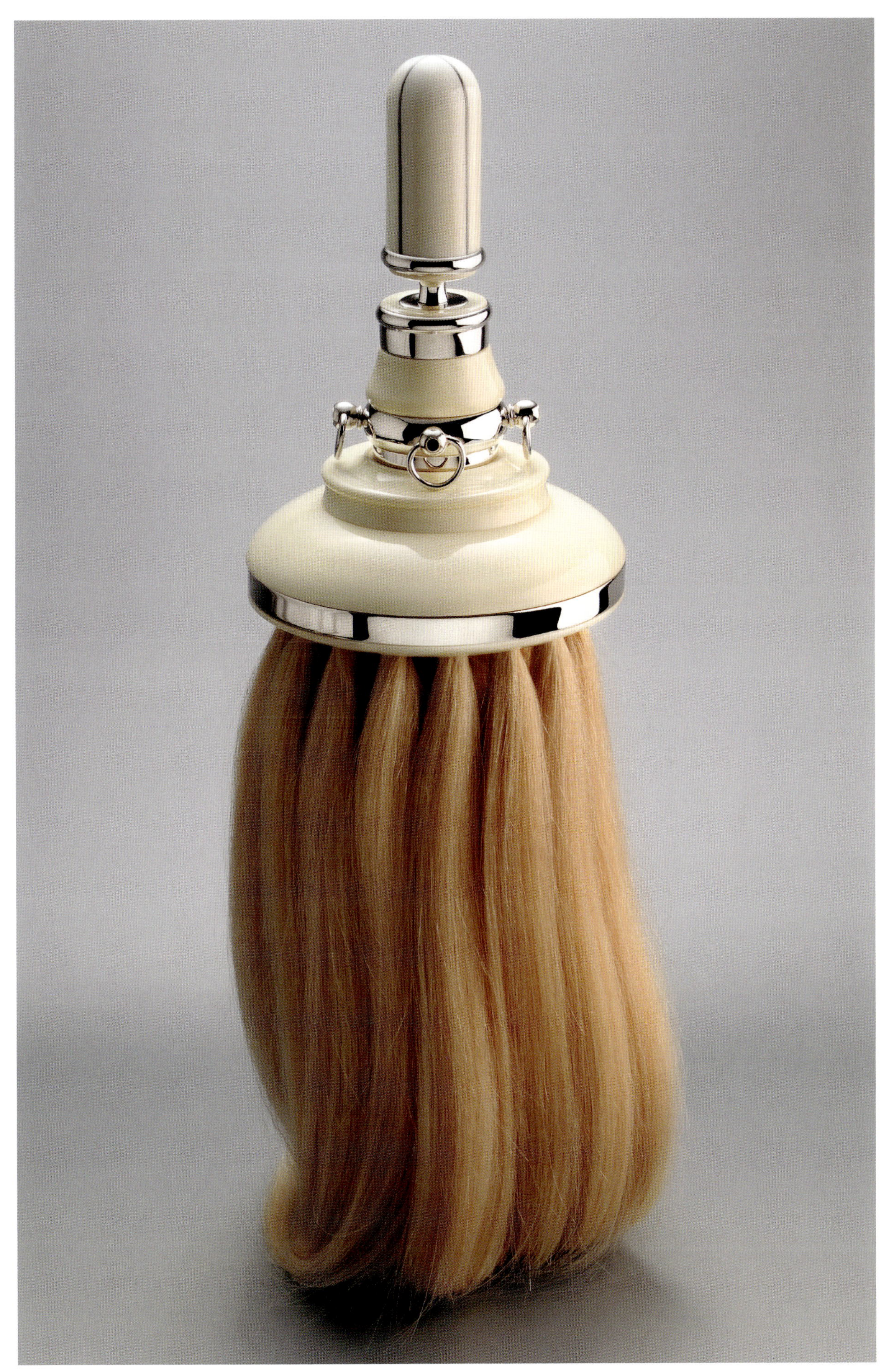

*THE OBJECT OF ITS
OWN GRACE*, 2012
Plastic, rhodium-plated
silver, human hair.
240 x 150mm

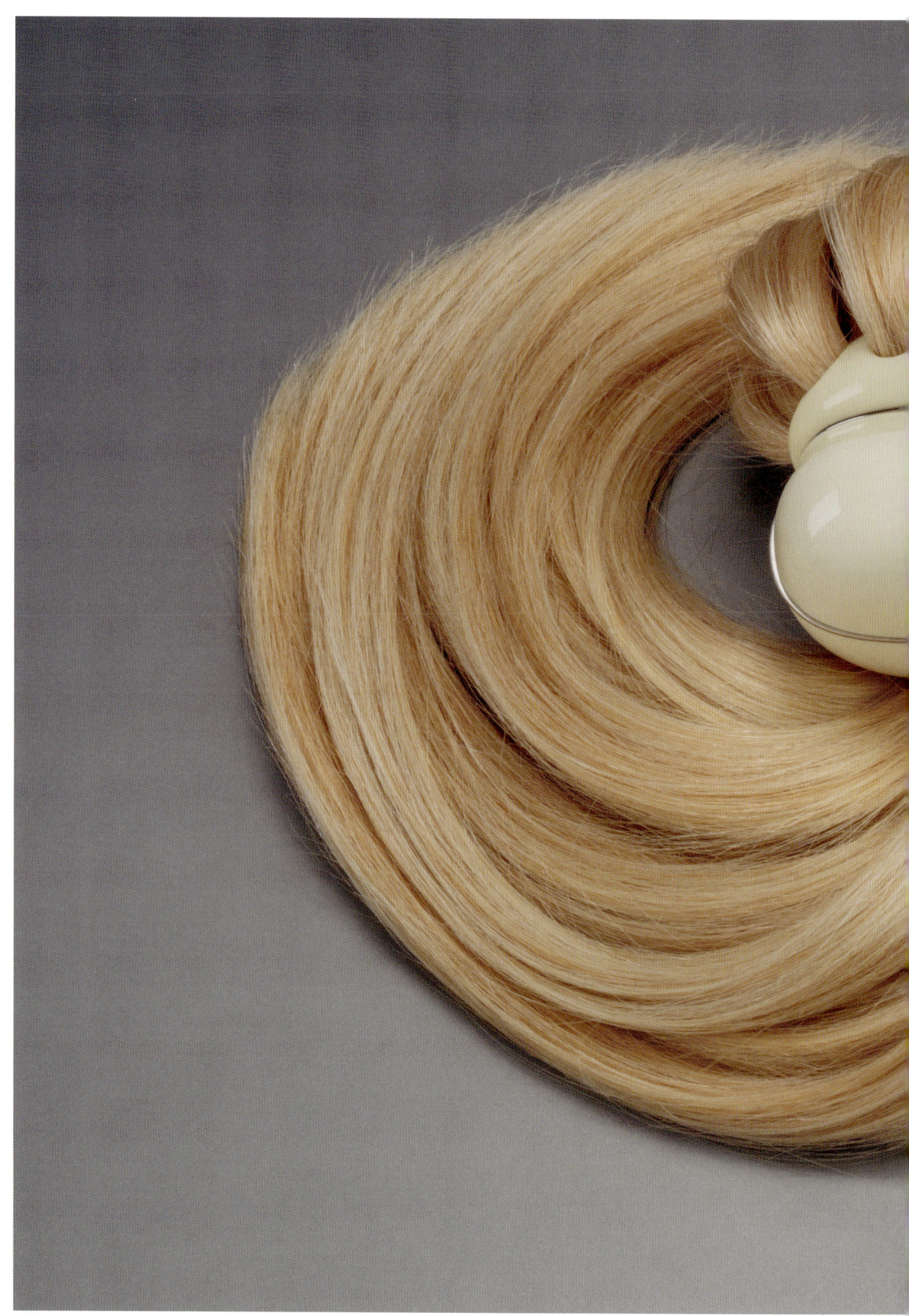

BLONDE BOMBSHELL,
2013
Plastic, rhodium-plated
silver, human hair.
220 x 70 x 70mm

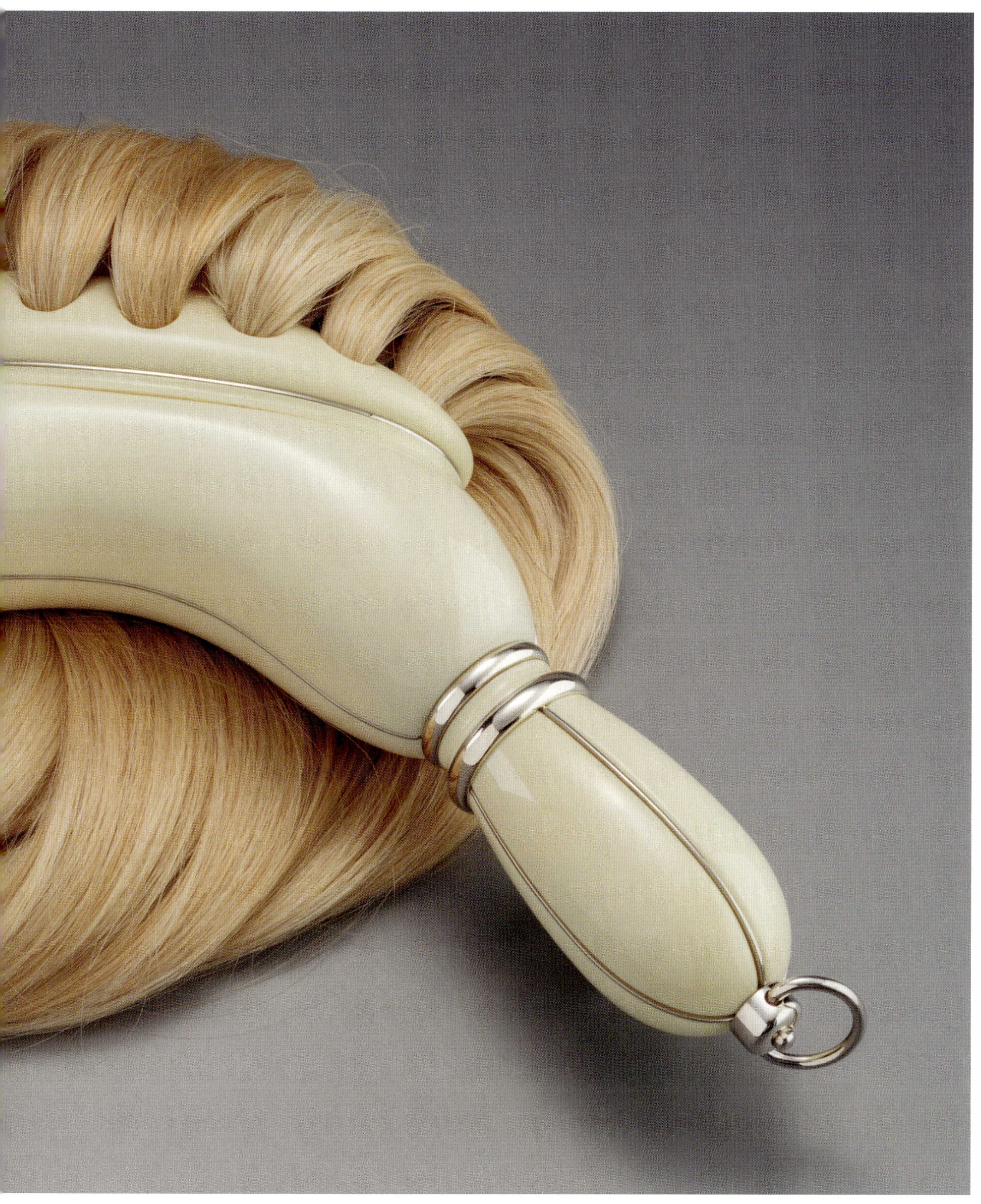

BRA PAD BABY, 2014
Fabric, wax, metal
findings, human hair.
210 x 160 x 90mm

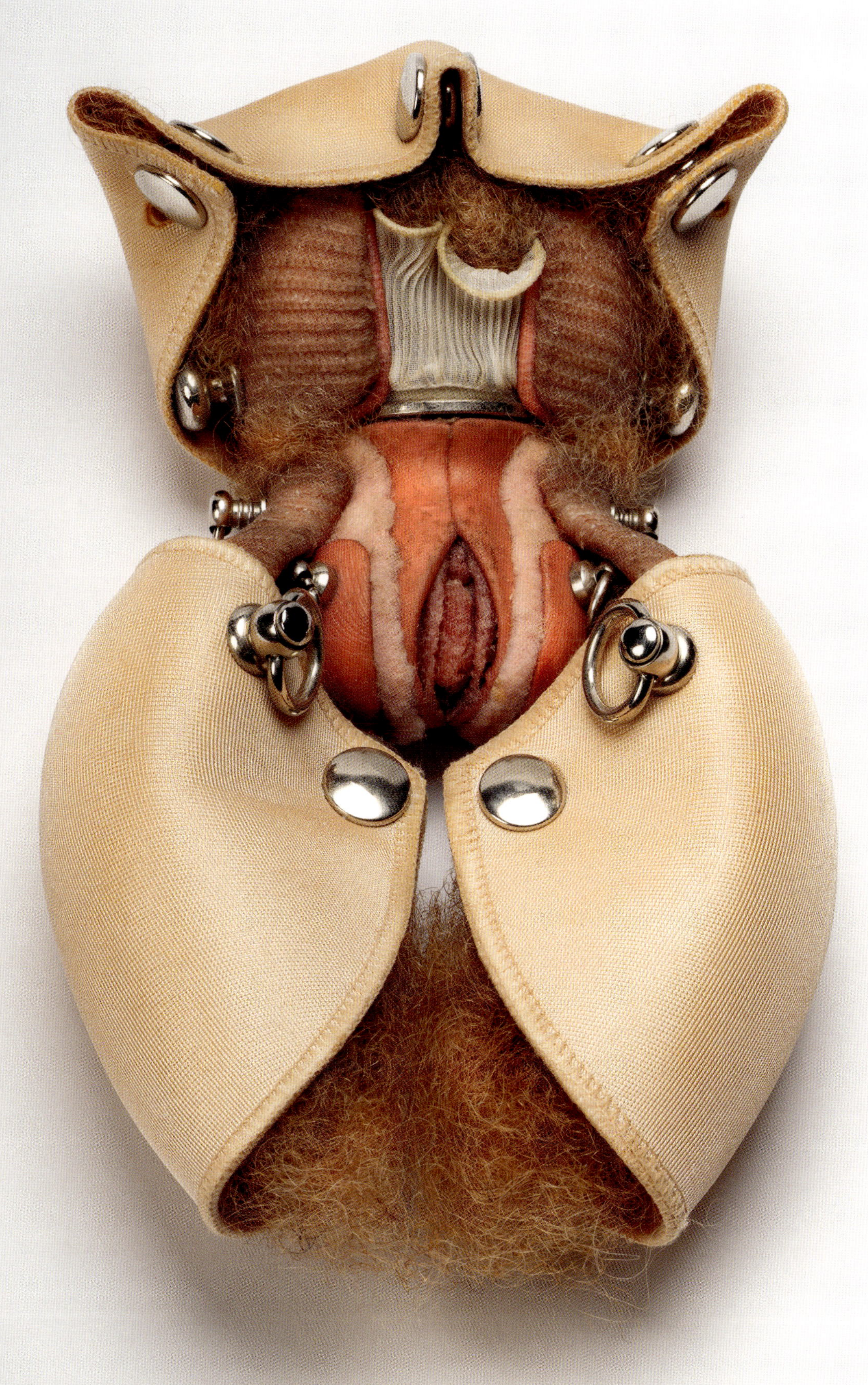

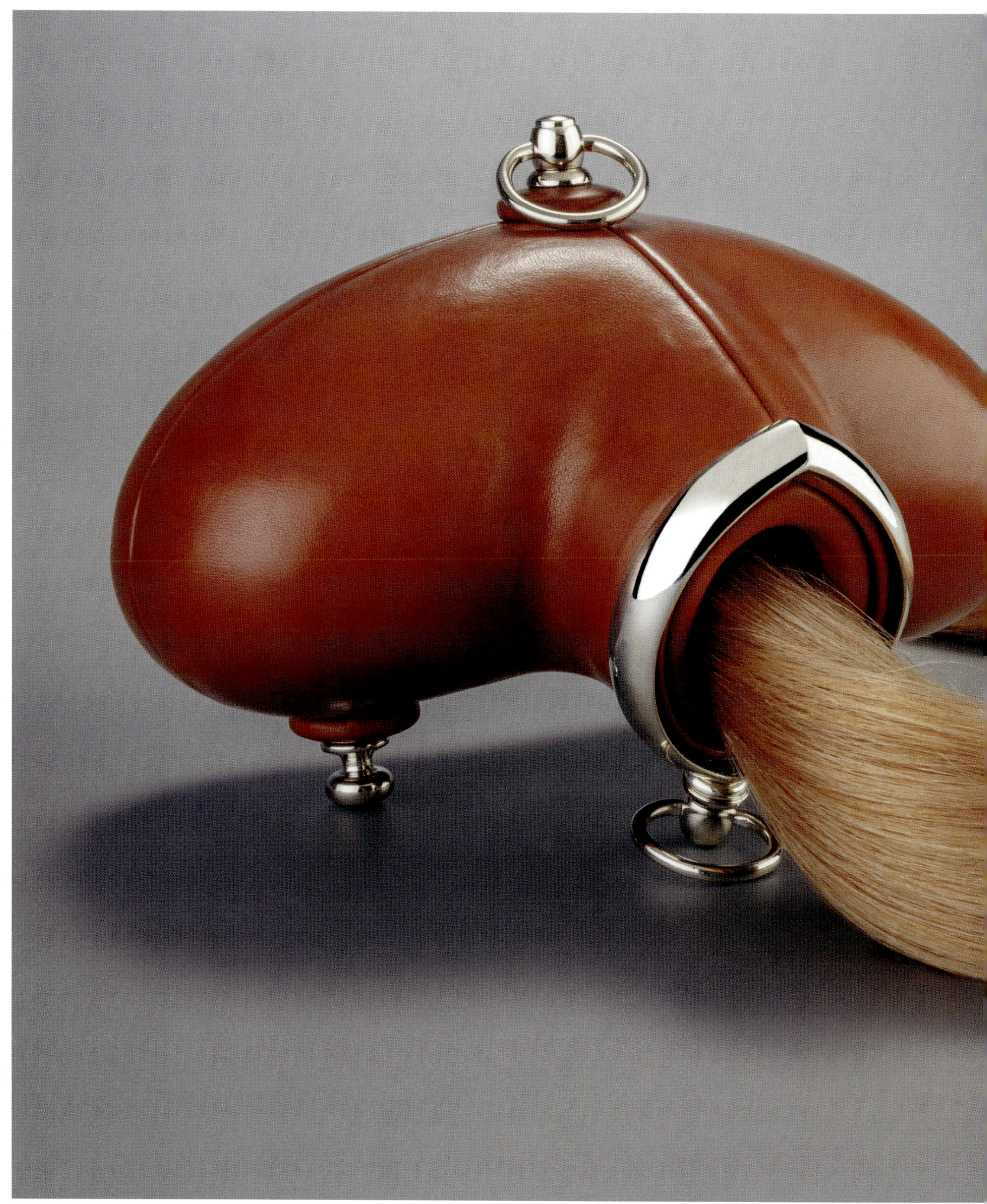

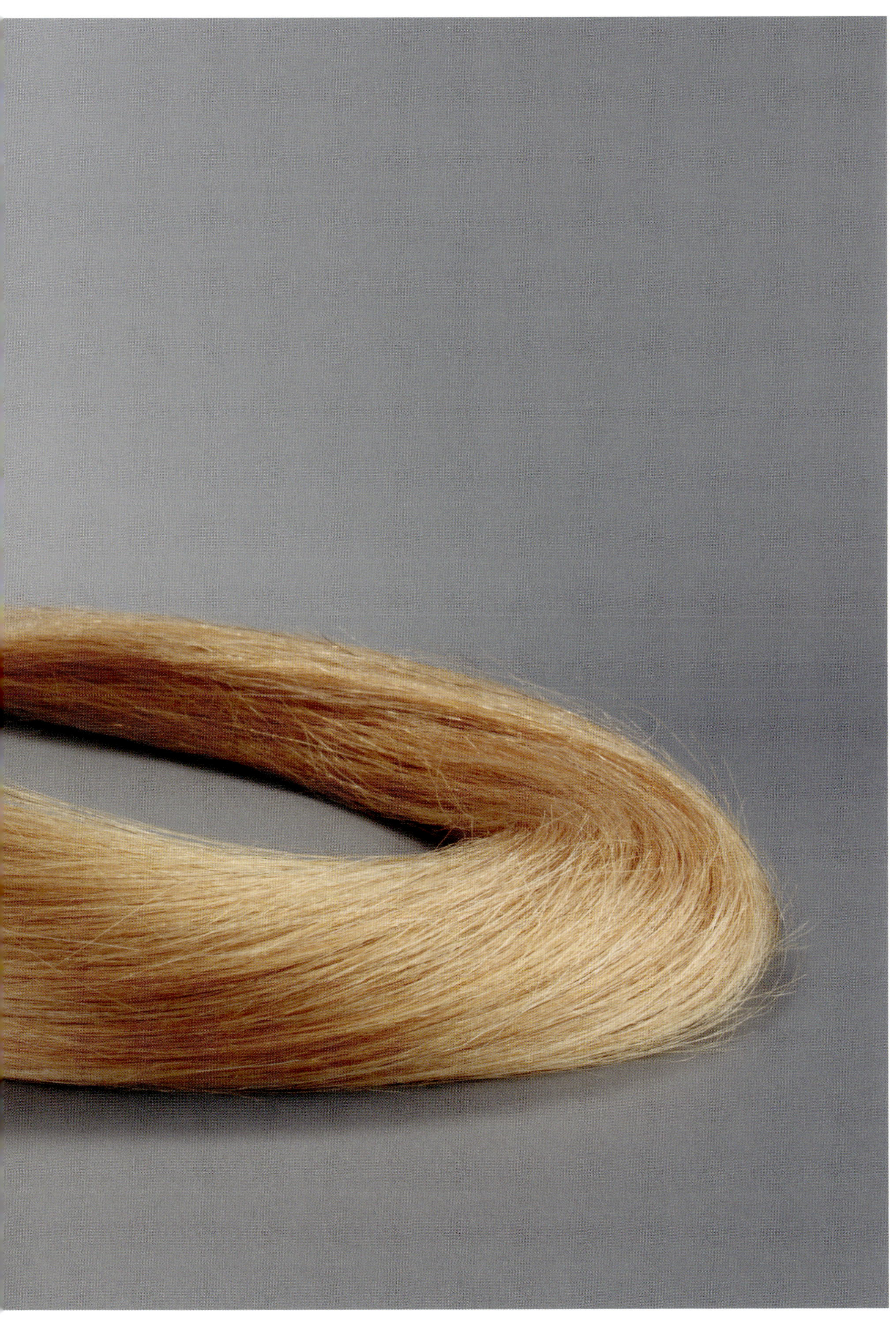

BOX BROWNIE, 2013
Leather, resin, silver,
metal findings, human
hair.
100 x 170 x 140mm

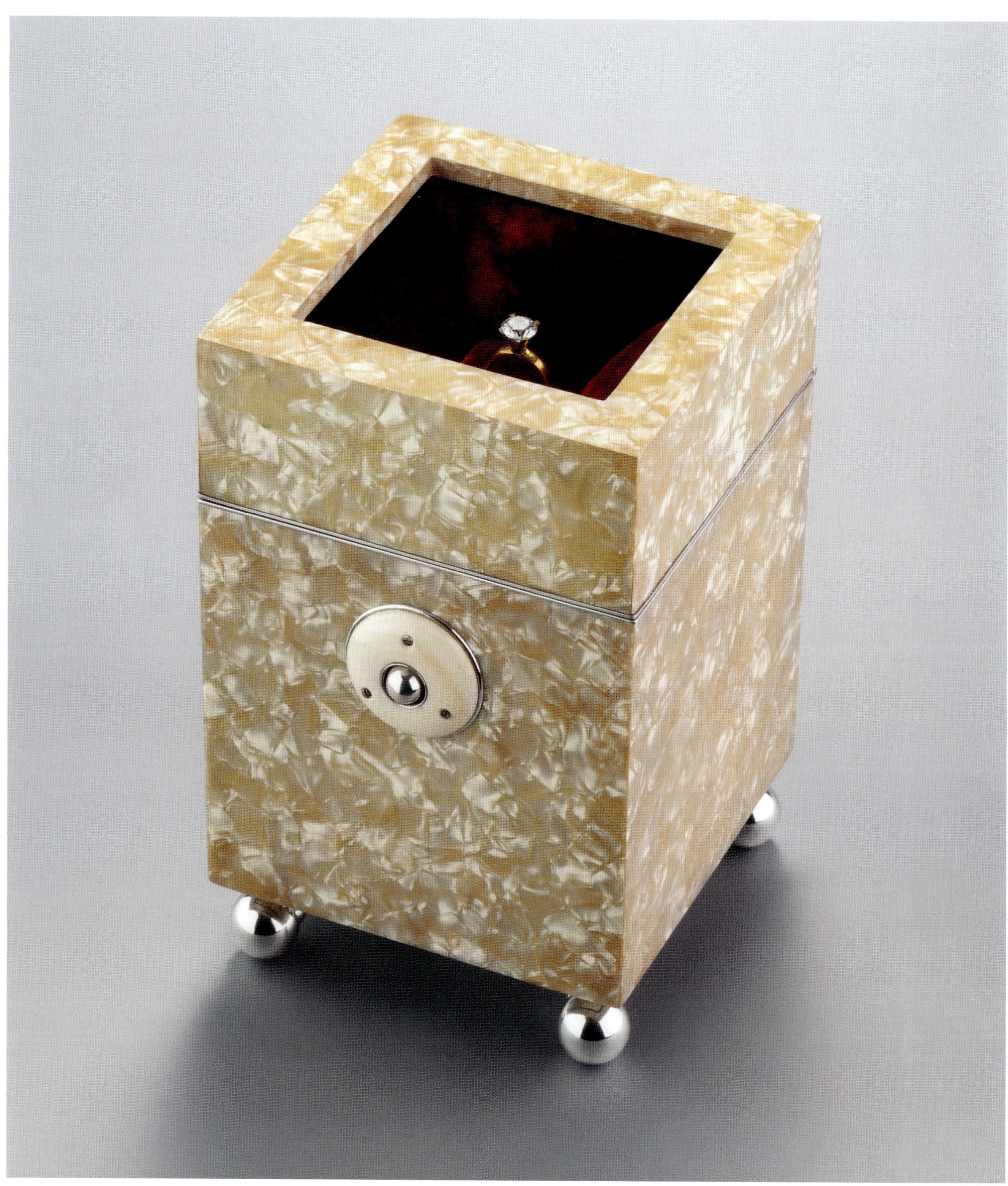

Above and opposite
THE FAMILY JEWELS, 1999
Music box, cellulose
nitrate veneer, MDF,
velvet, plastic, cubic
zirconia, spinel, silver,
22ct. gold, Sankyo music
box movement, tune:
"Somewhere Over the
Rainbow". Collaboration
with Rebecca Scott.
200 x 140 x 140mm

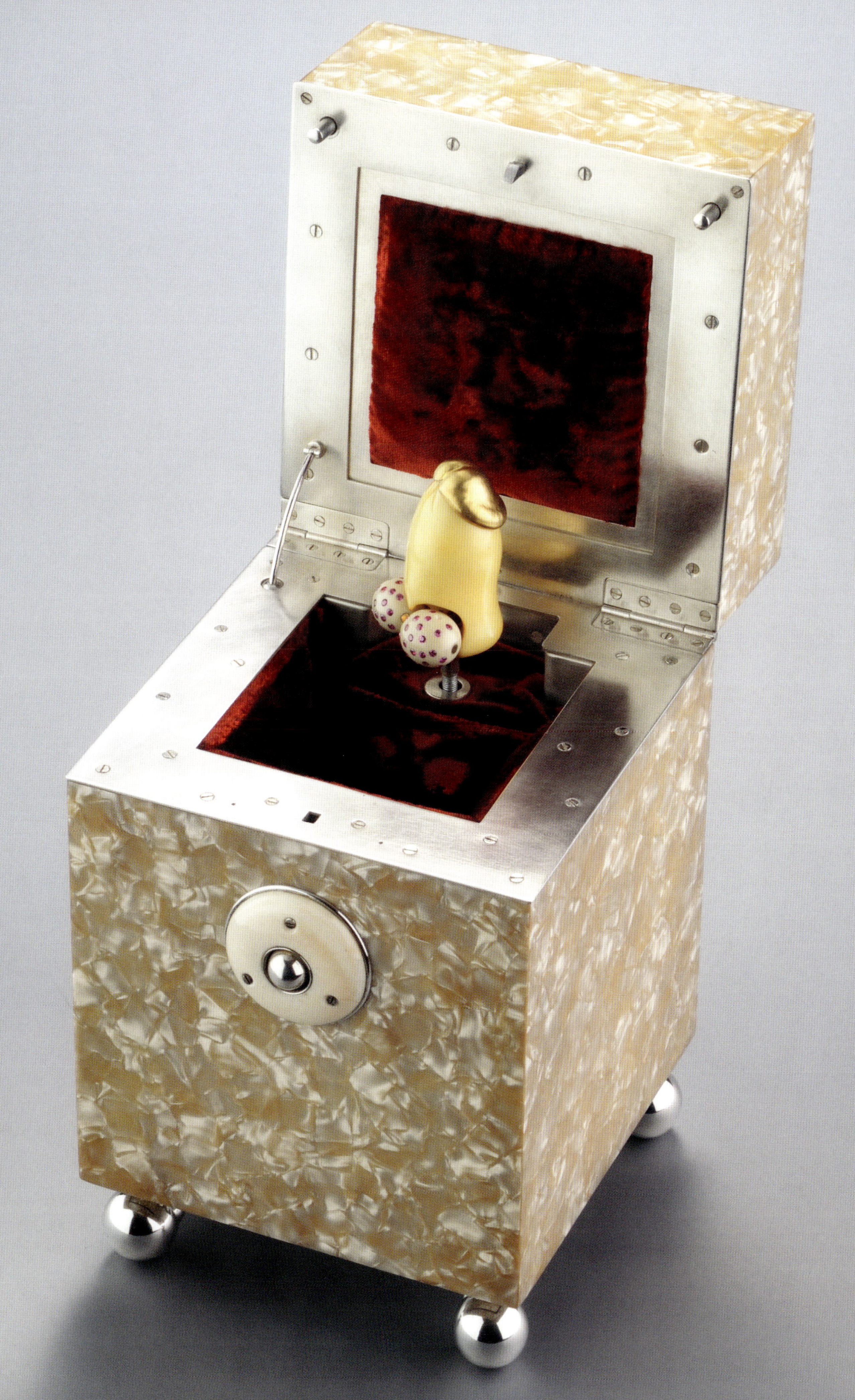

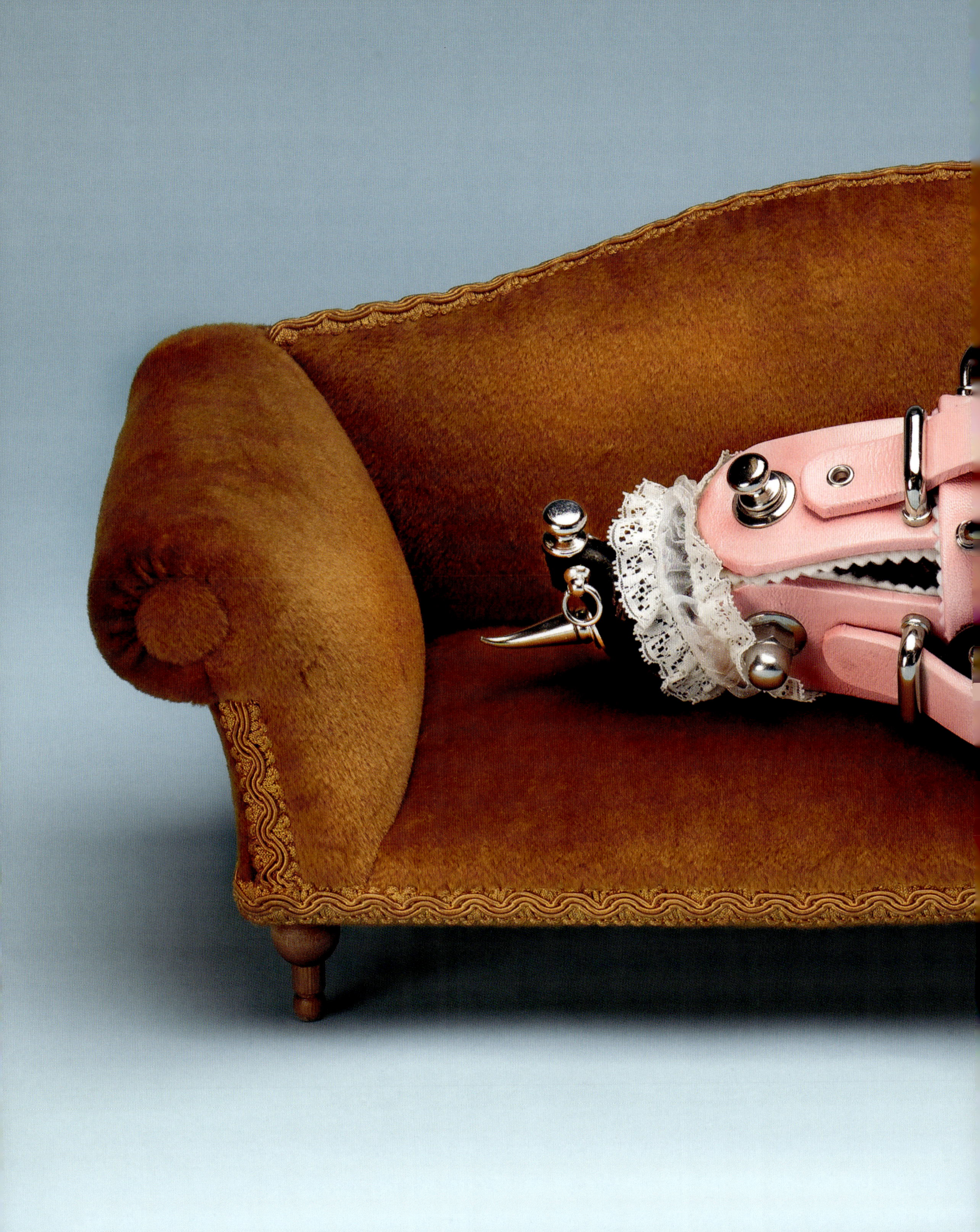

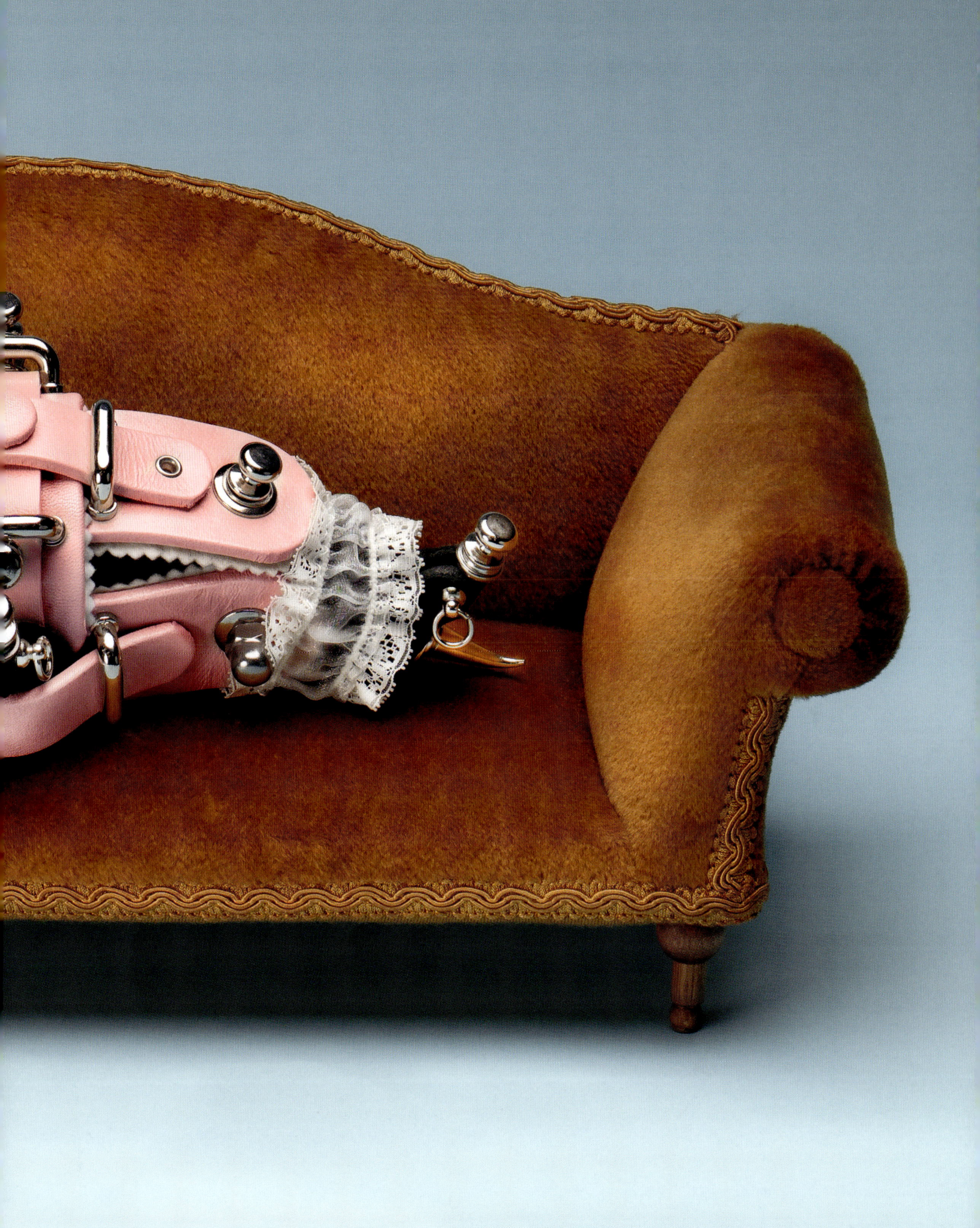

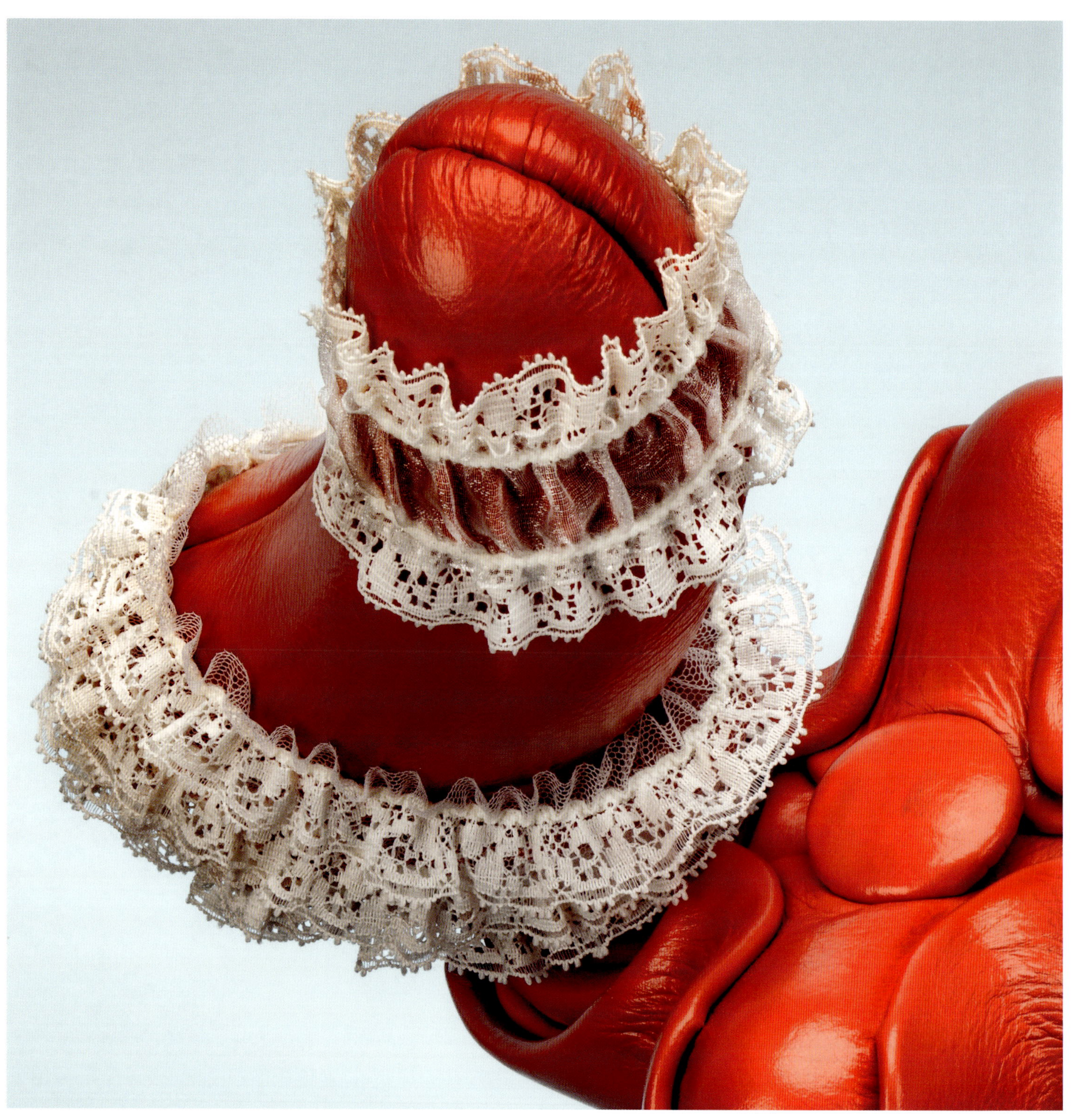

previous pages,
HURLY-BURLY, 2024
Doll house sofa, leather,
fabric, rope, metal
findings.
360 x 140 x 150mm

above and opposite
COCK-A-HOOP, 2010–24
Wood, leather, fabric
paint, metal findings.
250 x 150 x 300mm

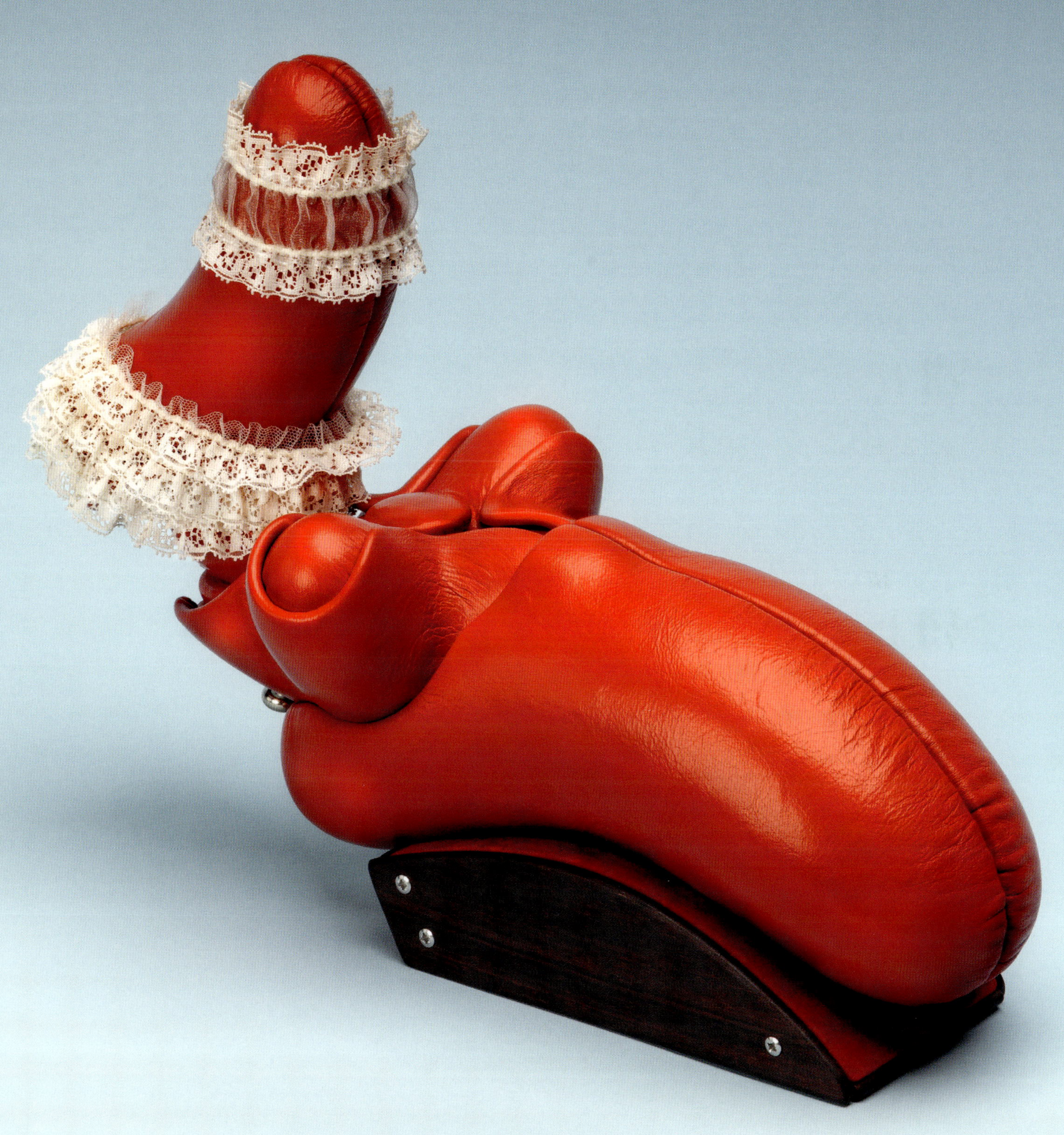

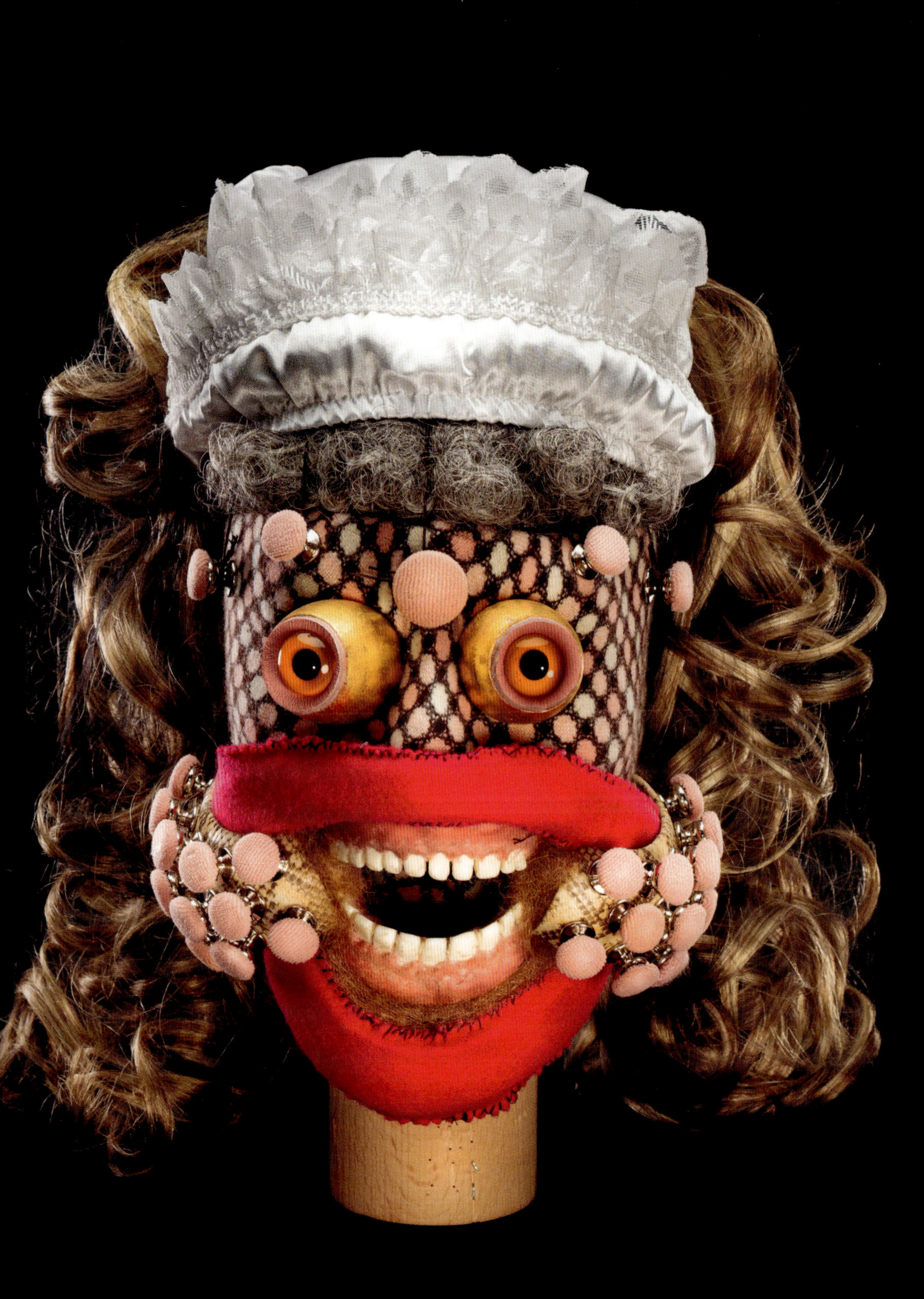

left
GYM BUNNY, 2020
Display dummy head,
fabric, knickers, plastic,
wax, wig, glass, gold
leaf, metal findings.
300 x 270mm

opposite
THE ART DIRECTOR,
2020
Display dummy head,
fabric, leather, wax,
rubber, gold leaf,
synthetic hair, metal
findings.
350 x 320mm

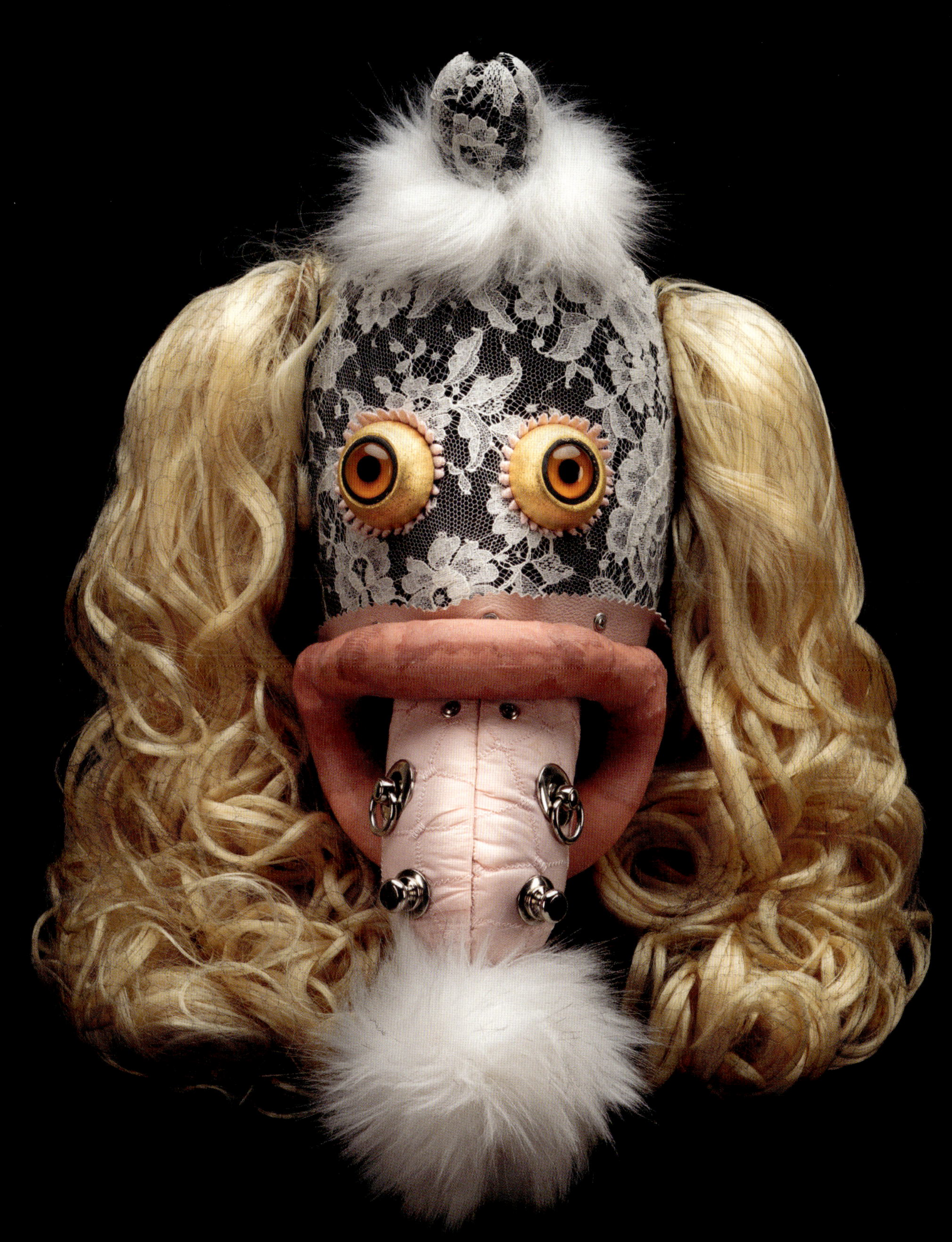

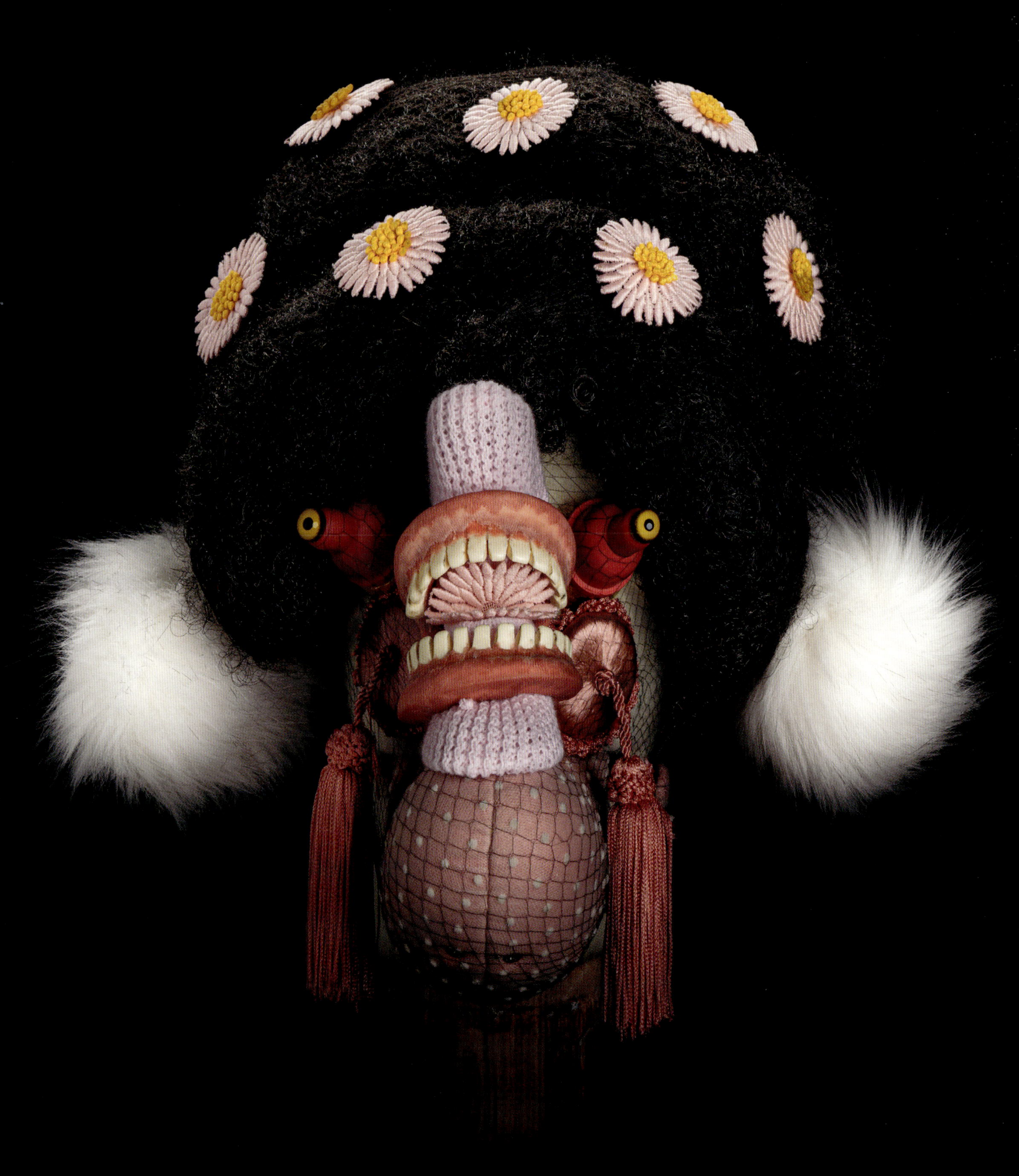

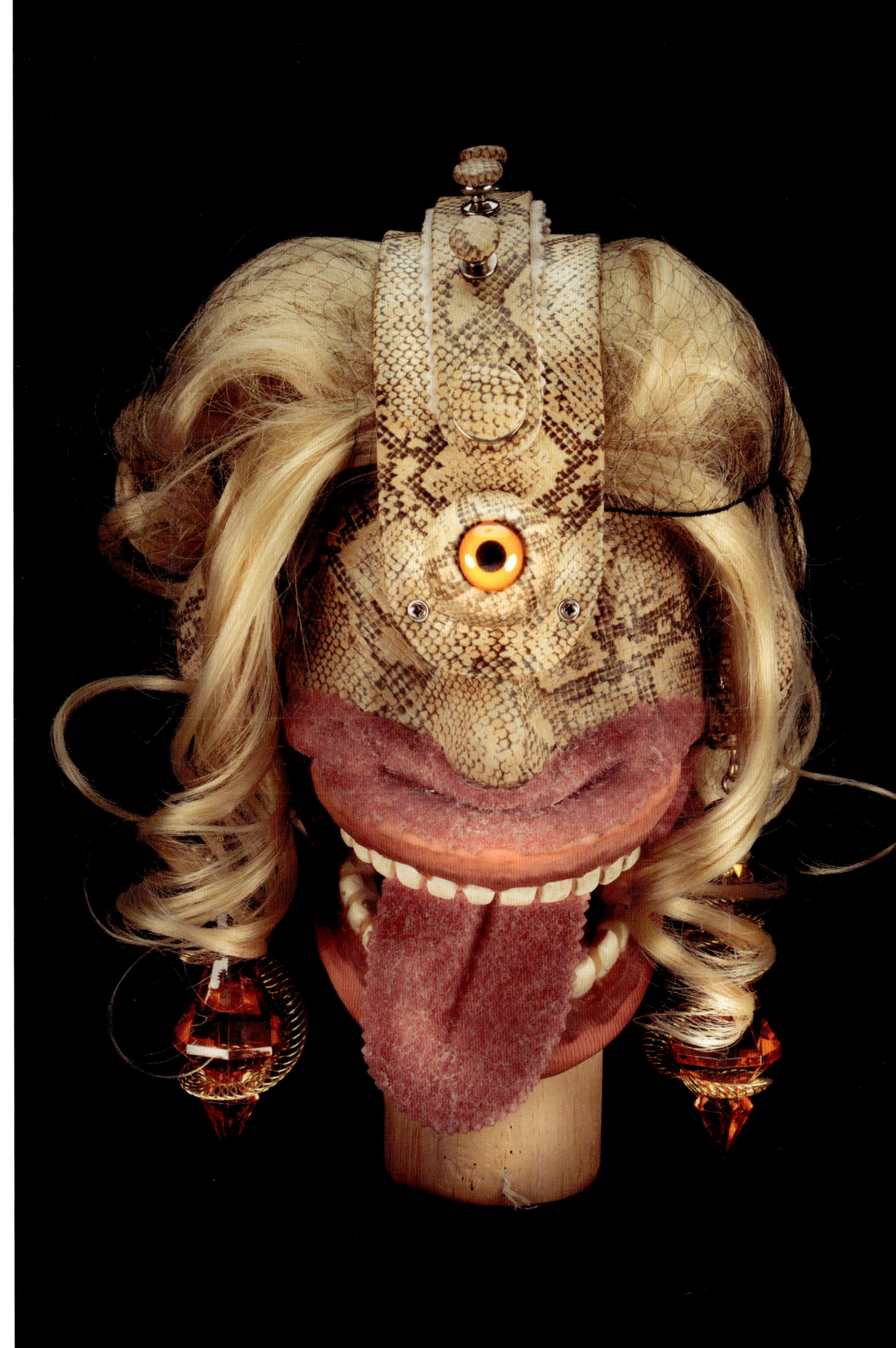

opposite
CRISP & KINKY, 2019
Display dummy head,
afro wigs, plastic, wax,
rubber, glass, pom
poms, tassels.
380 x 360mm

right
HANDBAG CYCLOPS,
2021
Display dummy head,
fabric, fake snakeskin,
wax, plastic, glass,
metal findings.
300 x 270mm

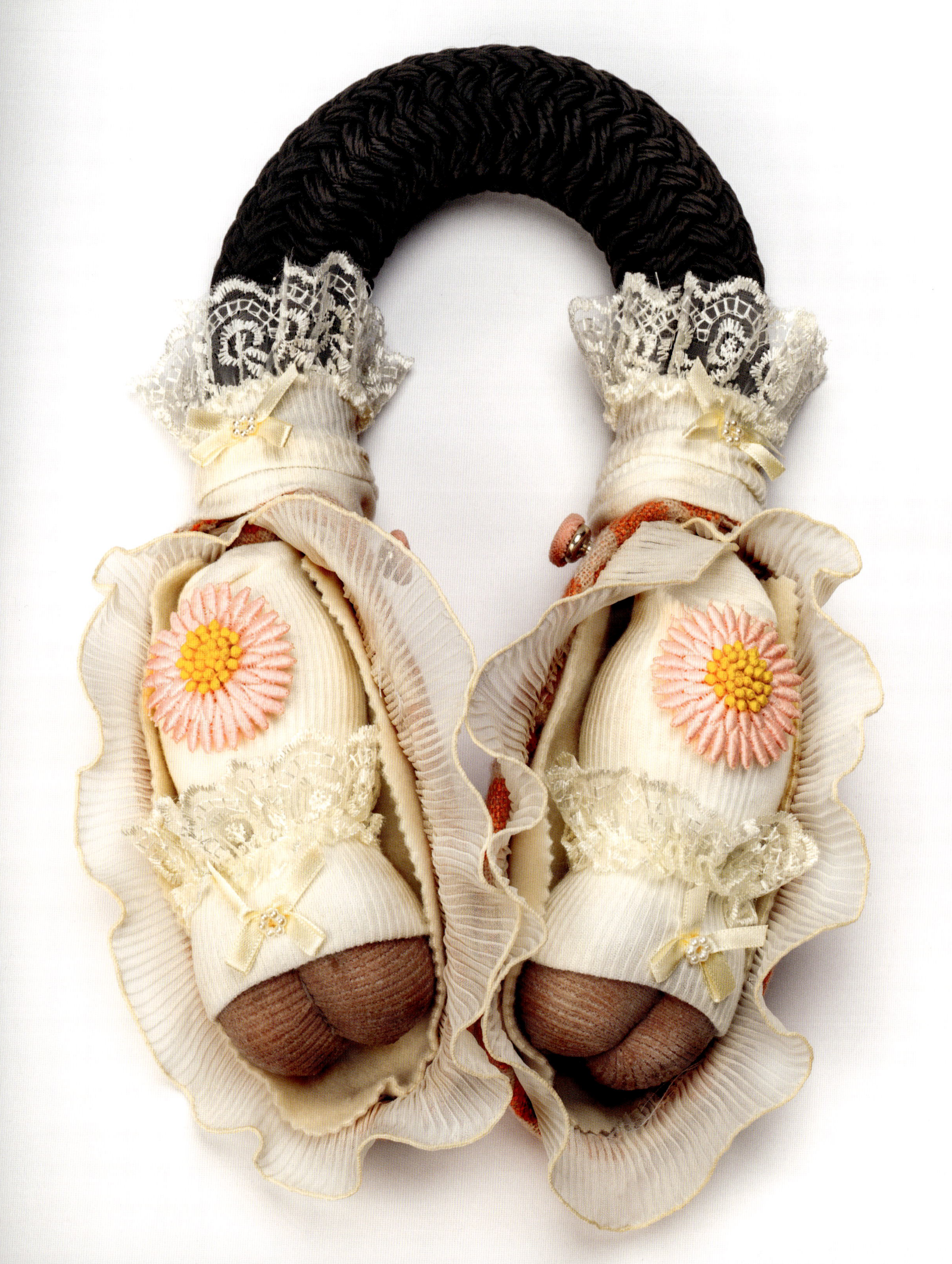

STRONG BABY FETISH,
2024
Fabric, rope, wax,
socks, metal findings.
380 x 220 x 100mm

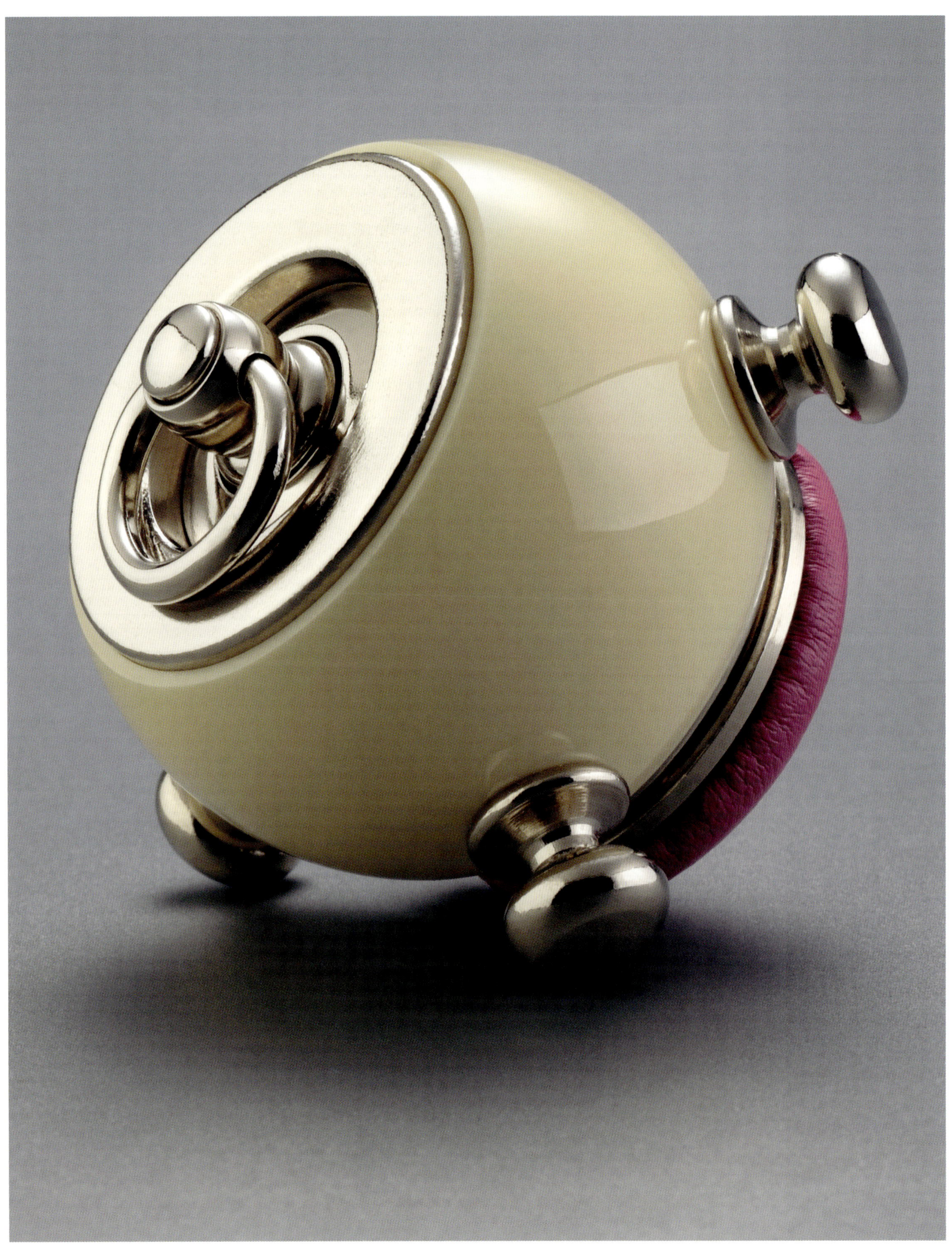

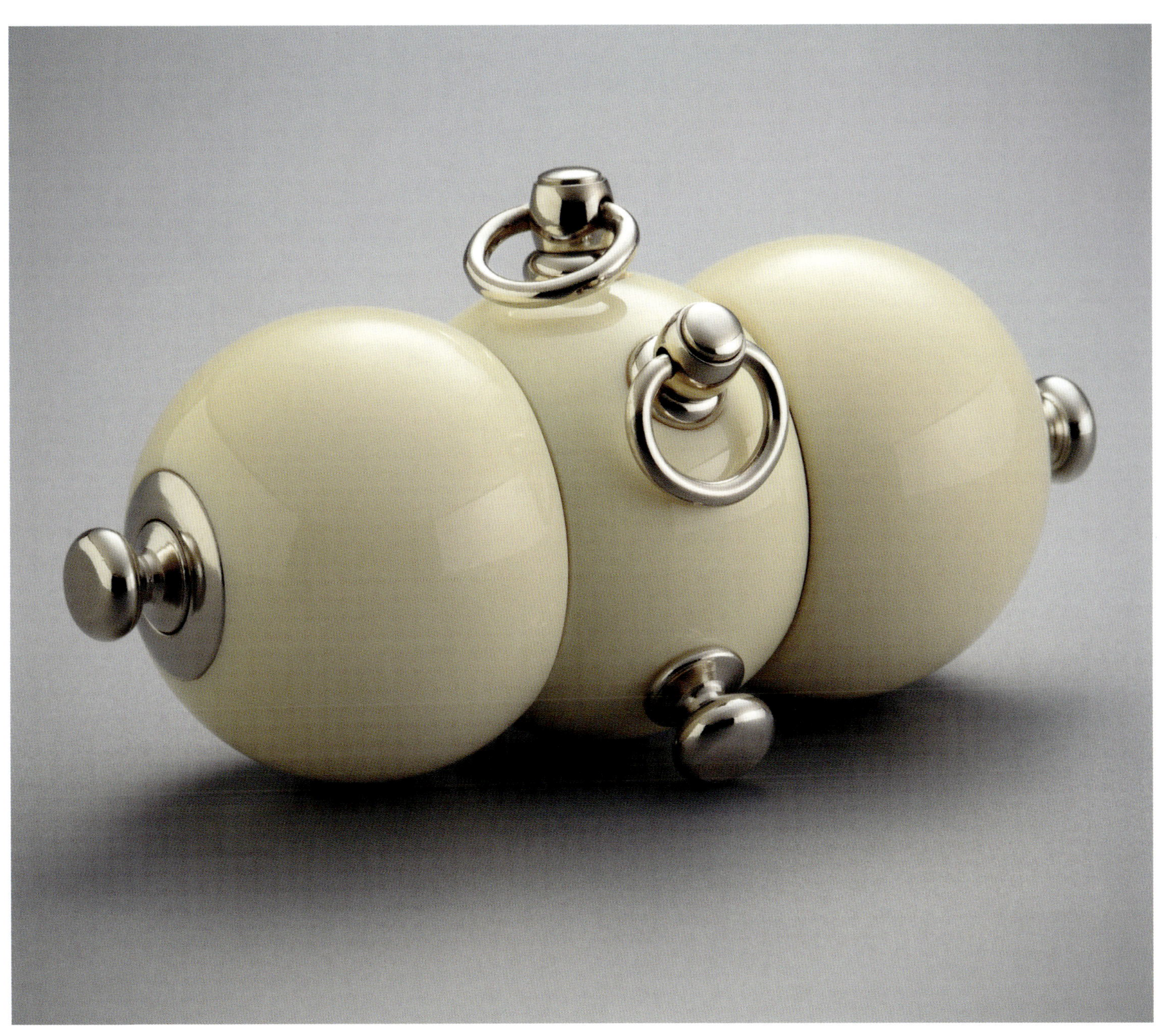

opposite
*WHITE BUTTON
FETISH*, 2013
Cue ball, leather,
button, metal findings.
50 x 50mm

above
WHITE BALL FETISH,
2013
Cue balls, metal
findings.
120 x 50mm

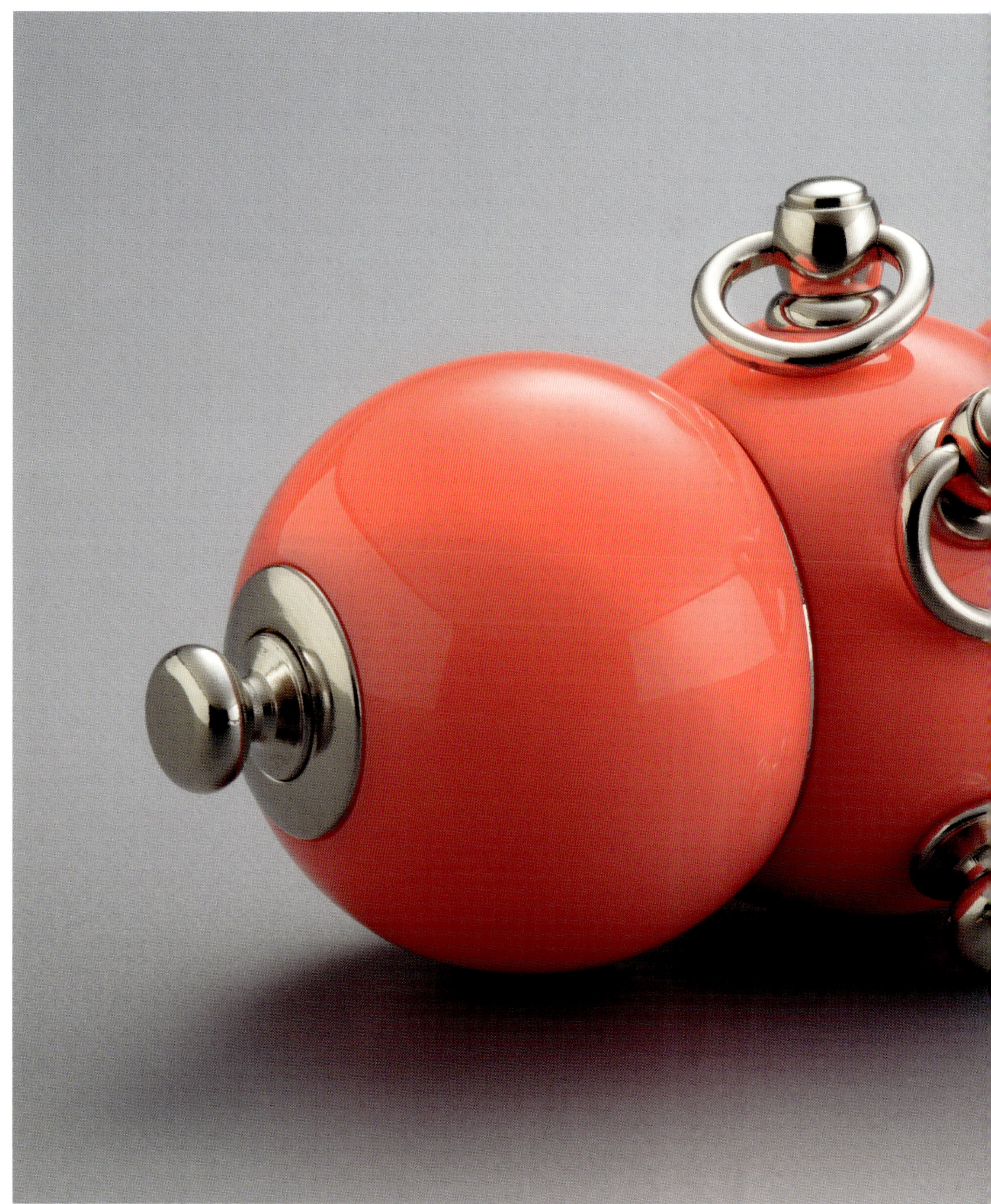

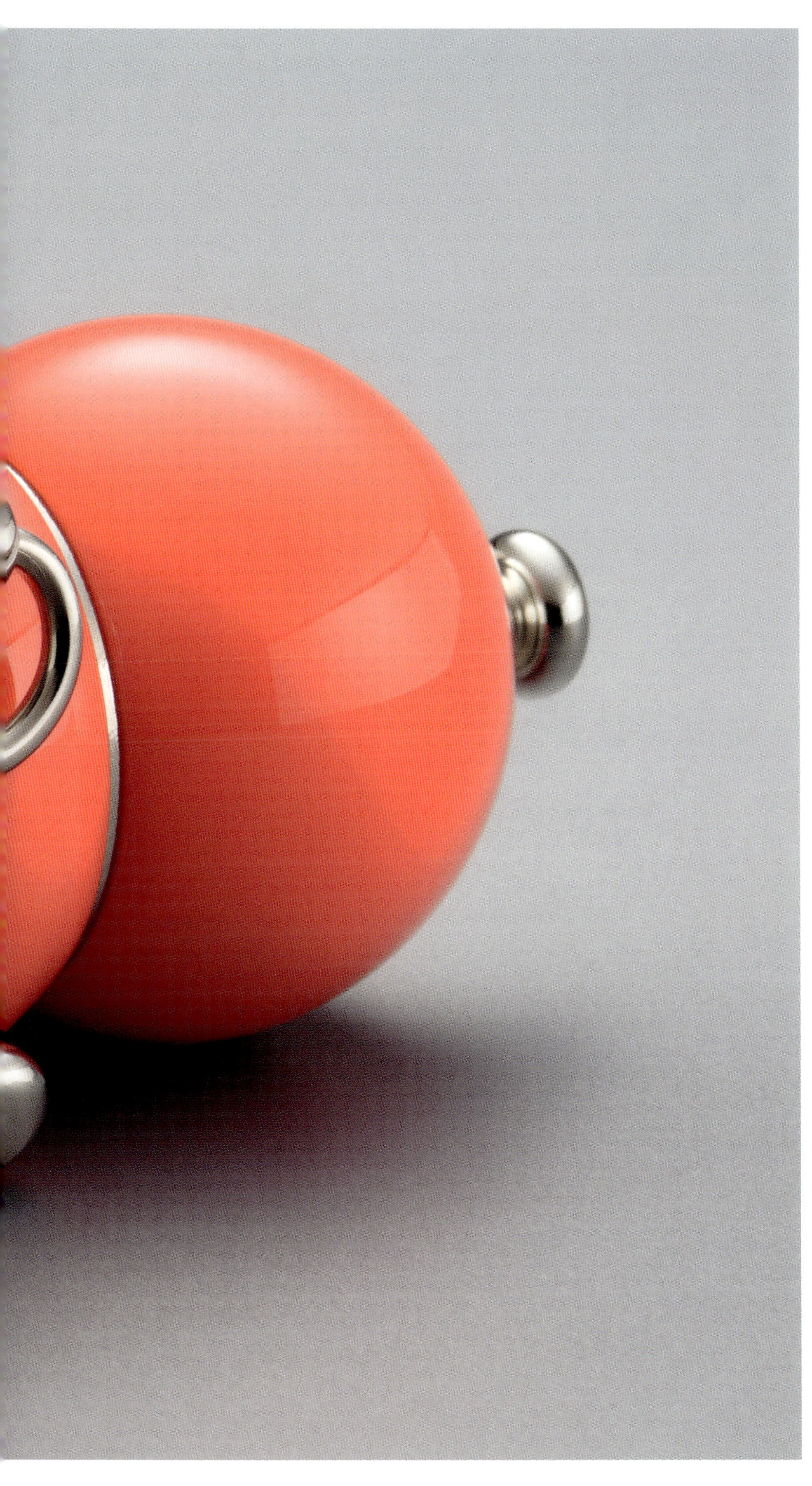

PINK BALL FETISH, 2013
Cue balls, metal
findings.
120 x 50mm

FUCKBUNNY FETISH,
2015
Fabric leather, rope,
hair bun, buttons,
metal findings.
620 x 130 x 90mm

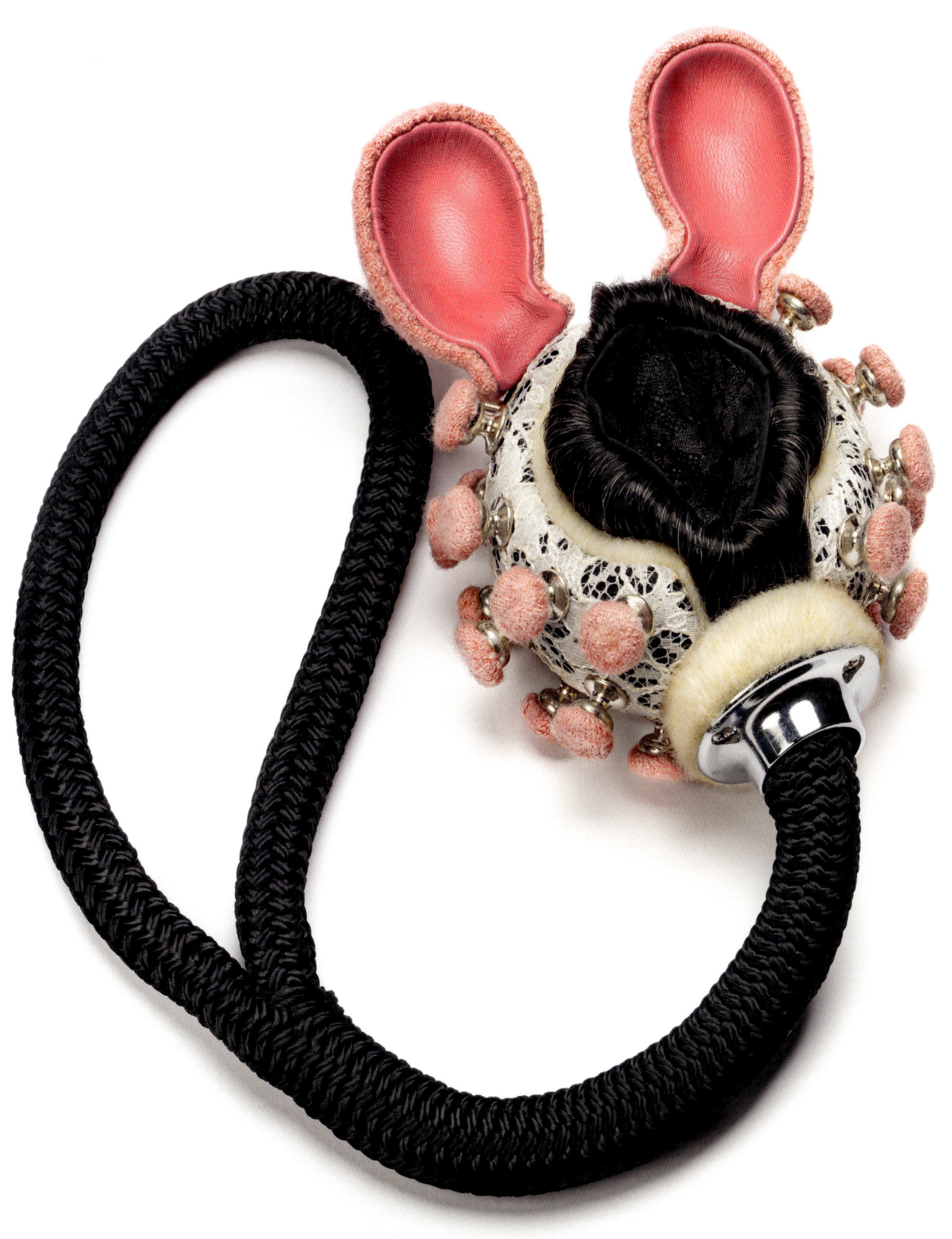

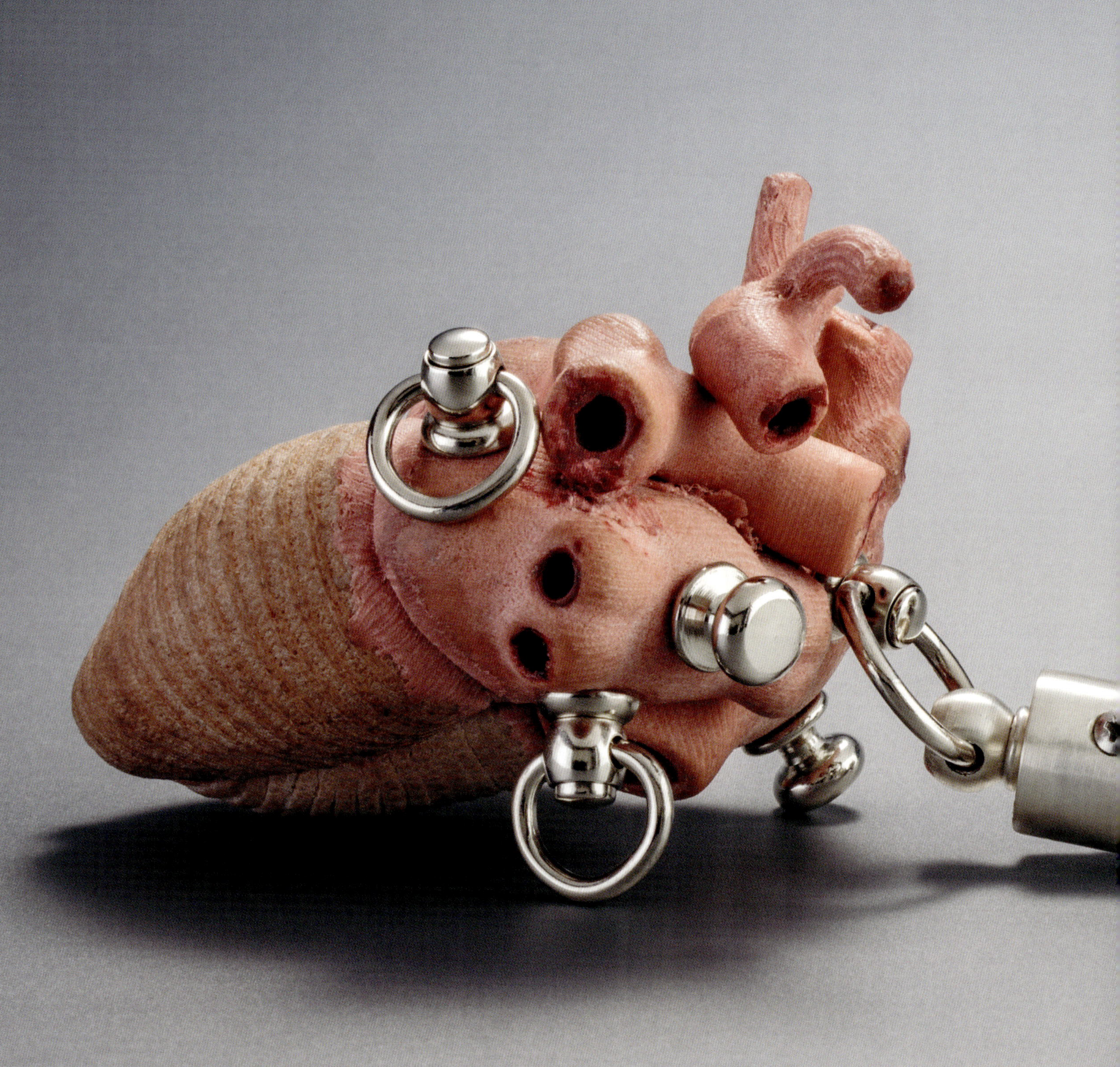

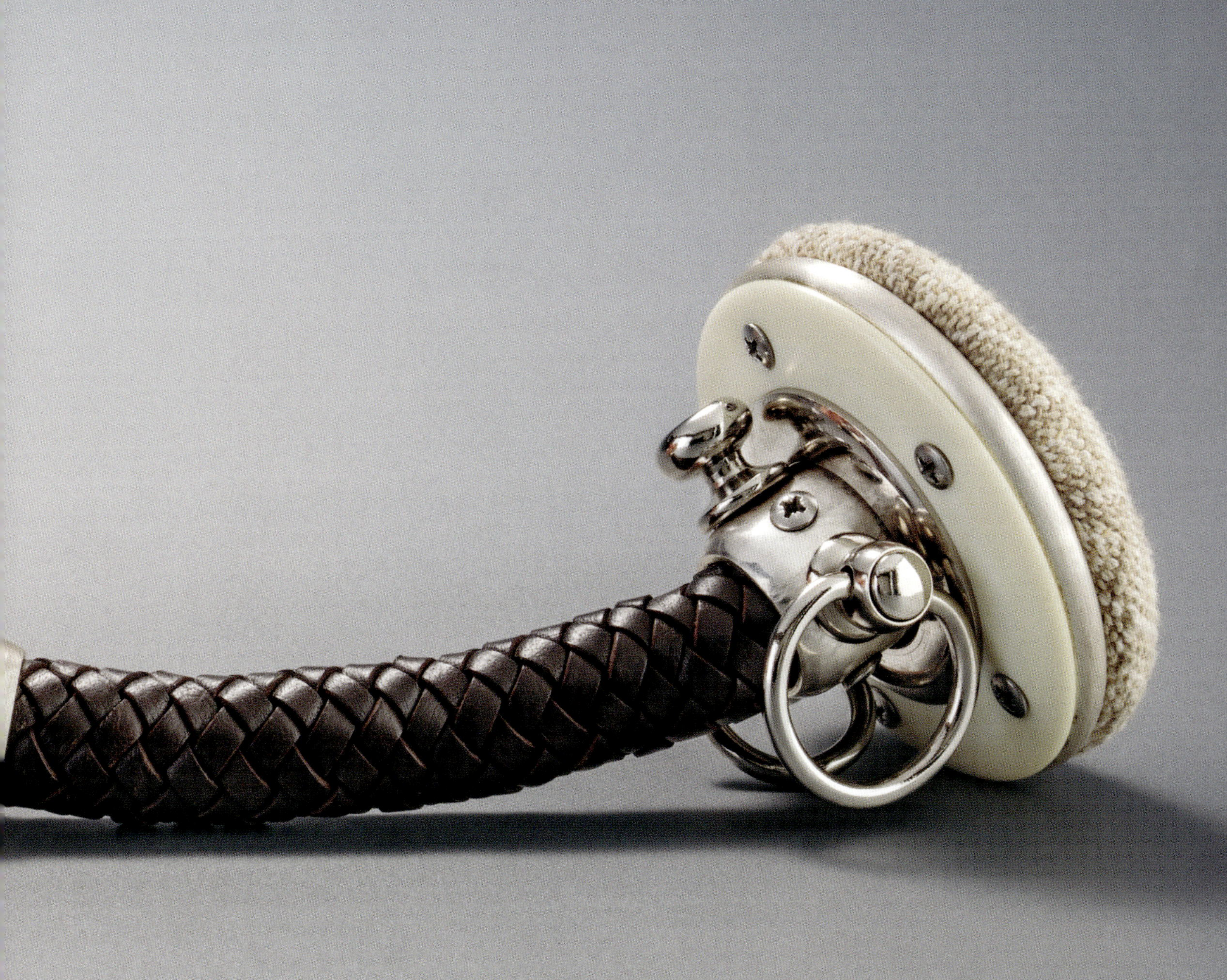

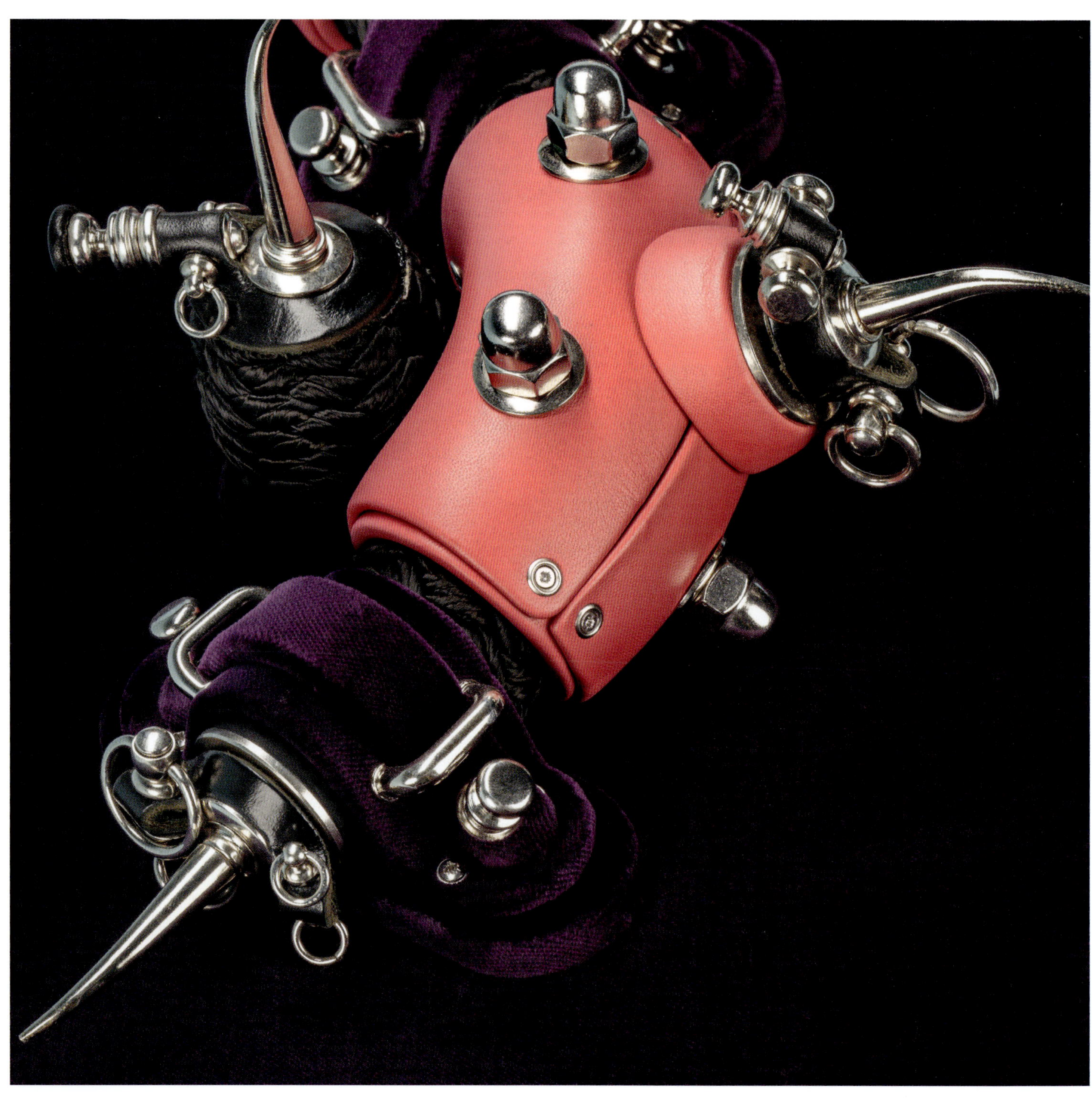

previous pages
WAR HEART, 2014
Resin, wax, fabric,
plastic leather, silver,
metal findings.
60 x 90 x 800mm

above and opposite
SPIKY COMMUNION,
2024
Wood, leather, rope,
velvet, nuts and bolts,
metal findings.
800 x 300 x 250mm

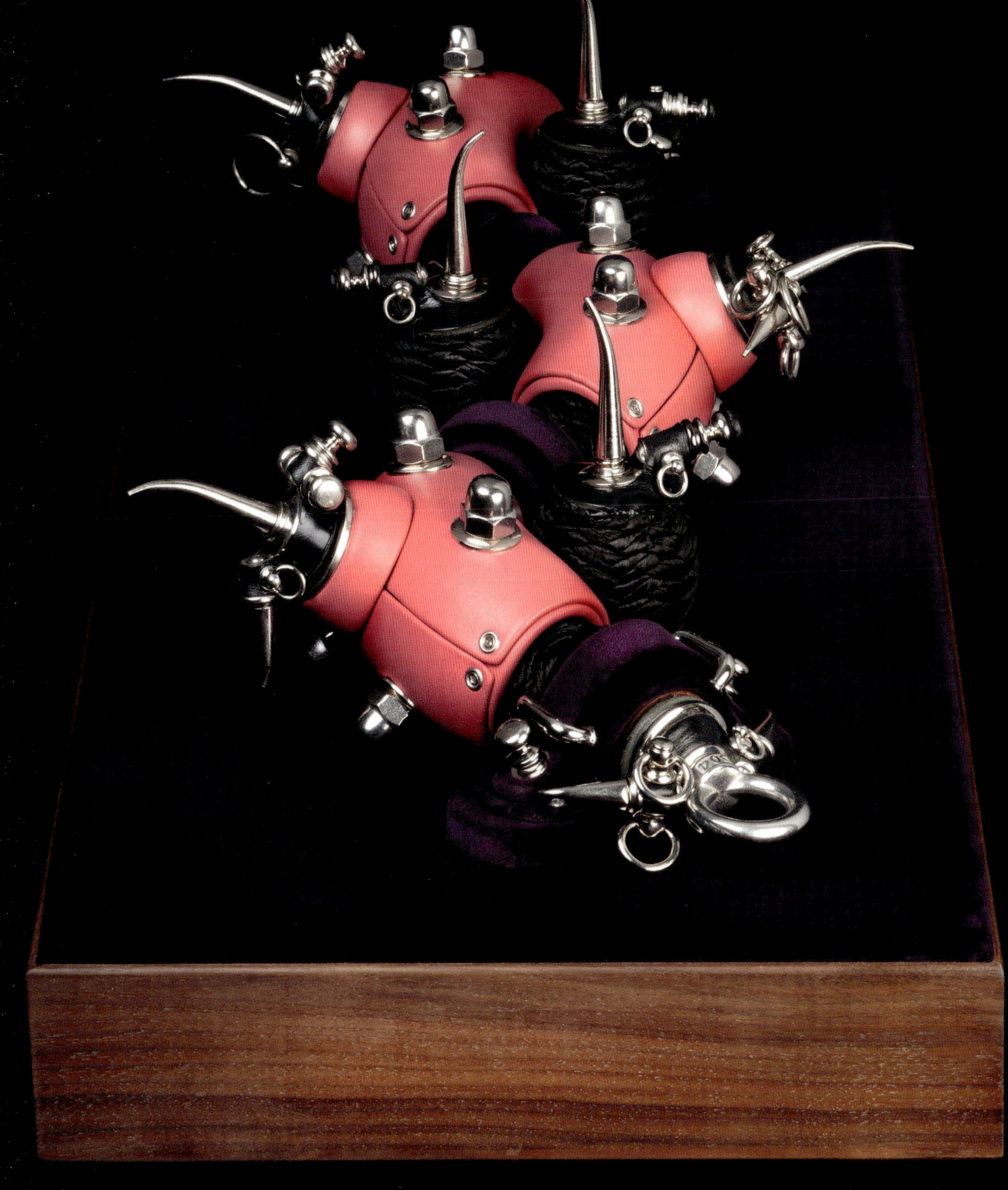

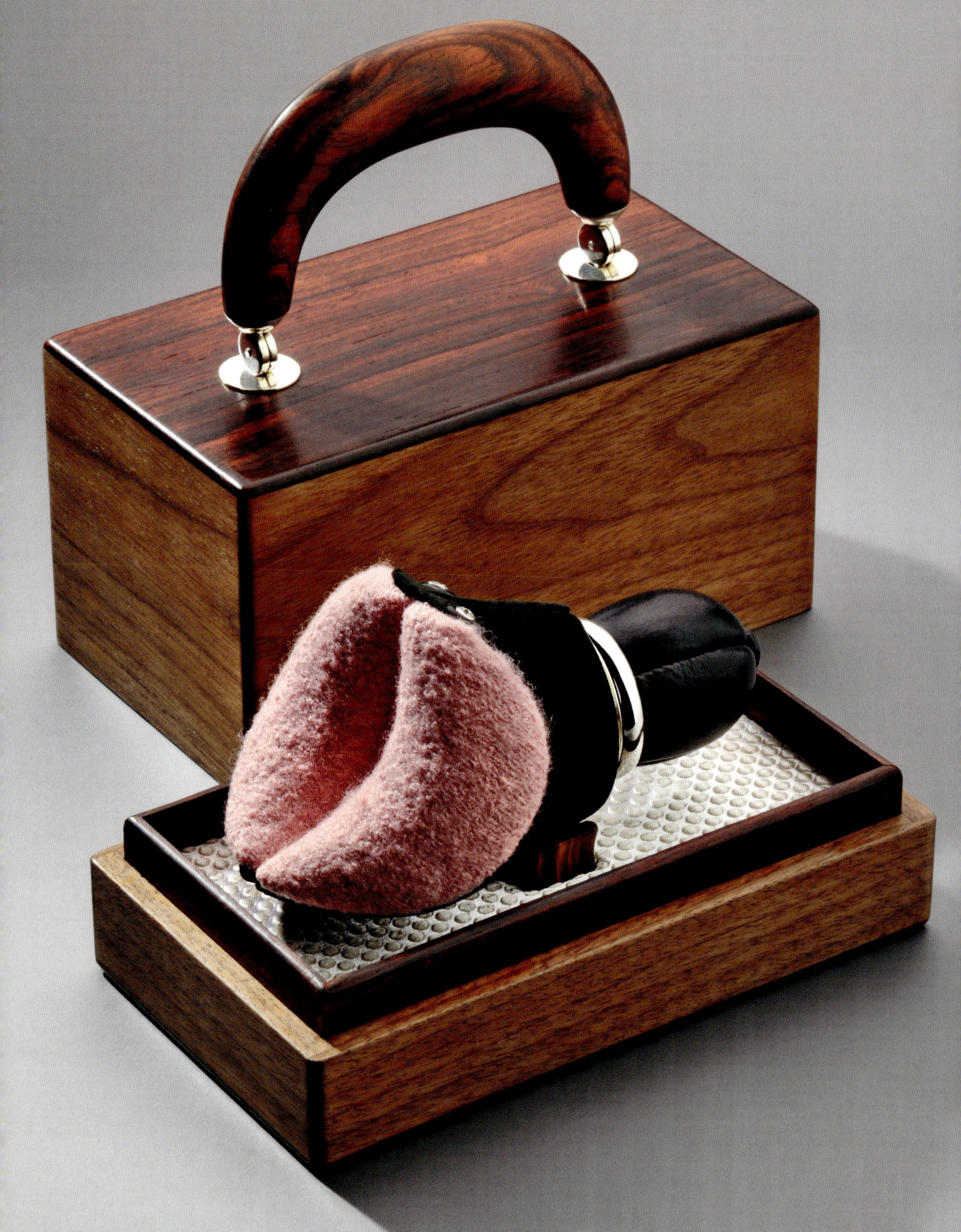

opposite and below
SEX OBJECT, 2012
Wood, leather, fabric,
silk, silver.
190 x 100 x 135mm

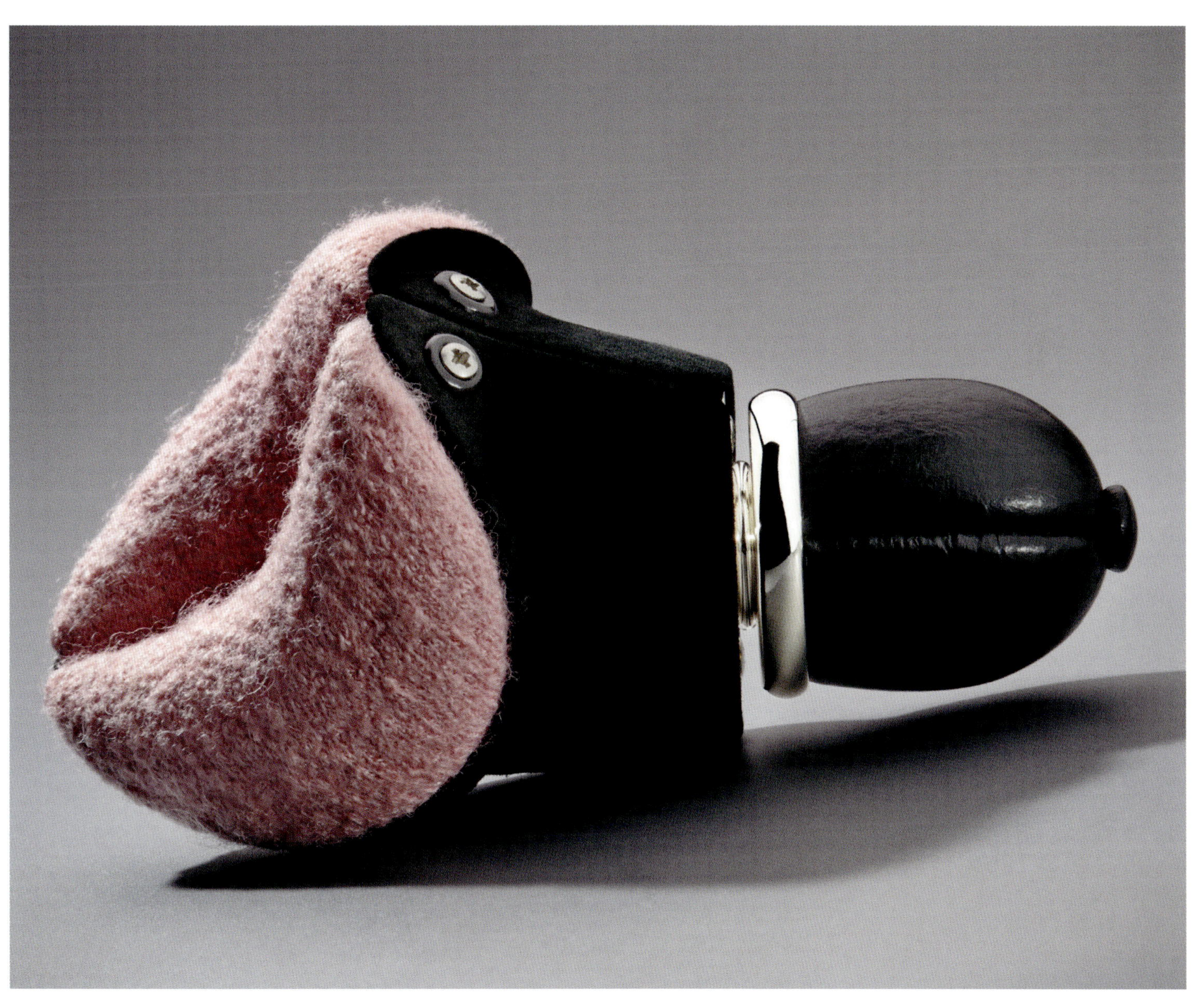

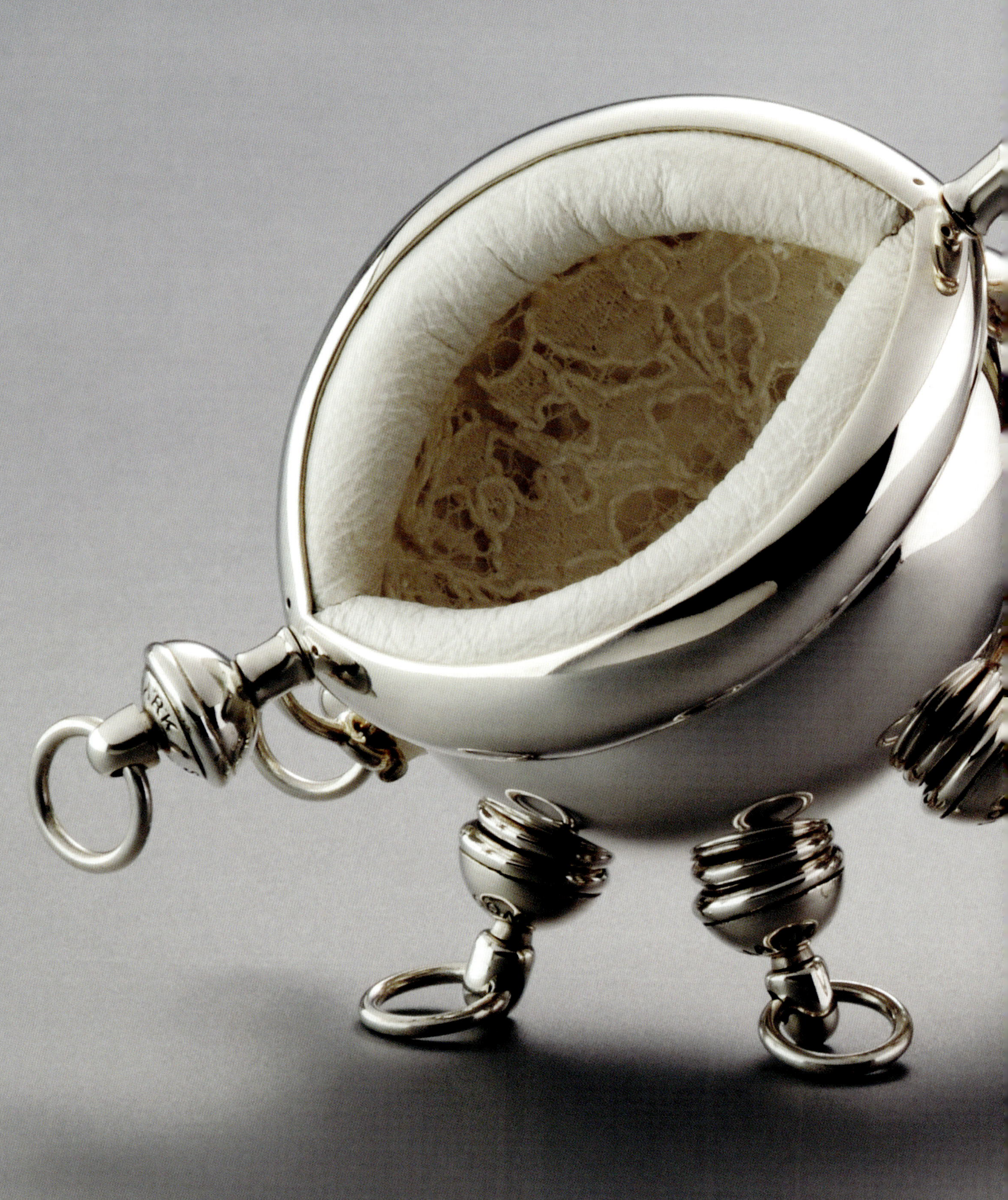

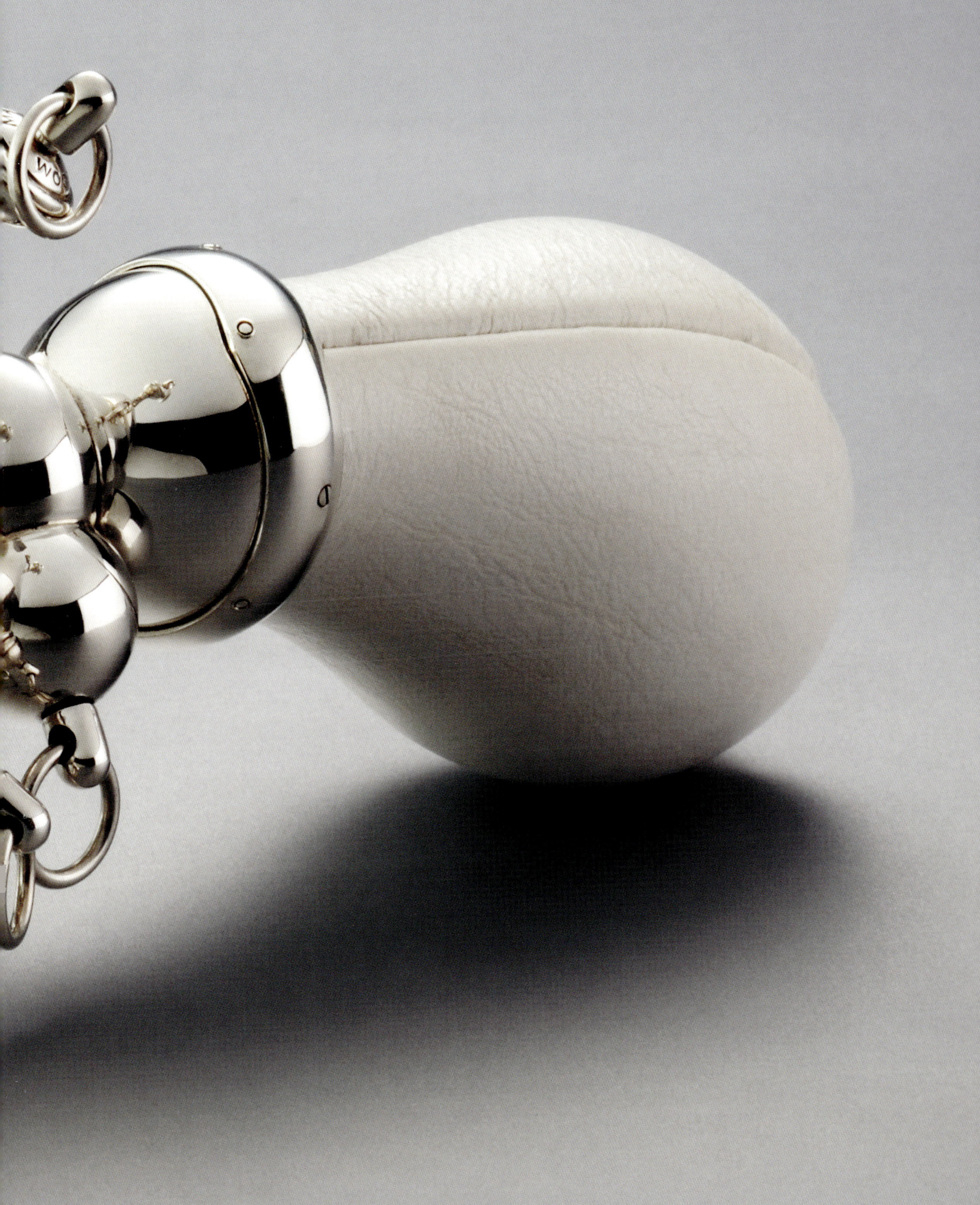

previous pages
*A SUNDRY FEMALE
OBJECT*, 2003
Silver, leather, wood,
lace.
230 x 110mm

opposite
*FRIEDA'S DOGTAIL
FETISH*, 2016
Dogtail, fabric, wax,
synthetic hair, paper
flowers, metal findings.
400 x 120mm

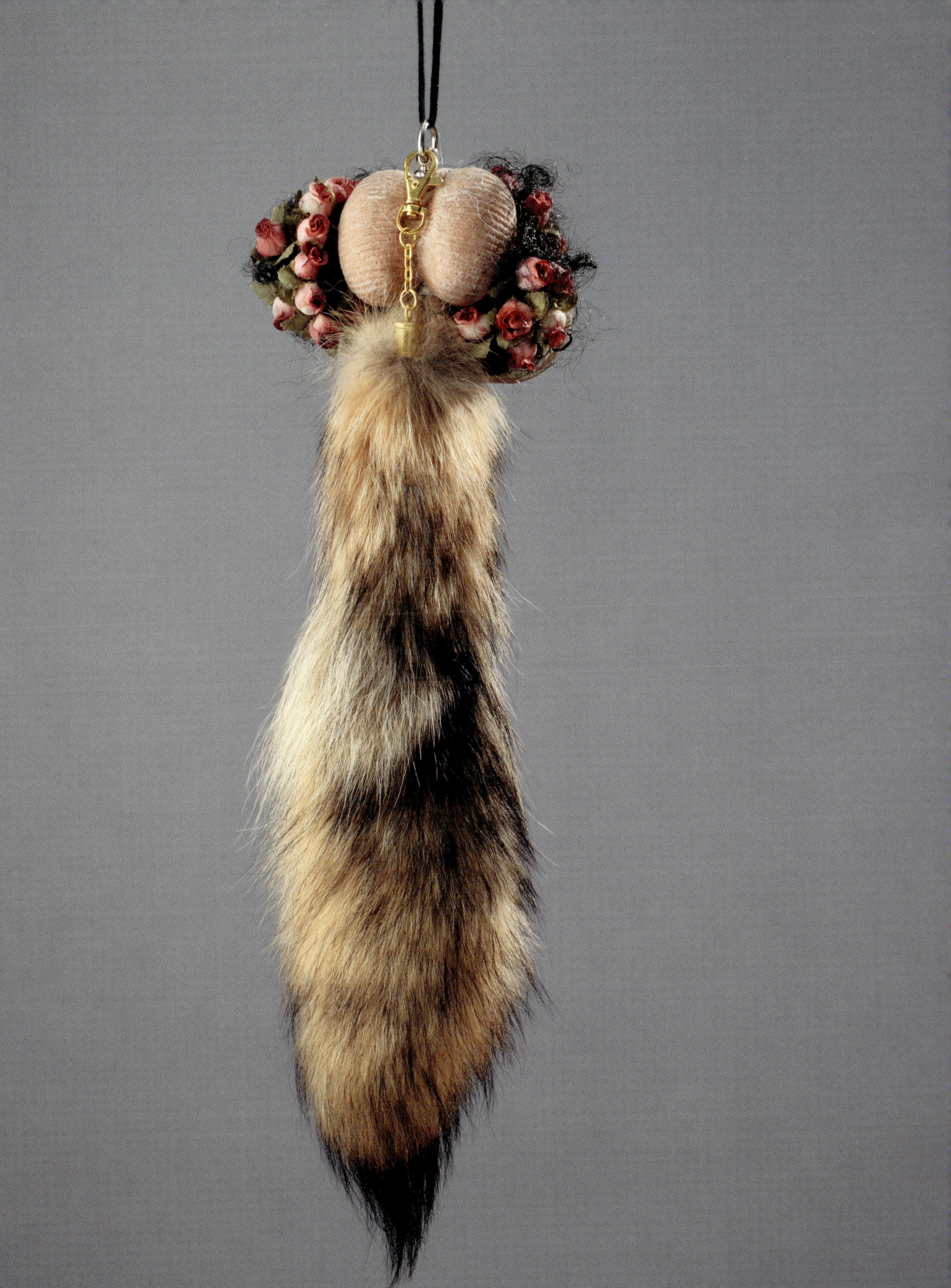

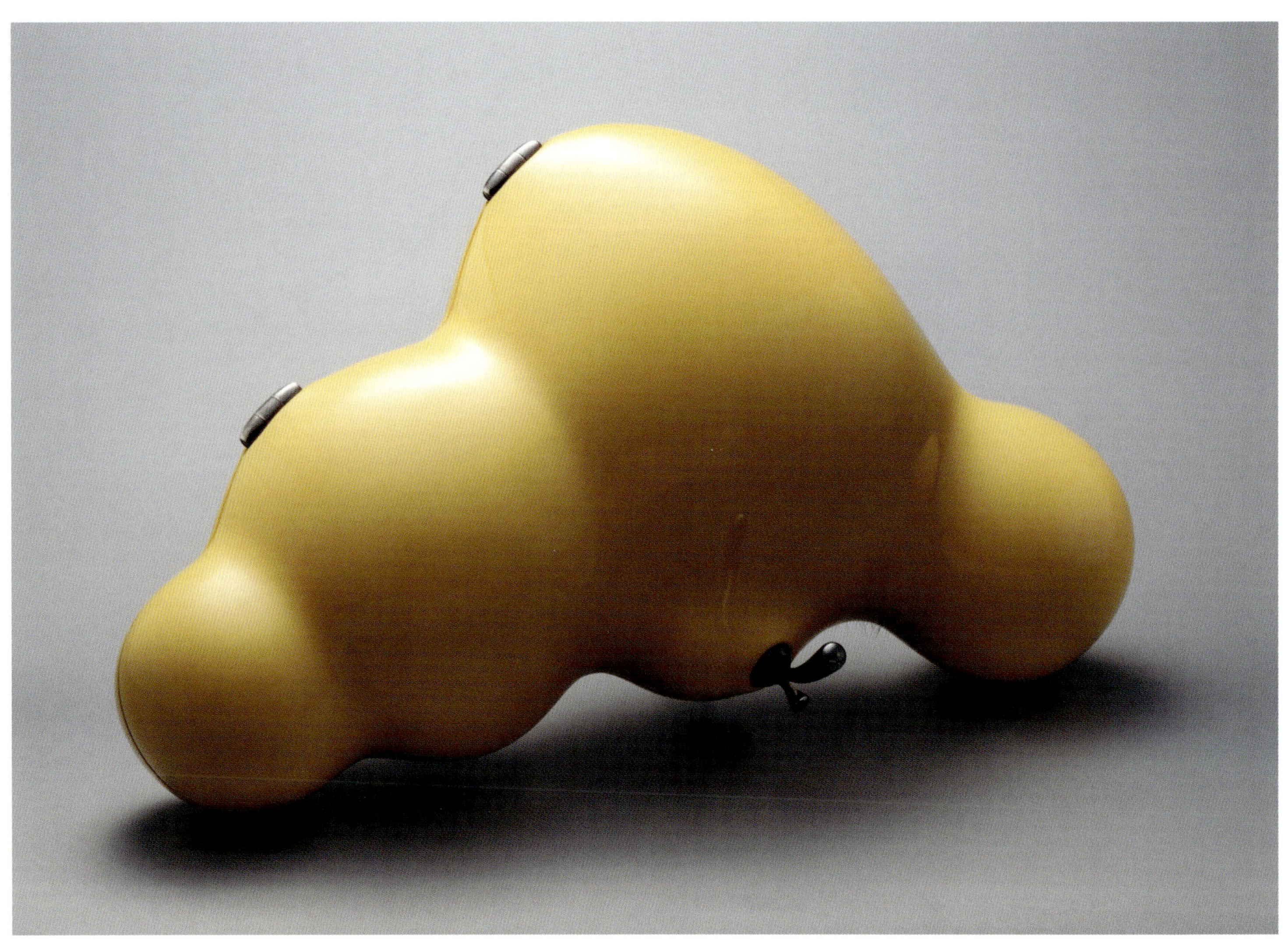

above and opposite
SPIRIT OF ECSTASY,
1999
Phenolic plastic, gold-
plated silver, 22ct. gold,
synthetic rubies, gelatin
capsules, coloured sand;
case: carved epoxy
putty, paint, silver fur.
300 x 150mm

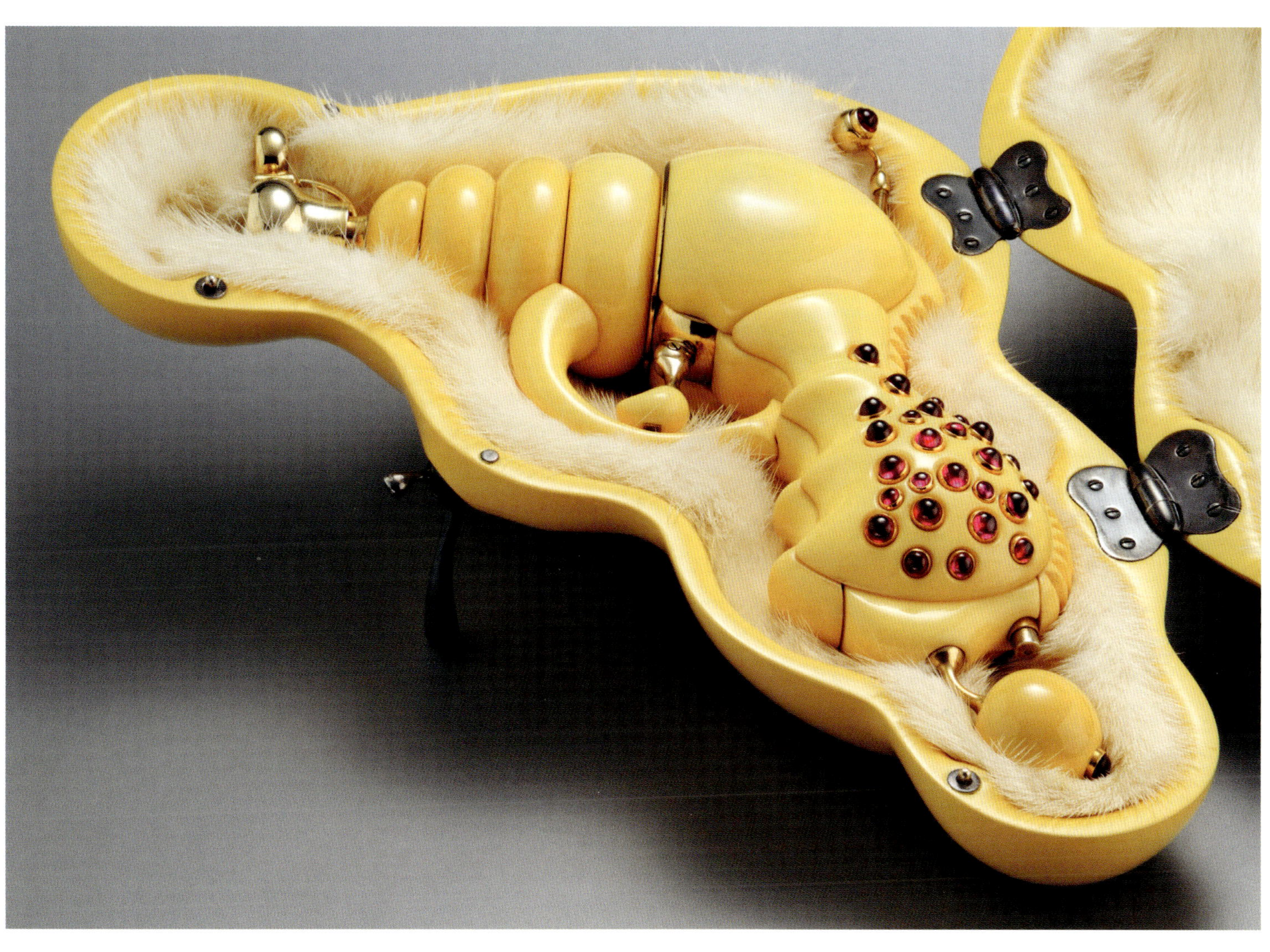

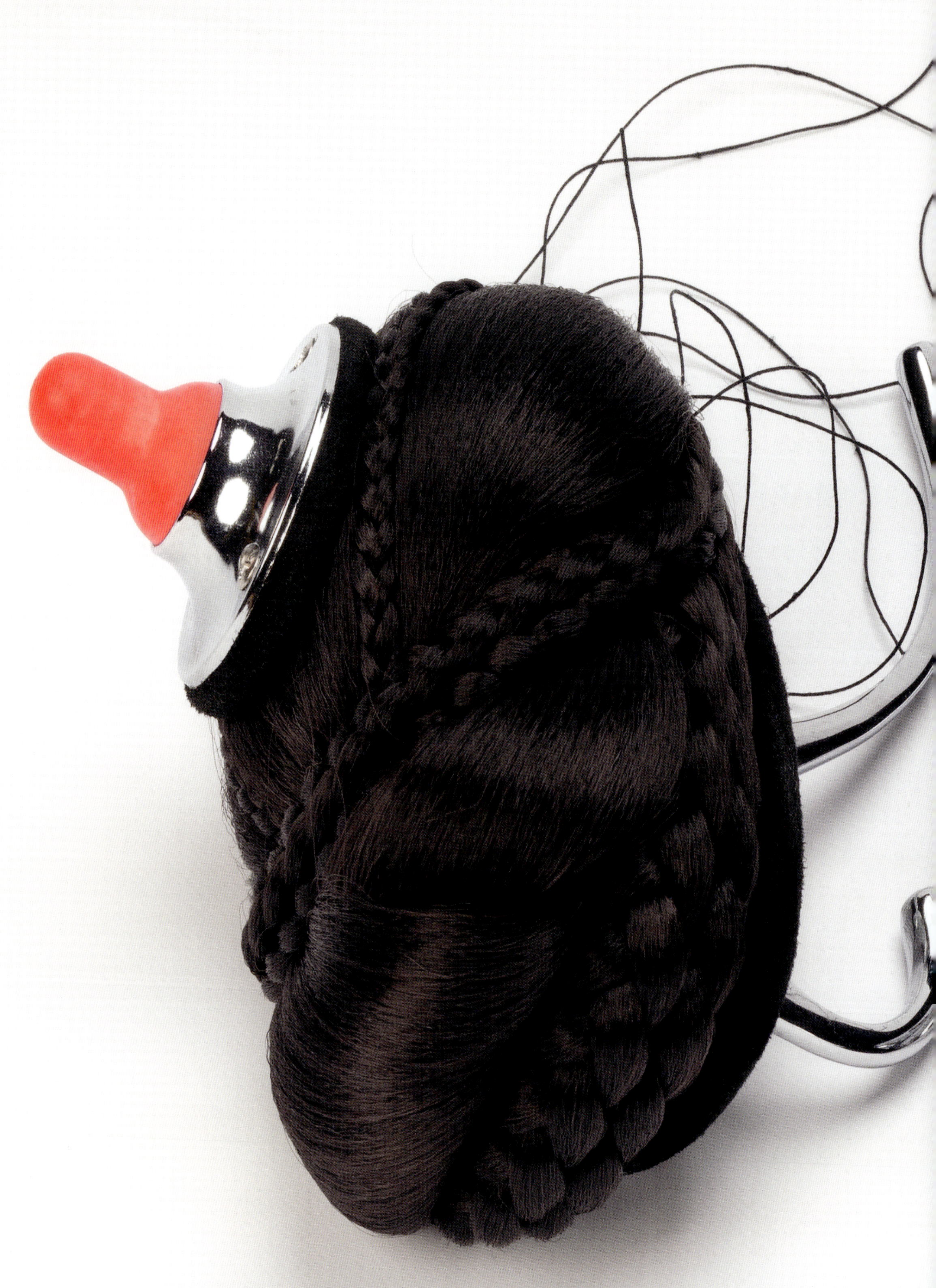

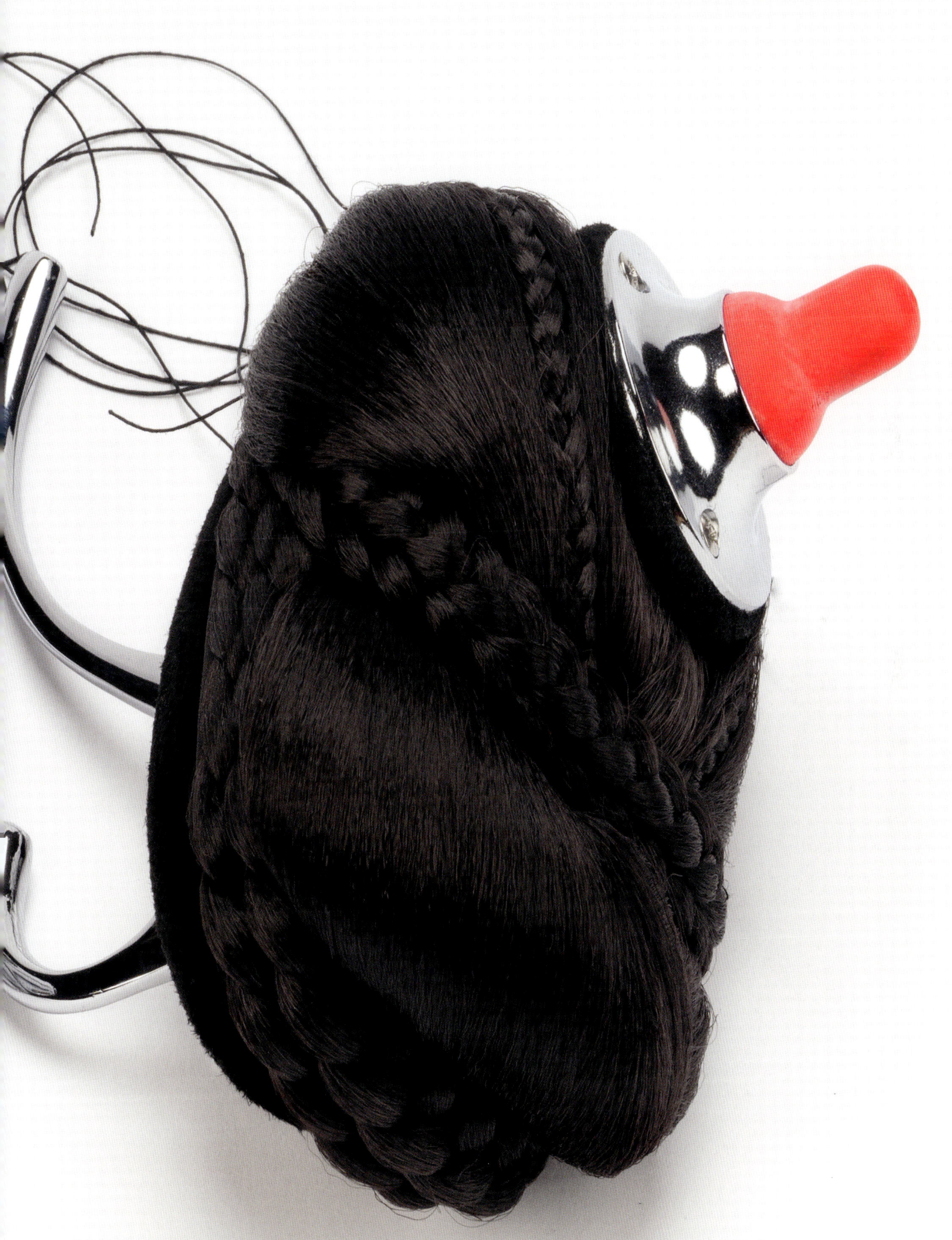

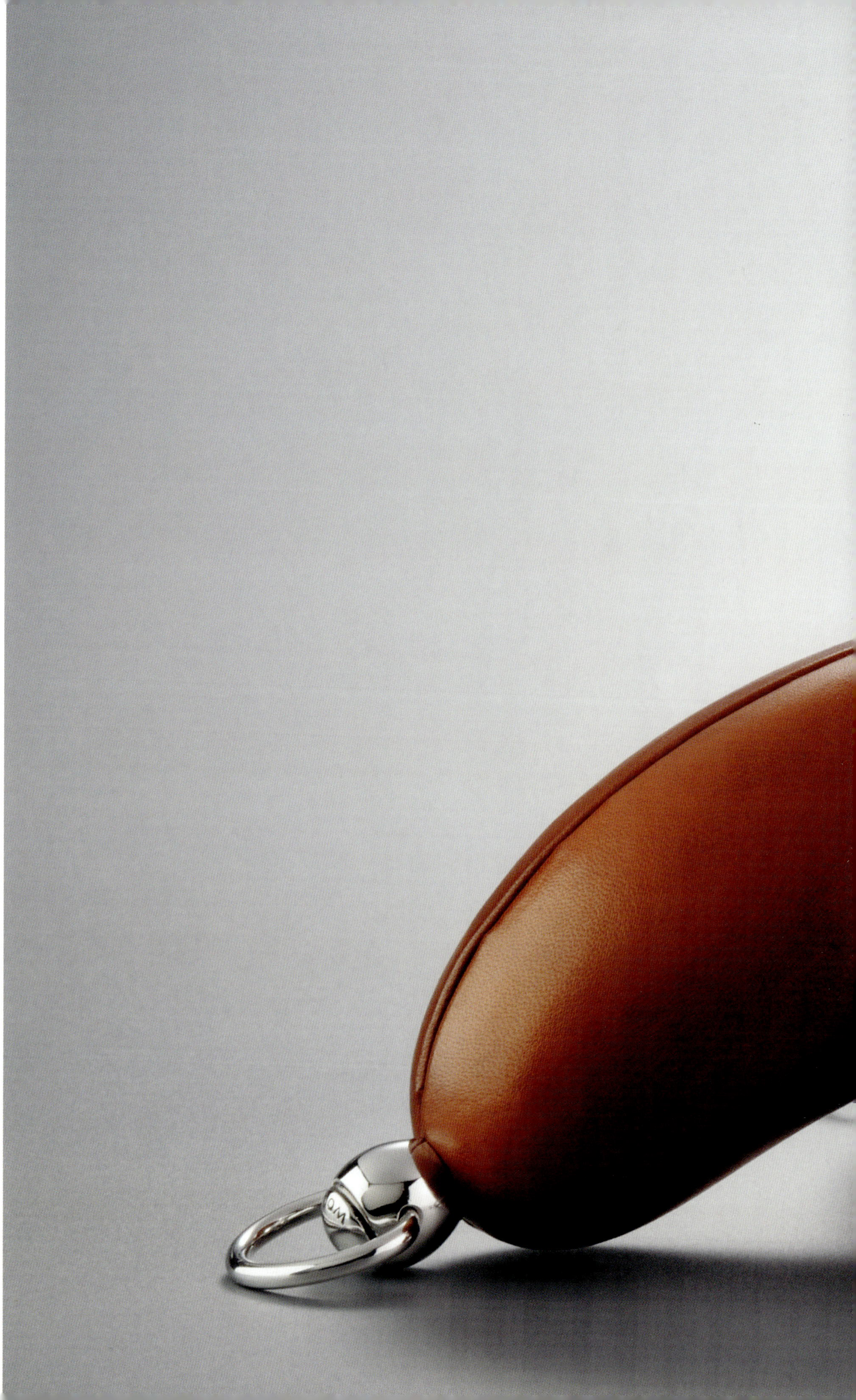

previous pages
HONOURED GUESTS,
2023
Hair buns, coat hooks,
rubber, thread, metal
findings.
140 x 200 x 85mm

right
*KILL 'EM ALL, GOD
WILL KNOW HIS OWN*,
2009
Resin, leather,
rhodium-plated silver.
200 x 140 x 140mm.

overleaf
*AND YOU HAVE
FATHERED SERVANTS*,
2009
Resin, leather, silver.
280 x 150 x 150mm

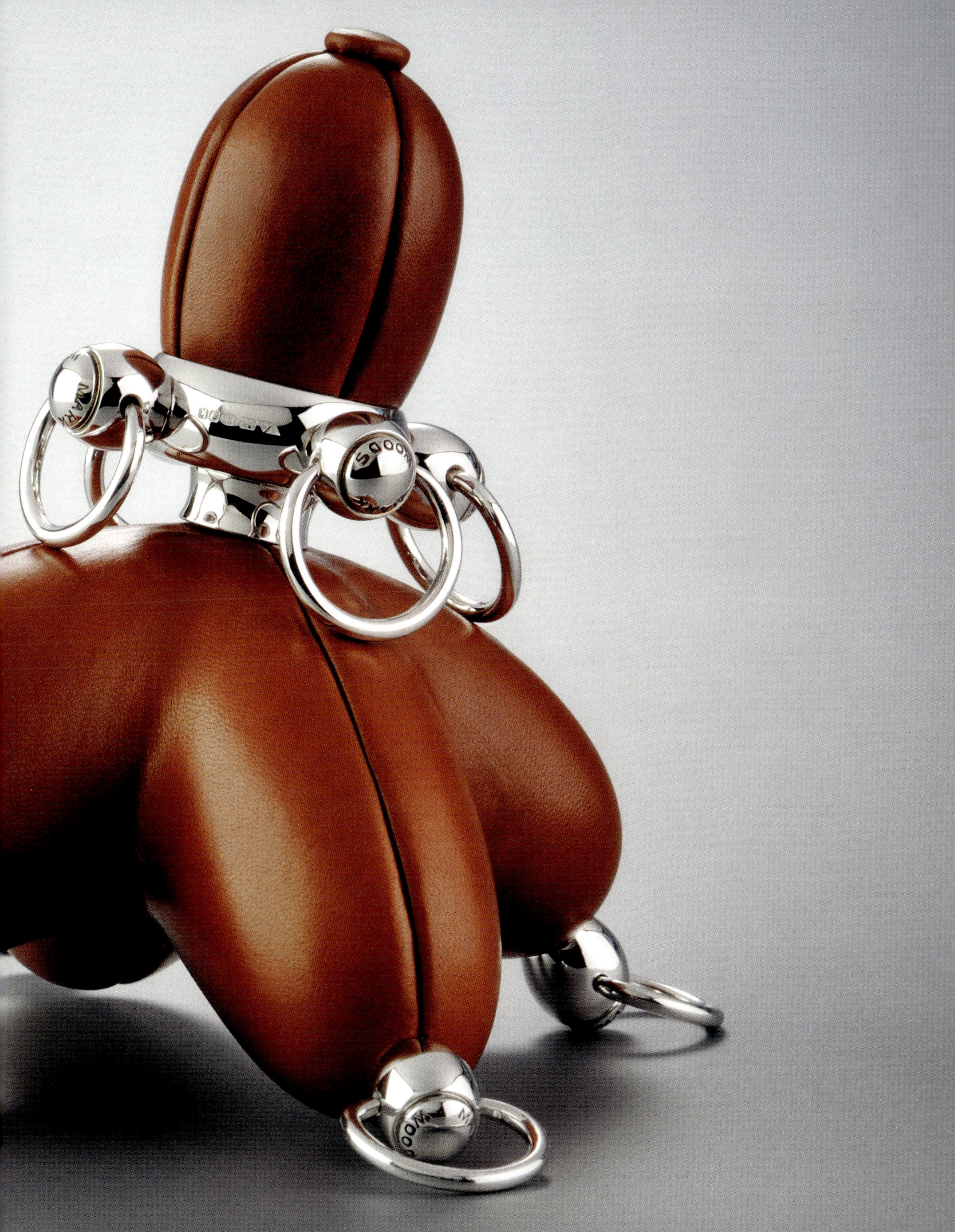

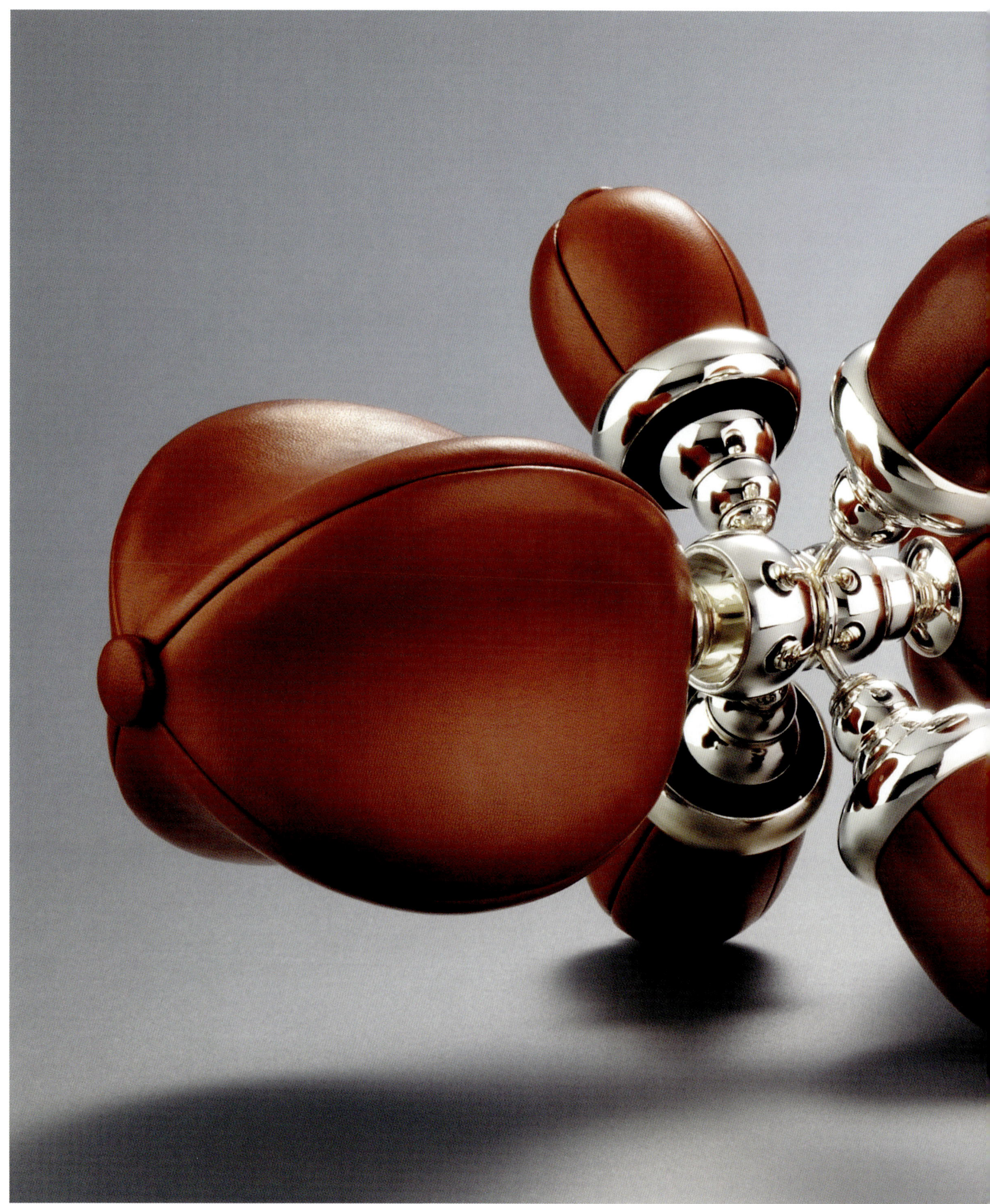

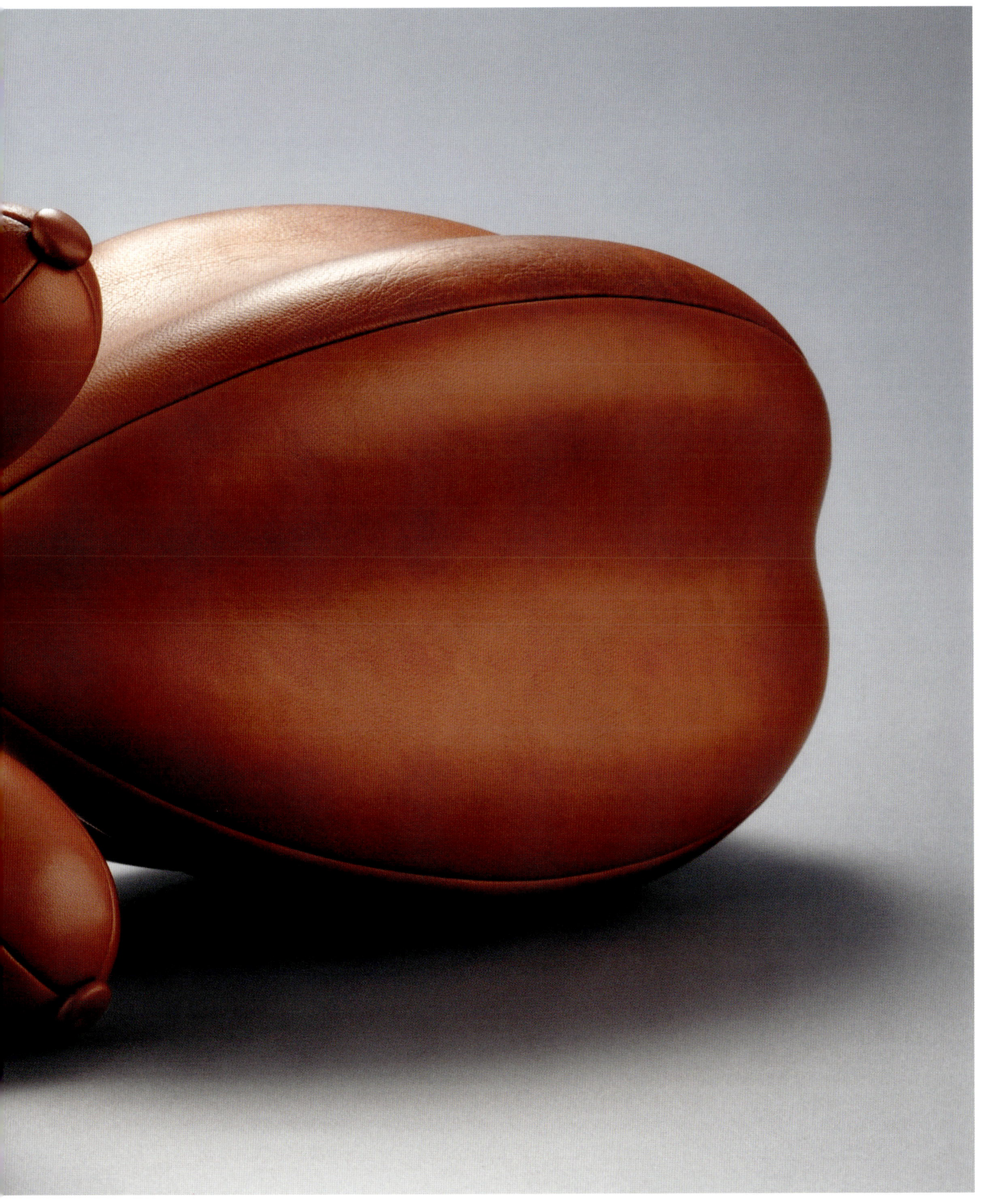

*THE WORD MADE
FLESH,* 2013
Walnut, cocobolo,
velvet, lace, resin,
plastic, rhodium-
plated silver.
280 x 150 x 85mm

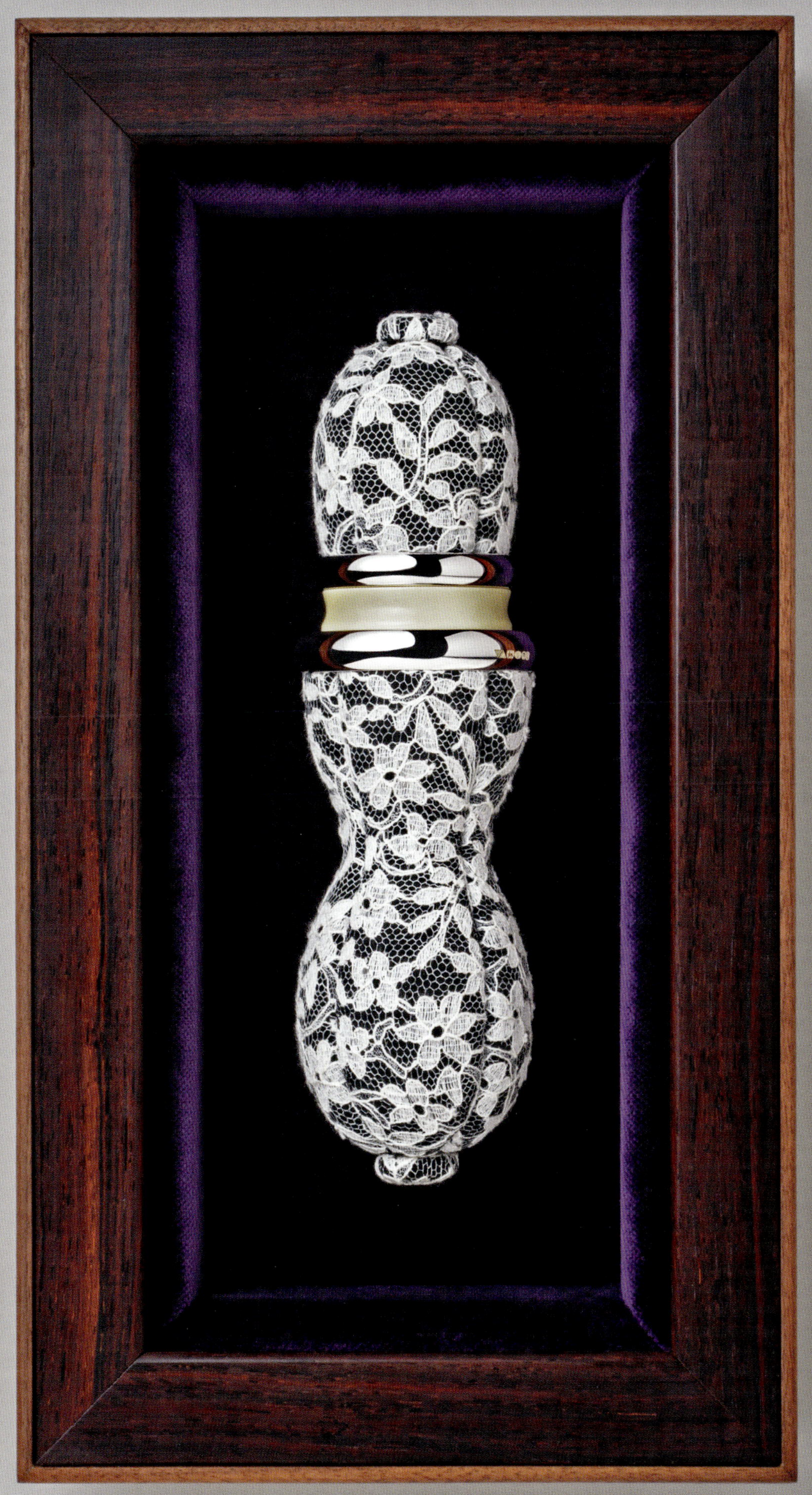

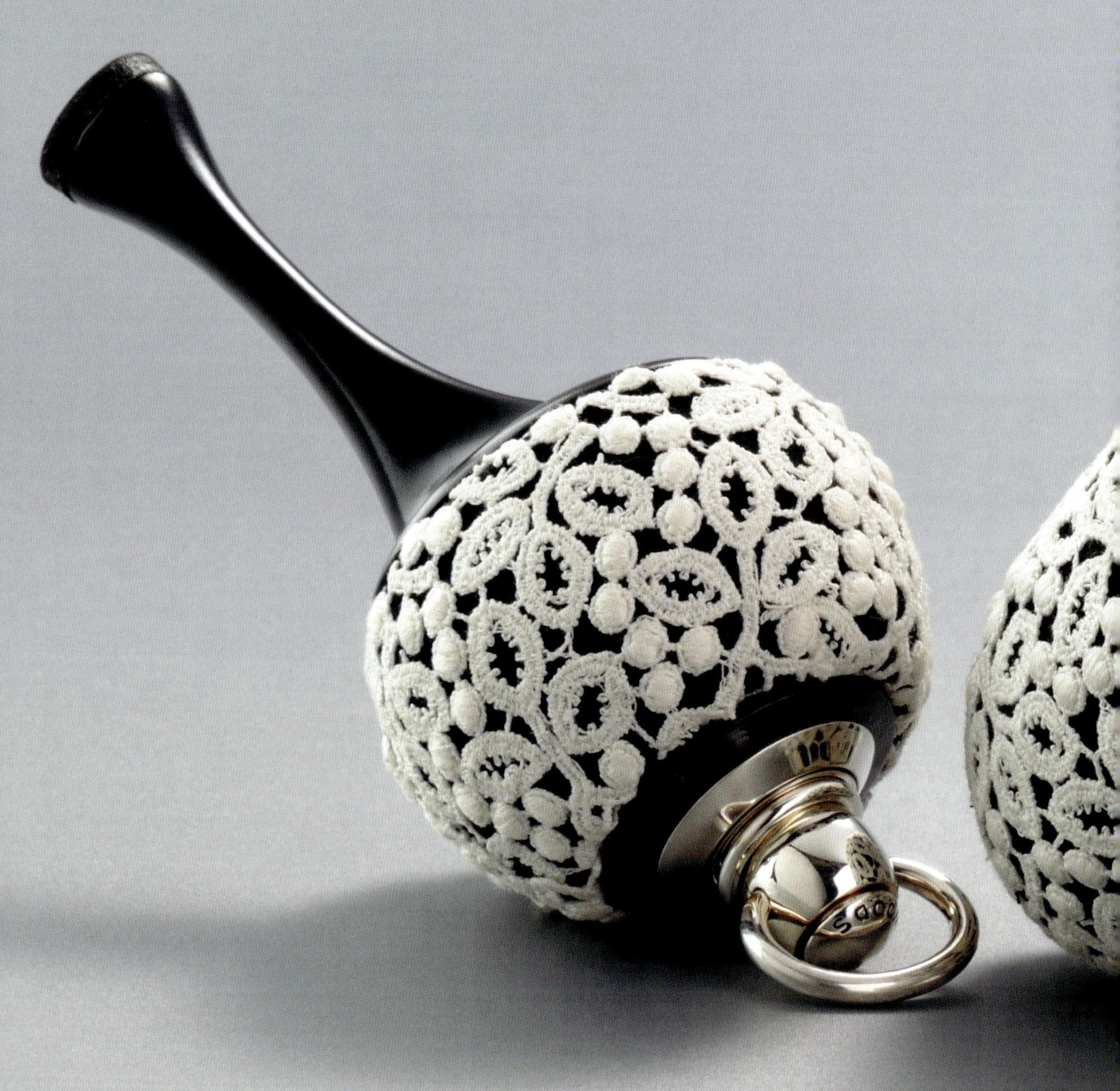

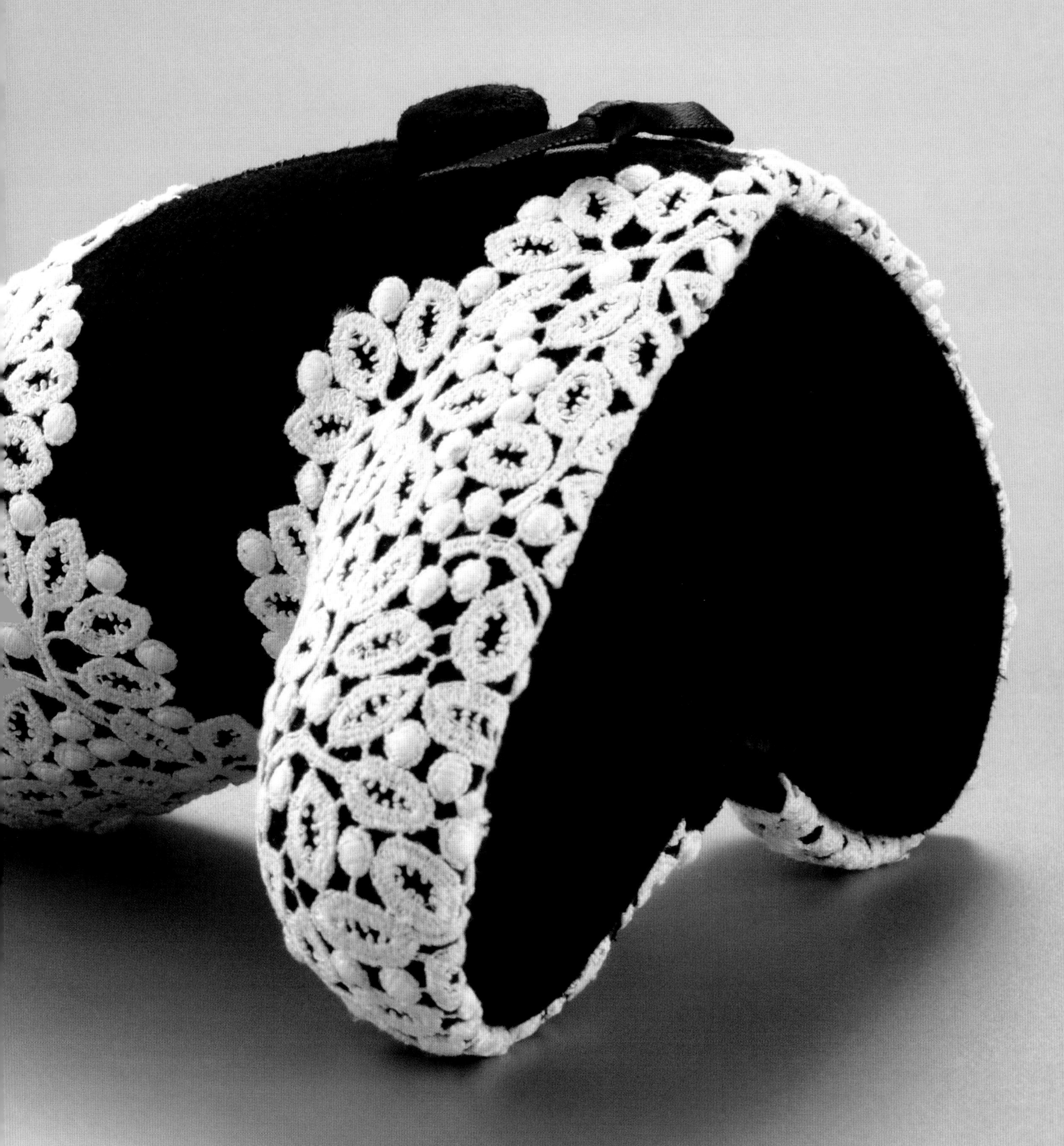

previous pages
ROMANTIC MISOGYNY,
2006
Leather, lace, wood,
paint, plastic, silver.
110 x 150 x 85mm

below and right
LOVE WARS, 1999
Gold-plated silver,
velvet, MDF, paint.
270 x 150 x 85mm

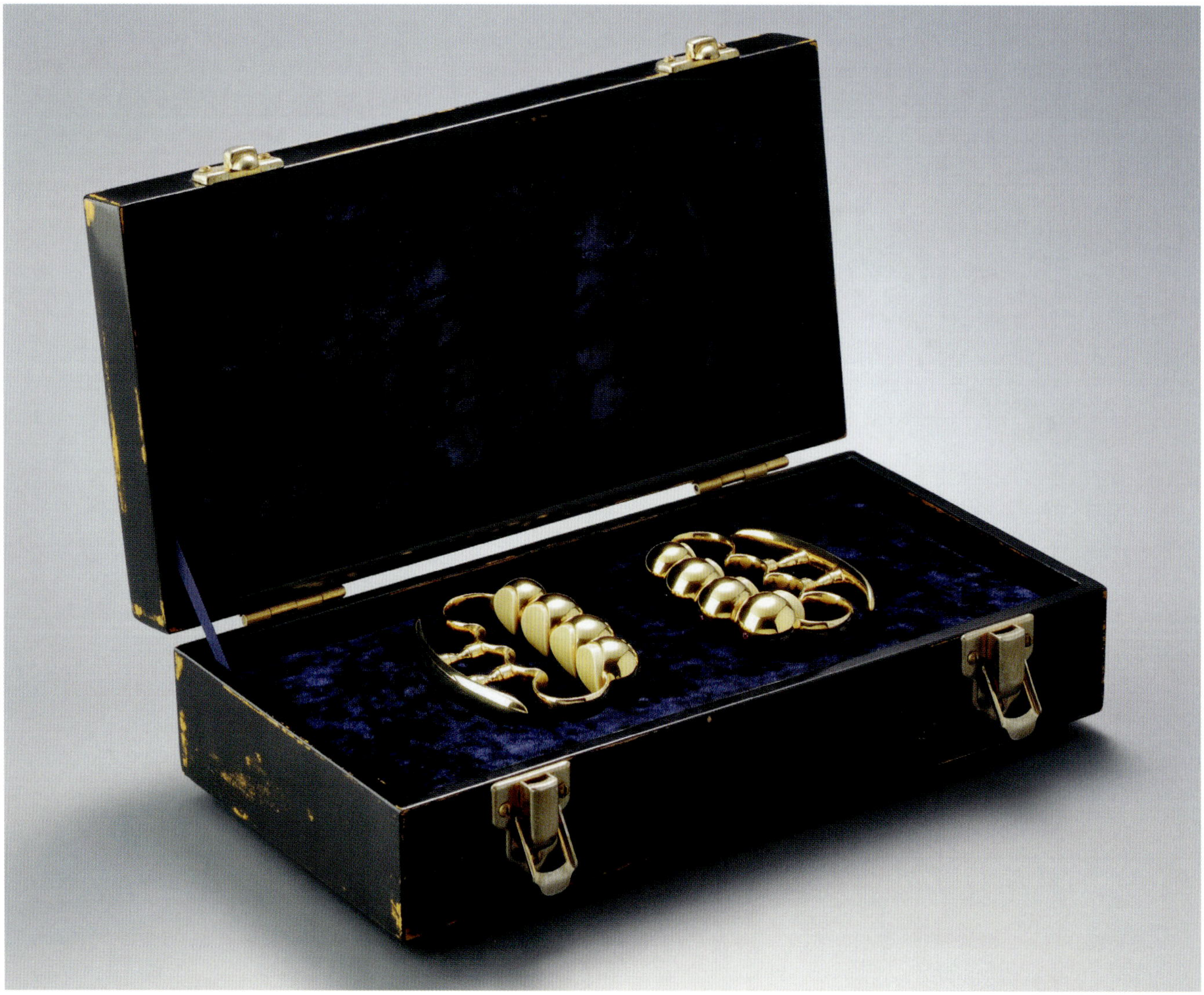

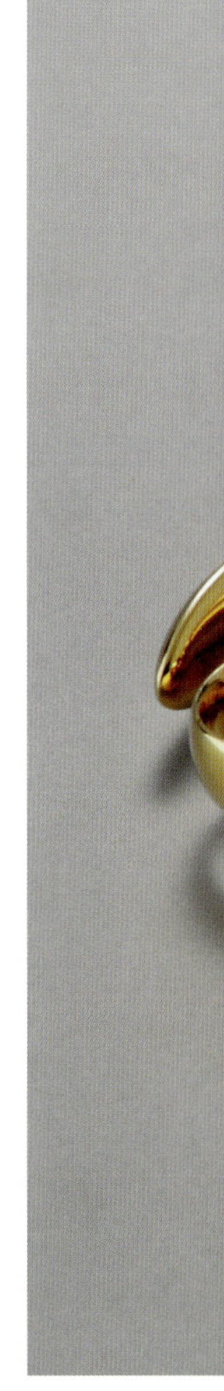

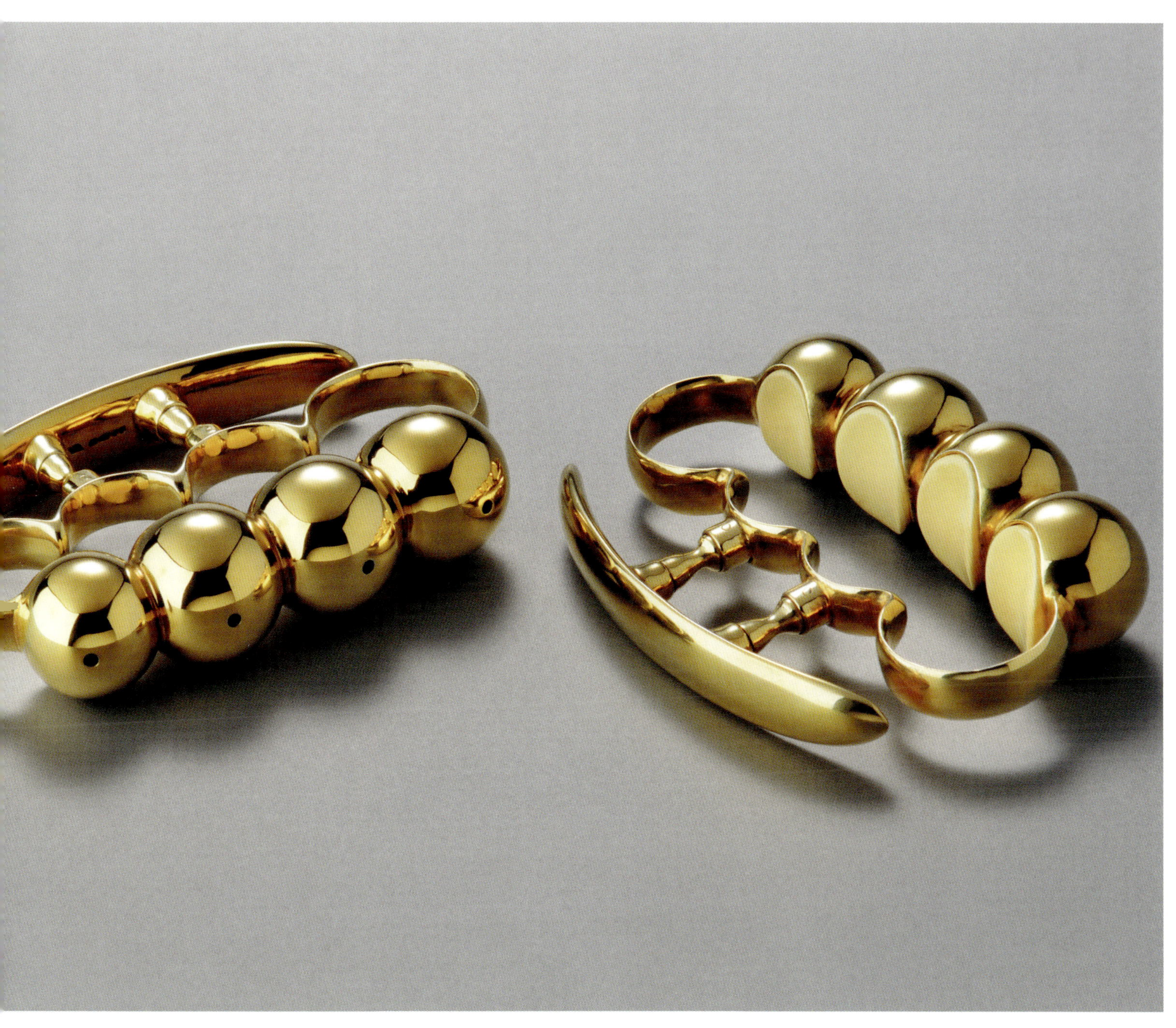

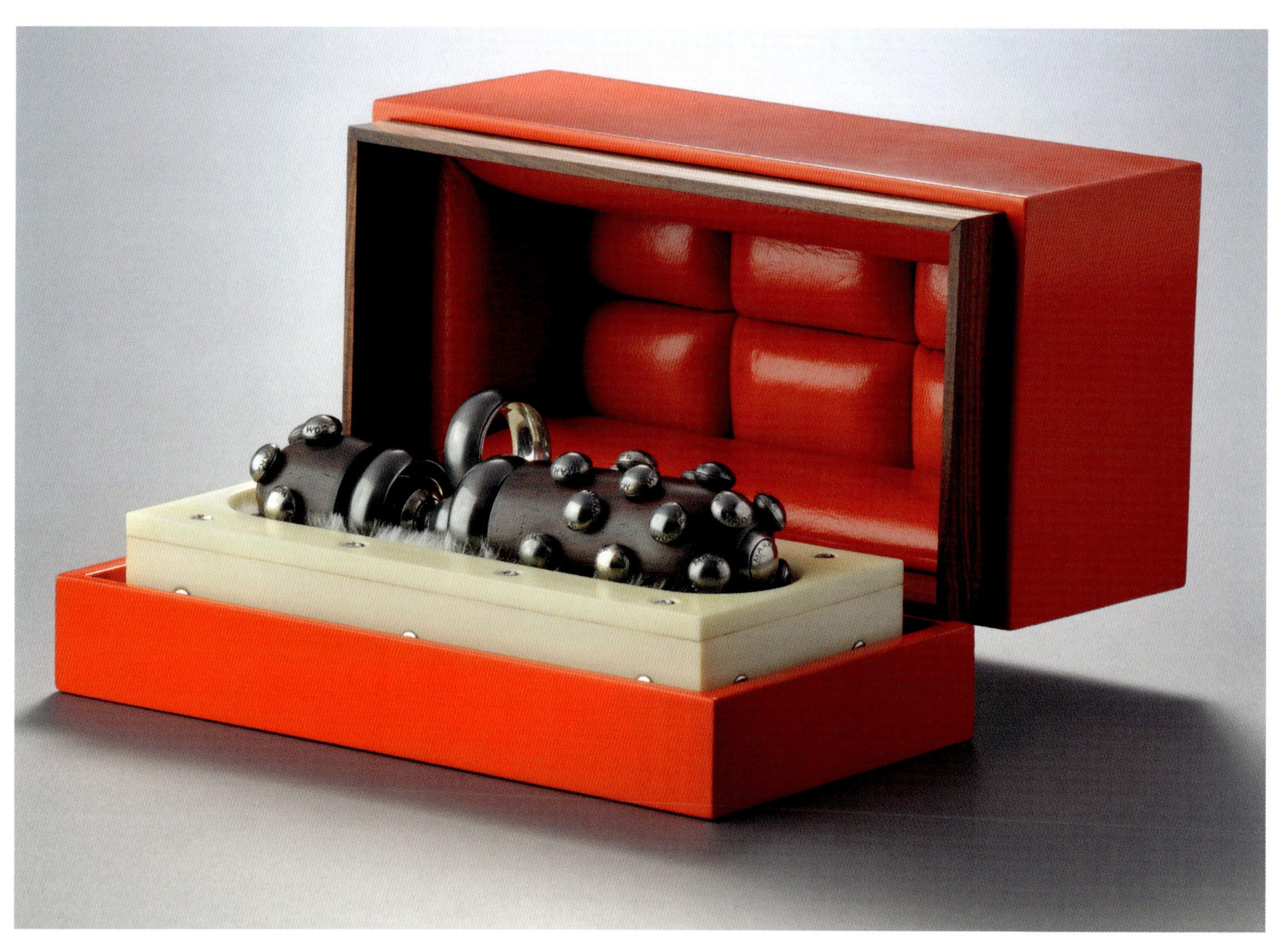

COSH, 2009
Oxidised silver,
cocobolo hardwood,
phenolic plastic, MDF,
paint, leather.
200 x 140 x 70mm

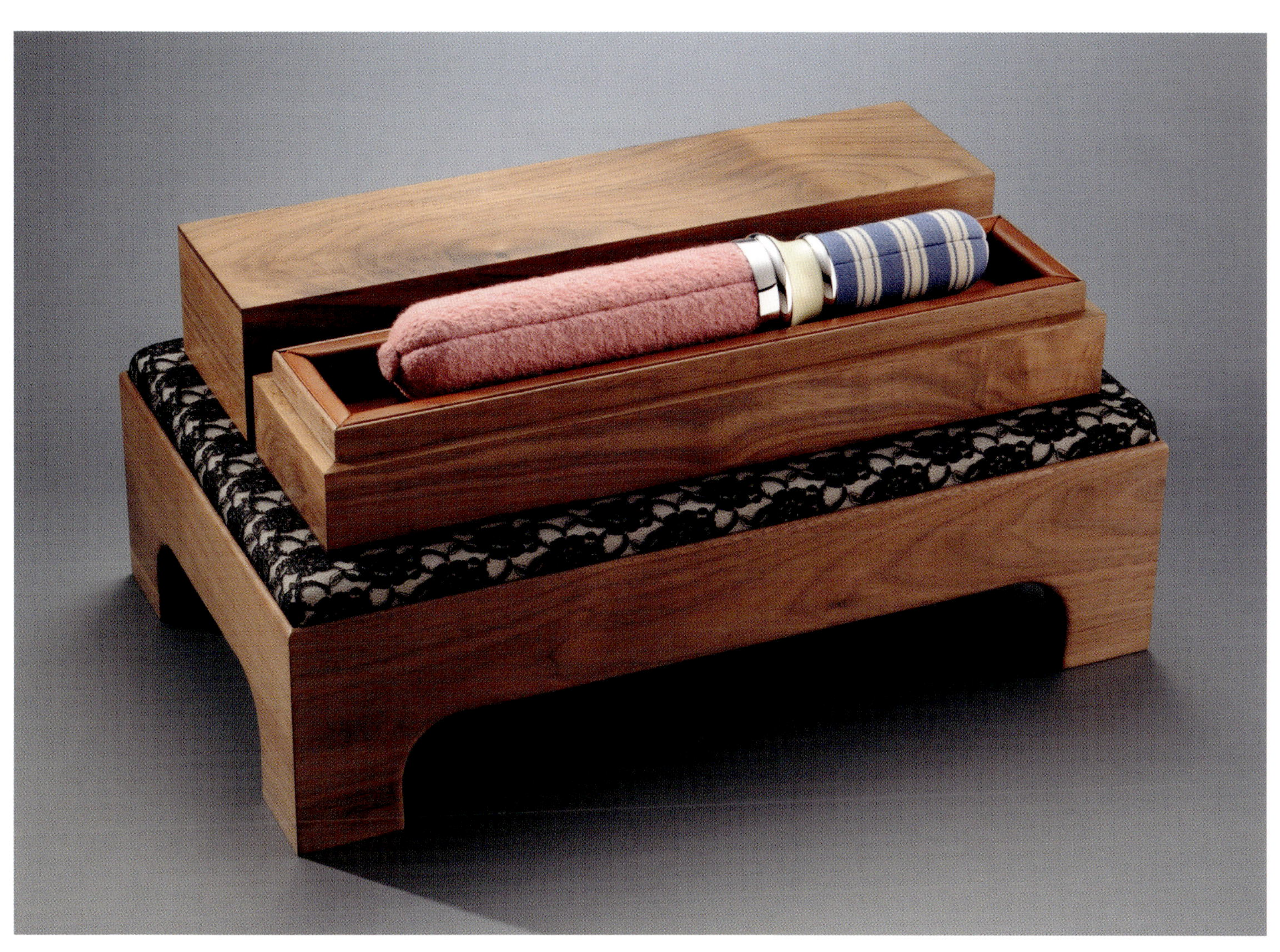

BEAUTY IS A MODERN
DOMAIN, 2011
Walnut, fabric, leather,
plastic, rhodium-plated
silver, felt.
450 x 260 x 200mm

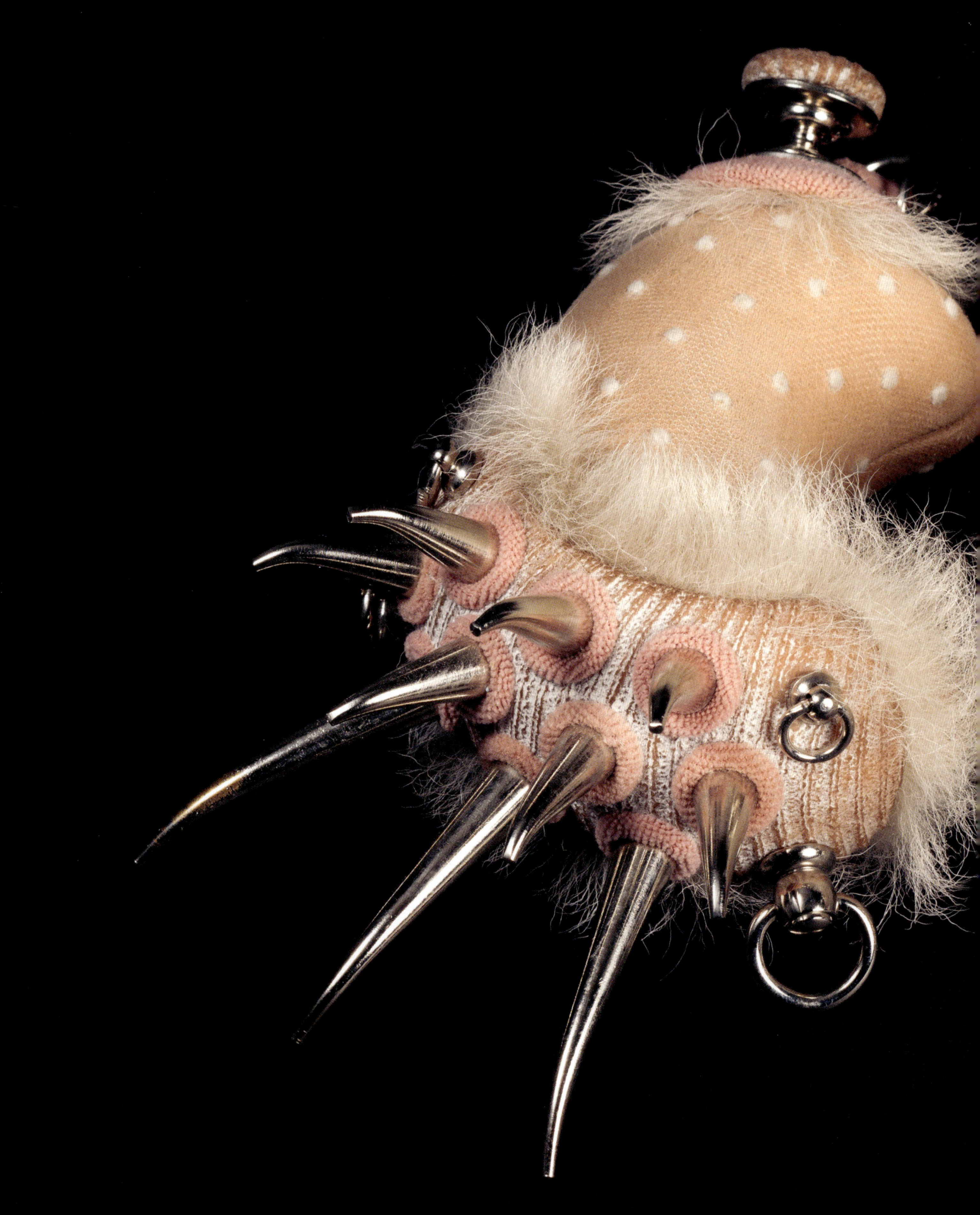

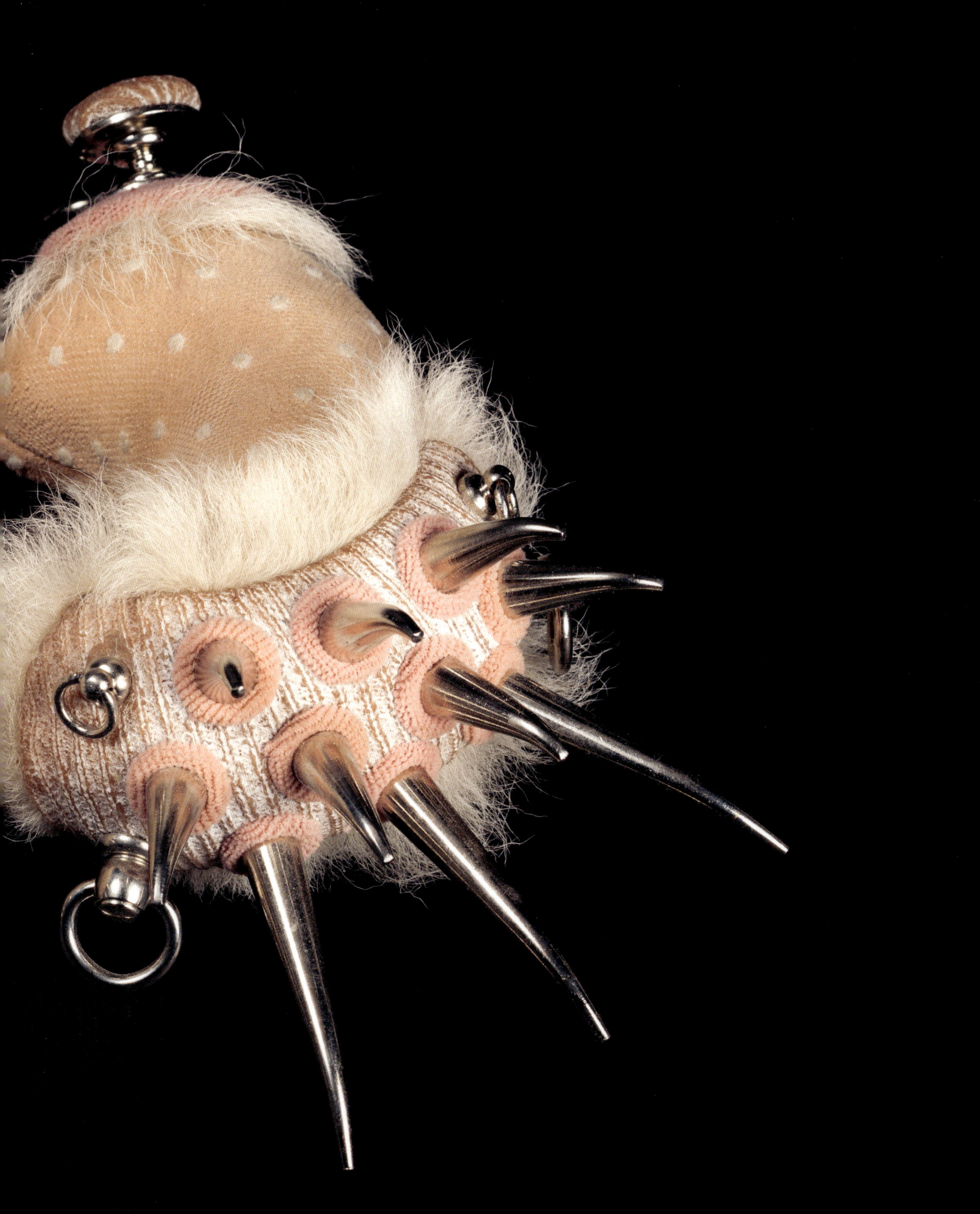

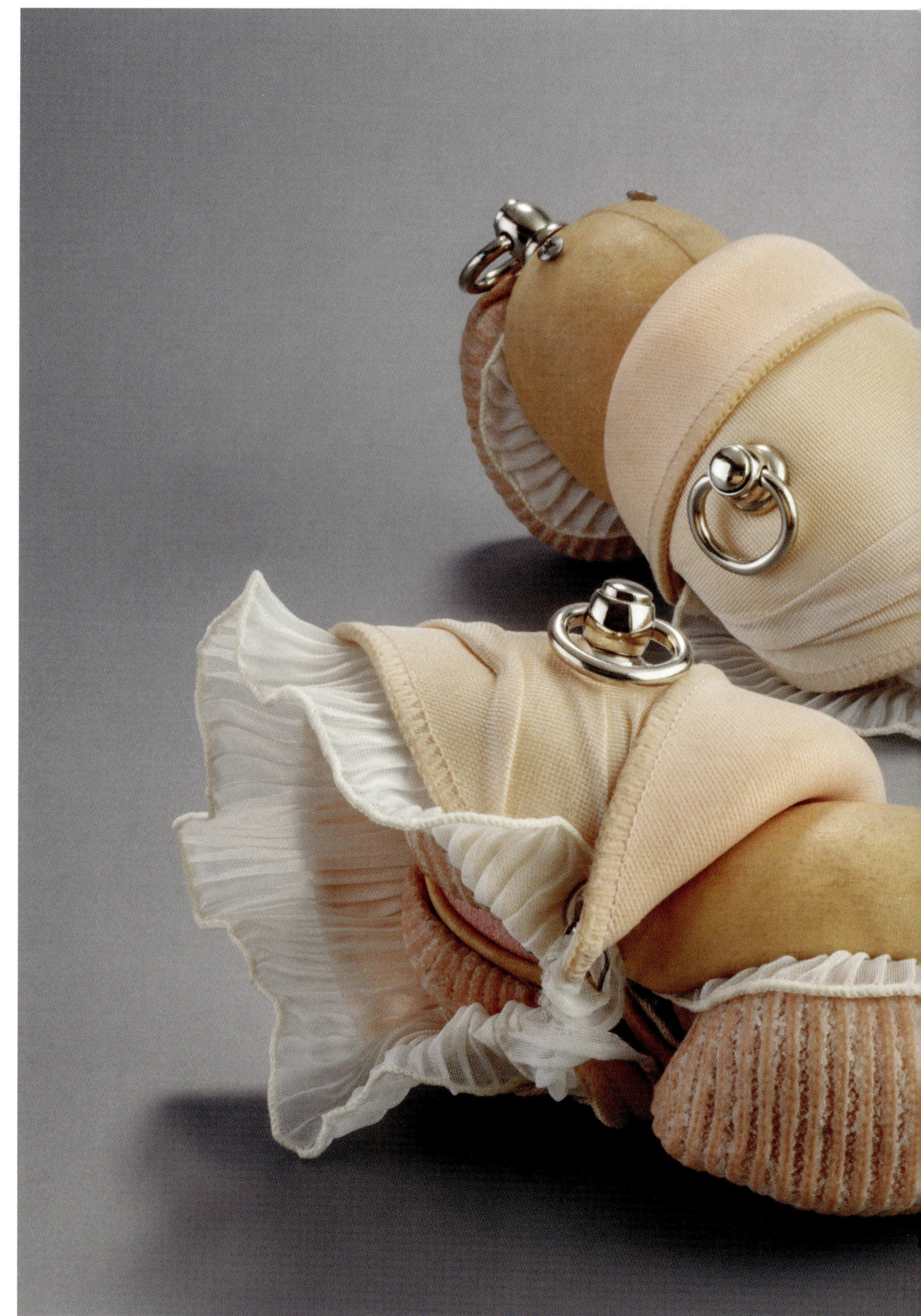

previous pages
SUCK, 2017
Resin, leather, fabric,
wax, fur, metal
findings.
230 x 250 x 70mm

right
LIL' CUTIE BALLS, 2014
Plastic, fabric, wax, bra
pads, metal findings.
130 x 95 x 80mm

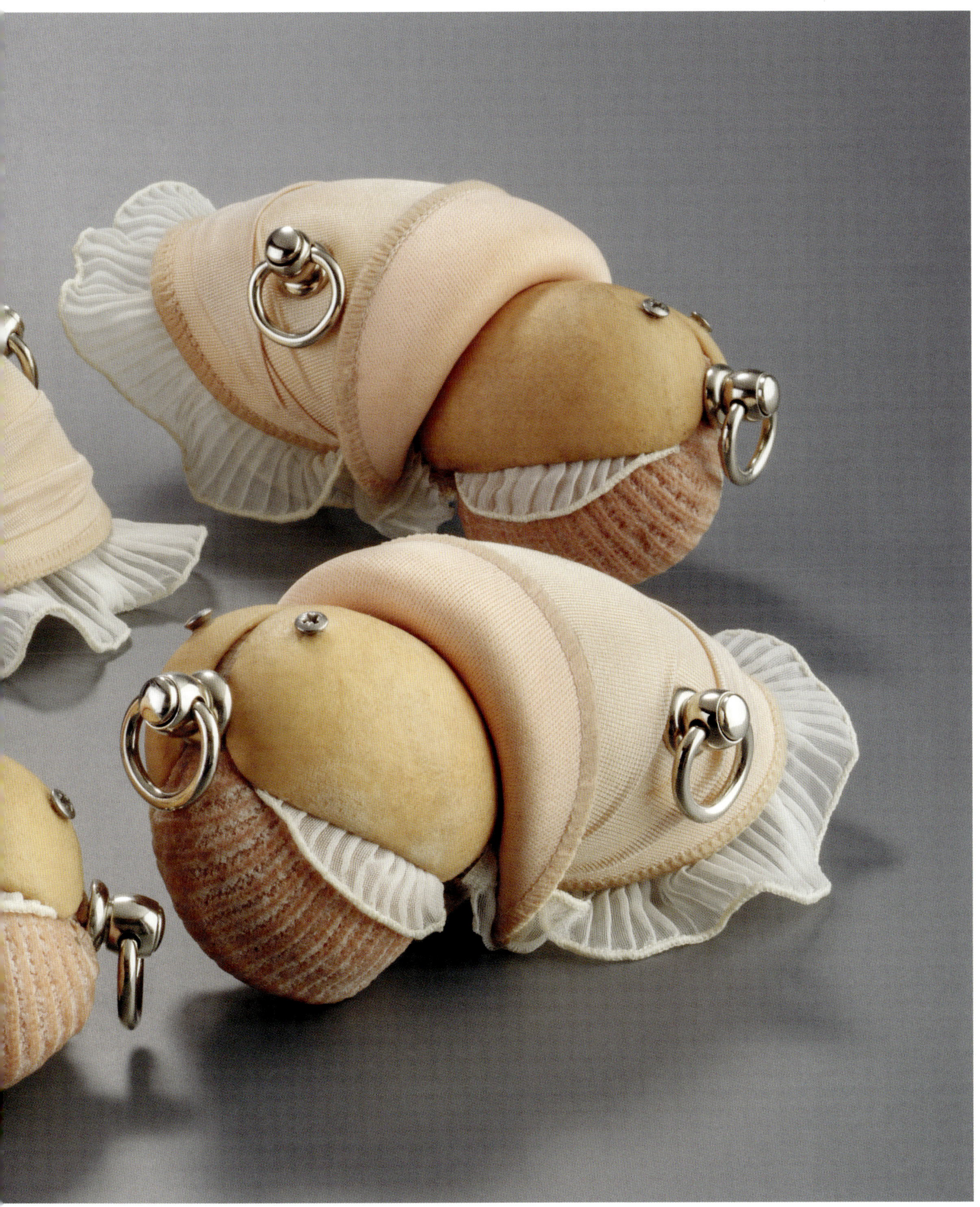

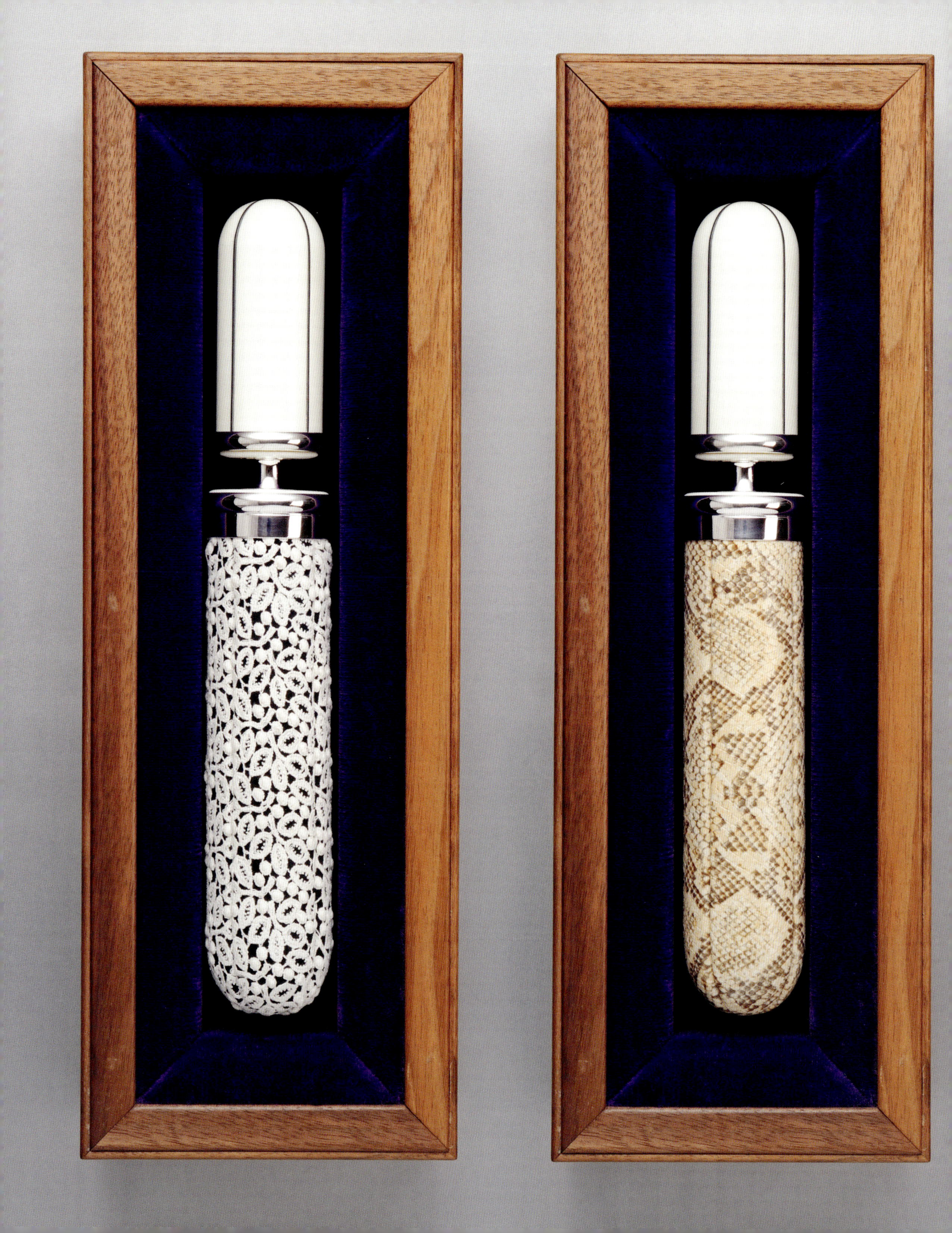

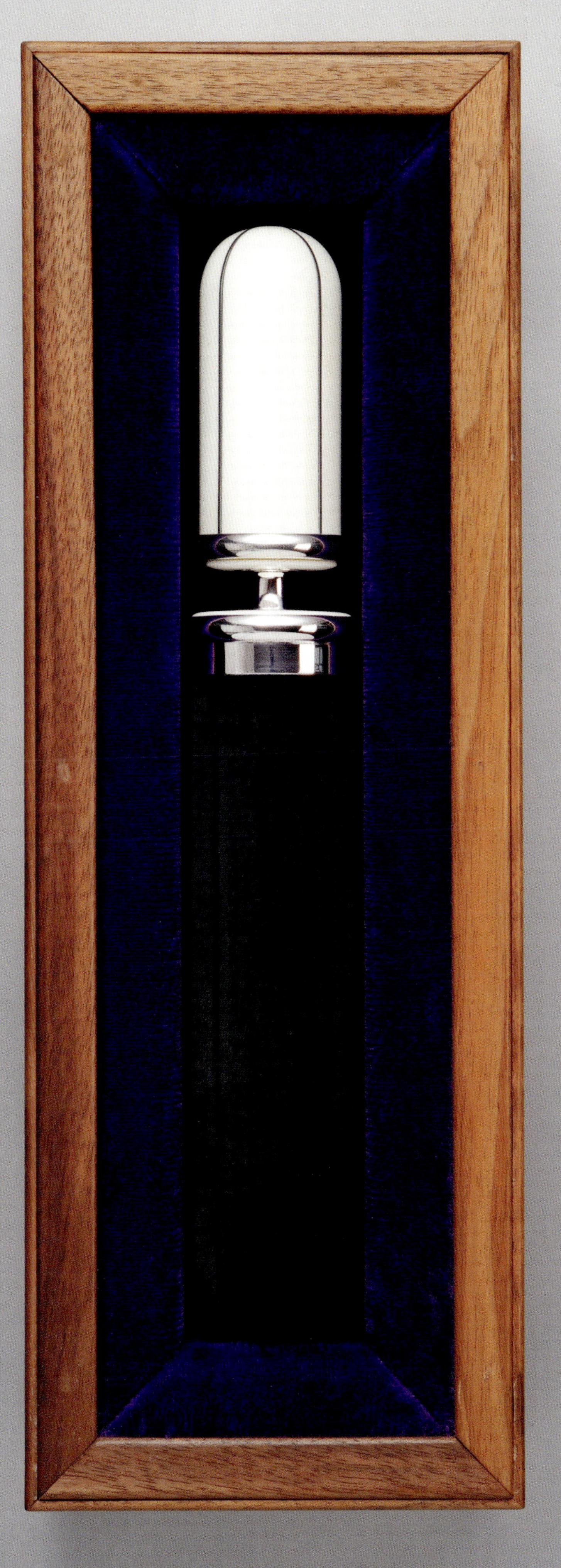

*WHO'S AFRAID OF
SUEDE, SNAKESKIN
& LACE?*, 2011
Rhodium-plated silver,
phenolic plastic, fake
snake, velvet, American
walnut.
380 x 140 x 95mm

opposite
FAKE BUN FETISH, 2014
Fake hair bun, leather,
wax, metal findings,
human hair.
160 x 120mm

overleaf
BIB BABY, 2014
Baby collar, fabric, felt,
leather, wax, metal
findings, human hair.
380 x 160 x 130mm

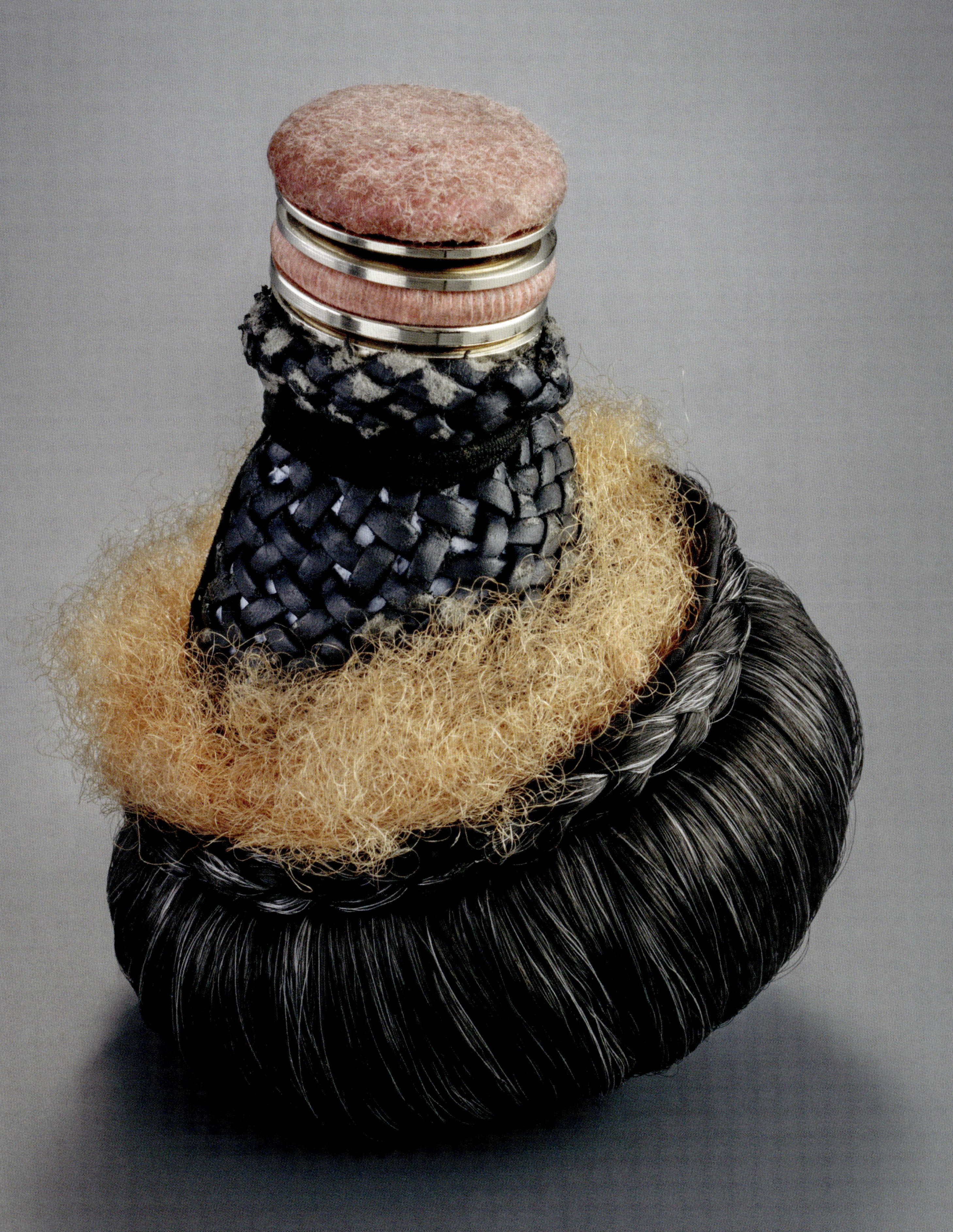

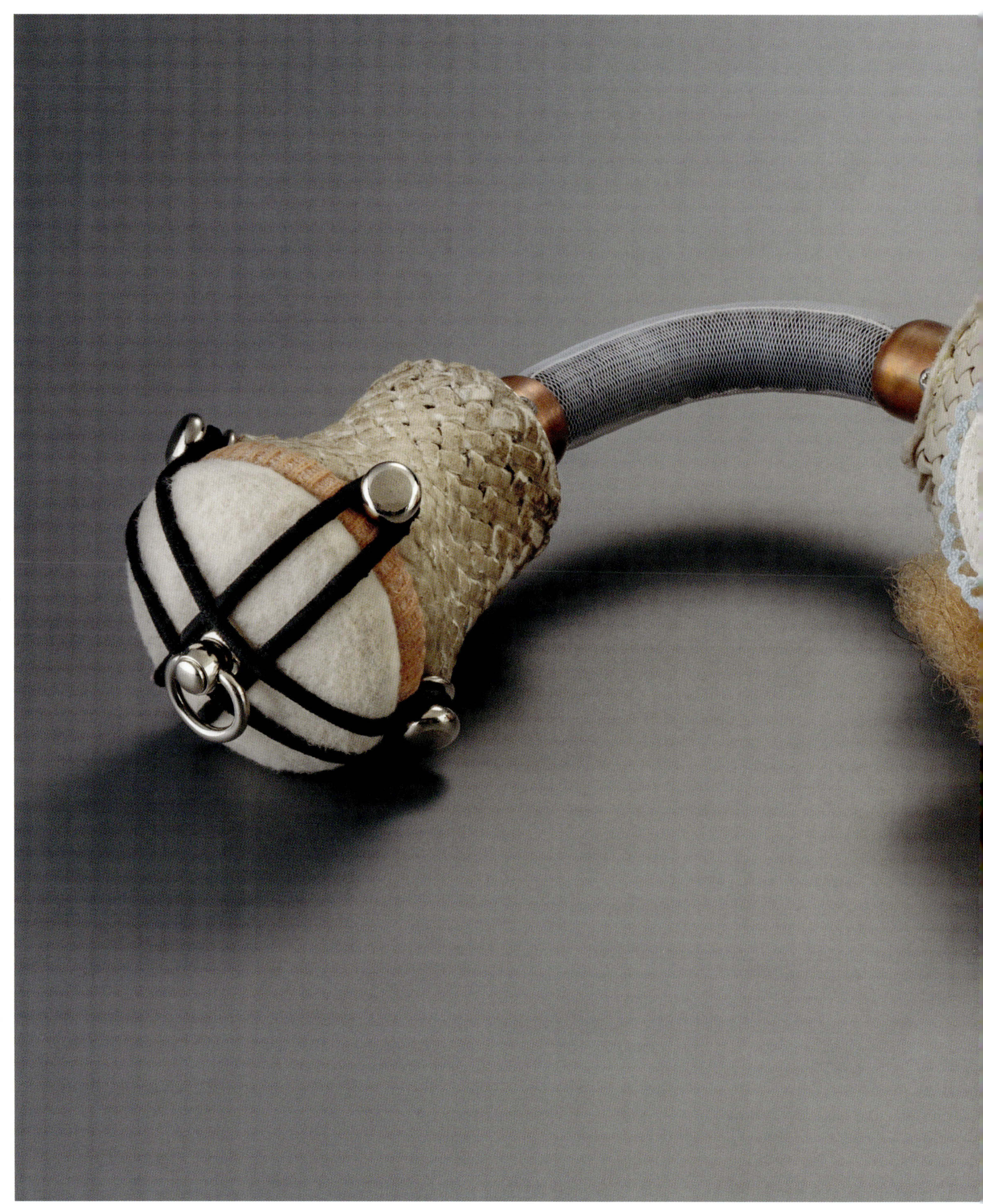

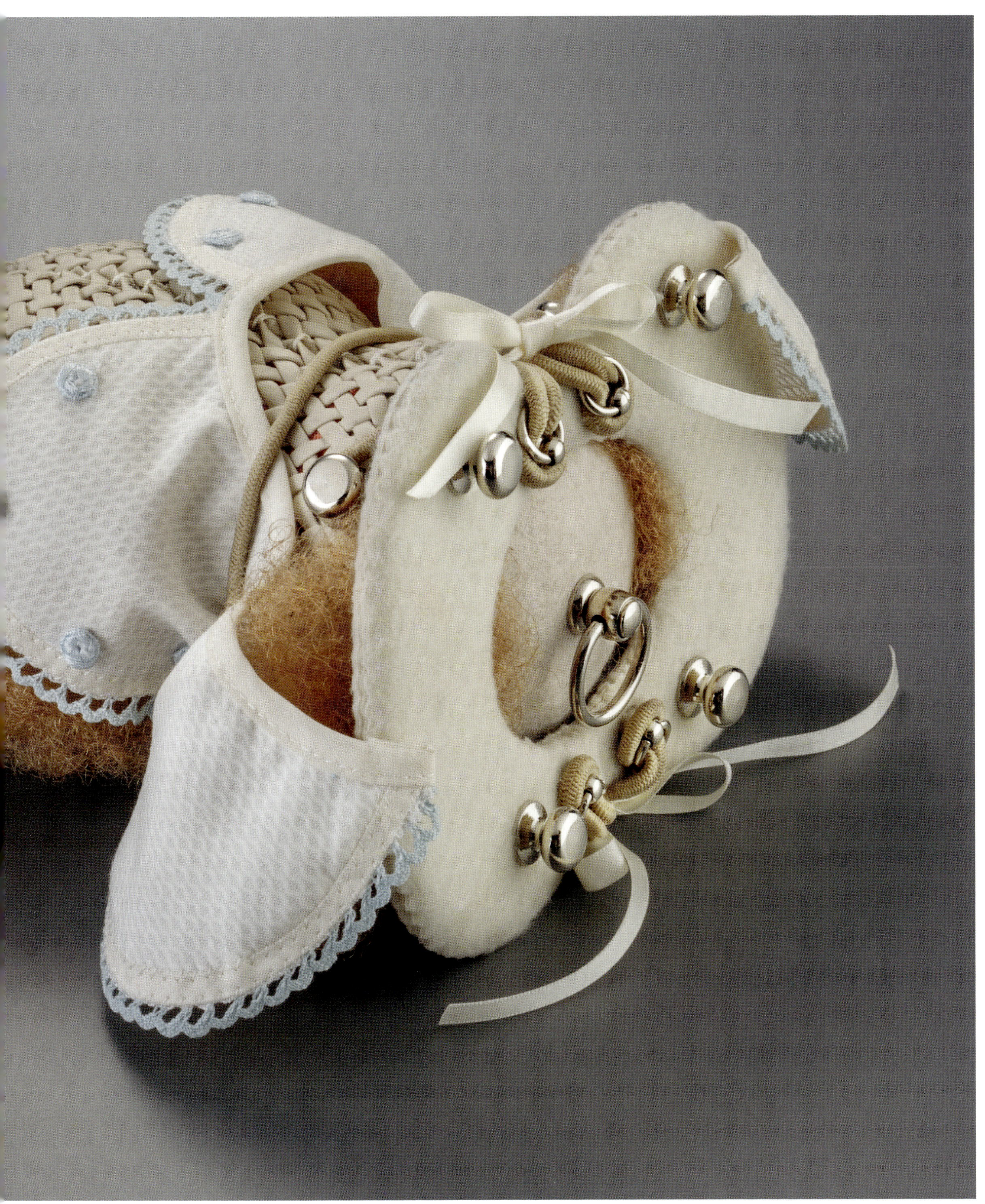

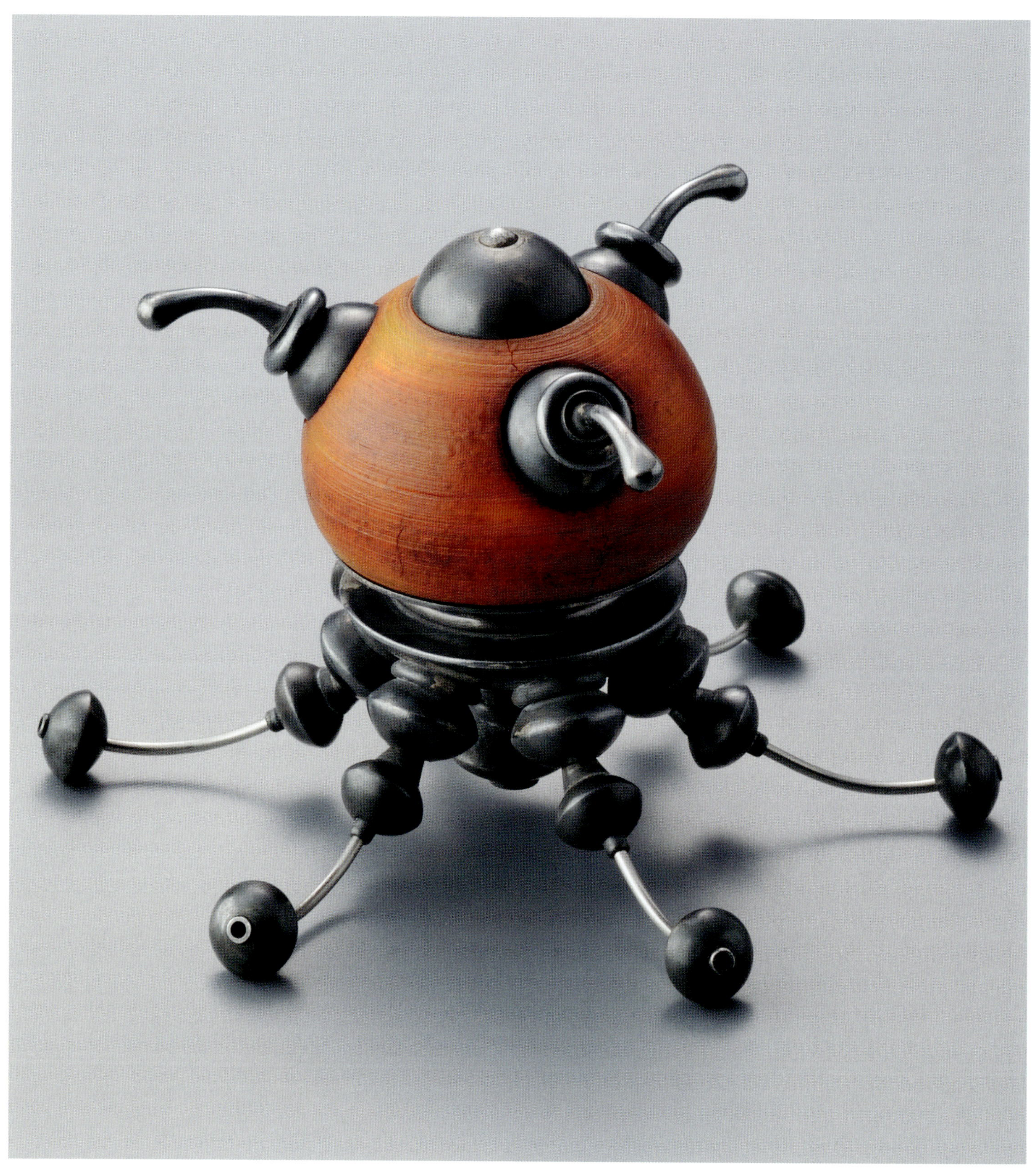

*VIRUS, BABY TOOTH
CONTAINER*, 1999
Cue ball, oxidised
silver, stainless steel.
110 x 100mm

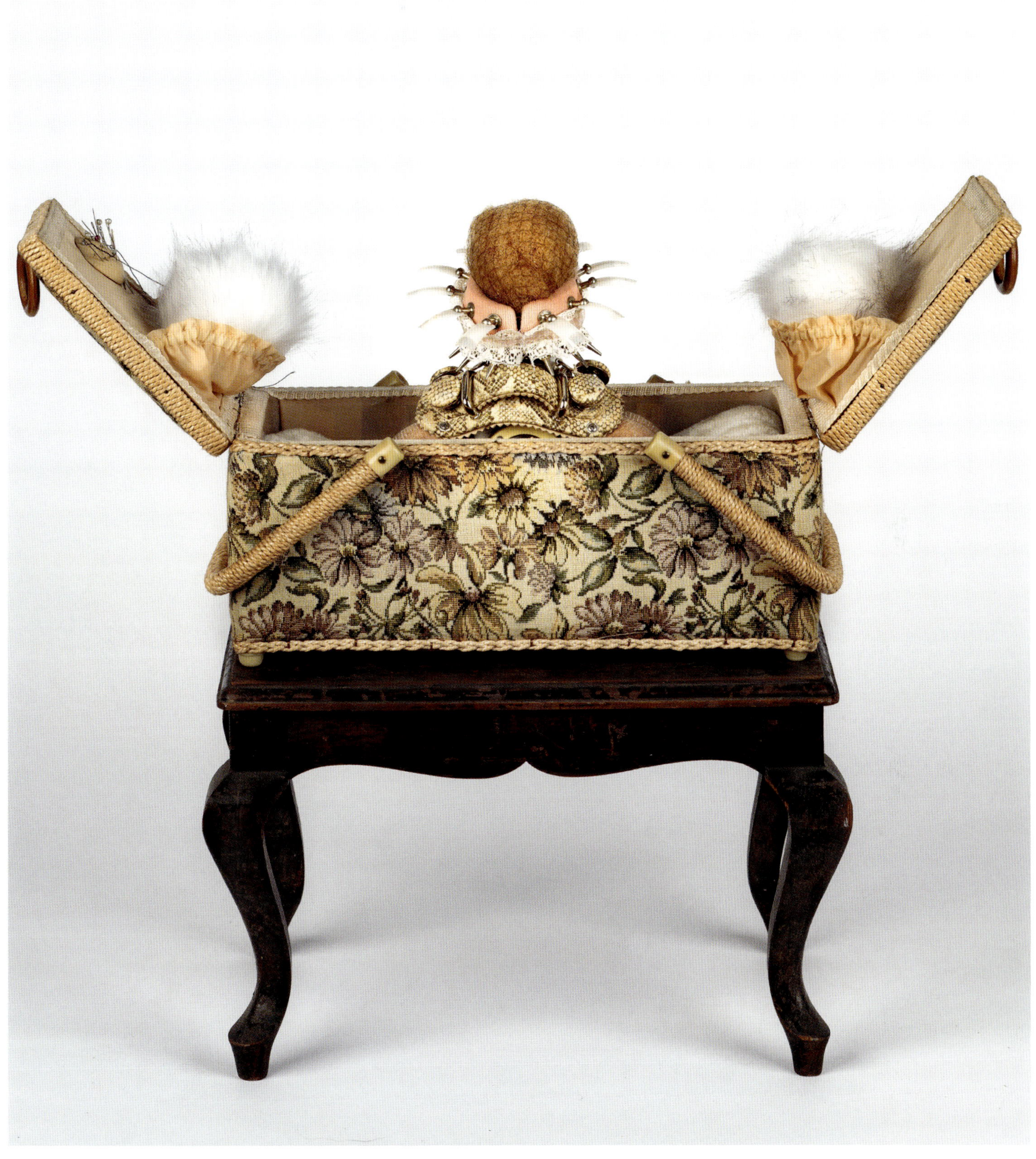

SEWING BOX FETISH,
2024
Vintage sewing box,
pom poms, fake
fingernails, fabric, wax,
hair net, human hair,
metal findings.
610 x 220 x 300mm

PINK & FRIENDLY, 2013
Fabric, wood resin,
silver, velvet.
200 x 140 x 130mm

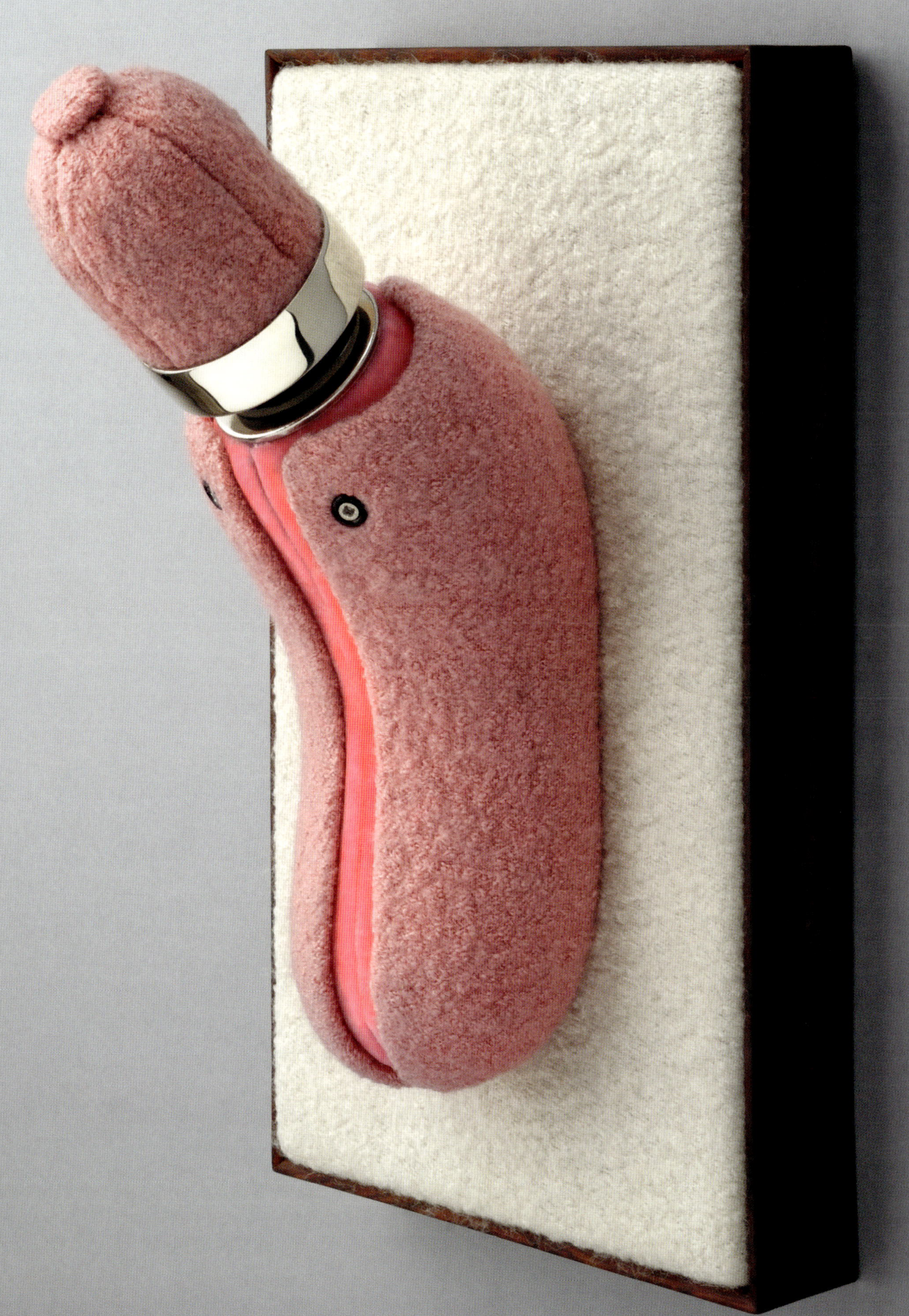

JEWELLERY

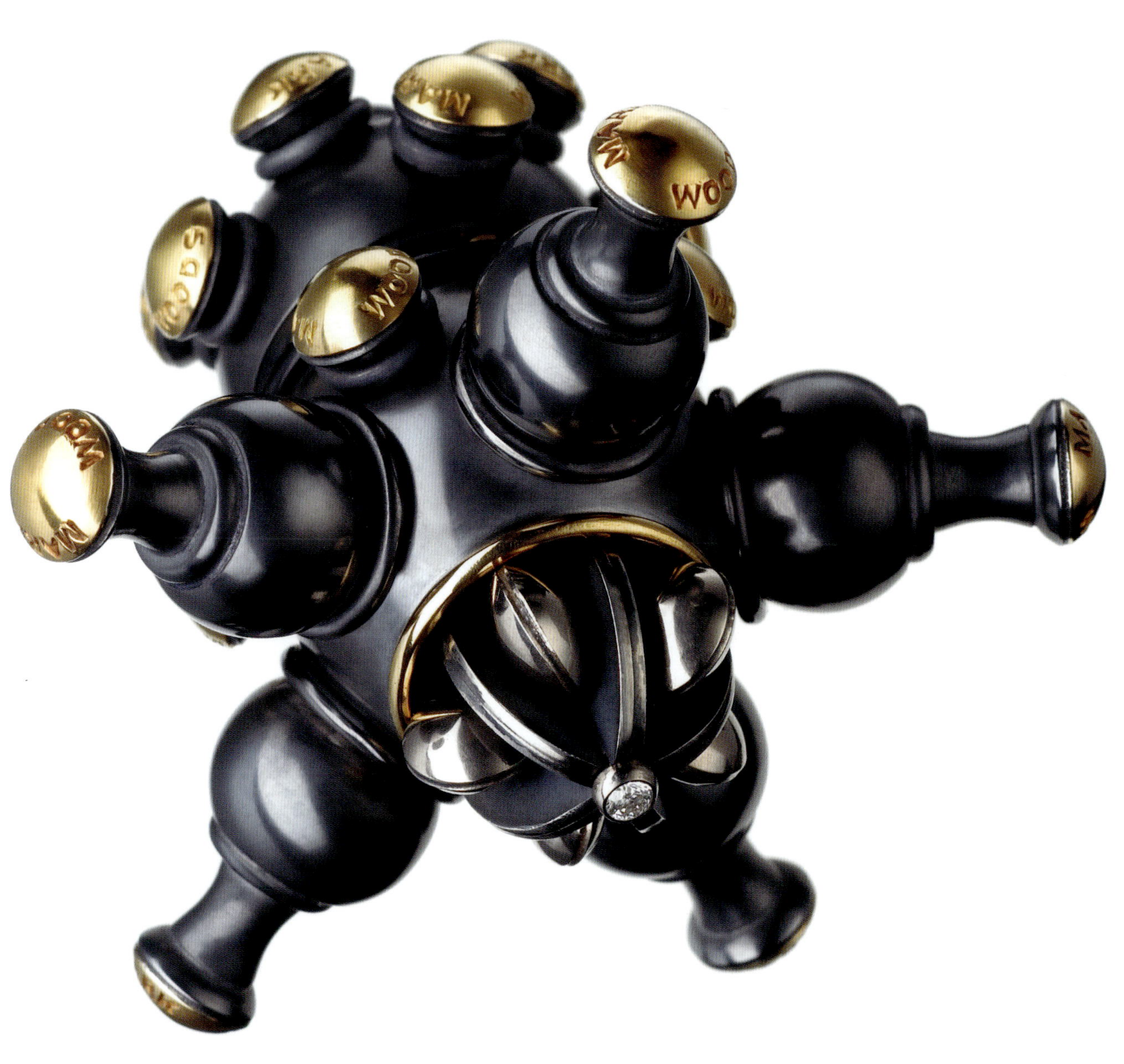

MEDIATOR BEAD, 2008
Oxidised silver, 22ct.
gold, 18ct. white gold,
diamond.
80 x 85mm

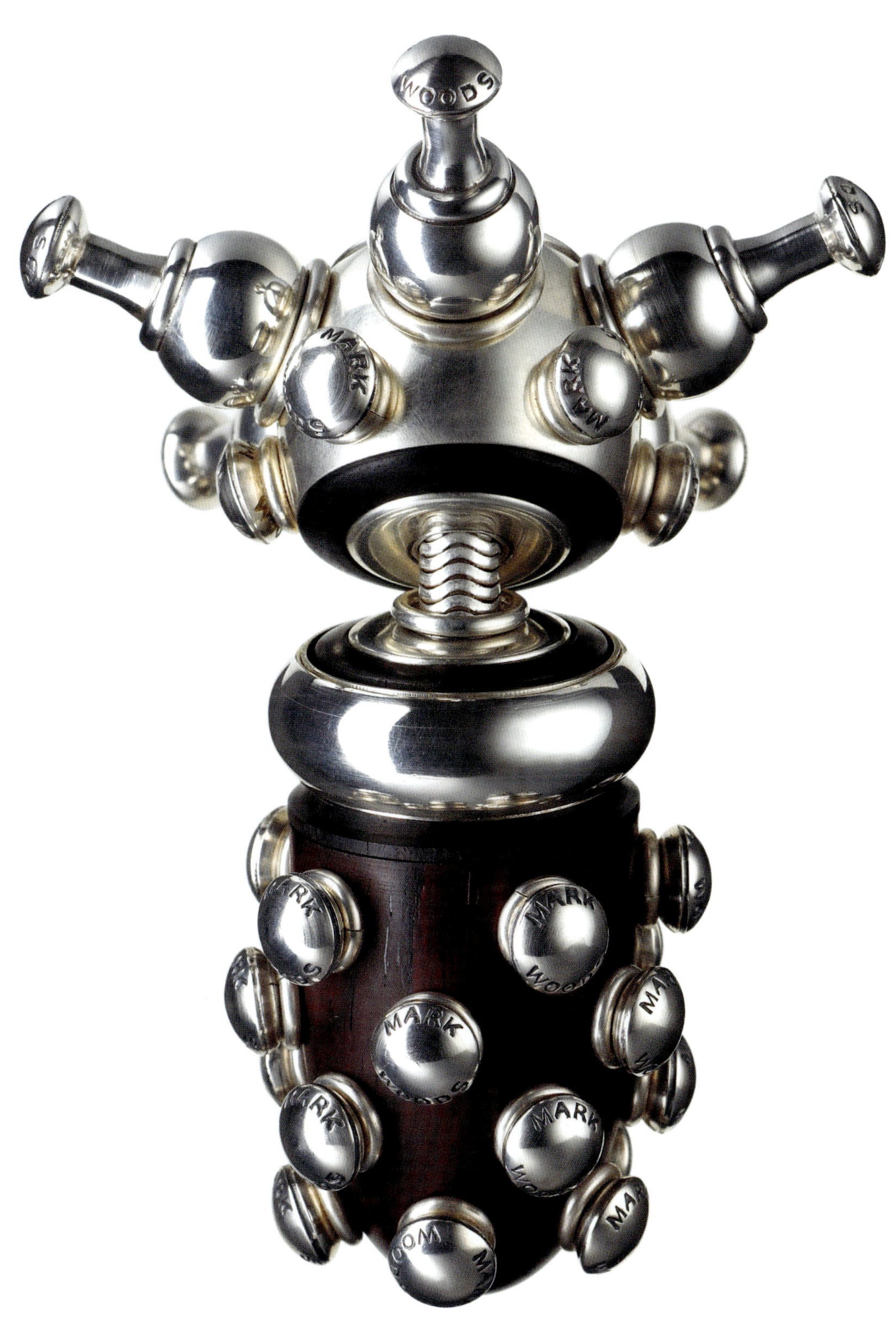

COCOBOLO MEDIATOR
BEAD, 2008
Silver, ebony, cocobolo.
110 x 80mm

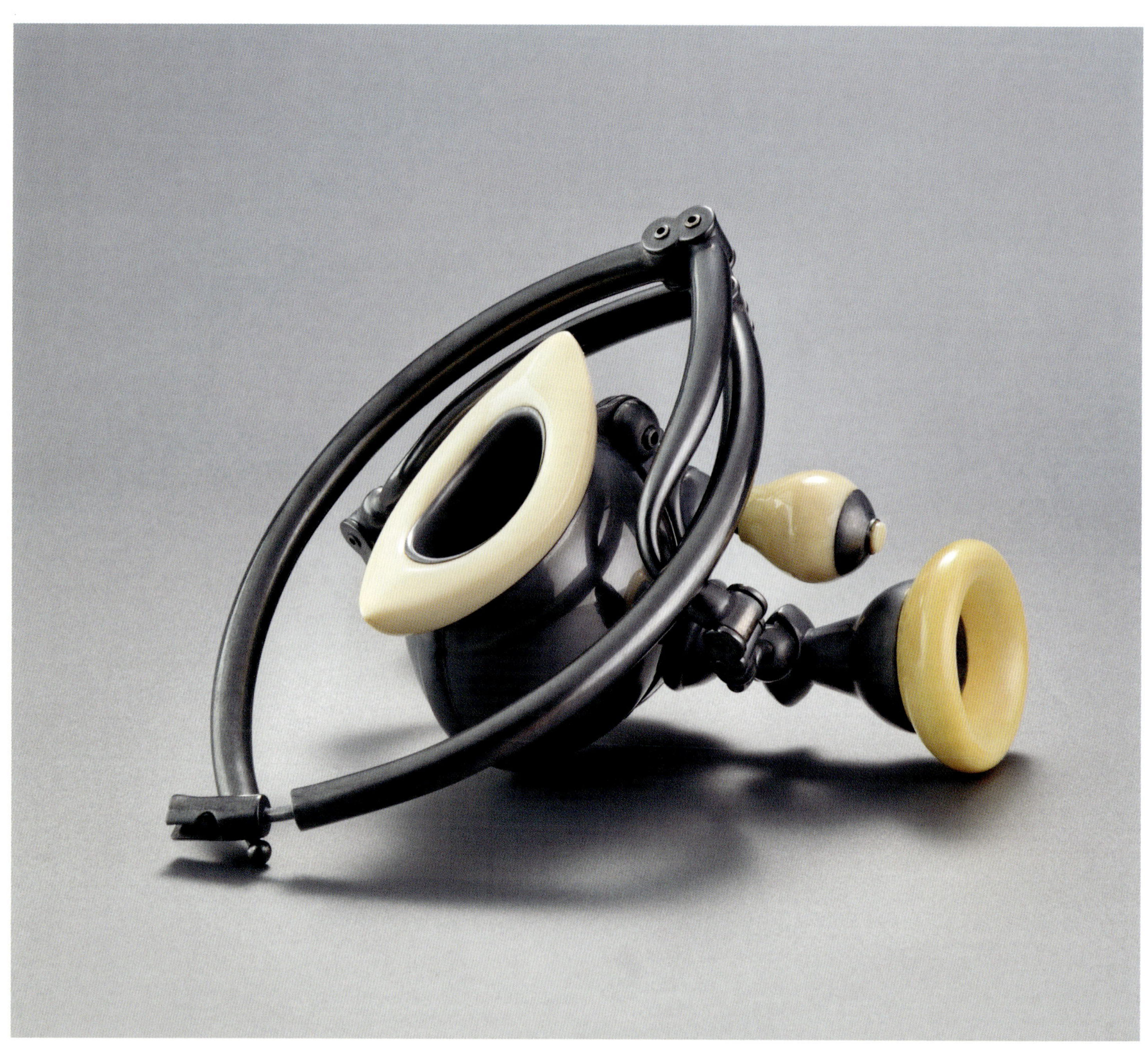

HOLE II, NECK-PIECE,
1996
Oxidised silver,
phenolic plastic.
145 x 190 x 48mm

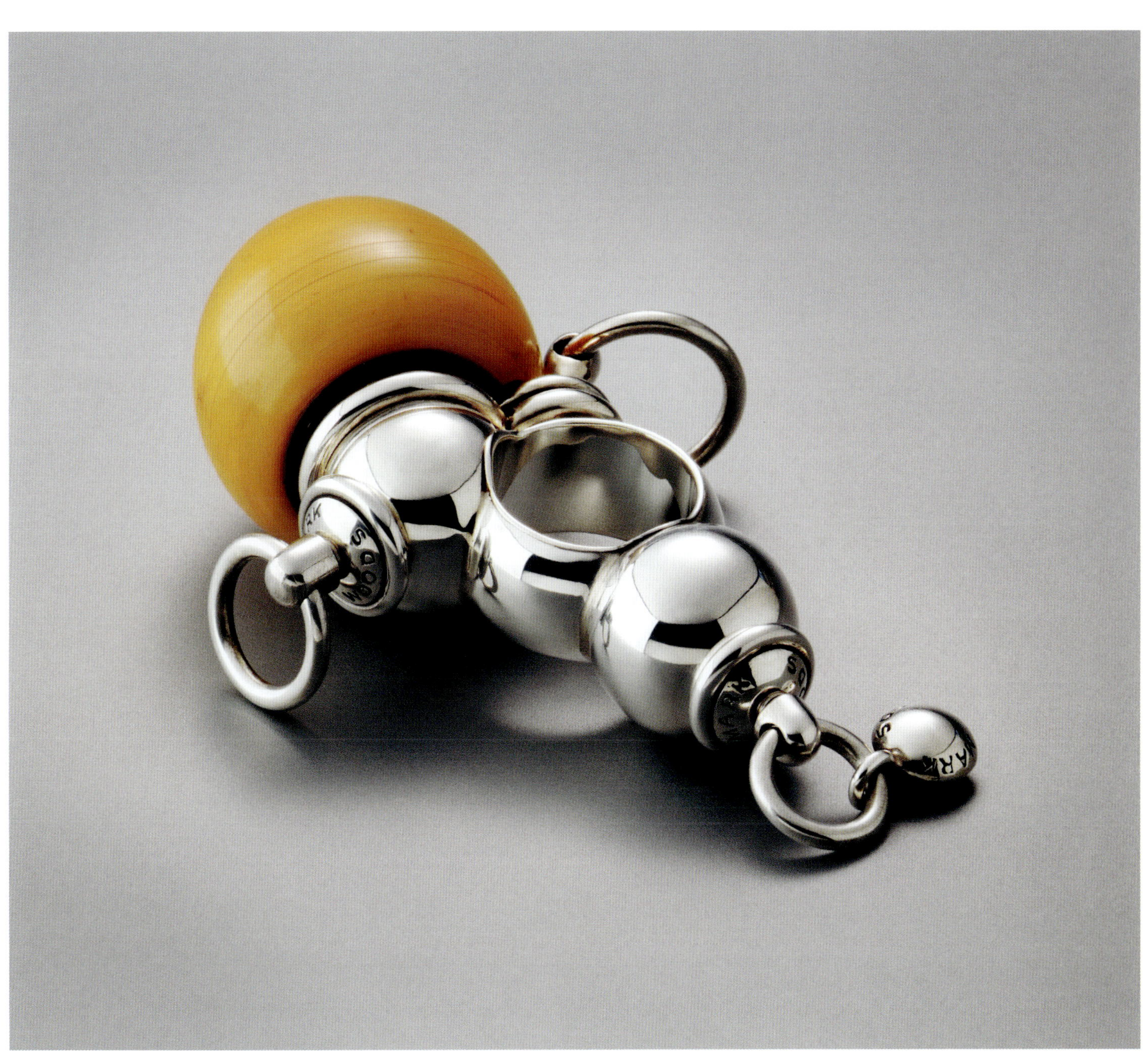

RING, 2005
Silver, phenolic plastic.
110 x 80mm

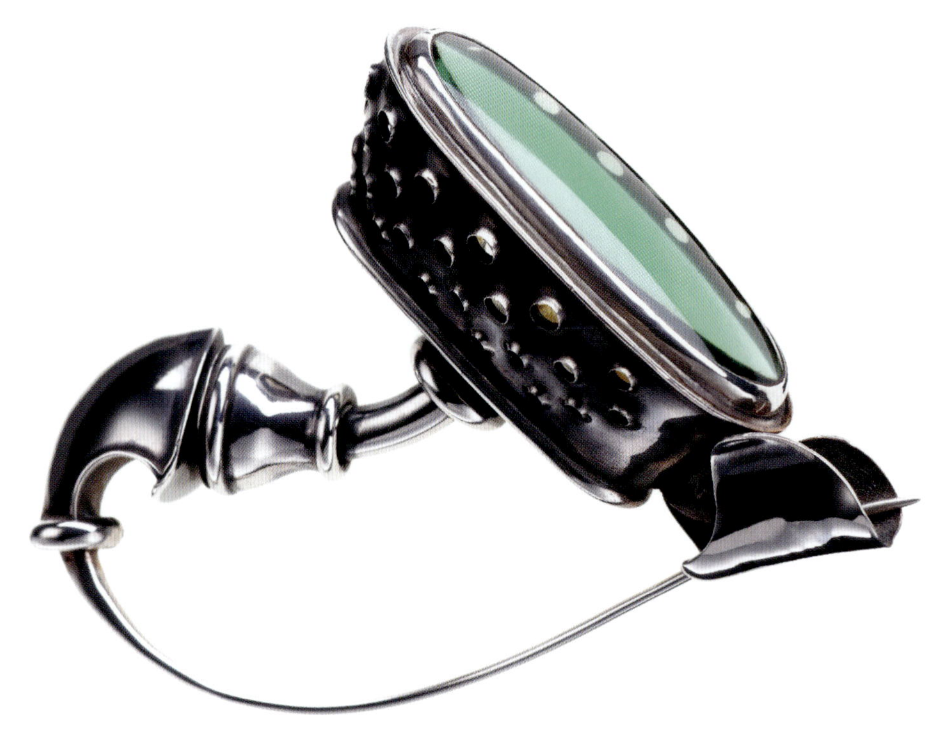

BROOCH, 1994
Oxidised silver, Tiffany
lamp glass.
78 x 30mm

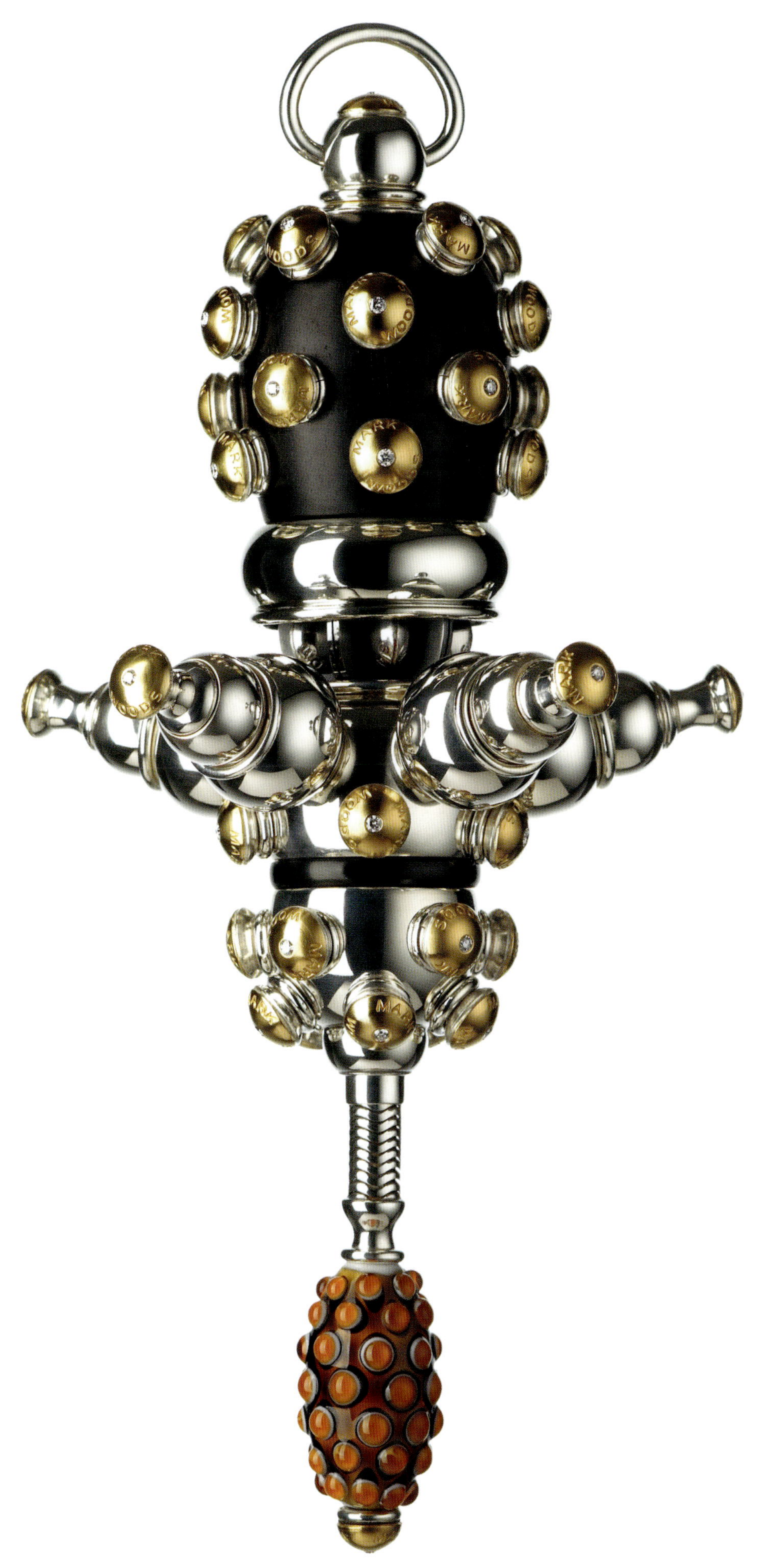

*FRUIT FROM THE
GARDEN OF EARTHLY
DELIGHTS*, 2010
Silver, 22ct. gold,
diamonds, ebony,
Venetian glass bead.
200 x 95mm

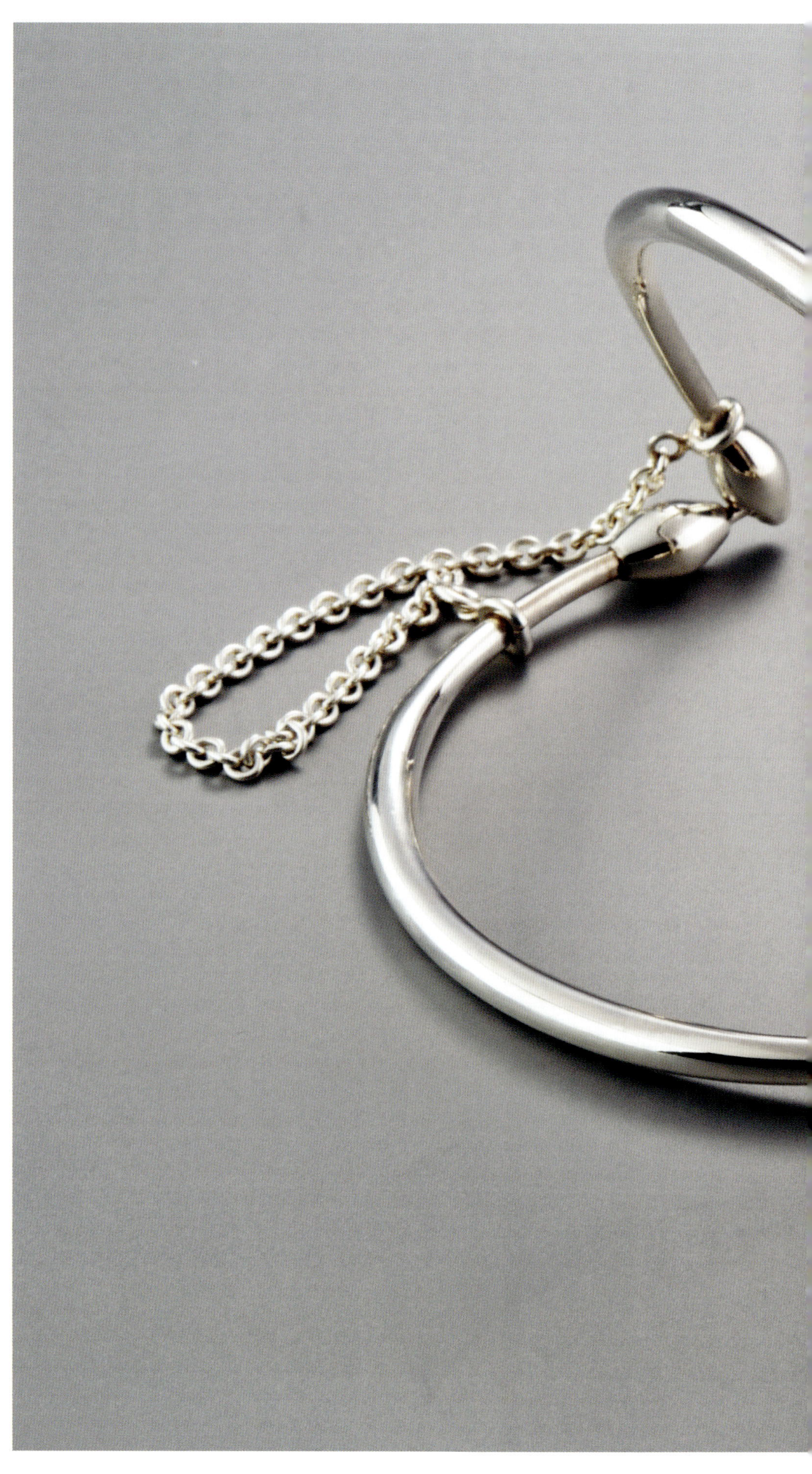

HOLE, NECKPIECE, 1995
Silver, phenolic plastic.
145 x 190 x 48mm

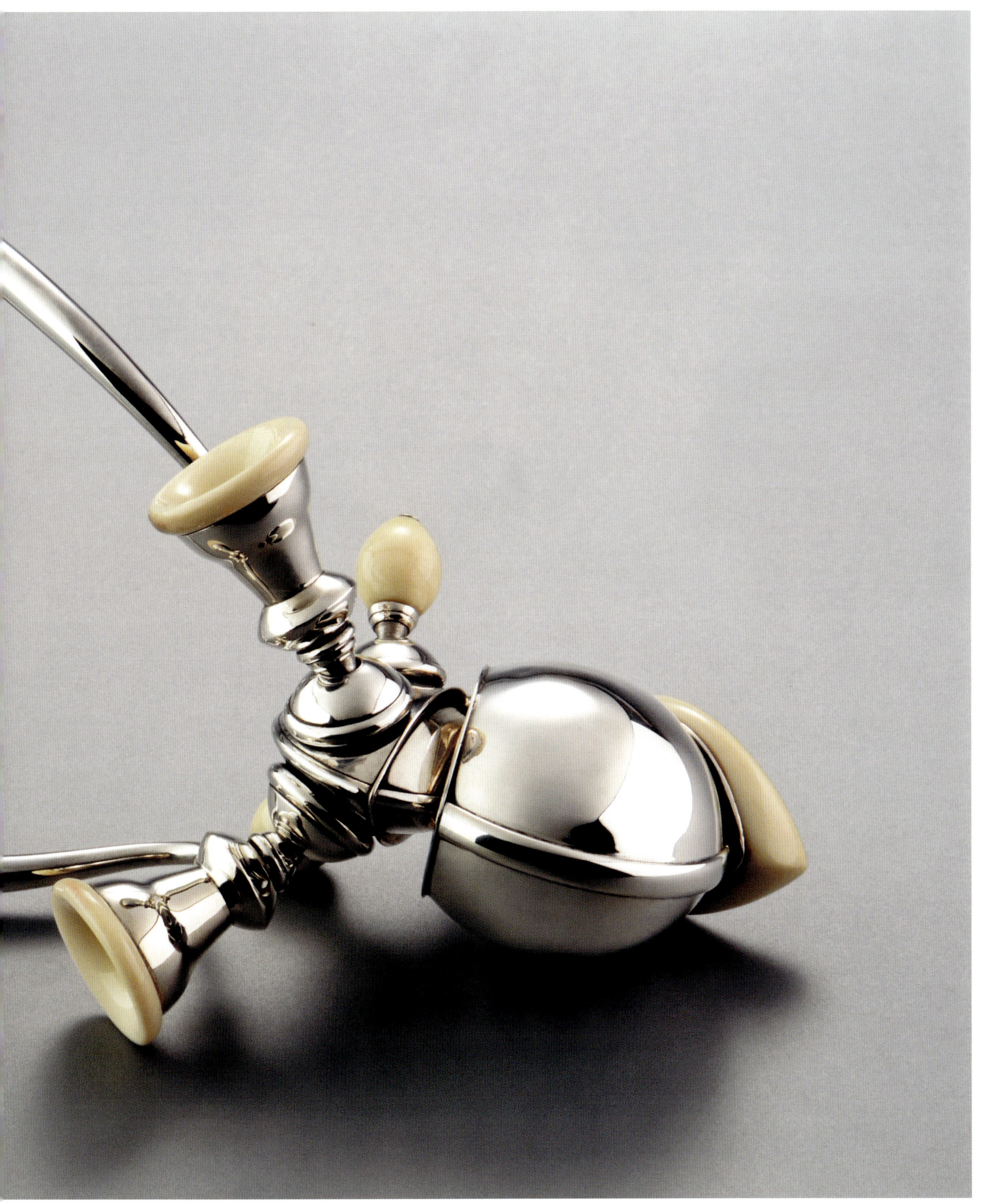

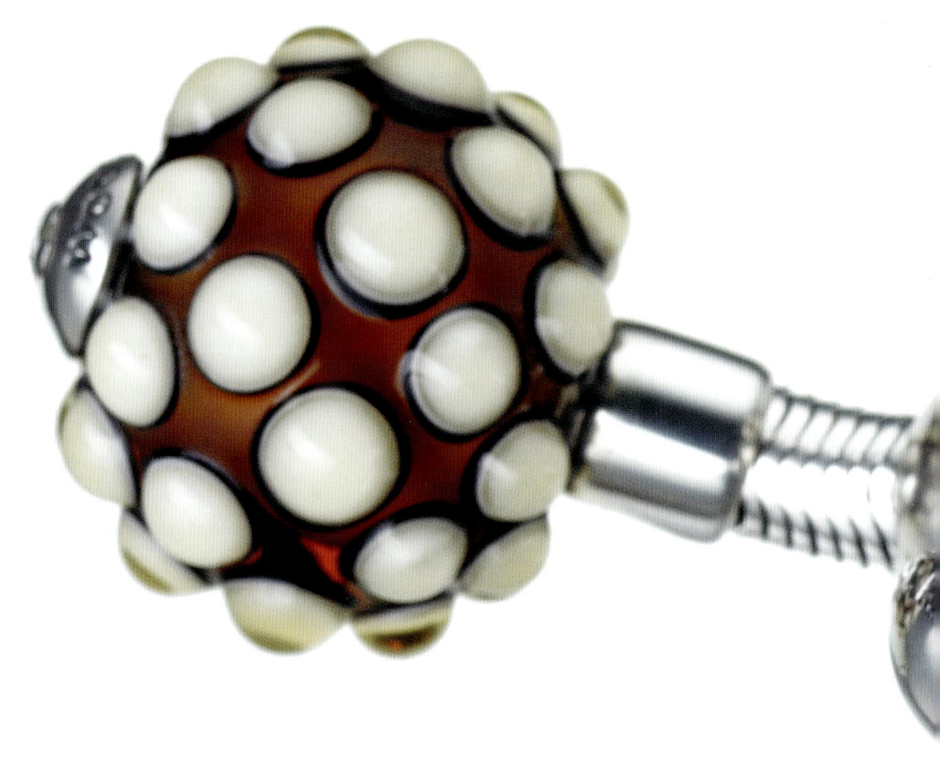

MEDIATOR BEAD, 2008
Silver, Venetian bead.
105 x 80mm

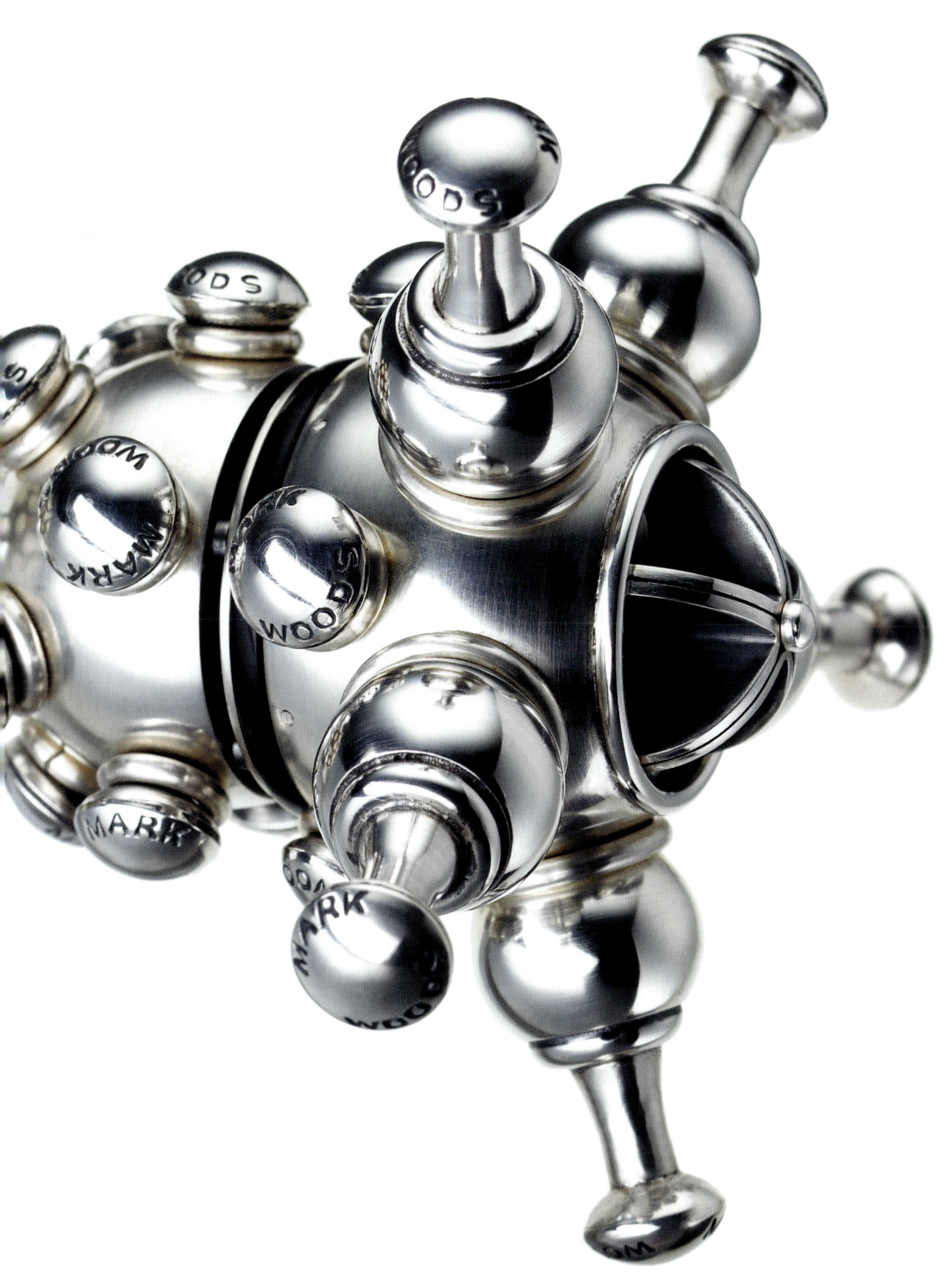
WOODS
MARK
WOODS
MARK
WOODS

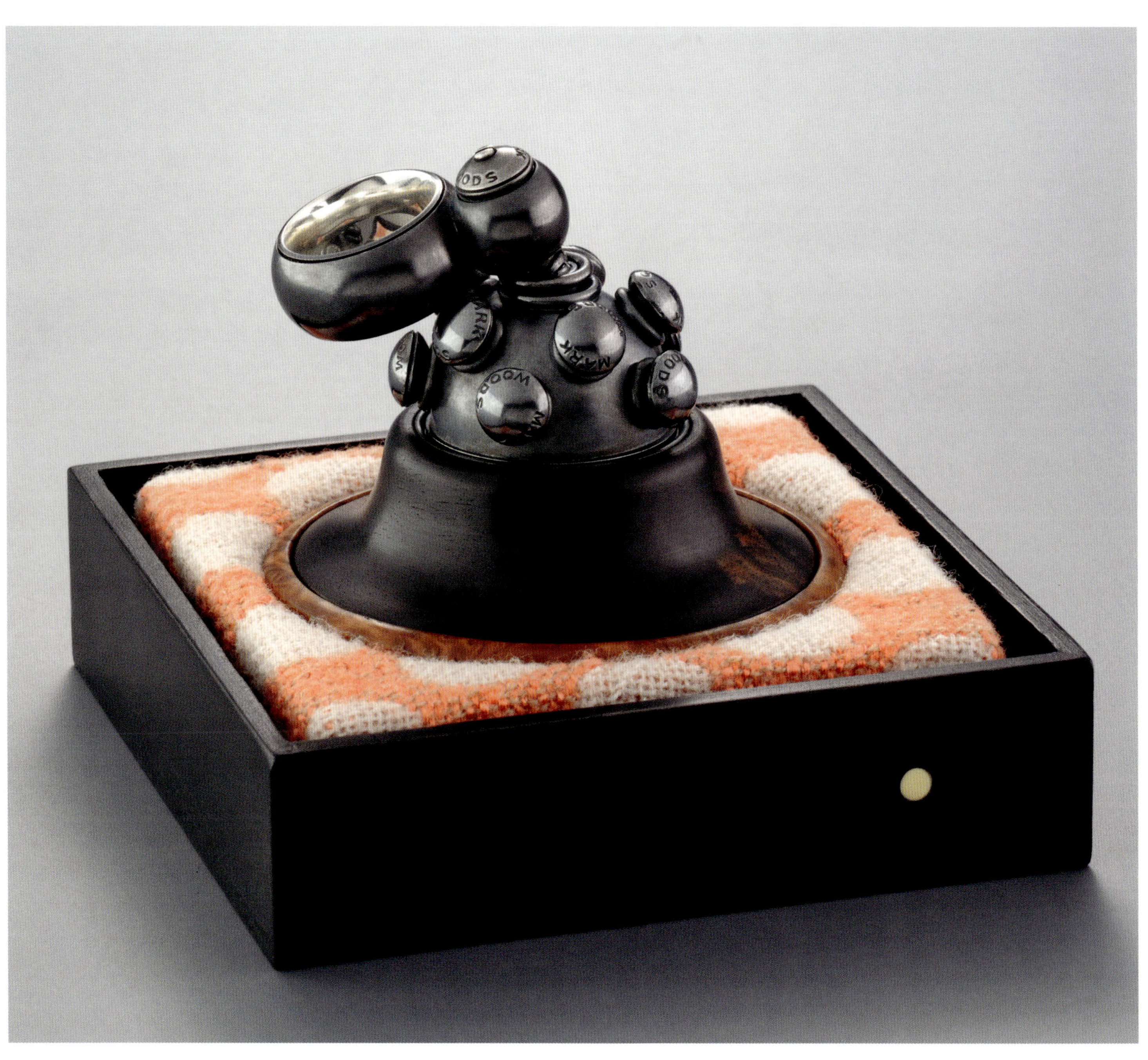

BEAD RING, 2006
Oxidised silver,
plastic, ebony, burr
wood, fabric, ebonised
plywood.
100 x 100 x 110mm

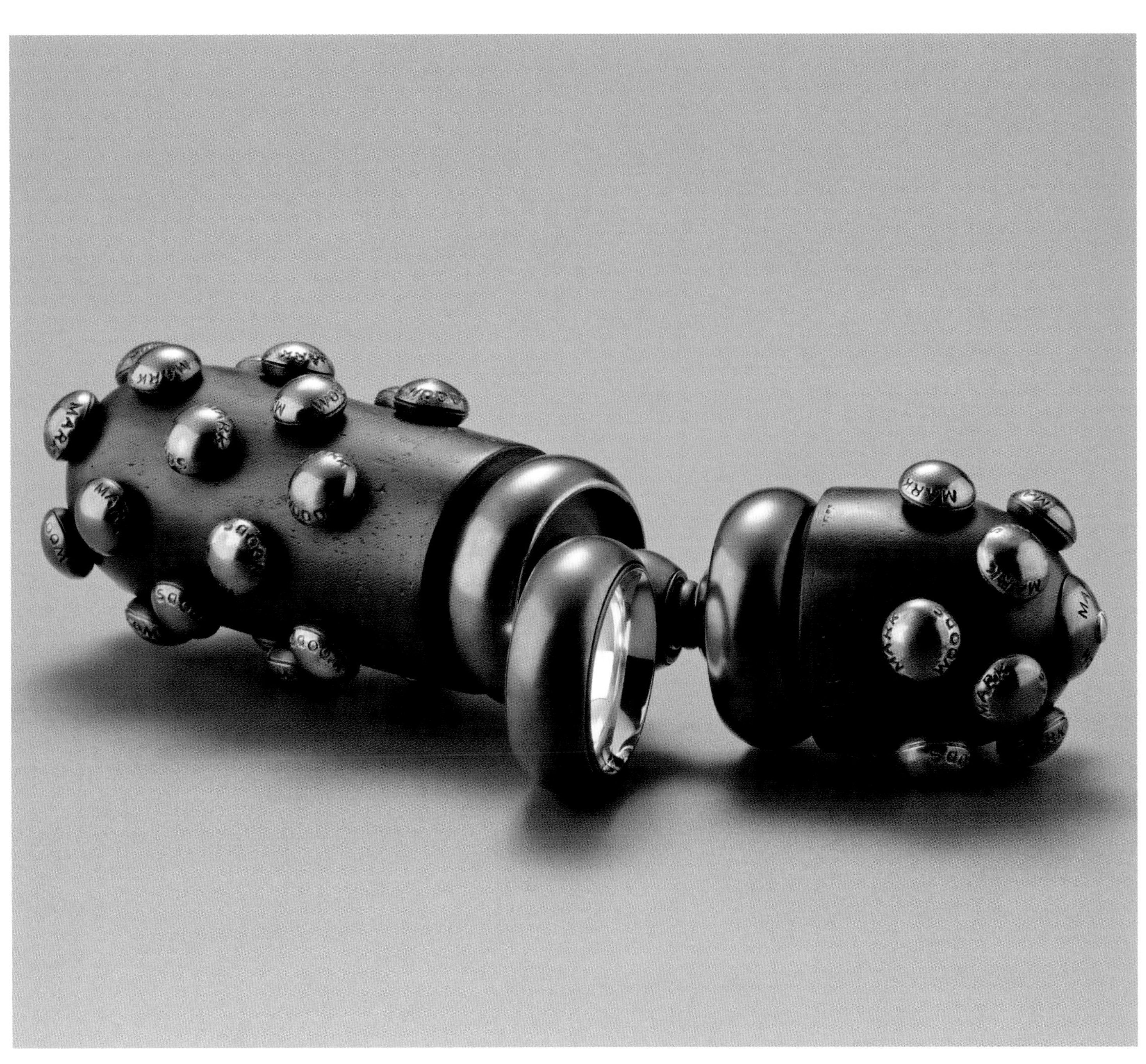

COSH, 2009
Oxidised silver,
cocobolo hardwood.
145 x 48mm

opposite, top left
MARS ATTACKS, RING,
1994
Silver, inlaid plastic.
52 x 60mm

opposite, top right
RING, 2002
Silver, 22ct. gold.
60 x 38mm

opposite, bottom left
RING, 2001
Silver, plastic.
35 x 38mm

opposite, bottom right
RING, SPOTTY
WOBBLER, 1995
Silver, inlaid plastic.
70 x 48mm

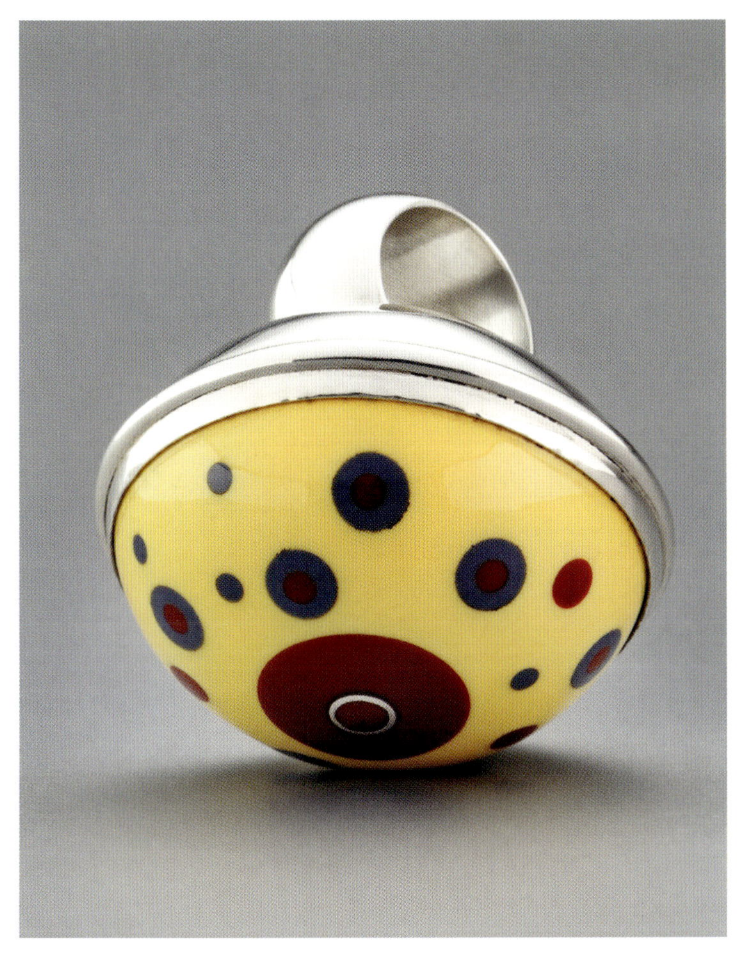
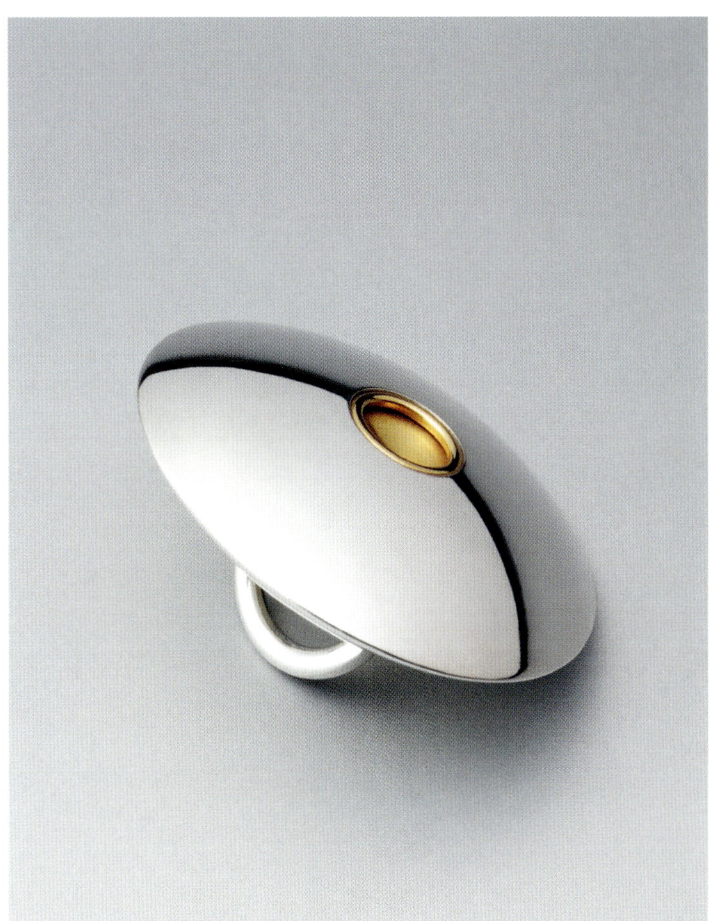
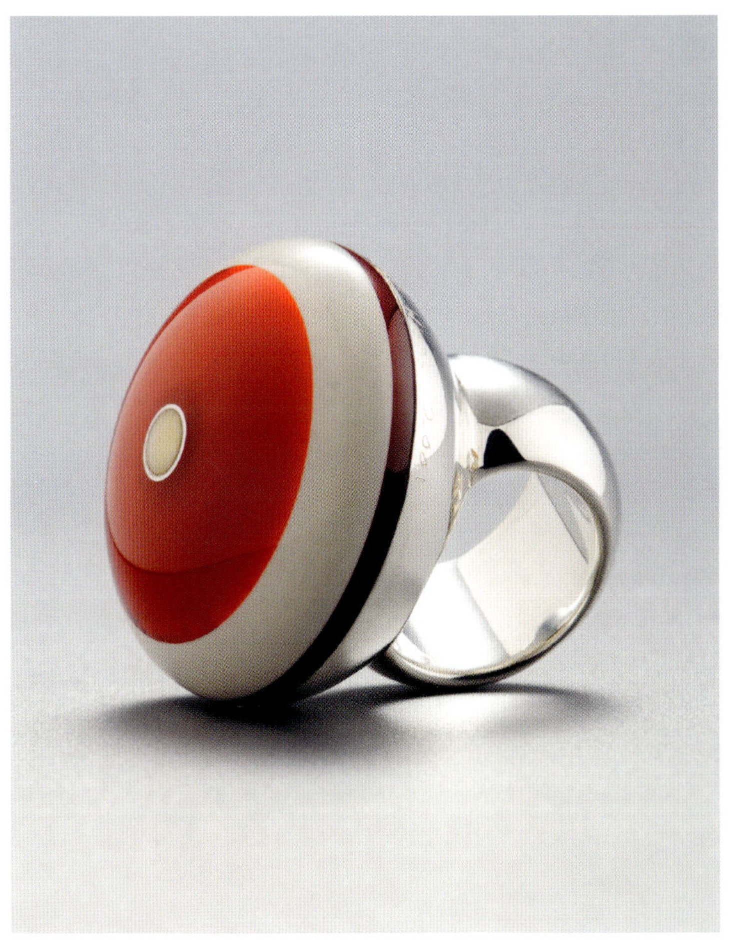
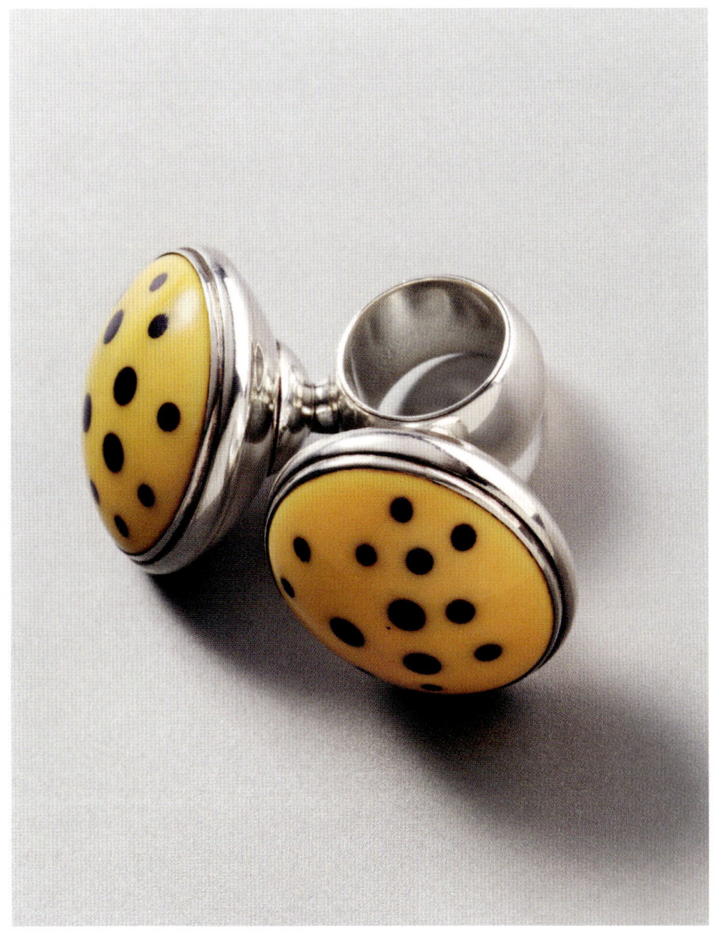

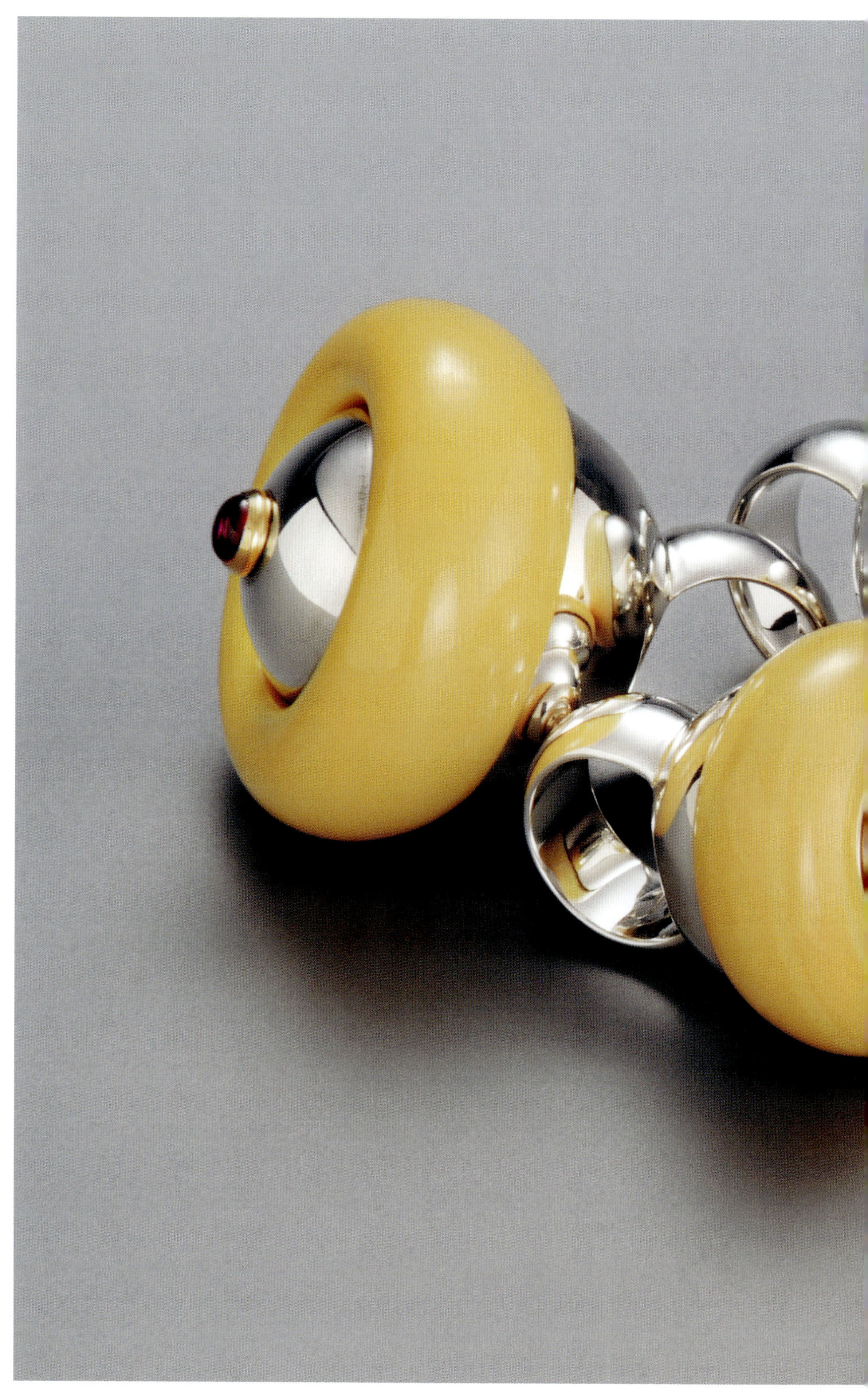

RINGS, EAT ME, 1999
Silver, 22ct. gold,
synthetic rubies,
phenolic plastic.
Dimensions variable

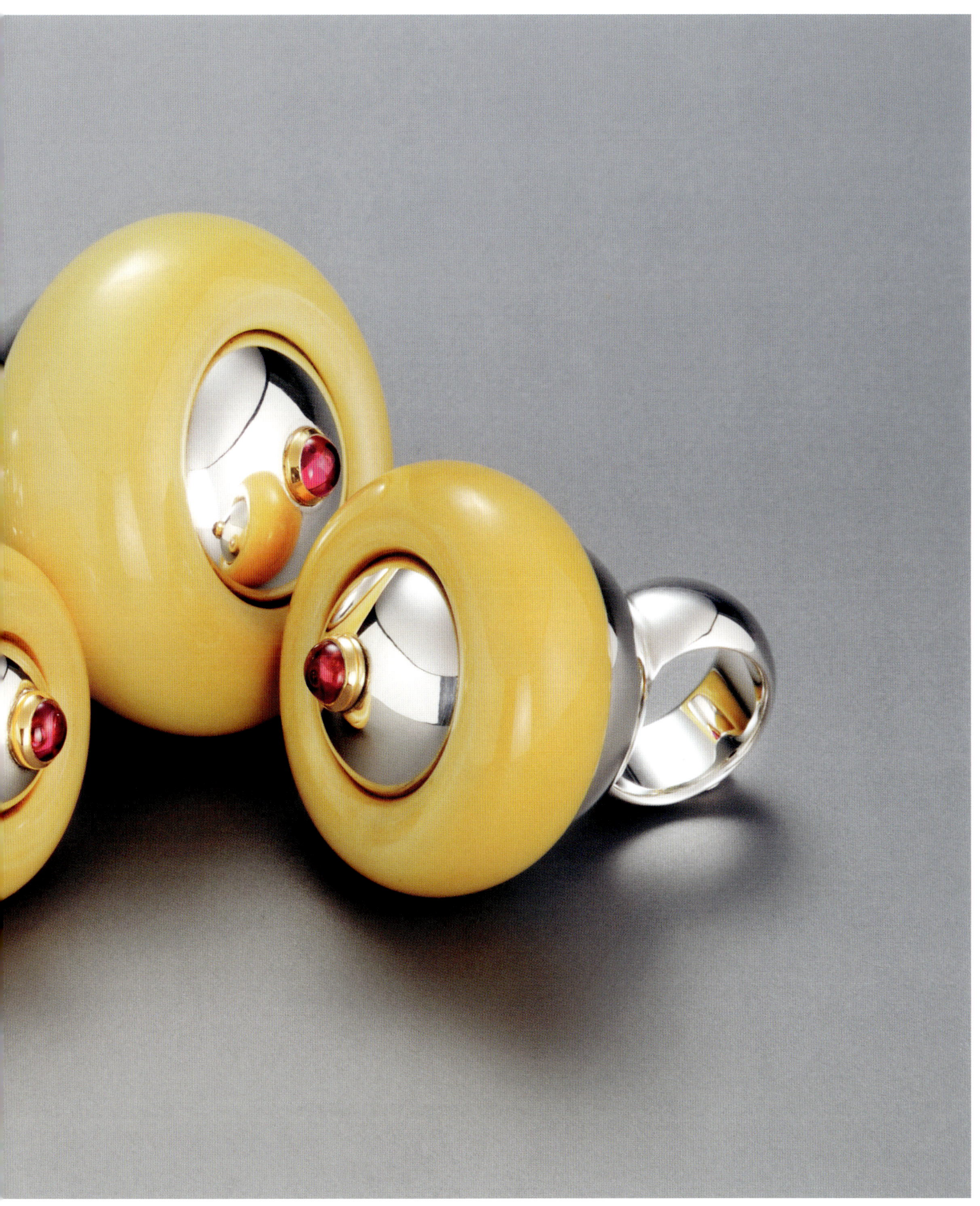

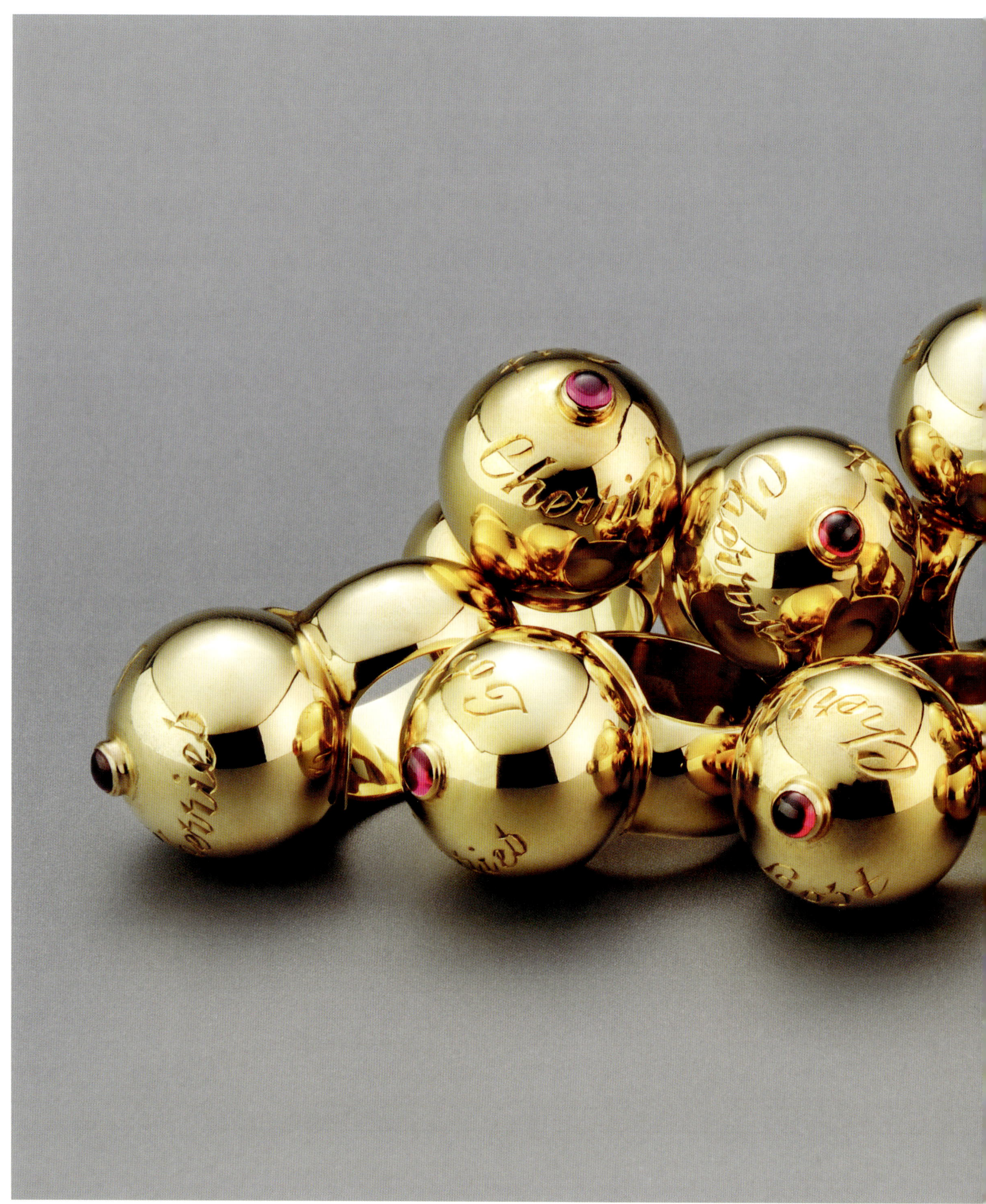

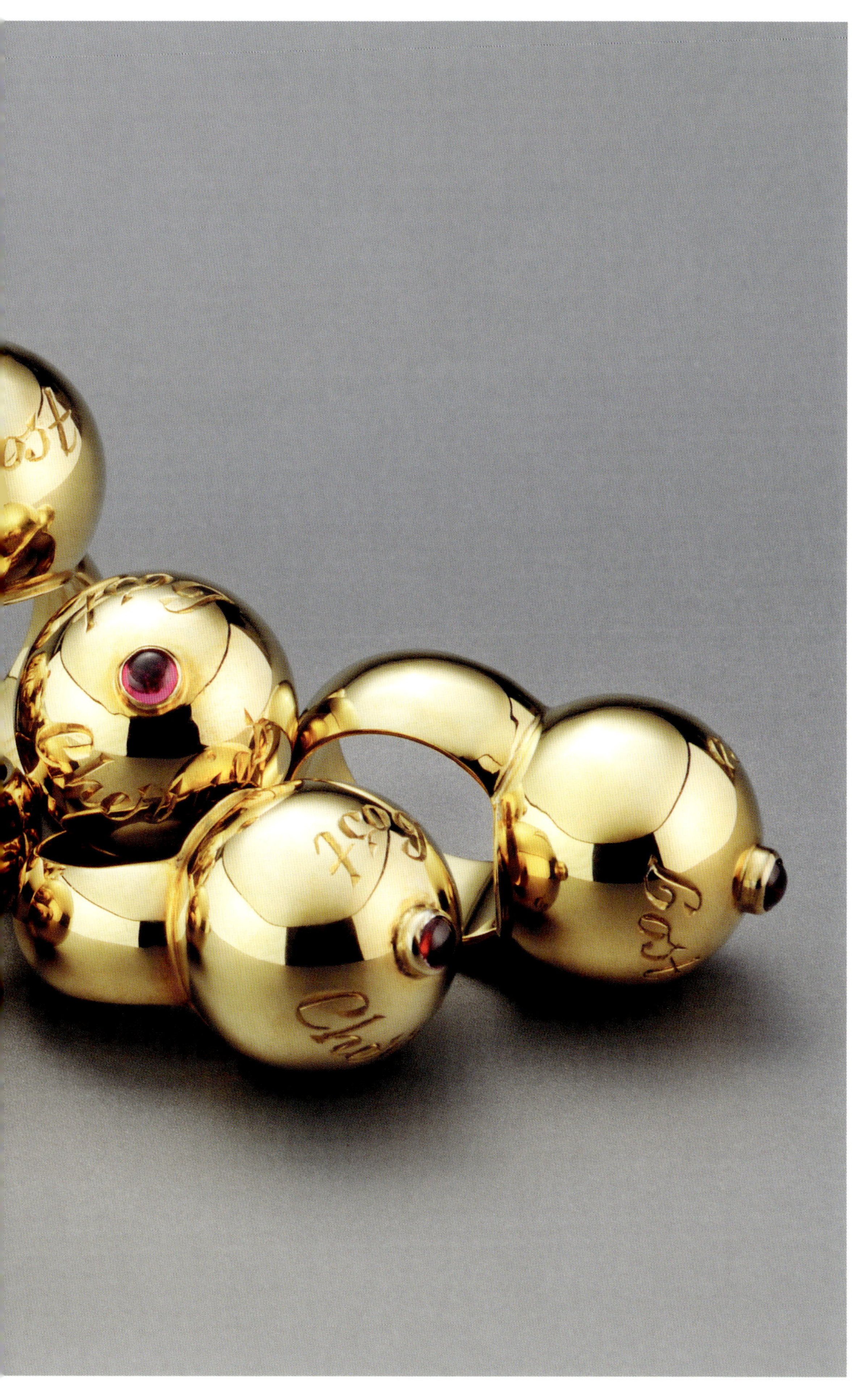

RINGS, LOST
CHERRIES, 1999
18ct. gold-plated silver,
synthetic rubies.
Dimensions variable

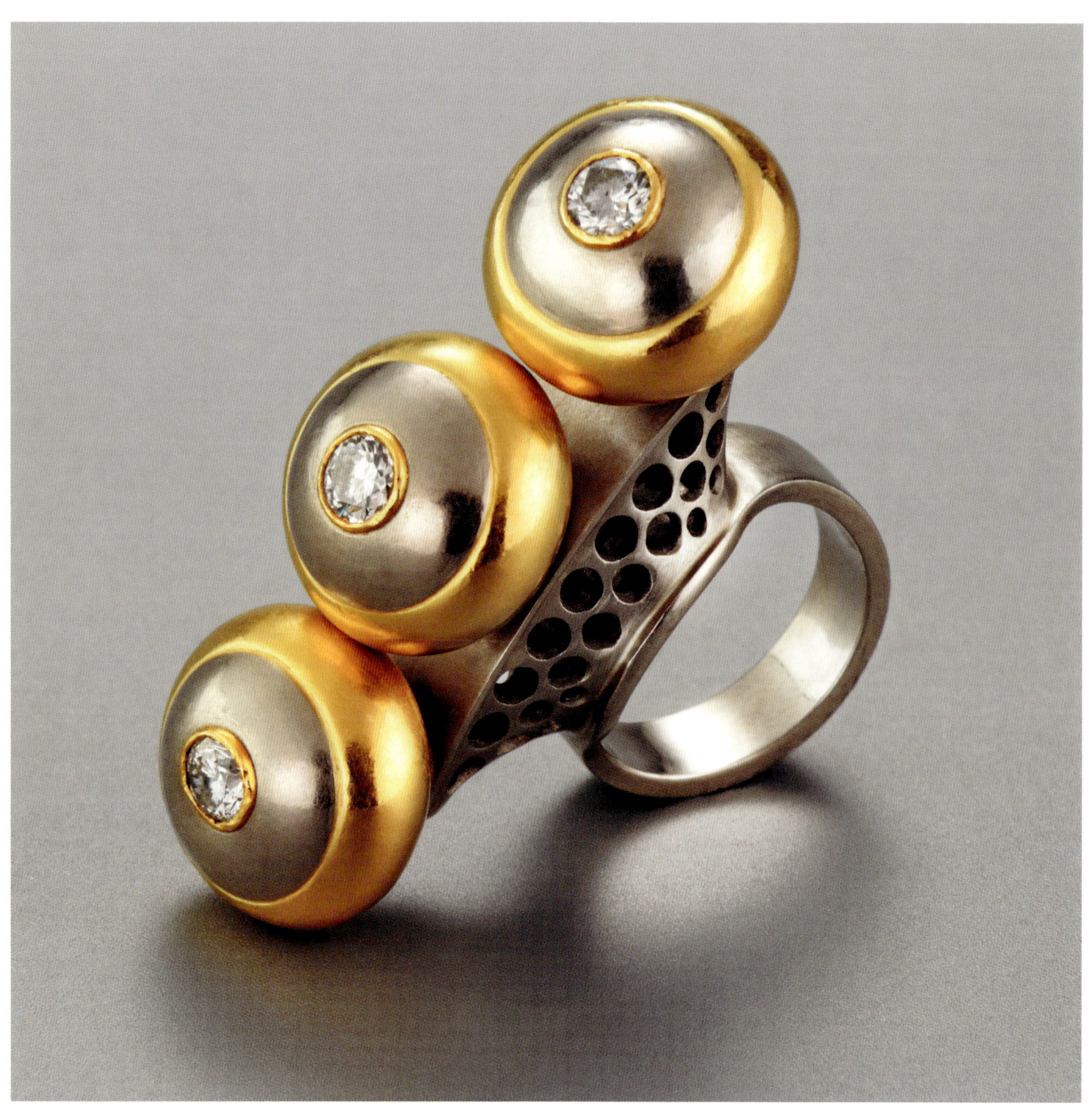

ENGAGEMENT RING,
1998
22ct. gold, 18ct. white
gold, diamonds.
46 x 15mm

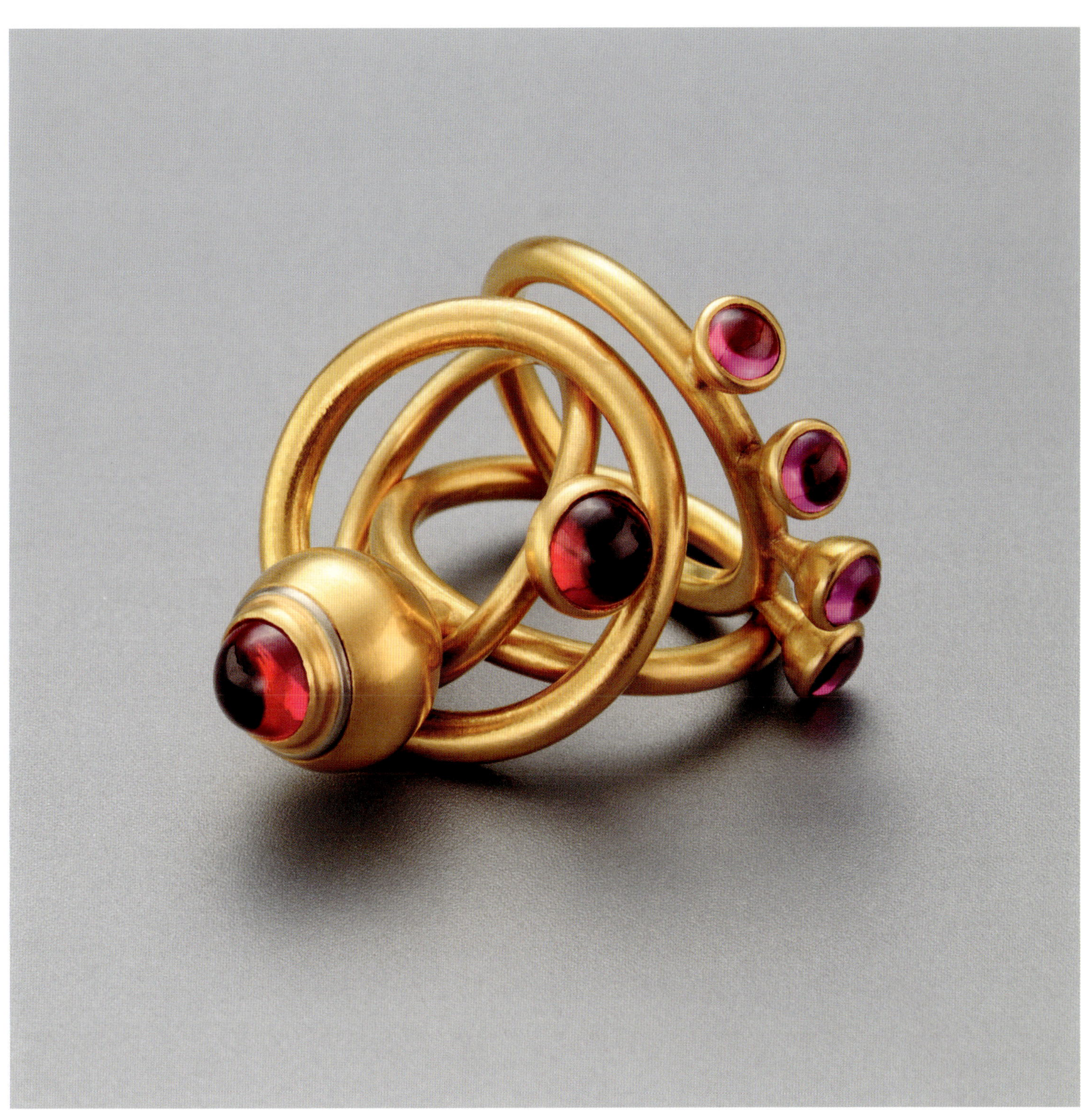

THREE RINGS, 1999
22ct. gold, synthetic
rubies.
Dimensions variable

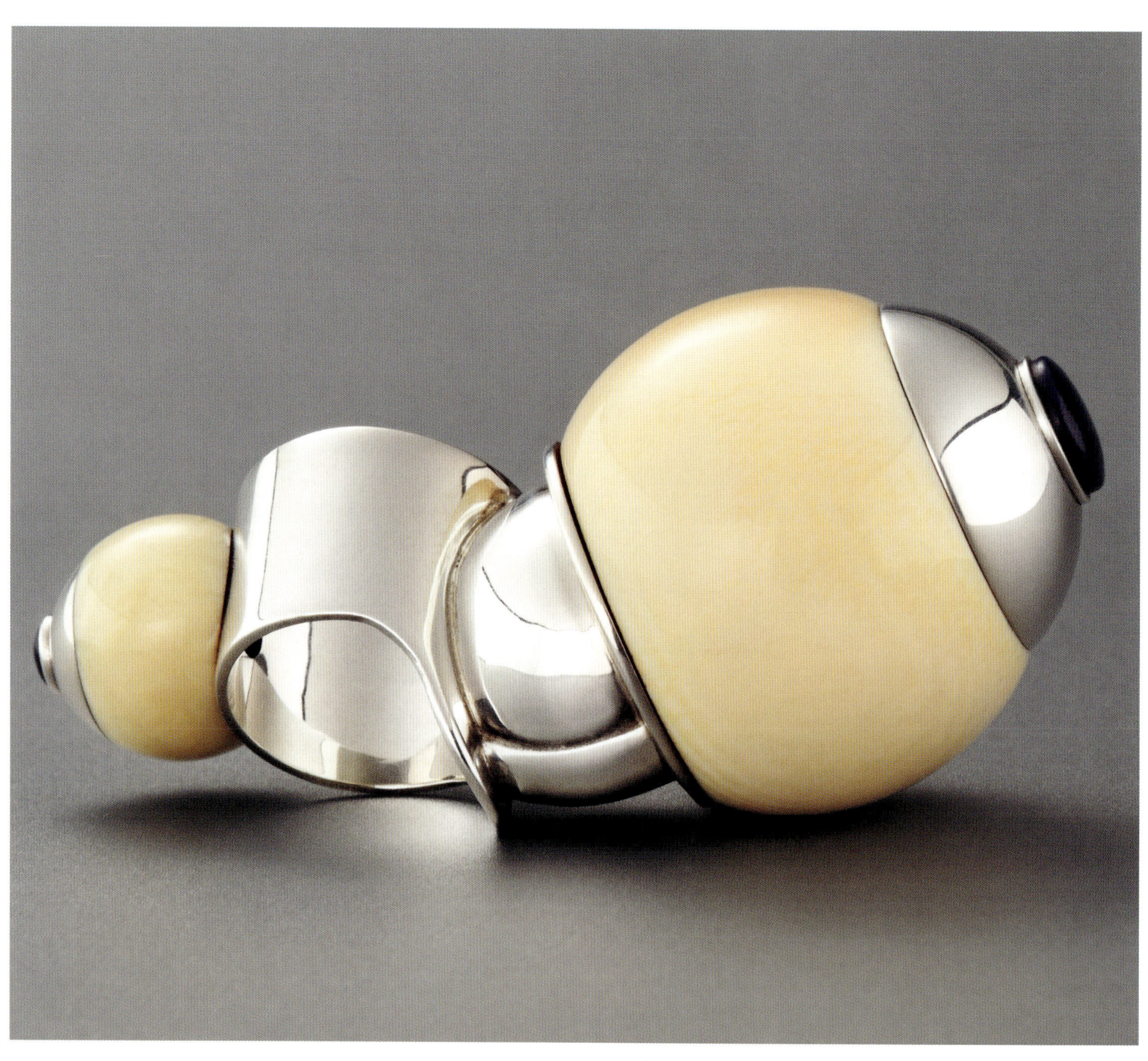

SLANTY EYEBALL,
RING, 1994
Silver, ivory, plastic.
70 x 32mm

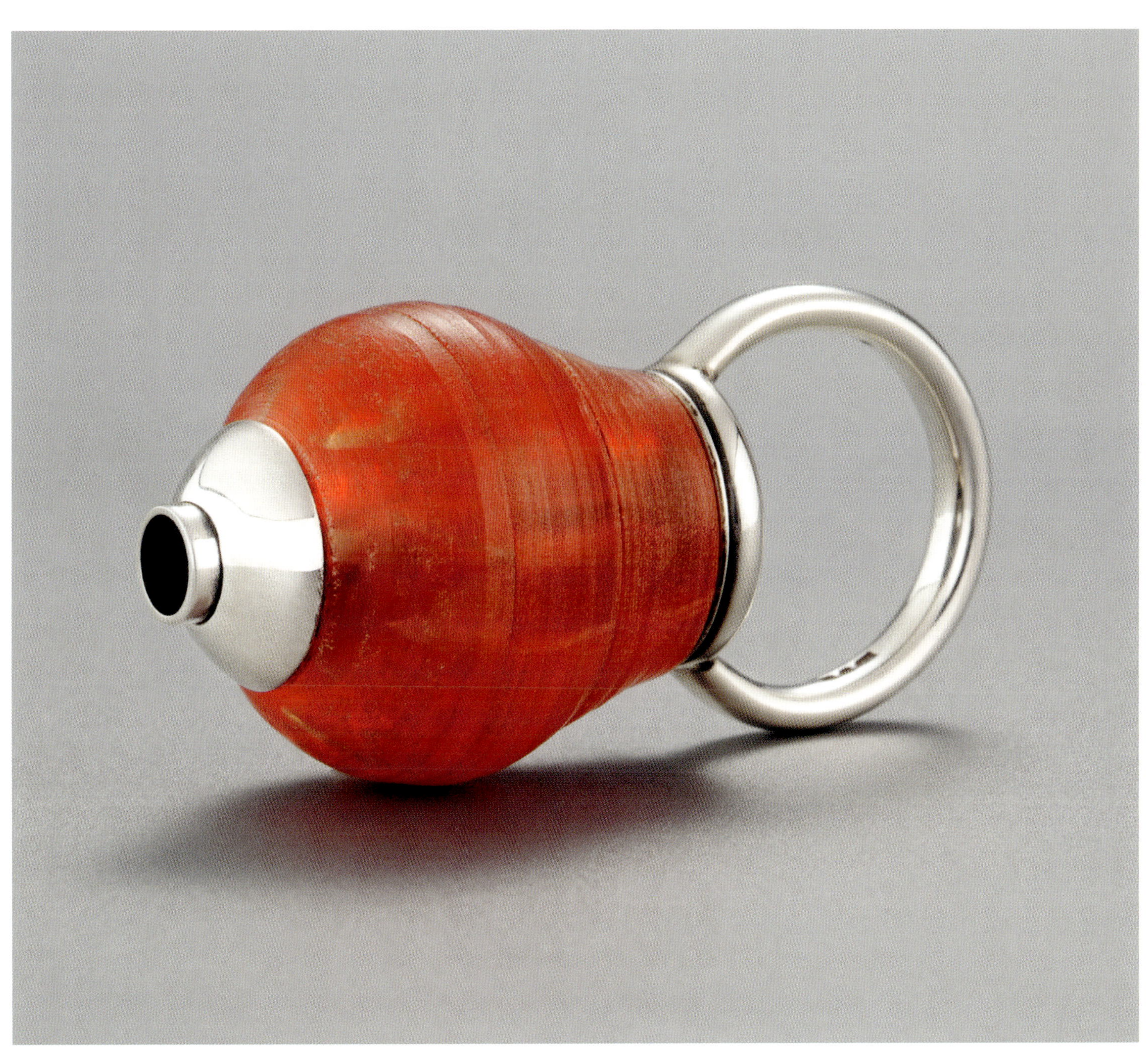

133

opposite, top left
RING, 2002
18ct. white and yellow
gold, diamond.
30 x 25mm

opposite, top right
THUMB RING, 2002
Silver, 18ct. gold.
52 x 32mm

opposite, bottom left
ACORN RING, 1998
Silver, caseinate plastic.
46 x 25mm

opposite, bottom right
RING, 1998
Silver, phenolic plastic.
70 x 32 x 39mm

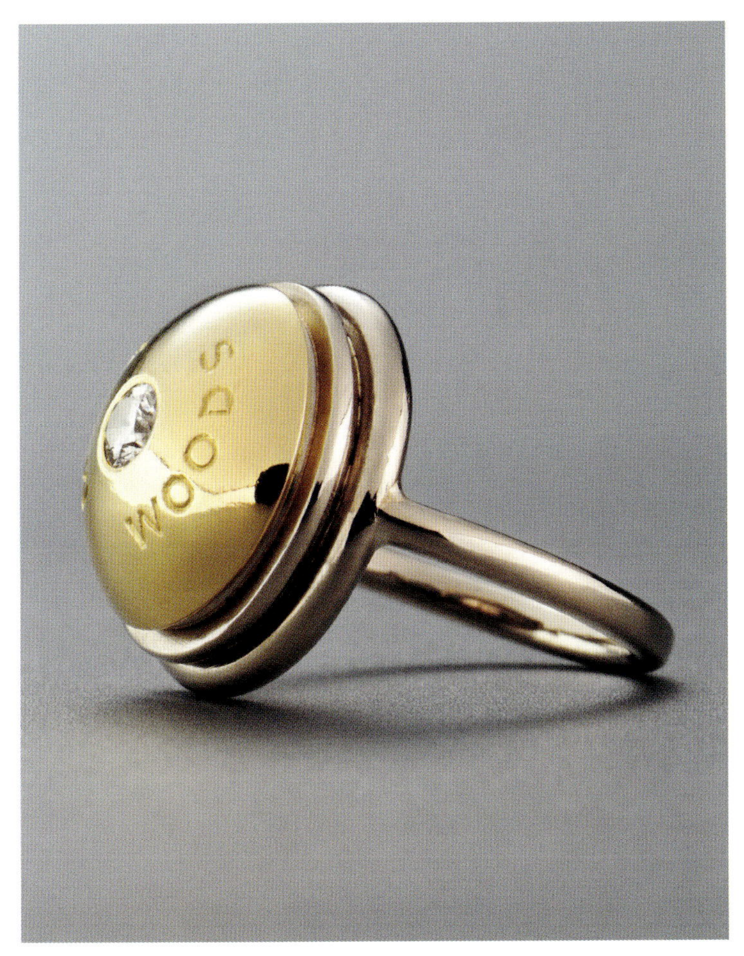

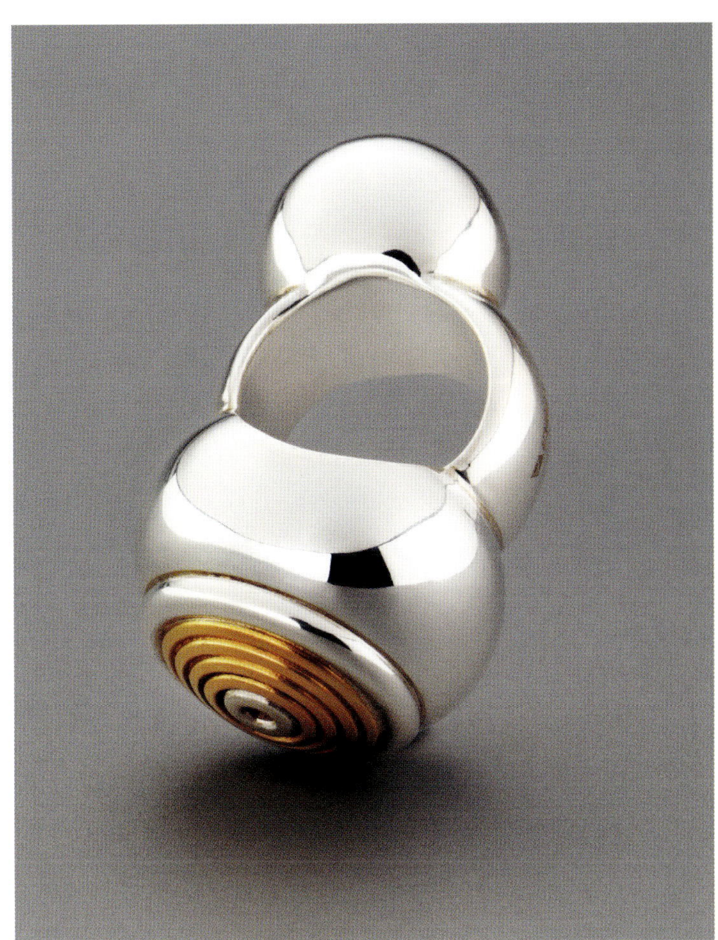

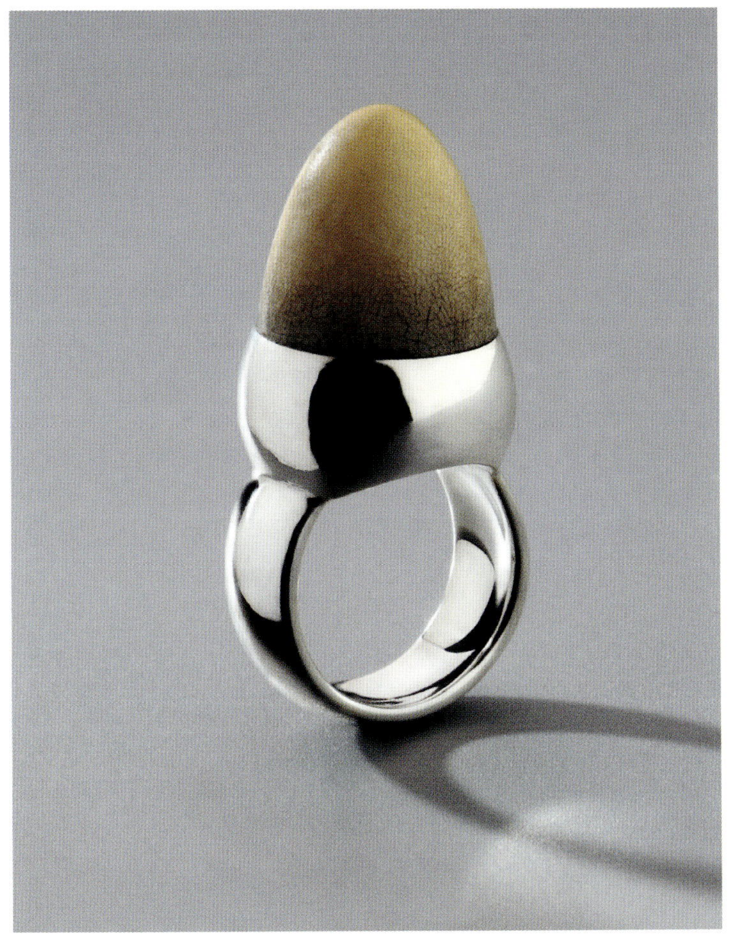

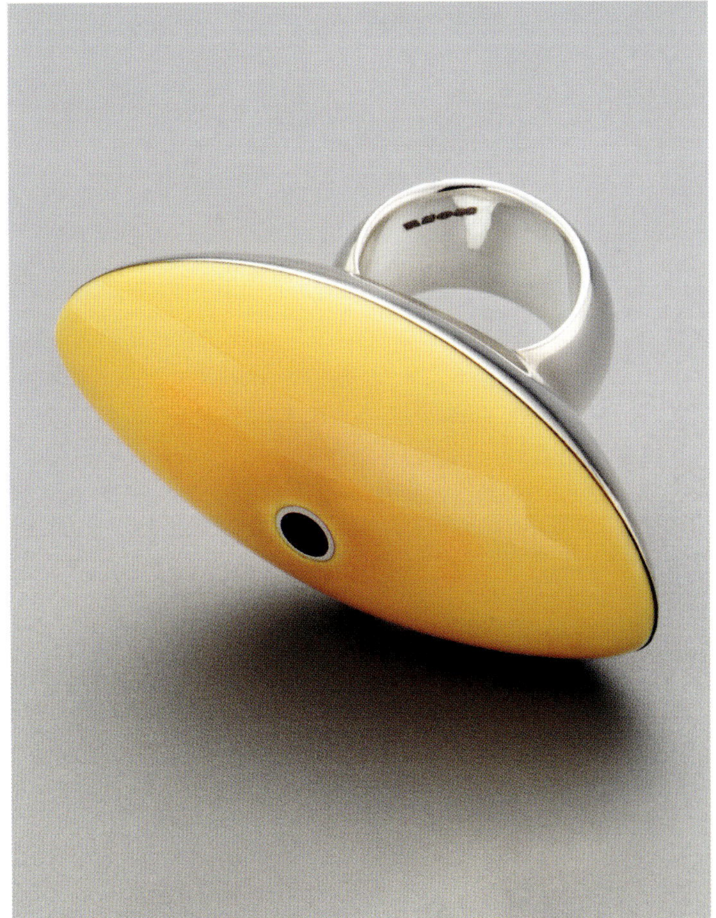

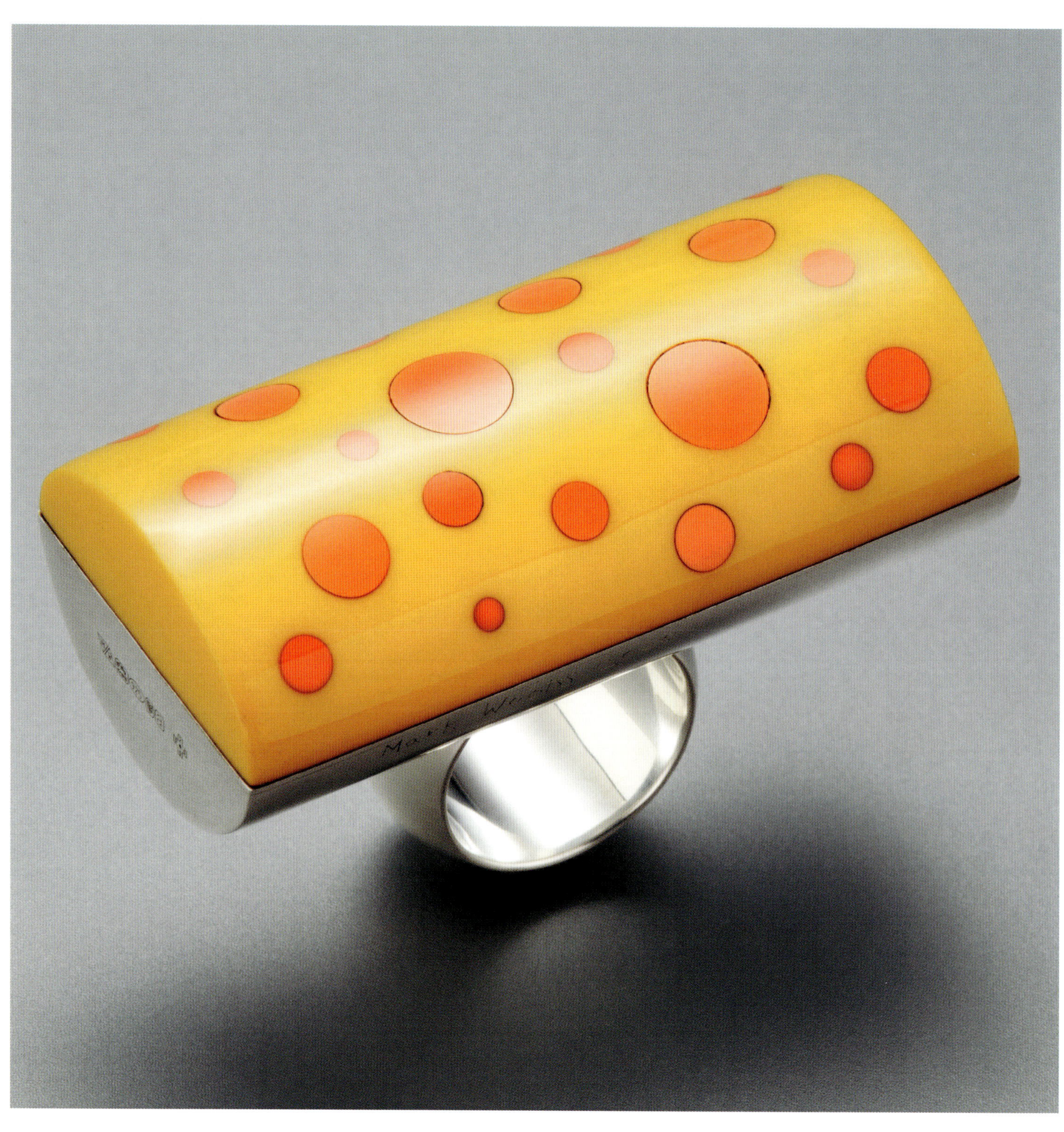

RING, 2002
Silver, inlaid plastic.
55 x 50 x 43mm

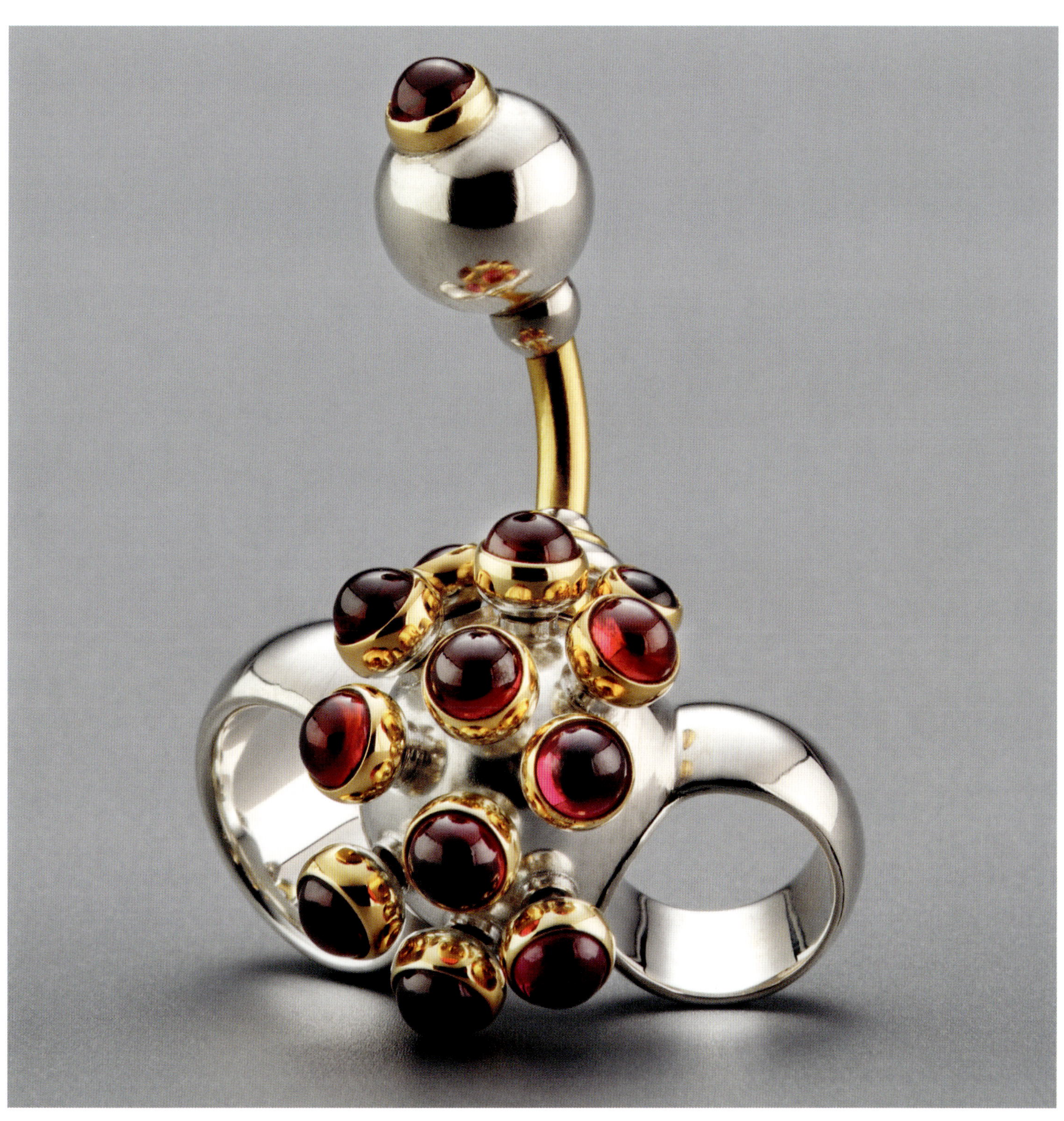

FLESH GORDON RING,
1999
Silver, 22ct. gold,
synthetic rubies.
60 x 38 x 42mm

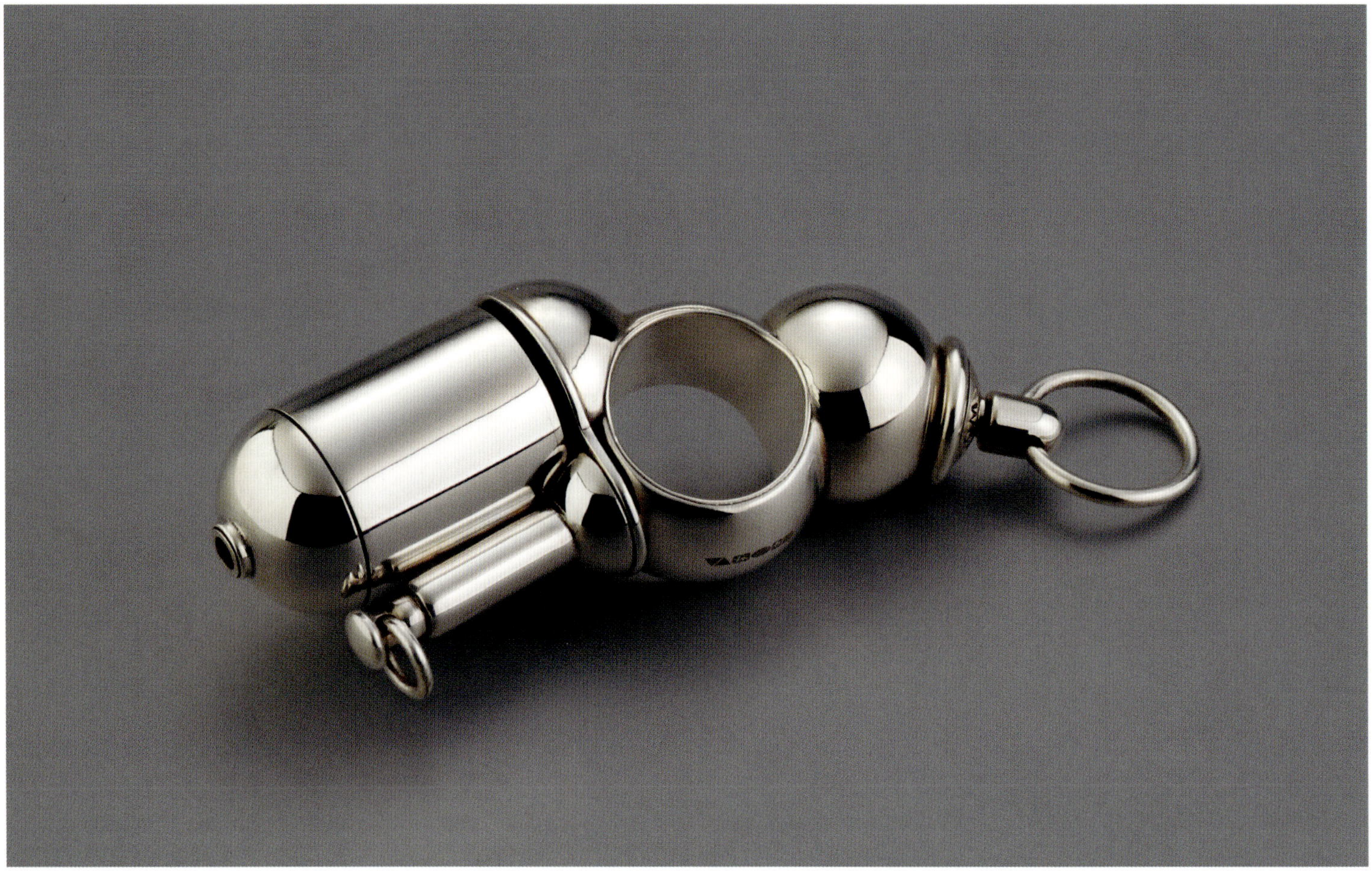

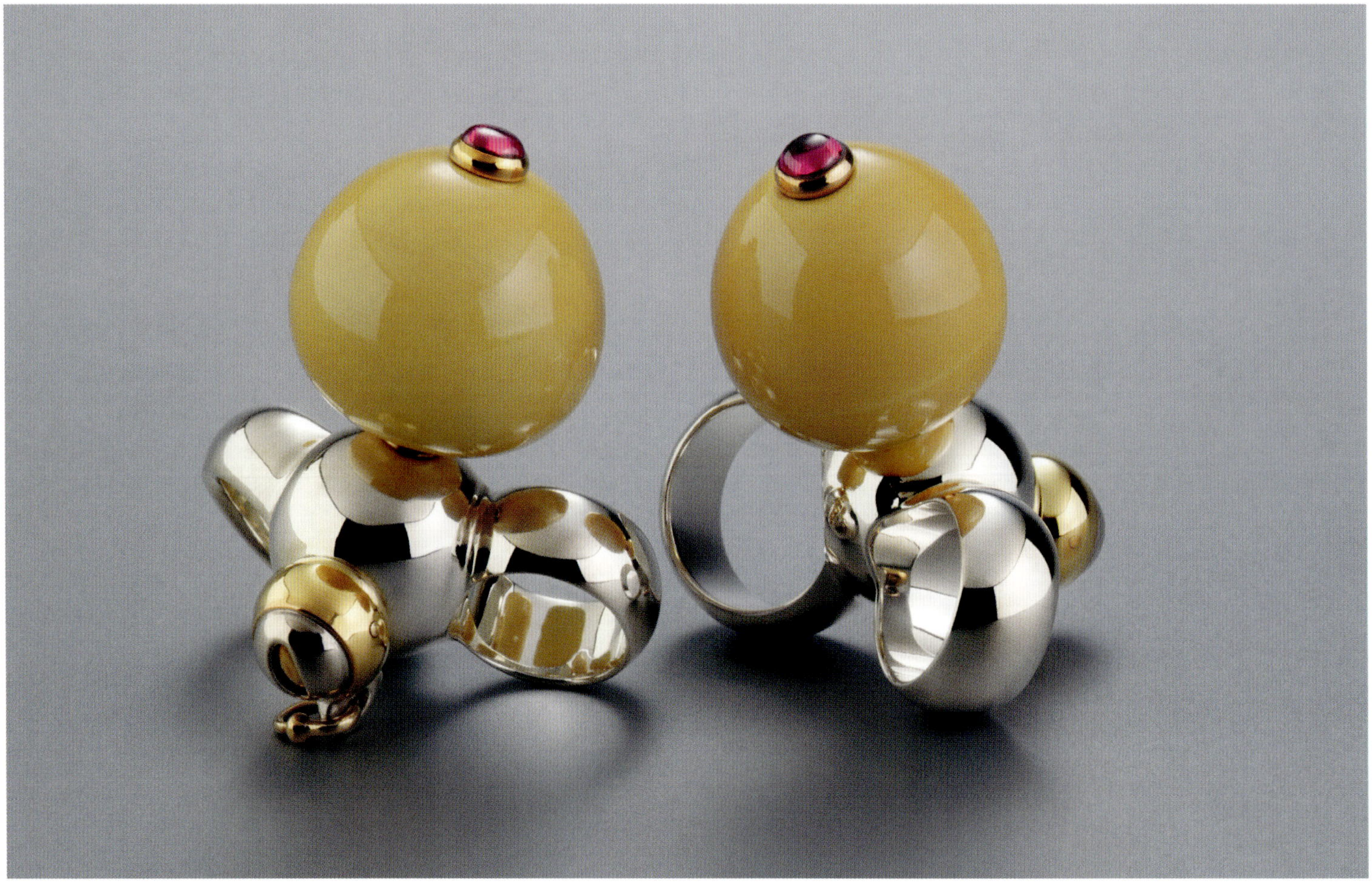

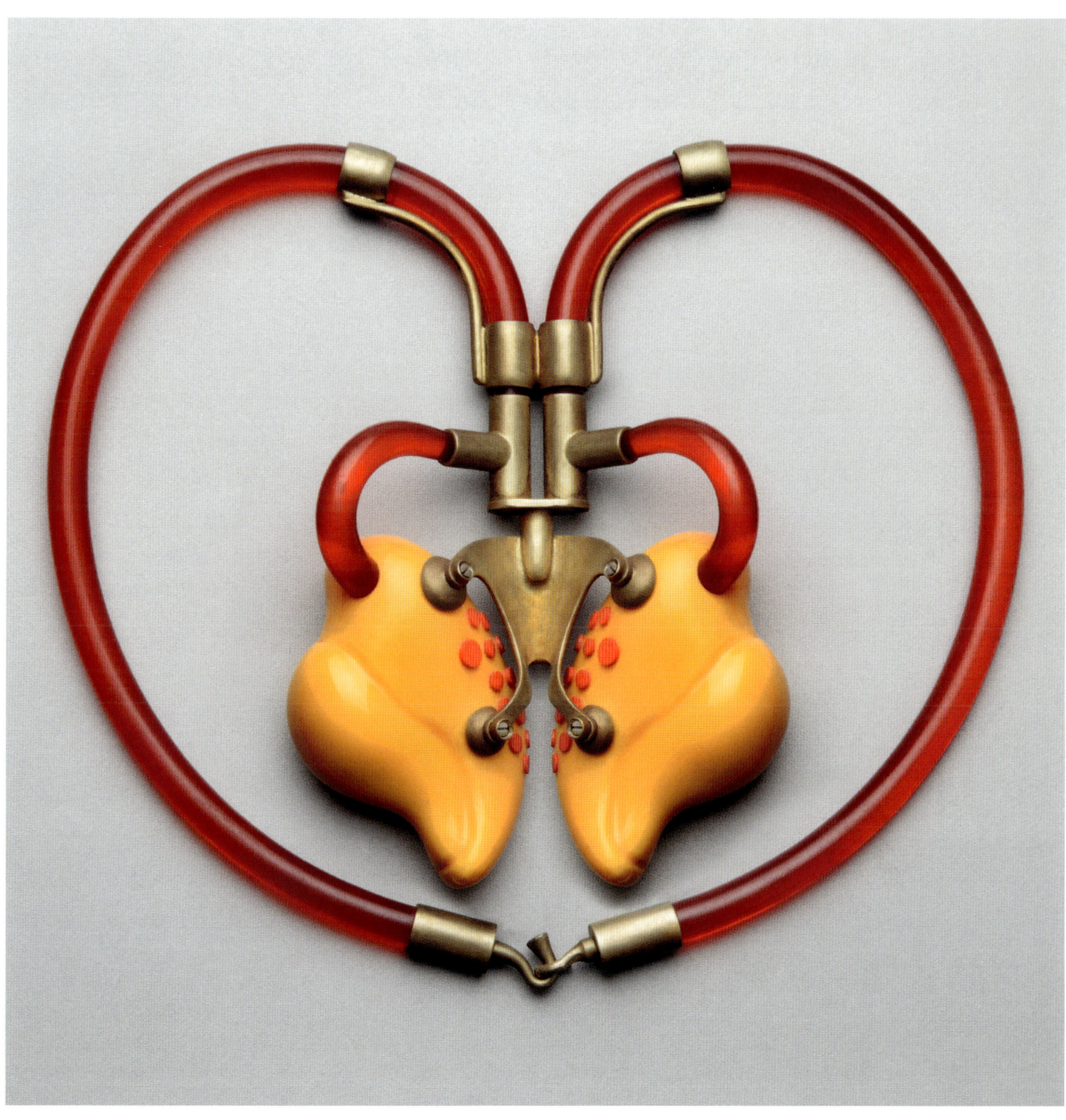

opposite top
VICKY AMBERY'S
SMITH & WESSON
RING, 2004
Silver.
80 x 25 x 40mm

opposite bottom
YOU & ME, RING, 1999
Silver, 22ct. gold
synthetic rubies,
phenolic plastic.
78 x 28 x 50mm

above
WEDDING NECKPIECE,
1998
18ct. gold plate on
silver, carved and inlaid
phenolic plastic, red
plastic tubing.
145 x 135 x 48mm

HOW TO FASHION A MAN
Michael Petry

Mark Woods is a cis gendered, white, straight, working-class man. He grew up under the watchful eye of his prison warder father, who demanded Woods conform to gender stereotypes. Woods is 63 years old, and has been married to artist Rebecca Scott for 27 years. These historic and current factors come into play in his work.

Woods started as a maker (late 1980s) and was well known in the jewellery world as someone of considerable skill. His rings and objects, with a clear erotic charge, were in high demand. Viewers placed them on their bodies. Woods showed at Electrum Gallery, where I came across his work. The idea that *fine art* was something different and better than *craft* has its Western roots in misogyny and Kant (1724). Craft in the West is very much at odds with Eastern tradition. A Japanese tea cup or piece of calligraphy can be seen as an important work, as "sublime" as any "work of art". The academic discussion surrounding artist versus maker was very prevalent in the late 1980s. Galleries such as Electrum, Galerie Ra (Amsterdam) and Galerie Marzee (Nijmegen) were at the forefront.

Woods was apprenticed to a boat-builder on the Isle of Wight where his father was a "screw" at Parkhurst Prison. He then moved to London to study jewellery. Woods' jewels were a bit like him – handsome, wild and a bit dangerous. He also spent a formative year in prison, commenting that in many ways he allowed himself to be caught as a form of humiliation for his father. What could be worse for a warder than to have a child in prison? Woods is not sure how much he meant to hurt him, but it was a serious way of rebelling.[1] His jewellery, meanwhile, rebelled against current trends and *good taste*. The work was as impolite as talking about sex in church (though we now know so much sexual activity took place there). Woods' works have the feel of fetish objects and are echt haptic. Engaging with the work is a bit like stroking a sleeping tiger – it feels amazing, but there is an element of fear attached.

Woods has said that prior to meeting his wife Rebecca, he was the sort of person no one should want to meet. Being a bad boy has its downsides. Artists are given a lot of freedom, but some abuse it, themselves and others. Tracey Emin, for example, has made a career out of her early life in Margate. Viewers are asked to see her as a universal every person, who lives, suffers and struggles on. Now that she is a wealthy artist, it is a harder trick to pull off. Woods' works speak a generalised language of desire. It has not been about him, whereas Emin's work is about her.

Woods' practice changed with his installation of provocative objects, "*To Have, to Hold*" (The Wapping Project, London, 2010). Crafted from gold, silver and platinum, and adorned with diamonds, rubies and precious stones, they explored Woods' fascination with the female form. These covetable objects were akin to the gynaecological instruments designed by Jeremy Irons in David Cronenberg's film *Dead Ringers* (1988). Woods showed the objects in a huge box covered in black rubber. The structure had small glass-fronted inserts where the pieces were placed. The rubbered space had a strong smell, as if entering the private collection of Hannibal Lecter. A sense of dread and excitement placed the visitor in the position of voyeur. A leather-handled whip of human hair, or a lace-covered dildo, glinted in the darkness, calling to be caressed.

Woods then made a series of free-standing boxes containing brightly lit scenes of desirable objects. Viewers peeped through a hole at the front of the boxes, much like experiencing Duchamp's *Étant donnés* (1946–66). Woods' boxes grew larger, filling entire rooms like his *Unchanging nature of the fetish object* for the "Nirvana. Strange Forms of Pleasure" exhibition (Mudac, Lausanne, 2013). There, a series of sexual automata spun around in a bright carnival atmosphere. The presentation of the objects had become much more part of a larger artistic whole – not an exhibition of craft objects, but an installation made up of them.

His photographic performances from 2019 incorporate his objects and set pieces, but only exist the second that the shutter snaps. An early image shows him in a fake fur coat astride a

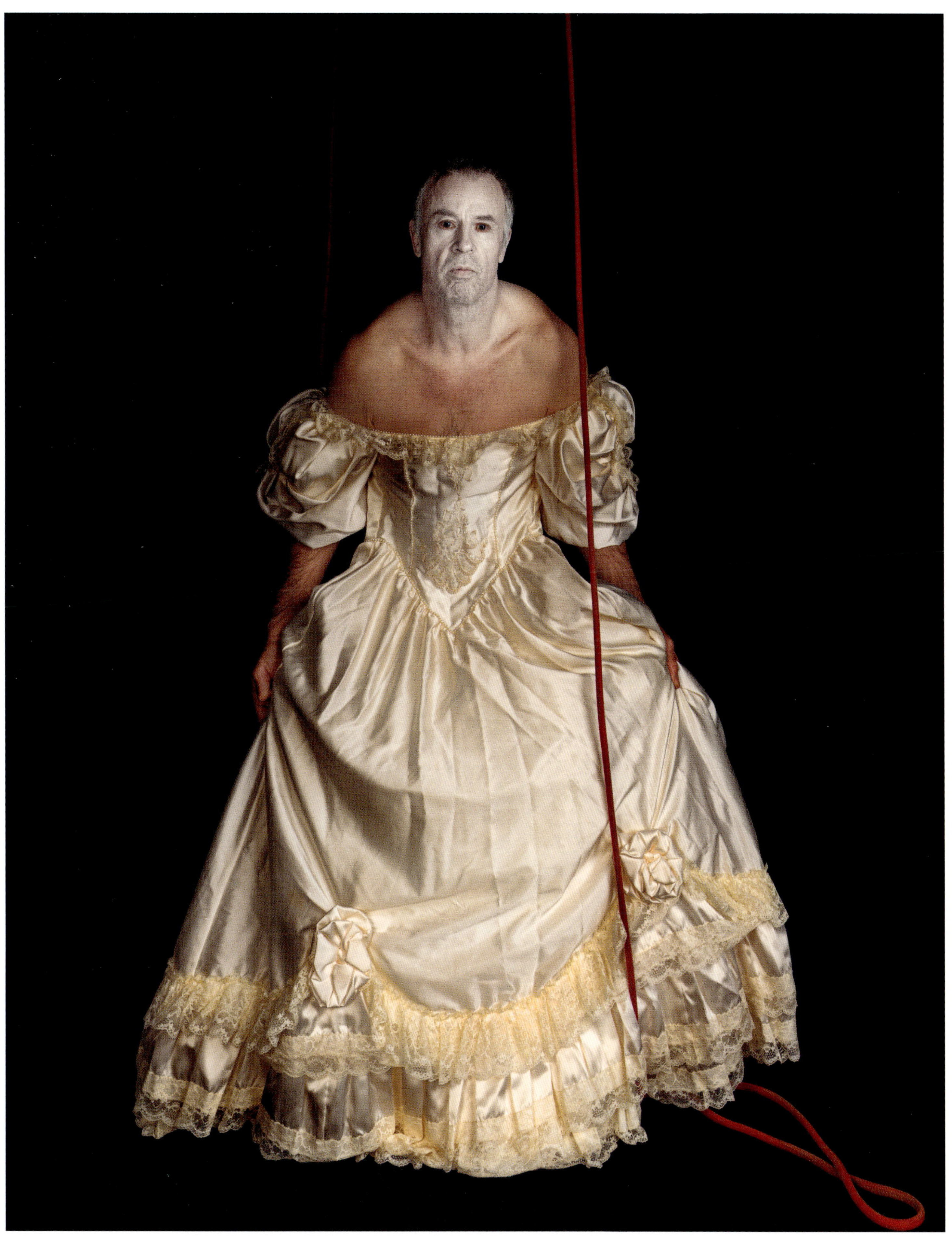

stool, legs open, wearing a wrinkled skirt or dress. He is barefoot and his head shaven; he could be a prisoner on the run. He clutches the coat's neck, wearing a big metal men's wristwatch. He stares at the camera. The image shows him as fully masculine but caught in some accidental cross-dressing, as if he has had no other choice than to don this garb.

Woods' photos include objects, looking like props that Geppetto (Pinocchio's elderly woodcarver creator) might have discarded as too rude. We see Woods wearing a cream Disney ballgown. Red ropes fall from the ceiling – they might entangle, trap or tie him up. "Cinderfella" is ready for the ball, but needs to shave his chest. Woods' look implores the viewer. The dress is wrinkled, as if pulled from a dressing-up trunk. Is this private play or performance for an envisioned/real audience? Woods presents himself to the viewer, hands spreading the skirt open. We see in the male body (in female clothes) how much flesh women expose as the norm. He is the "slutty" princess.

Give a girl the right kind of shoes and she can rule the world.
Marilyn Monroe

In another photograph Woods appears like the dreaded mother-in-law of bad sexist jokes. With his head tipped down his eyes look straight into the camera, giving him a stern look, as if he/she has caught the *viewer* doing something wrong. Woods wears the garb of an older middle-class matron, including a set of pearls, but his low-cut top shows chest hair. Sex is charged throughout this body of work. In another, we see the reverse of *Cinderfella* – Woods' naked buttocks and torso as he clutches the same gown from behind. Sprouting from his shoulders are stag horns that frame the back of his cropped head. The image evokes coitus with his other self, the more feminine or at least femininely dressed self of the earlier image. He looks like he is engaged in lumbering, or maybe drunken sex. Woods is clearly a middle-aged man, hairy in places unlike the groomed pelts of fashion models. He is not tanned. The look is raw. His blemishes are on show as are the wrinkles in his face. This is a man who has lived an event-filled life. The coldness of his stare fixes the viewer.

Fashion is the armor to survive the reality of everyday life.
Bill Cunningham

below and opposite
TO HAVE, TO HOLD,
2010.
Wapping project, London.

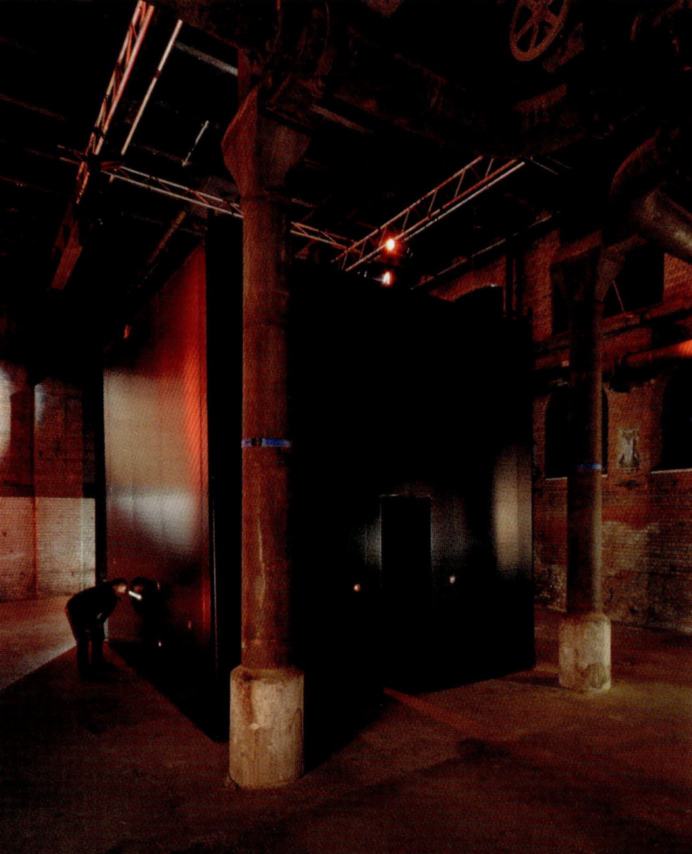

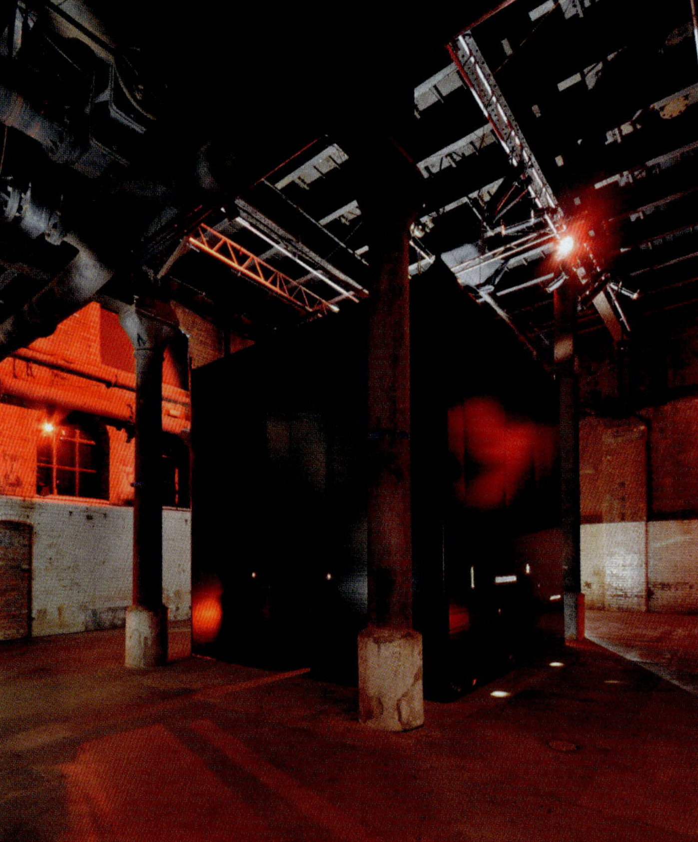

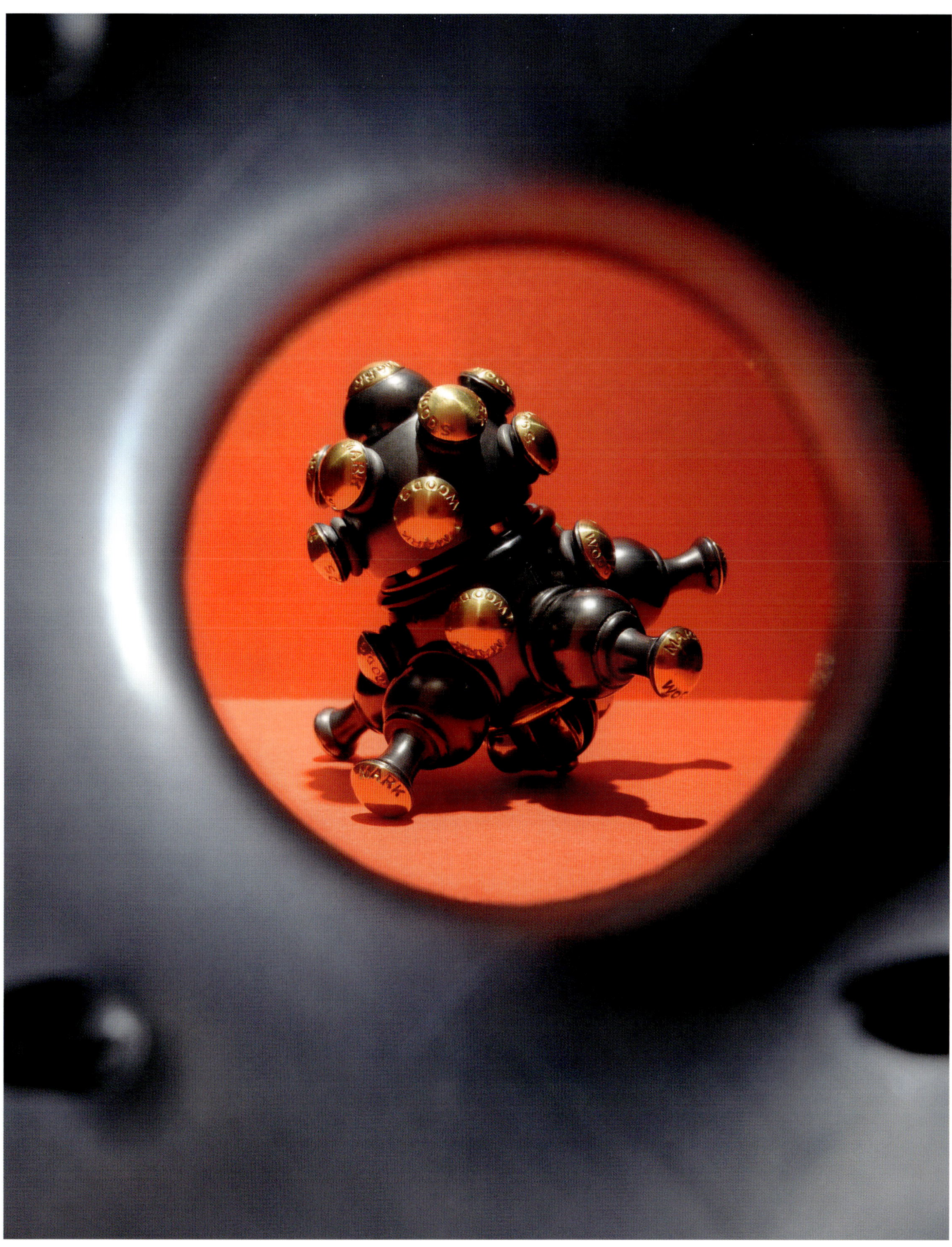

WOOD
MARK

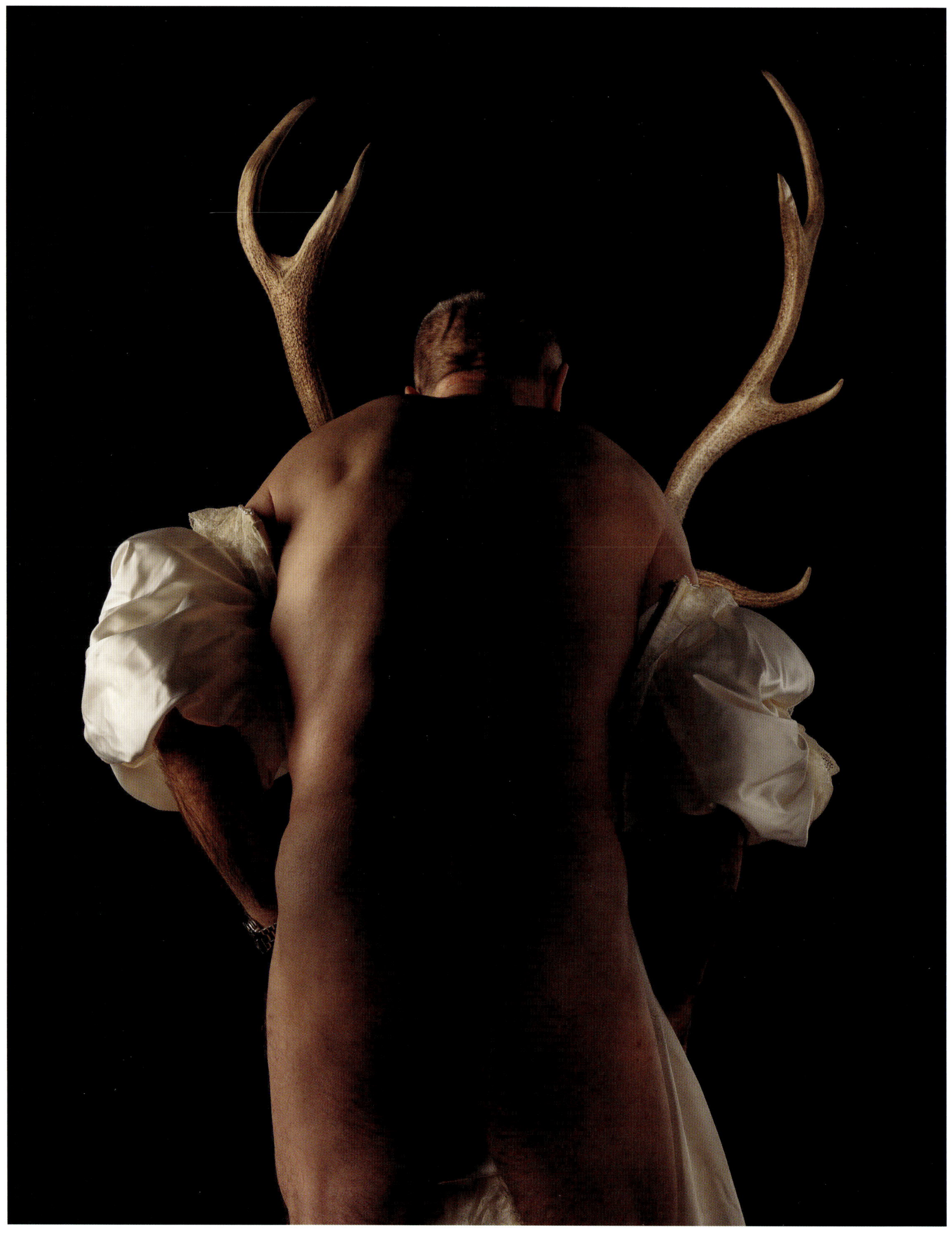

The images are sort of anti Pierre Molinier (1900–76), the erotic surrealist who made a series of black-and-white photographs of himself in his transsexual fantasies. Molinier is seen in these images as the petite madam dominatrix, alone or with many doll figures, recalling the surrealist images of Hans Belmer (1902–75). Molinier made these works to fulfil his sexual desires and, in the surrealist tradition, to address his subconscious needs. His *Cent Photographies Erotiques* (1965–76) were made with a remote-control shutter so that the images look like he/she is unaware of the viewer. The act of looking is eroticised by the artist, who passes that gaze onto the viewer. Molinier took great pains to look every bit a woman, with shaved legs, face and the addition of garb that feminised him further. Woods, however, appears like a bloke in a frock, along the lines of an English pantomime dame. Like Woods, Molinier was married to a woman. Molinier noted the dolls were not necessarily substitutes for women, nor was he a transsexual. He did not see himself as a woman, but simply a man erotically attracted to the legs and nipples of women (and men if also shaved). Molinier was clear in his own mind that his images were for *his* sexual and artistic satisfaction, and if viewers were shocked, so much the better.

Fashion is only the attempt to realise art in living forms and social intercourse.
Francis Bacon

Woods is not aiming to shock, nor is he attracted to transvestism. Woods does not dress as a woman outside of these photographs, or perhaps even *in* the images. He does not have sexual experiences with his wife (or anyone else) dressed in women's clothing or identifying as a woman. Woods is a man in his images, and it is the bold masculinity that makes the images so arresting. What is the core of this artistic endeavour? We will come to his own complex needs, but it is important to look at how these images function. Woods' images address a certain crisis in masculinity.

Another blokey artist dressing in women's clothes is Grayson Perry (b 1960), whose persona Claire appears like a large female child with a lot of money and imagination. Perry says she is a mid-40s matron, stout and English. Perry is married with a child, has been very open about wanting to dress in women's clothes from an early age, and sees himself as a transvestite. He attends art events as Claire, and she appears in his pottery and tapestry for which Perry won the 2003 Turner Prize. He has made television programmes about his cross-dressing desires, and appears in man drag – full leathers – as he is a keen motorcyclist. Perry is playing with gender roles in his work and life. His wife Philippa is a psychotherapist, who was aware of Claire from the start. Perry makes objects that were once considered craft (pots, tapestries), and has taken those forms into the world of *fine art*, as Woods has done with jewellery. Both artists ask the viewer to look at the content and the form, but not to make ingrained decisions about the work based on its form having long been seen as secondary.

We're all born naked, and all the rest is drag.
RuPaul

Challenging fashion convention in quite a different way was Leigh Bowery (1961–94), who grew up in a Melbourne suburb called Sunshine. Bowery lived to dress up. He was a striking figure at 6ft 3in before strapping on six-inch platformed boots. He made all his outfits, and with his partner Trojan they ran Taboo, one of London's top nightclubs in the 1980s. The whole of London's New Romantic tribe would weekly turn up to see what new outfits they were wearing and to show off their best efforts. I was a regular at the club where Boy George (Bowery's friend) called the then-closeted George Michael "a dirty little faggot". It was that sort of club.

Later, Bowery became known for daring and outrageous performances in prestigious galleries such as Anthony d'Offay. Yet it was out of costume, naked and exposed to the eye of Lucian Freud, that he found global fame. His own work was about covering up, but he allowed Freud to show him vulnerable. While Grayson Perry uses women's clothes to present as a woman, Bowery was not performing as a woman but as an artist. Woods, too, is performing as himself as an artist. Bowery's clothes are artworks with no gender (some are based on dresses or skirts, but are complete transformations). Woods is not aiming to come across as a woman in any way. He is always his masculine self in the clothes of a woman.

opposite
ANIMAL HUSBANDRY, 2019

below
Pierre Molinier, *TRIOMPHE*, c.1969–70
Black-and-white silver print.
112 x 141mm

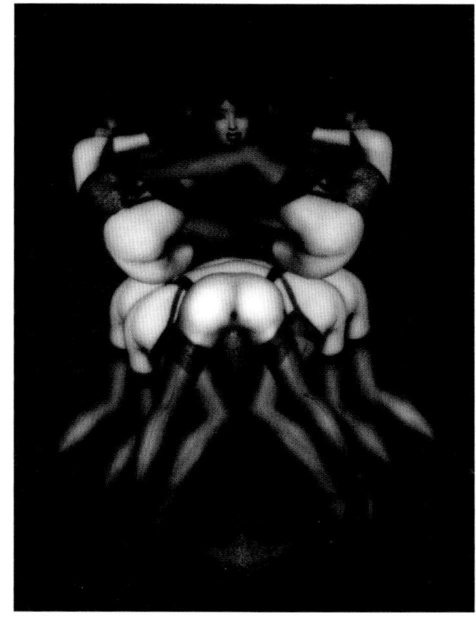

Woods says he wants to feel society's humiliation when a man gives up his patriarchal privilege and allows himself to be laughed at, to have a child stare and say "mummy, why is that man in a dress?".[2]

People will stare. Make it worth their while.
Harry Winston

Woods has stated that, with these images, he is seeking out in an attempt to control his desire (for women) and to overcome societal and family notions of emasculation.[3] His upbringing showed him how to be conventionally masculine, where the worst thing was to be a *sissy*, unmanly, or in any way womanly/feminine. This misogyny is not something he believes in, but there is a deep part of him that has been conditioned to feel that way. It is no wonder he took up Brazilian jiu-jitsu, and allowed himself to wind up in prison. Oscar Wilde had challenged English Victorian and Edwardian masculine ideals, contributing to the next generation being brought up in a world that stamped out any hint of homosexuality or unmanliness. Woods' father acted out gender norms that he was brought up in. Woods has taken time to find a way to rebel against his own masculinity.

Woods' earlier explicit objects were beautifully made, yet contained kernels of rebellion against these gender norms. More recently, by placing himself in "humiliating" scenes Woods transgresses personal, historic and societal norms within the safe space of art. This is not art therapy, but in touching vulnerable spaces Woods opens to the viewer possibilities of being outside the norm, and comfort. Woods documents the performance of masculinity and its alleged antithesis.

Bowery's polished photographic works (with professional photographers) always look like he is in command. He firmly holds the gaze of the viewer, and seems to ask: "So, you think you know what beauty is? Well, look at me. I am beautiful, maybe not the general ideal, but I am beauty itself, and don't even think about questioning me."

You have no sense of fashion … No, no that wasn't a question.
Miranda Priestly, The Devil Wears Prada

Woods' gaze is often uncertain, like a child caught in his mother's clothes. At the age of five, he found a pile of cardigans at home and tried them on, preening in a mirror. His parents happened upon him, and both laughed at him. He says he felt utterly humiliated – for wearing genderless sweaters. Today, gendered clothing is ever changing. Women wearing trousers in the early 20th century were said to be in men's clothes, but now sweat pants are sadly *de rigueur* for all. Perry talks about starting to cross-dress as a child with the support of his mother, but Woods has never been drawn to dressing as a woman. Woods knows we are looking at him and wondering what he is up to, and knows we also know he is not enjoying himself. So we keep uncomfortably asking, "What are you doing?" He wants us to engage in the humiliation of masculine desire and, if we look, we have done so. It is our looking that completes the transaction. We make him feel humiliated, whether we want to or not. Our only choice is to look away, and that too is a form of disgust that he thrusts upon us.

These images worry the viewer, because almost everyone can be humiliated, or shamed.

But what if the viewer does not want to partake in that humiliation? What if their interest is generic, or inquisitive? That is where the work functions as art, much like the *X Portfolio* images by Robert Mapplethorpe (1946–89) where someone is willingly being abused or debased. Mapplethorpe's images may be hard to look at (for many), but all involved in them are consensual adults. Humiliation, for pleasure or punishment, is imagined by those in the image. The viewer does not place their fist in someone's anus, but, in looking, confirms Mapplethorpe's incredible photographic eye and conceptual conceit that everything can be or maybe is beautiful. Looking is the only price the viewer pays. Mapplethorpe's are difficult works of art, and some will find in Woods' images, if not that level of discomfort, a certain something going against the grain. When a viewer sees extreme Mapplethorpe images they might go *ouch*, feeling an imagined pain, but they do not usually feel the pleasure that the person is also enjoying. These are sexual acts done to fulfil a fantasy, even if there is some or a lot of physical pain. Woods is only dressed as a sissy, or a princess, yet he and many heterosexual men might find that humiliation as extreme as in any Mapplethorpe image. Woods feels no physical pain, but psychic breaches are often more difficult to overcome than physical blows. His images function on many levels, yet remain firmly in the world of art.

**I think there is beauty in everything. What "normal" people perceive as ugly,
I can usually see something of beauty in it.**
Alexander McQueen

The response of the viewer, what they take away, is often key. Intentionality is usually additional information and not necessarily crucial to the work. Woods' work can be interpreted as misogynistic or homophobic. This is not his intent, but he understands that those interpretations might be overlaid on it. Men dressing in clothes seen to be female, even if not in an attempt to pass as a woman, can seem anti-women. Woods saying that he debases himself – being seen as a man caught in the viewer's gaze dressed as a woman – implies that he too might believe this is the worst thing that can happen to straight men. It suggests womanliness as a lesser to manliness. Woods could be accused of this, were he not so clear that this is not what he is doing or asserting. He is deconstructing these tropes, and in doing so applies them to himself, his father and the patriarchy. Woods admits he has been taught this misogyny and that it certainly affects him in and out of women's clothing, but it is important that a cis heterosexual man can think through this dilemma and in trying on the trope free himself from it.

As a queer man, I feel I have stolen much of the power the word "queer" has by using it myself, but that does not make me homophobic, nor is it internalised homophobia. All those who use queer theory wrest power from those who would use the word as a weapon. Cross-dressing could signal a homophobic slant to the work, but Woods isn't punching down at women or homosexuals, or making a joke about them or at their expense. This is about him and how he is aiming to free himself from outmoded ideas about manliness. Unlike Perry, who is also attracted to women, Woods does not want to dress as one, nor have any sexual activity dressed as one. He is also not taking a swipe at those who do. It is an edgy enlightened body of work likely to cause offence, as many will not want to see a cis heterosexual man enter this arena of discourse. Gender, and its multifaceted, multilayered domains, has seen few such men feel confident enough to engage it.

But a man who can dress looking like an East End gangster, a Russian or African mobster in fake furs, or someone's auntie at a bar mitzvah, often in the same photograph, clearly knows that everything is up for grabs. Woods never looks beautiful in these works; he is not aiming at that sort of flattery. Not for him the androgony of Molinier, or the odd constructed unworldliness of Bowery, or the comic nature of Perry. He is carving out another way to make images of heterosexual men that aims to be free from patriarchal constraints. It is a call for freedom and compassion for himself, other men and women, of any gender or sexuality. It is a difficult project, and he might not succeed in every image he makes, but the concept, the effort, and the intentionality are something viewers rarely see.

Notes
1   Mark Woods in conversation with Michael Petry, 15 April 2024.
2   Mark Woods in conversation with Michael Petry, 15 April 2024.
3   Mark Woods in conversation with Michael Petry, 15 April 2024.

PHOTOGRAPHS

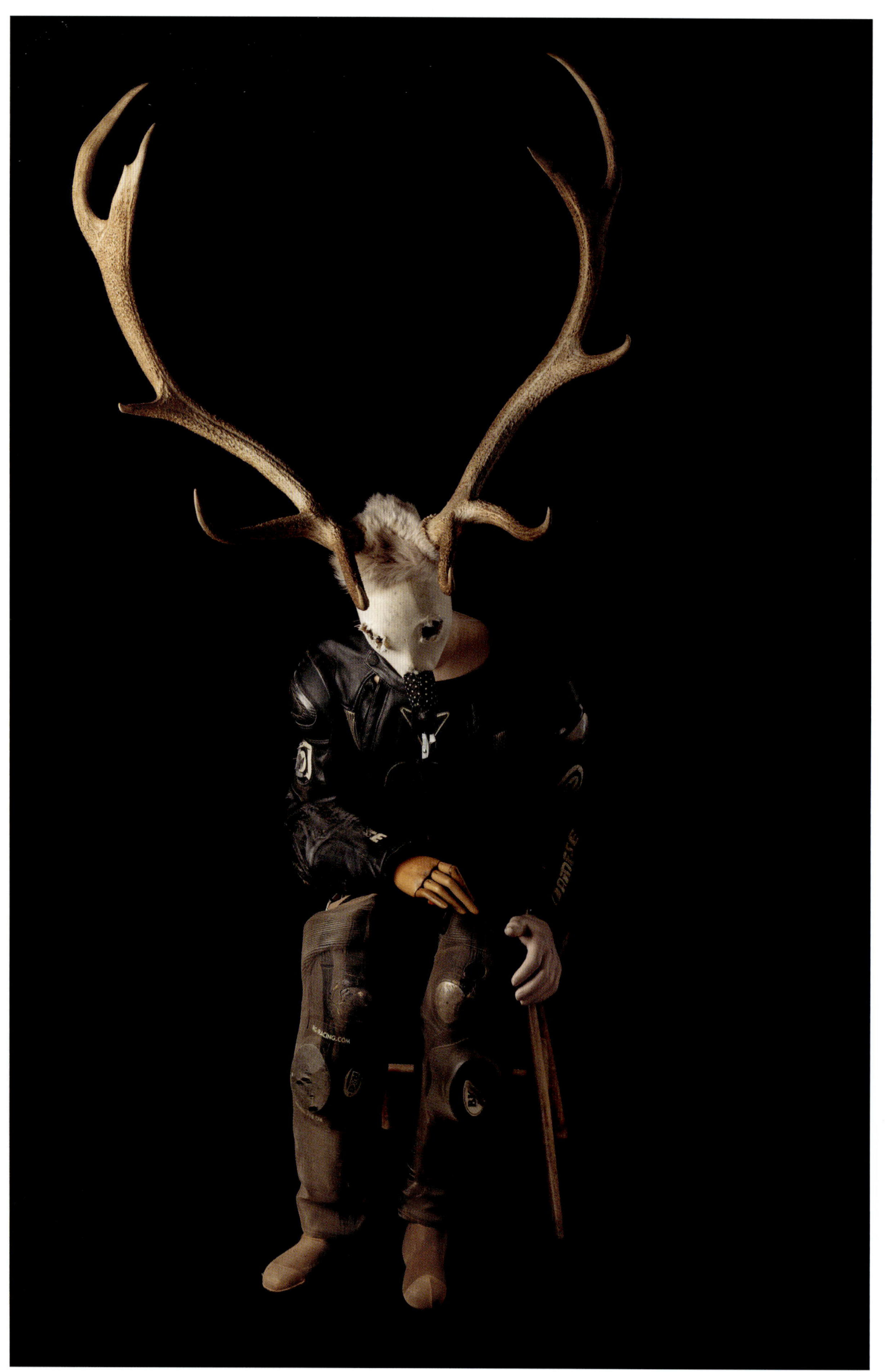

left
MALE POTENCY, 2020
Photographic print.
Dimensions variable

opposite
BOSCH MAN, 2020
Photographic print.
Dimensions variable

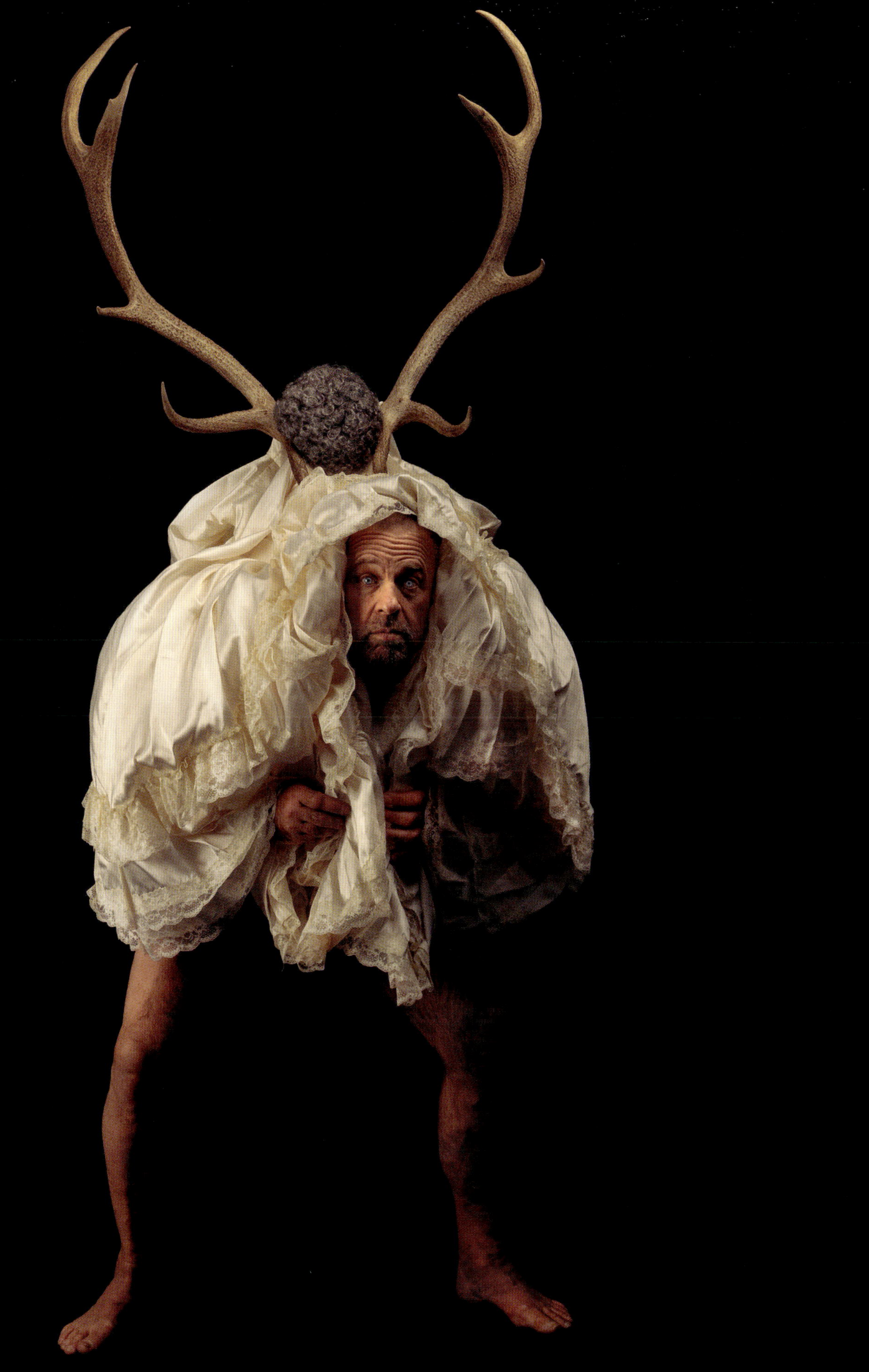

LEATHERJACKET, 2023
Photographic print.
Dimensions variable

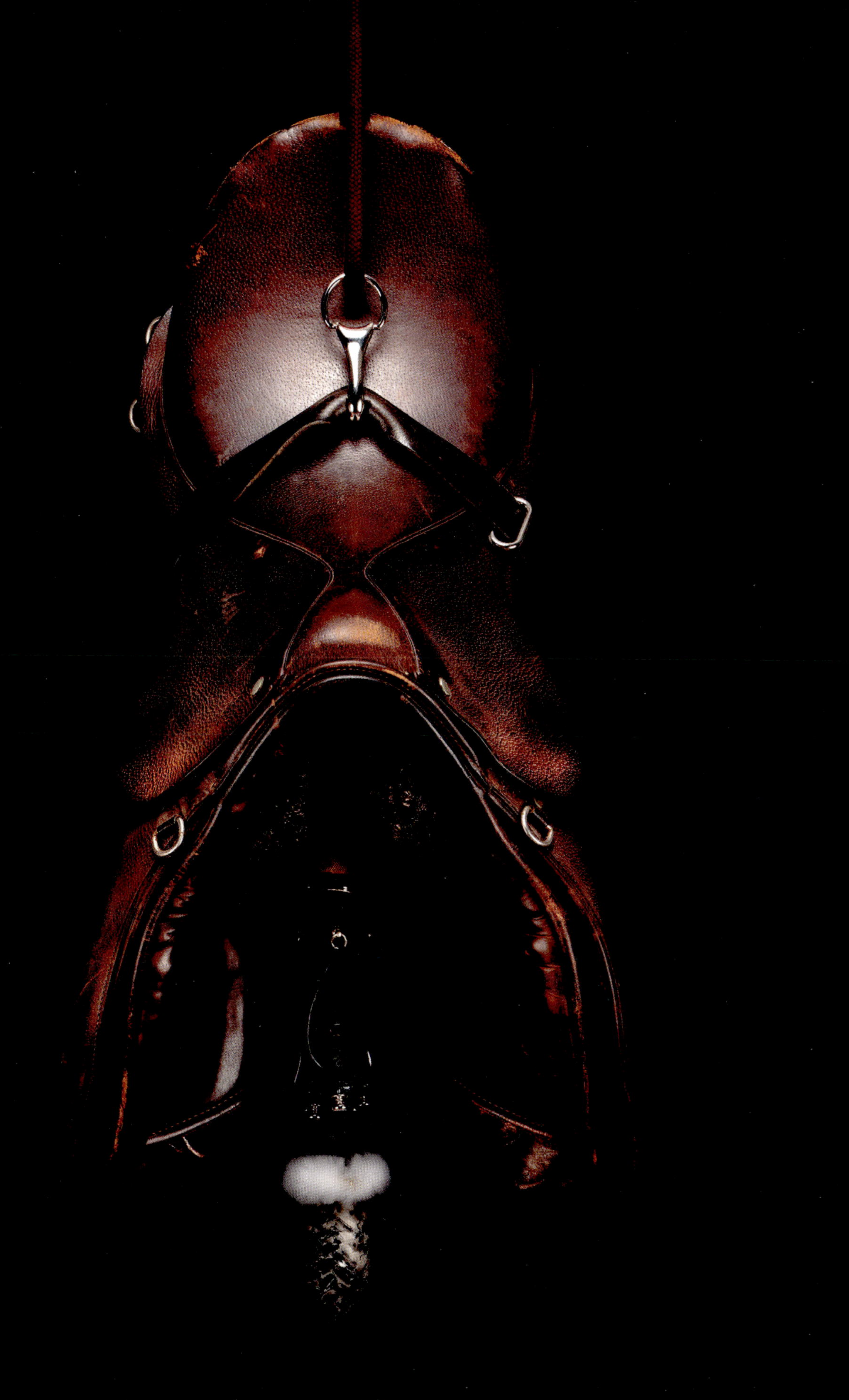

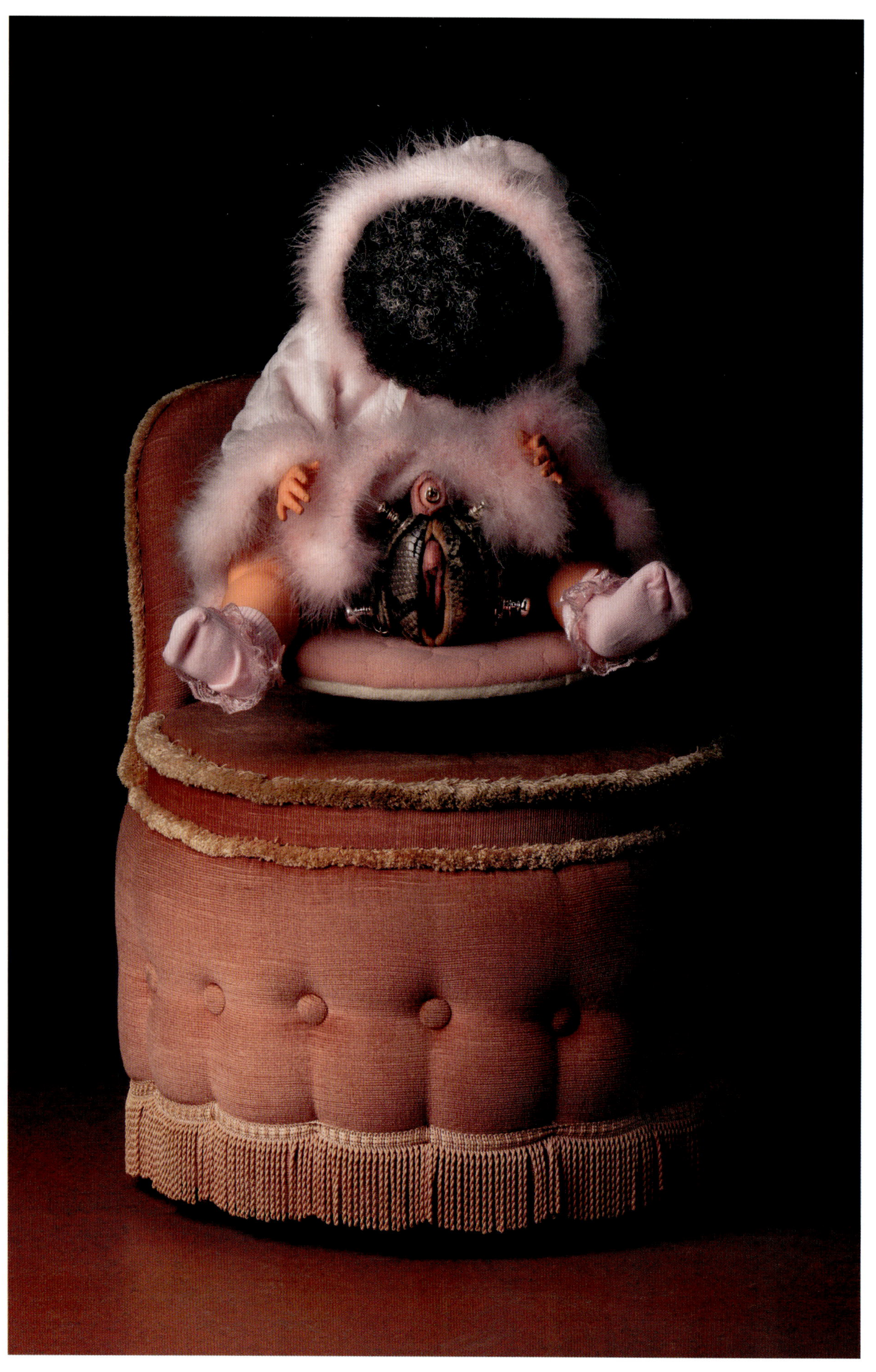

left
CENTREFOLD, 2021
Photographic print.
Dimensions variable

opposite
HORSE, 2021
Photographic print.
Dimensions variable

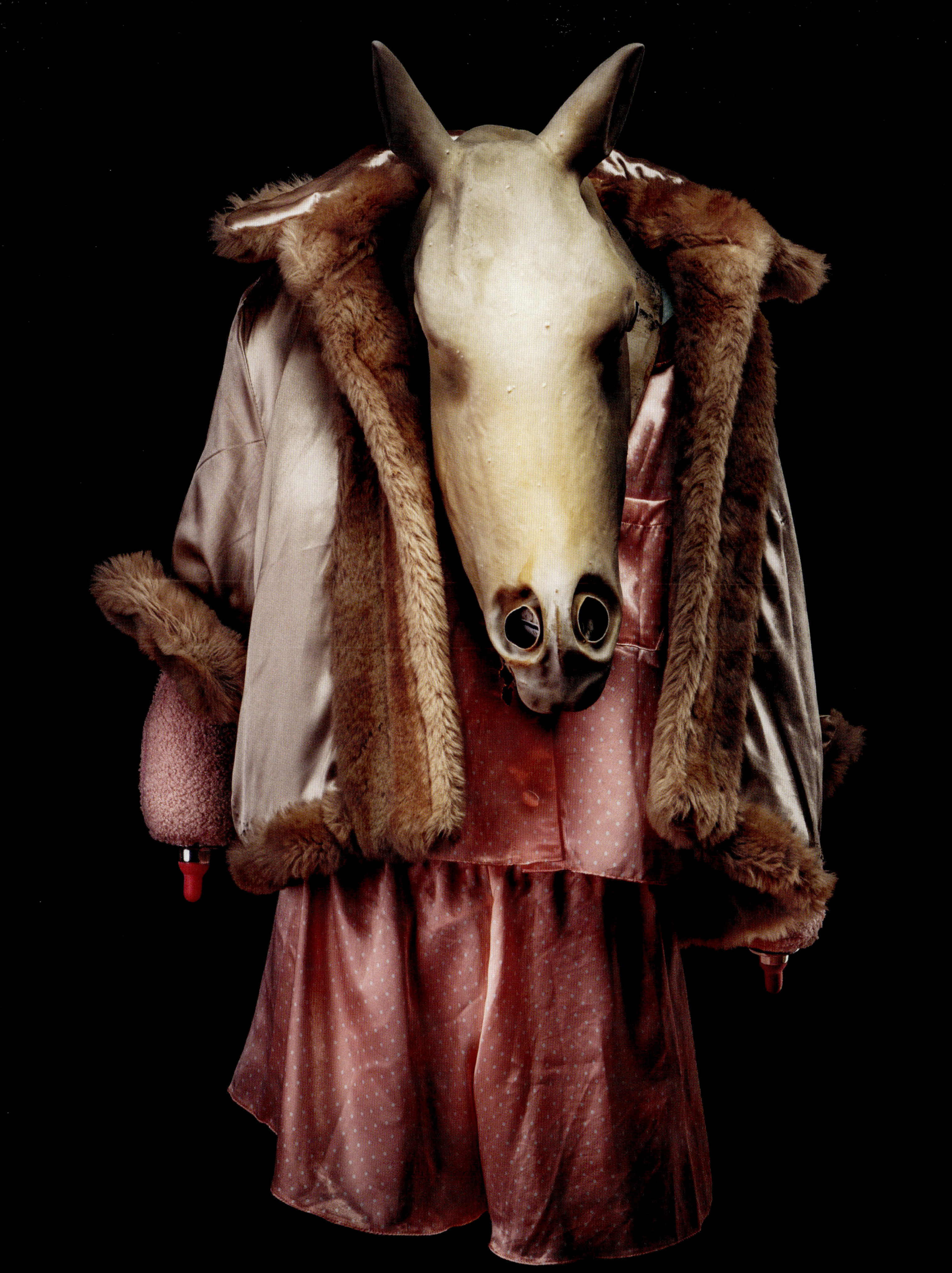

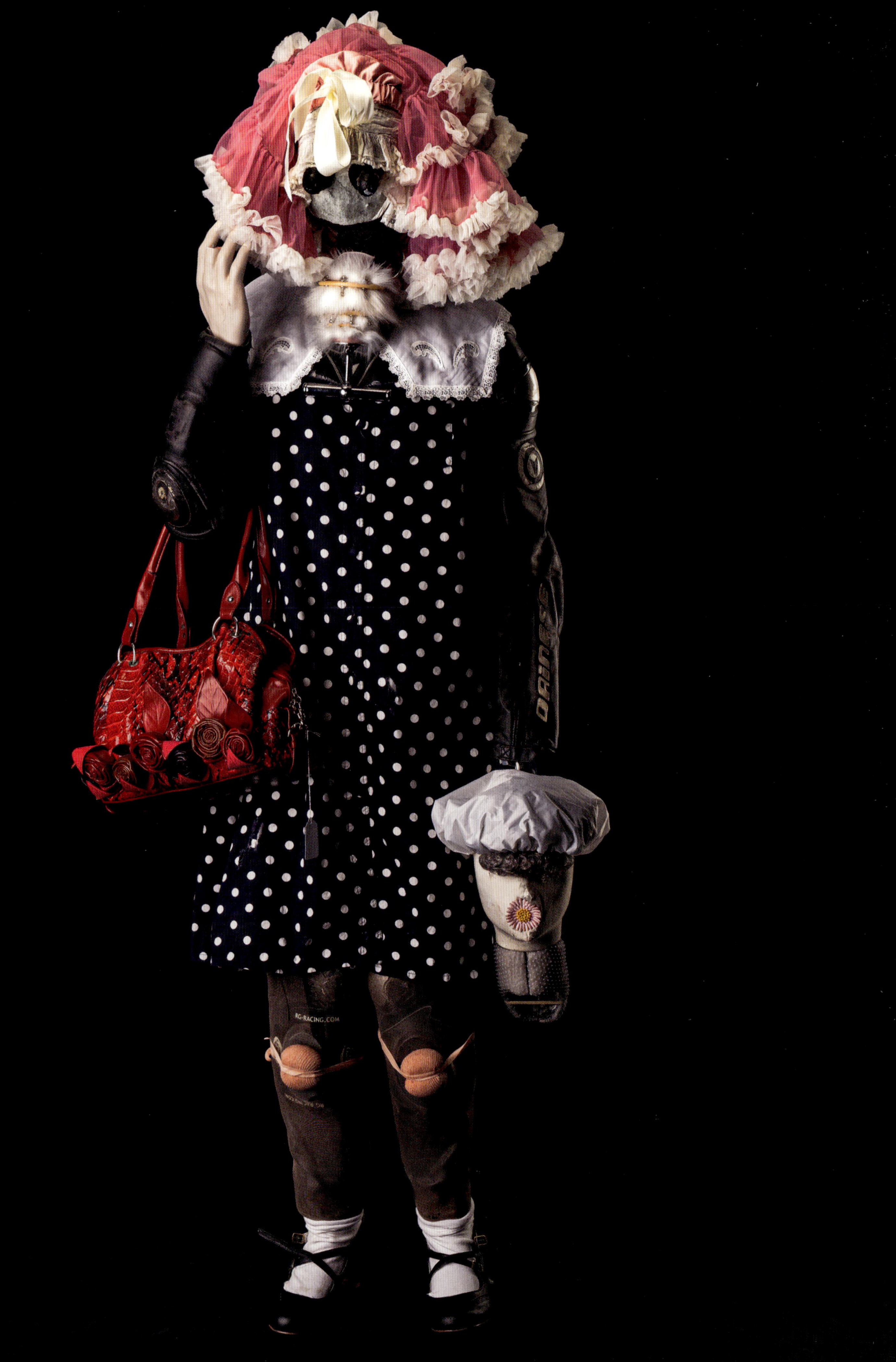

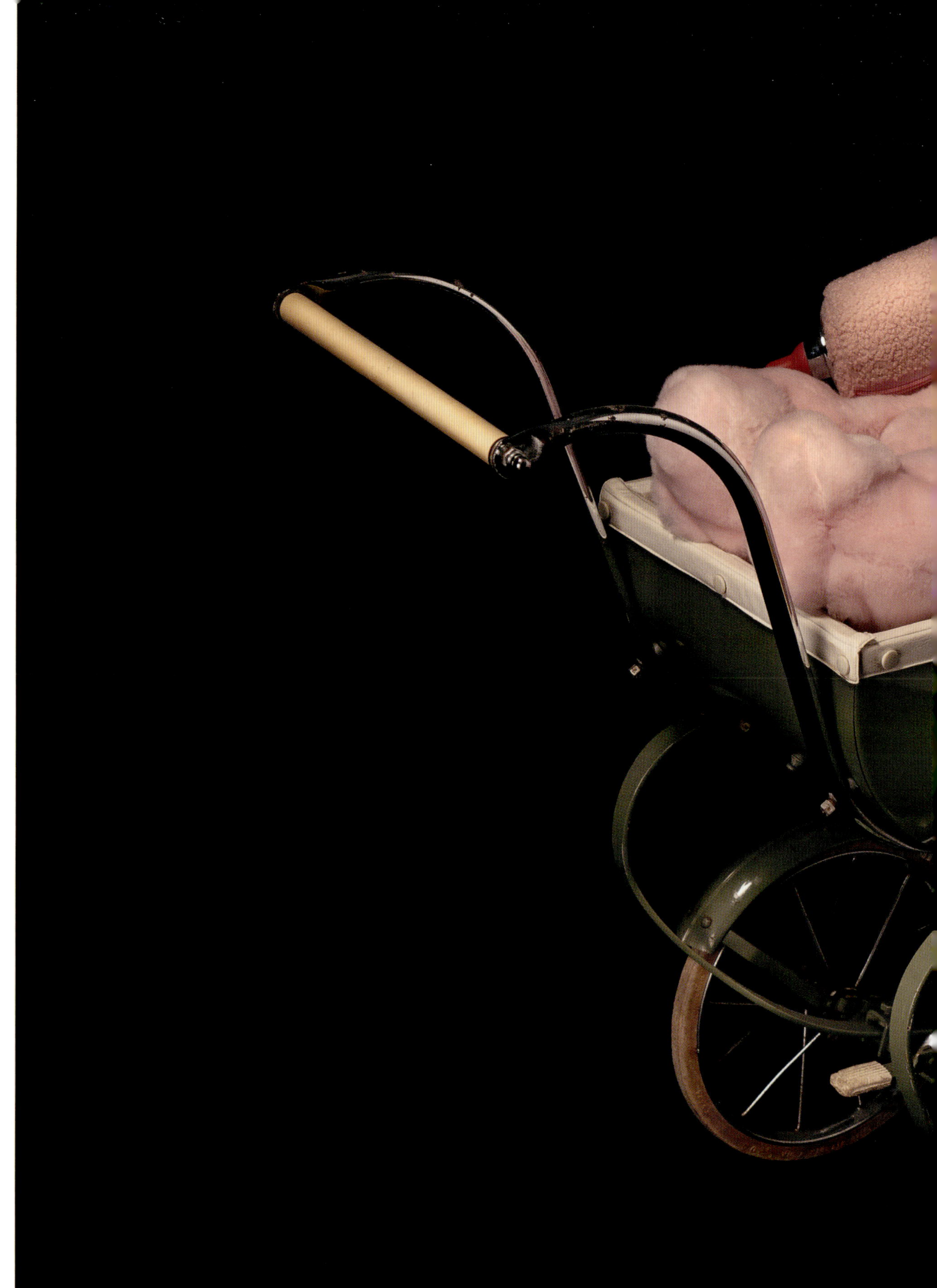

PRAM MONSTER, 2021
Photographic print.
Dimensions variable

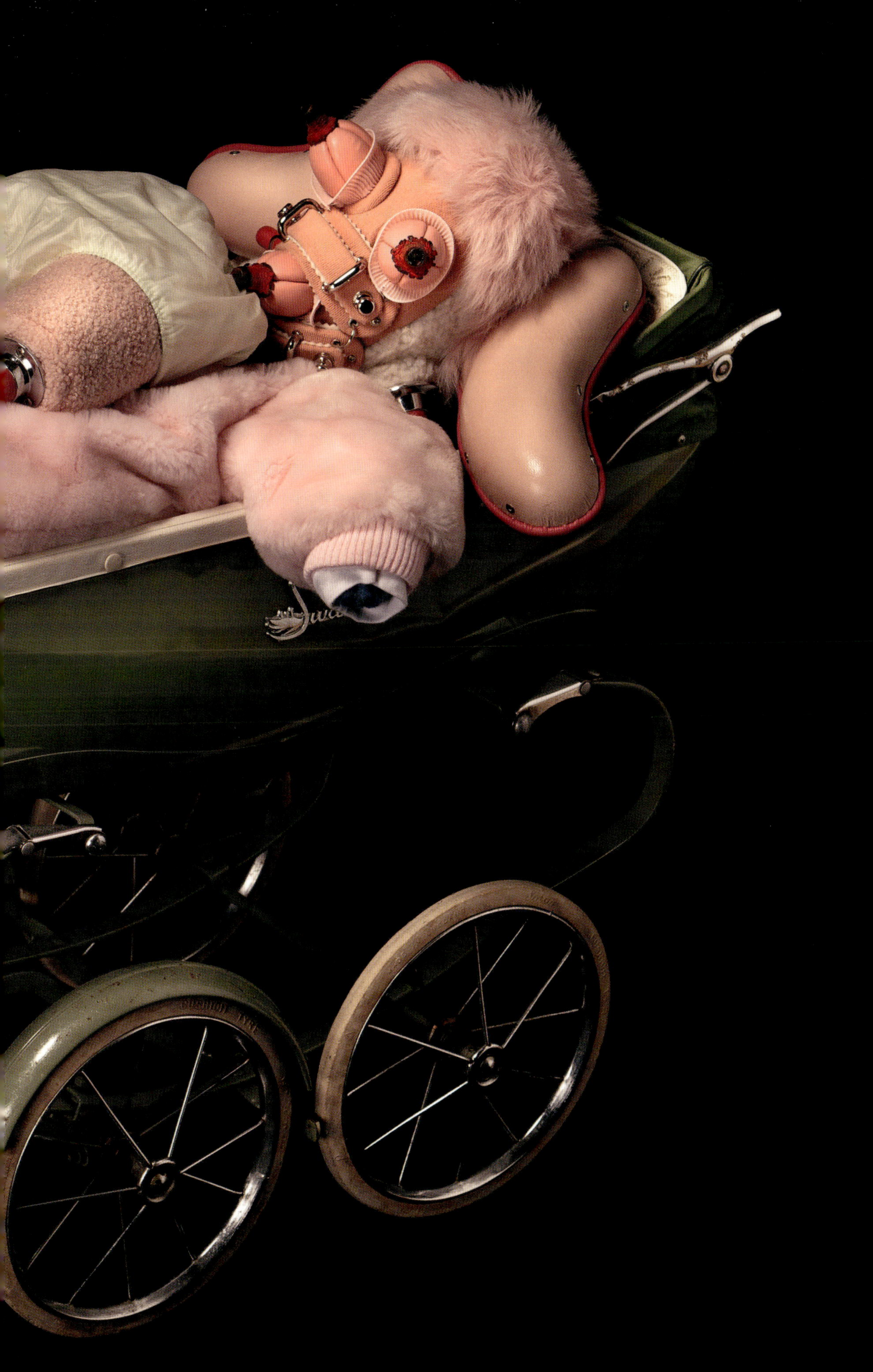

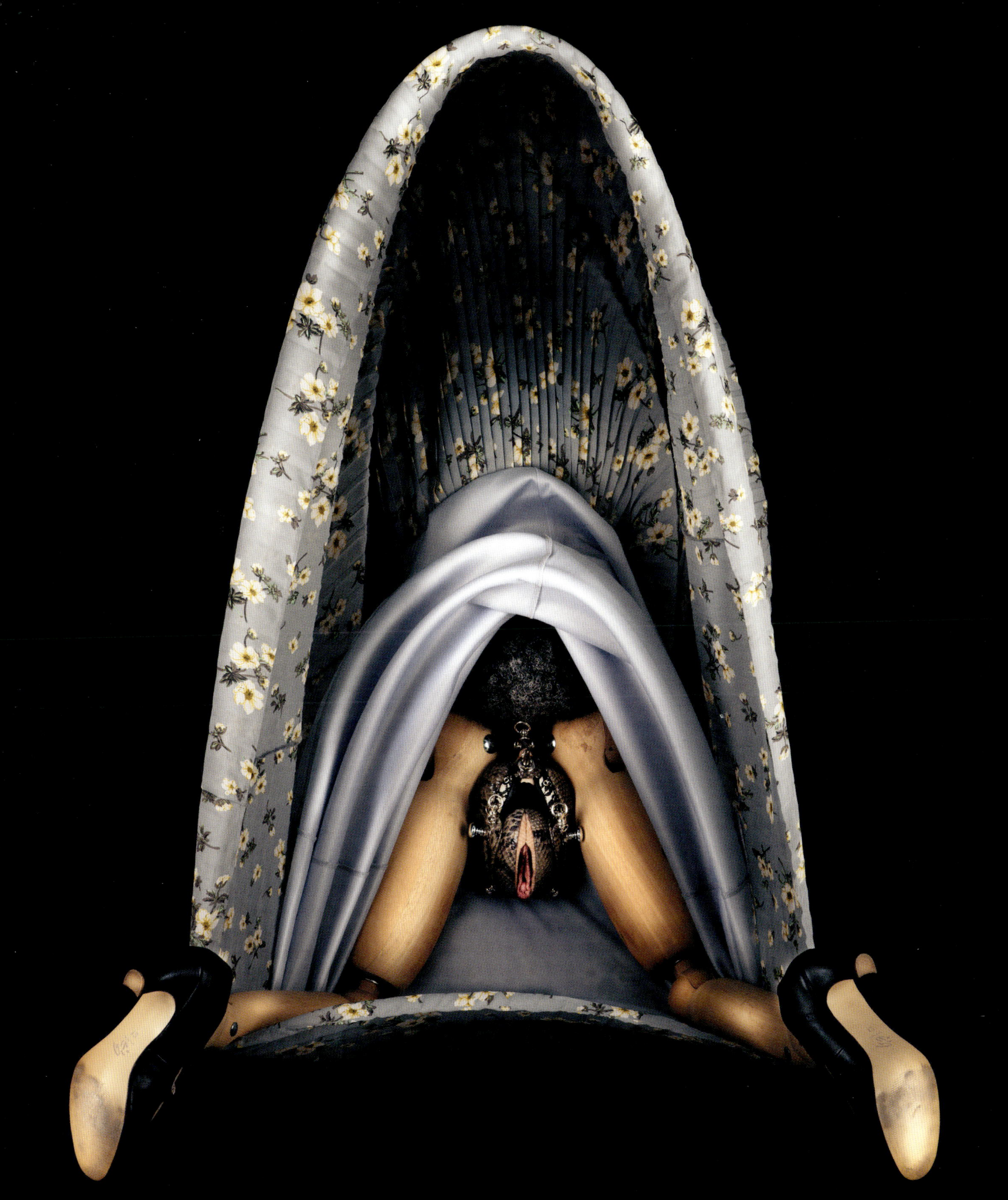

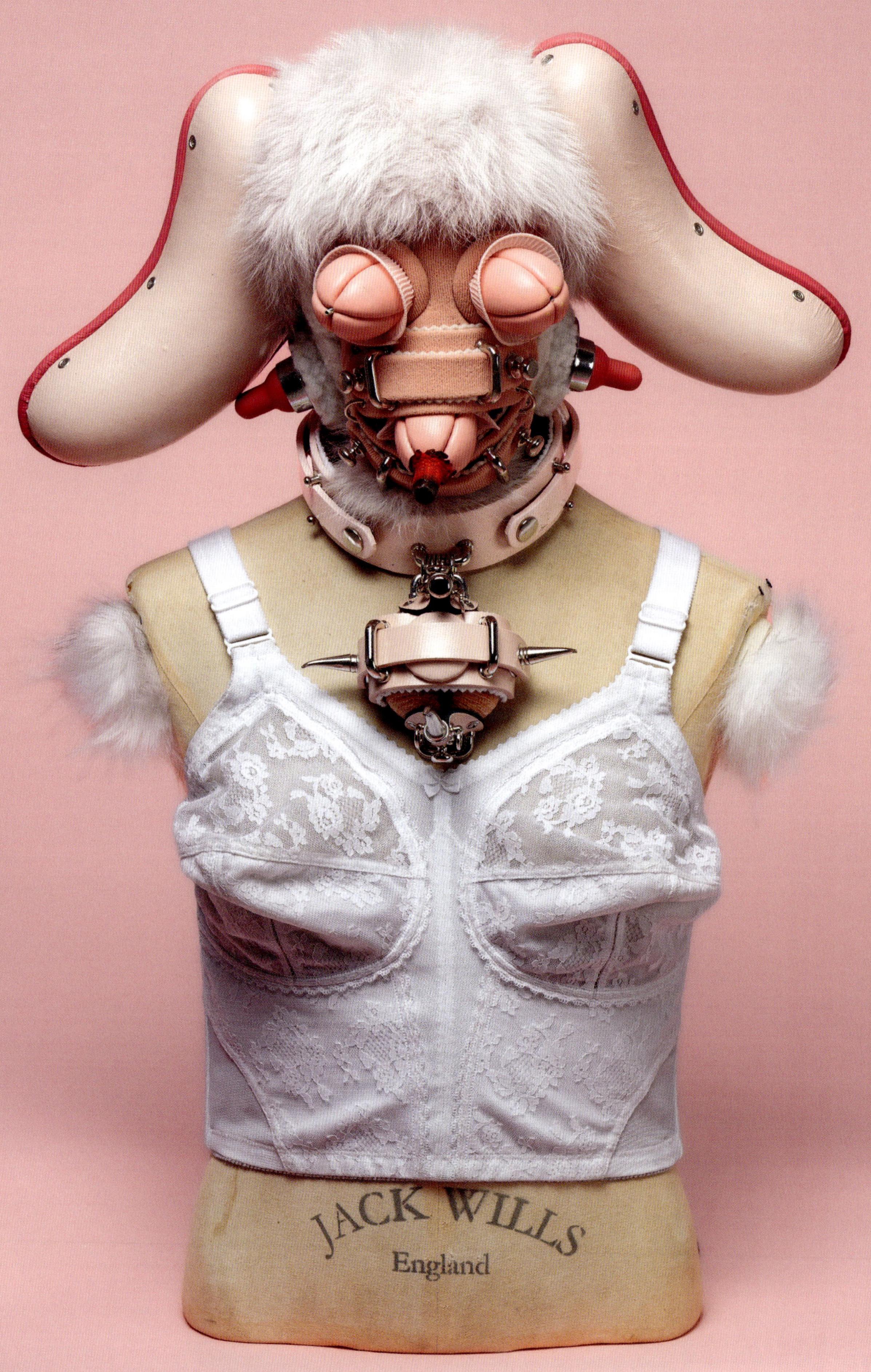

JACK WILLS
England

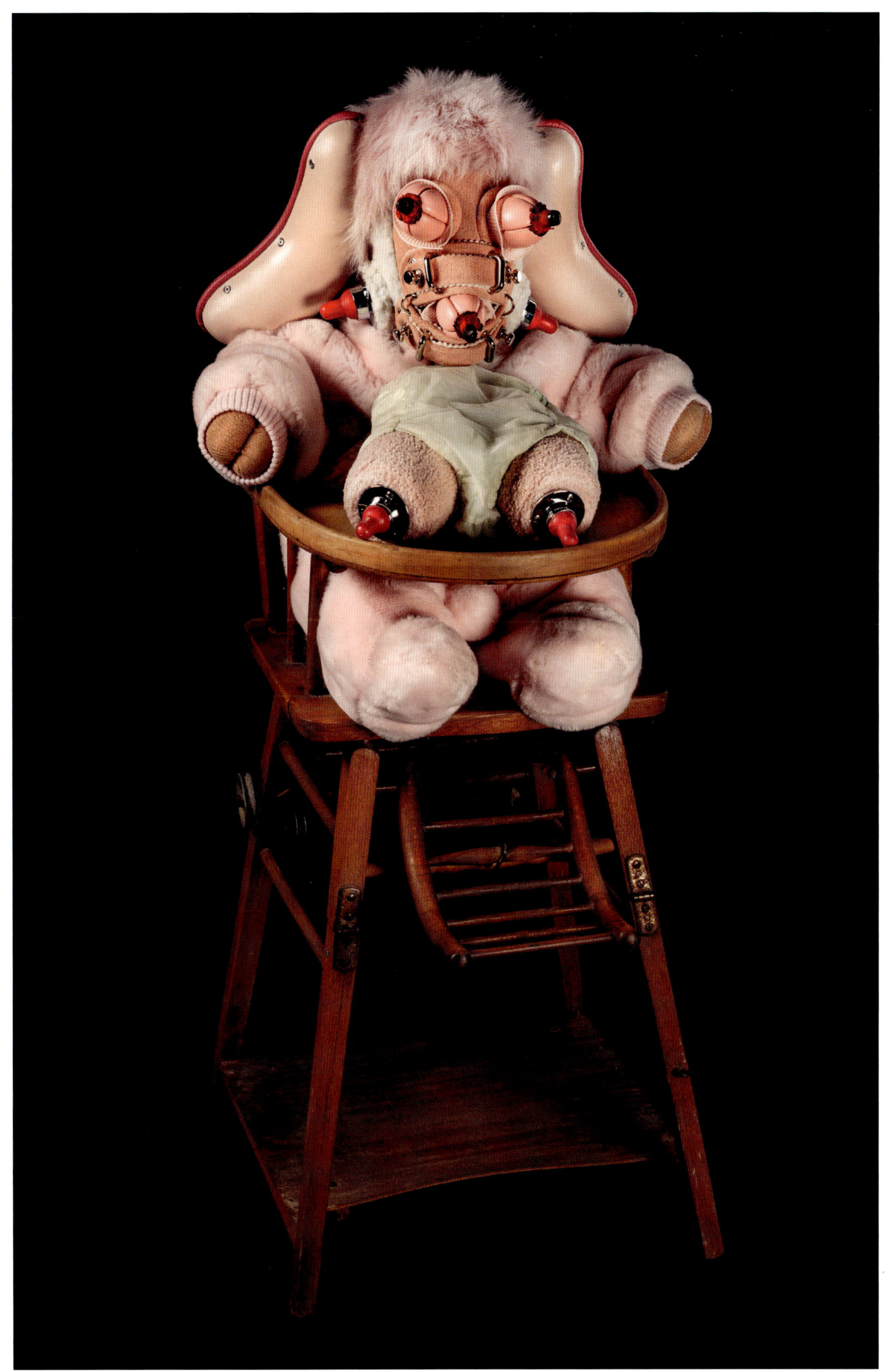

opposite
*GOATHERD POSTER
GIRL*, 2023
Photographic print.
Dimensions variable

right
HIGHCHAIR MONSTER,
2021
Photographic print.
Dimensions variable

163

NATURAL BLONDE,
2019
Photographic print.
Dimensions variable

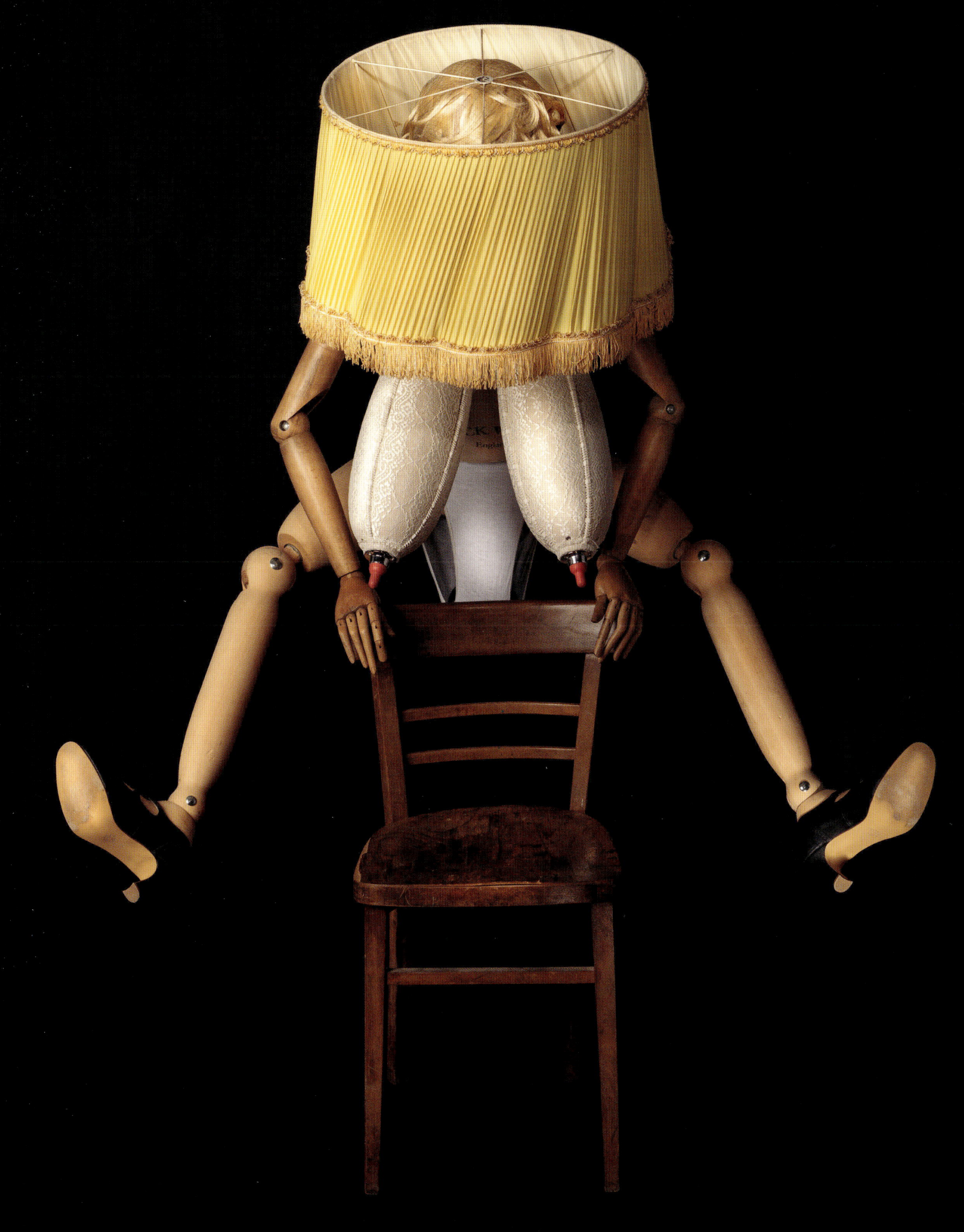

SELF-PORTRAITS

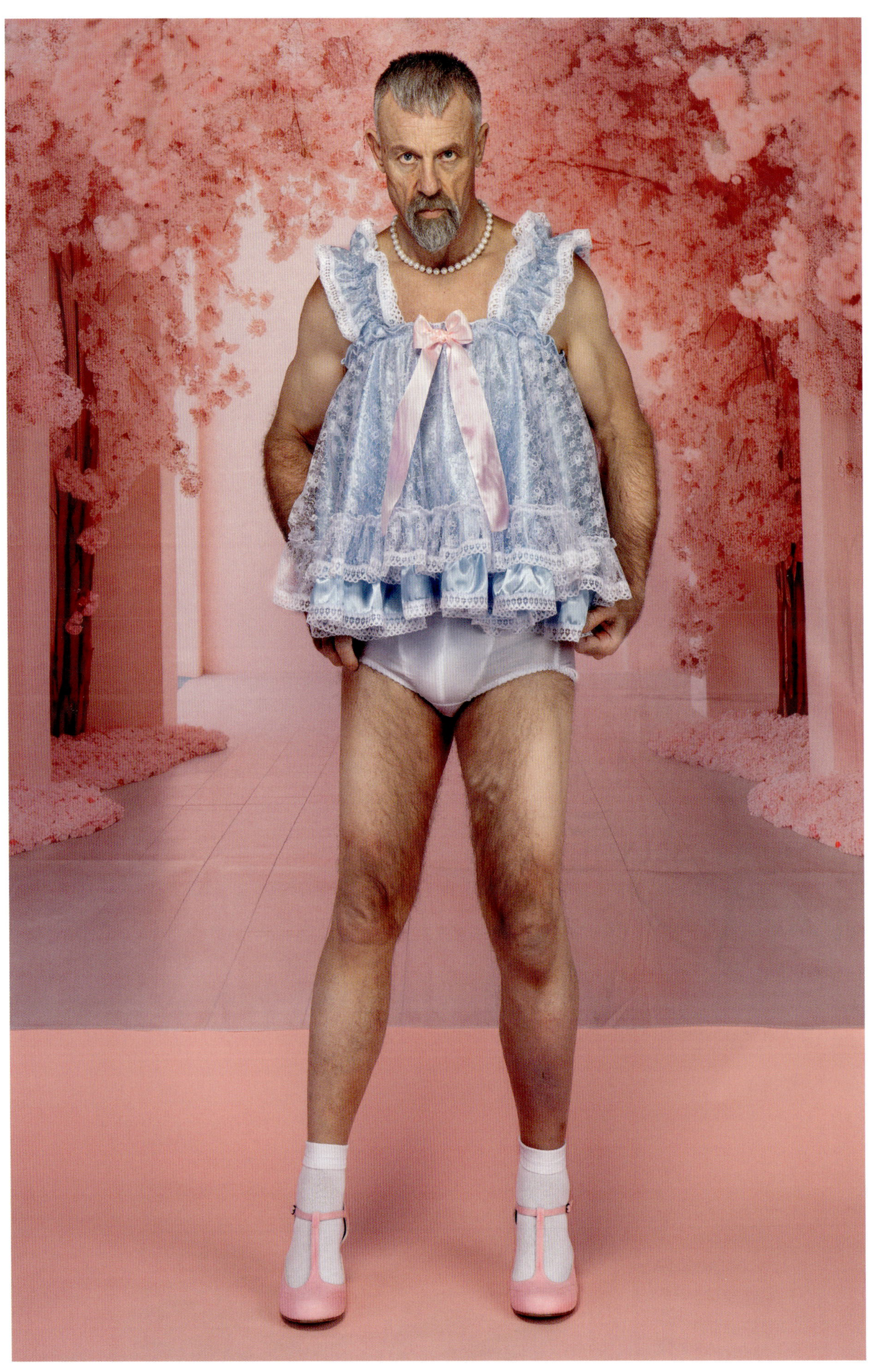

BABYDOLL, 2024

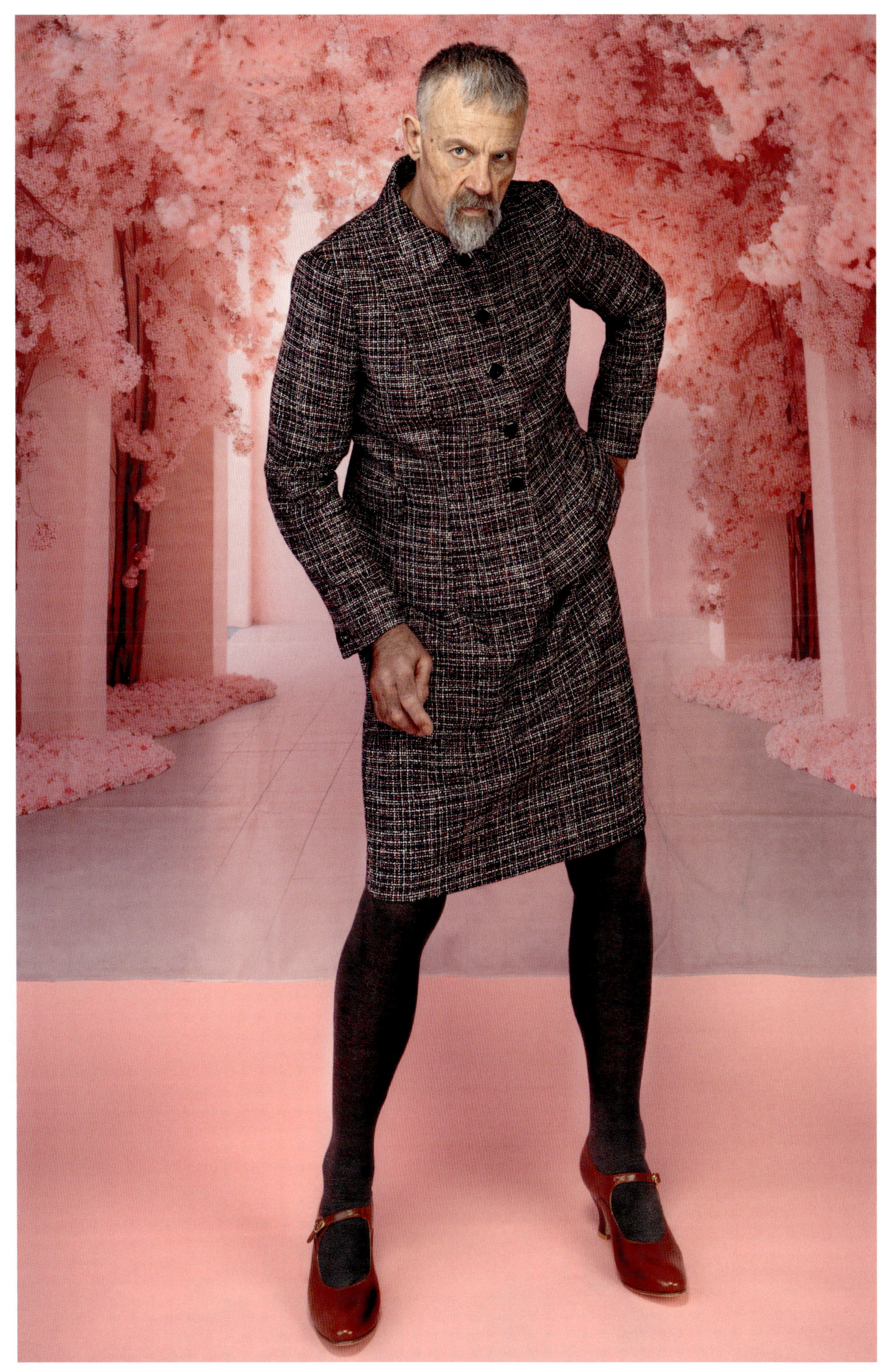

GONNA BRING HOME
THE BACON, 2024

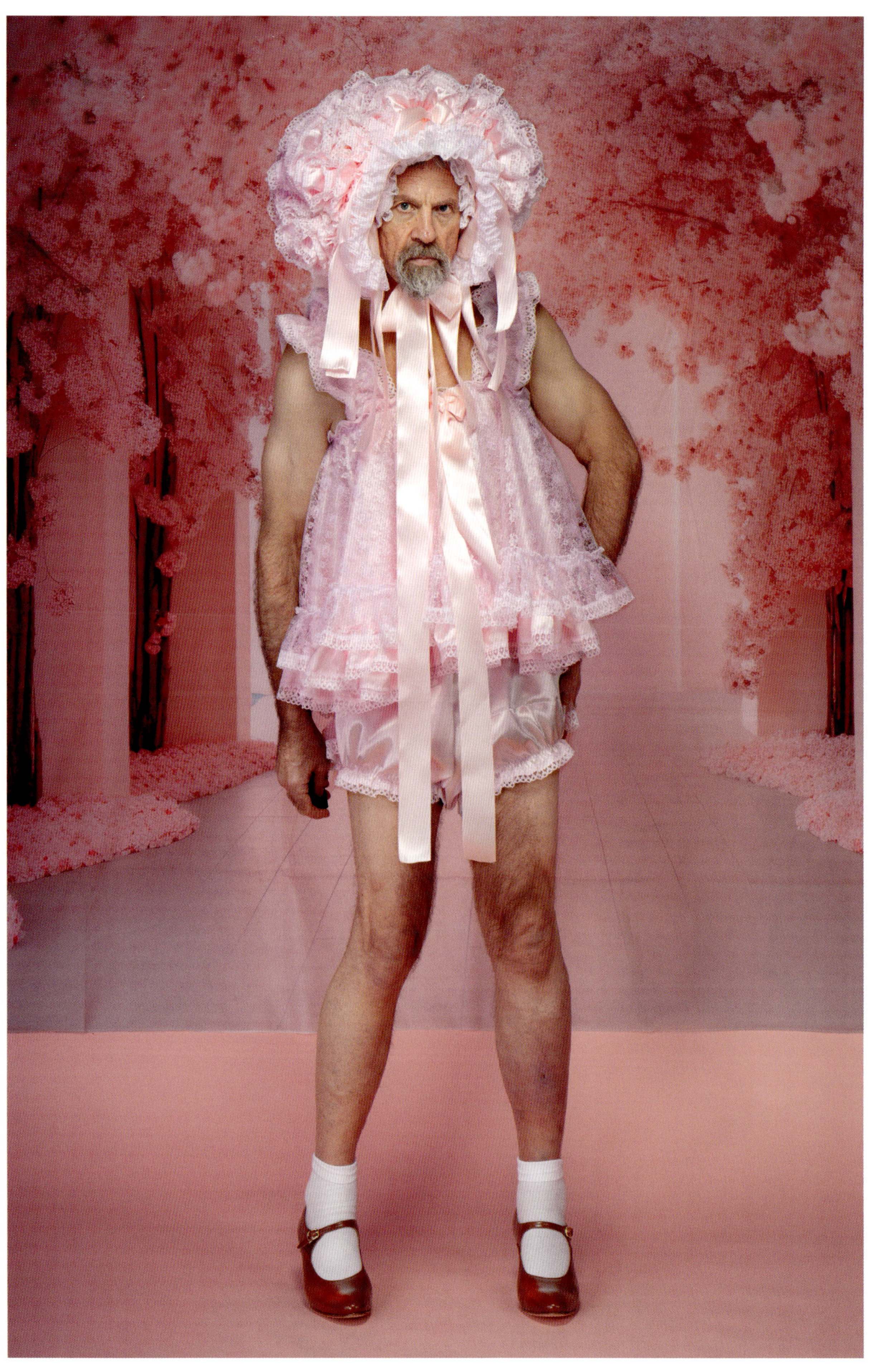

NYLON BON-BON, 2024

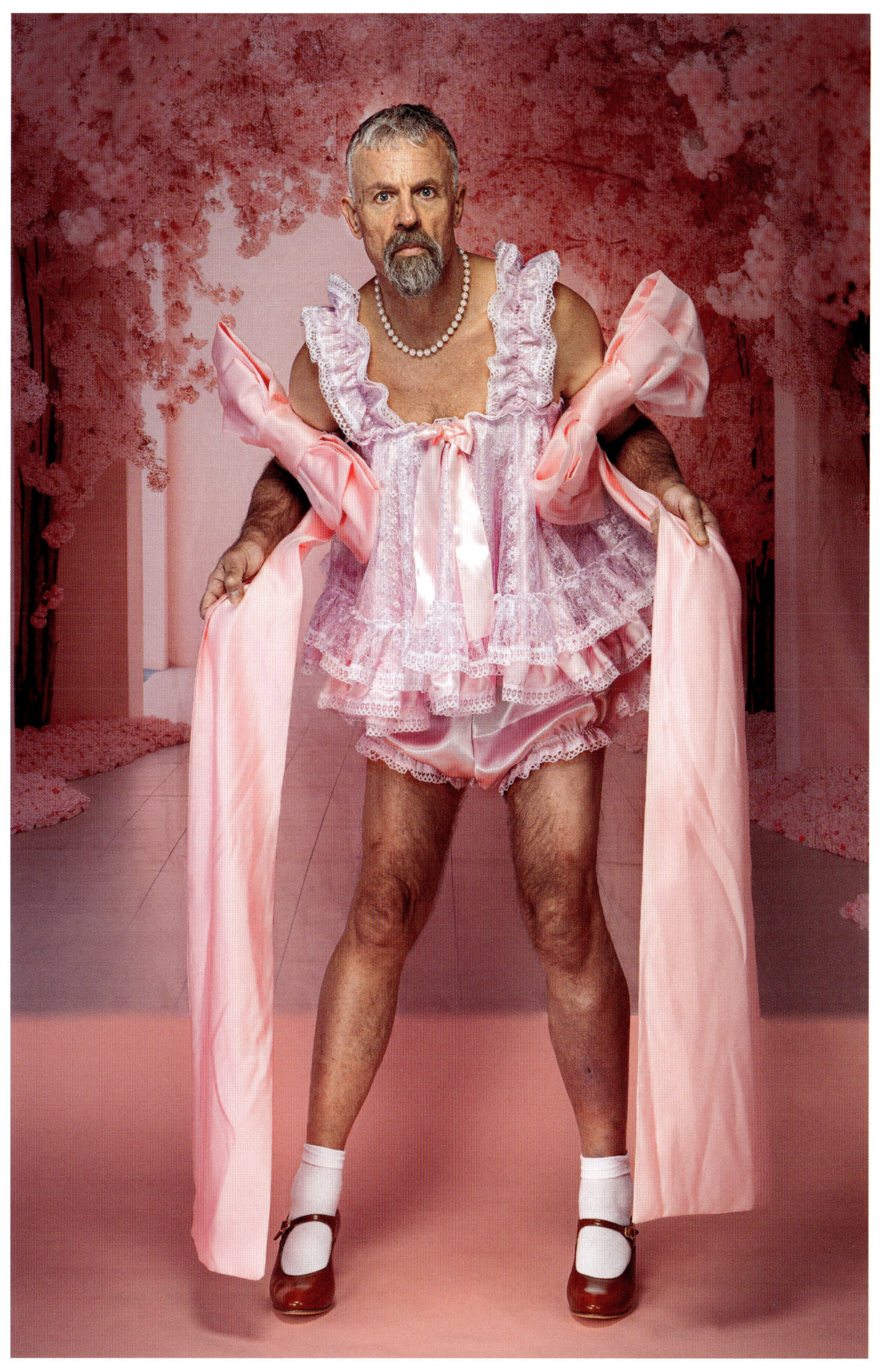

FAIRY GODMOTHER, 2024

CINDIE BRINGS A GIFT,
2022

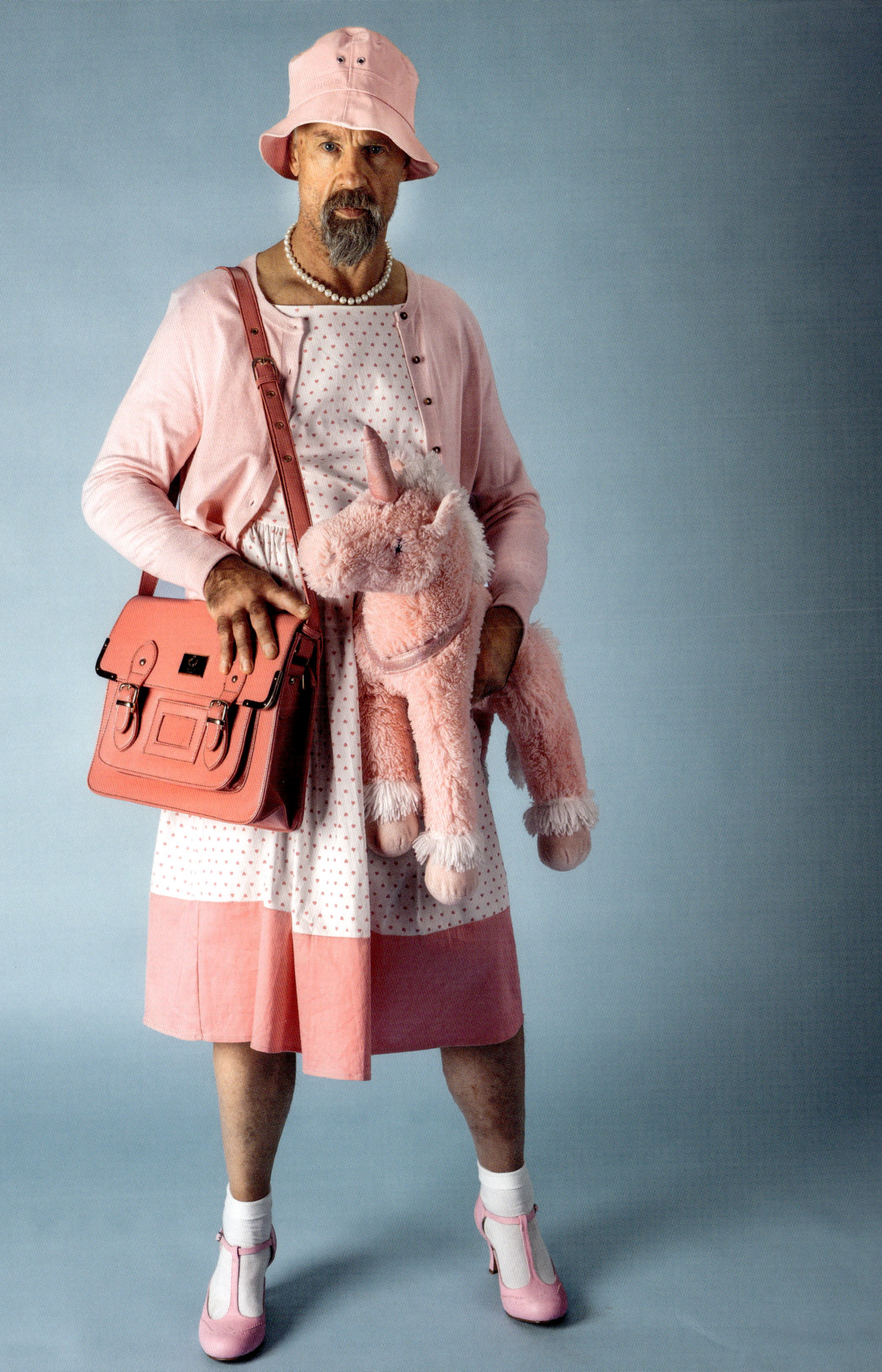

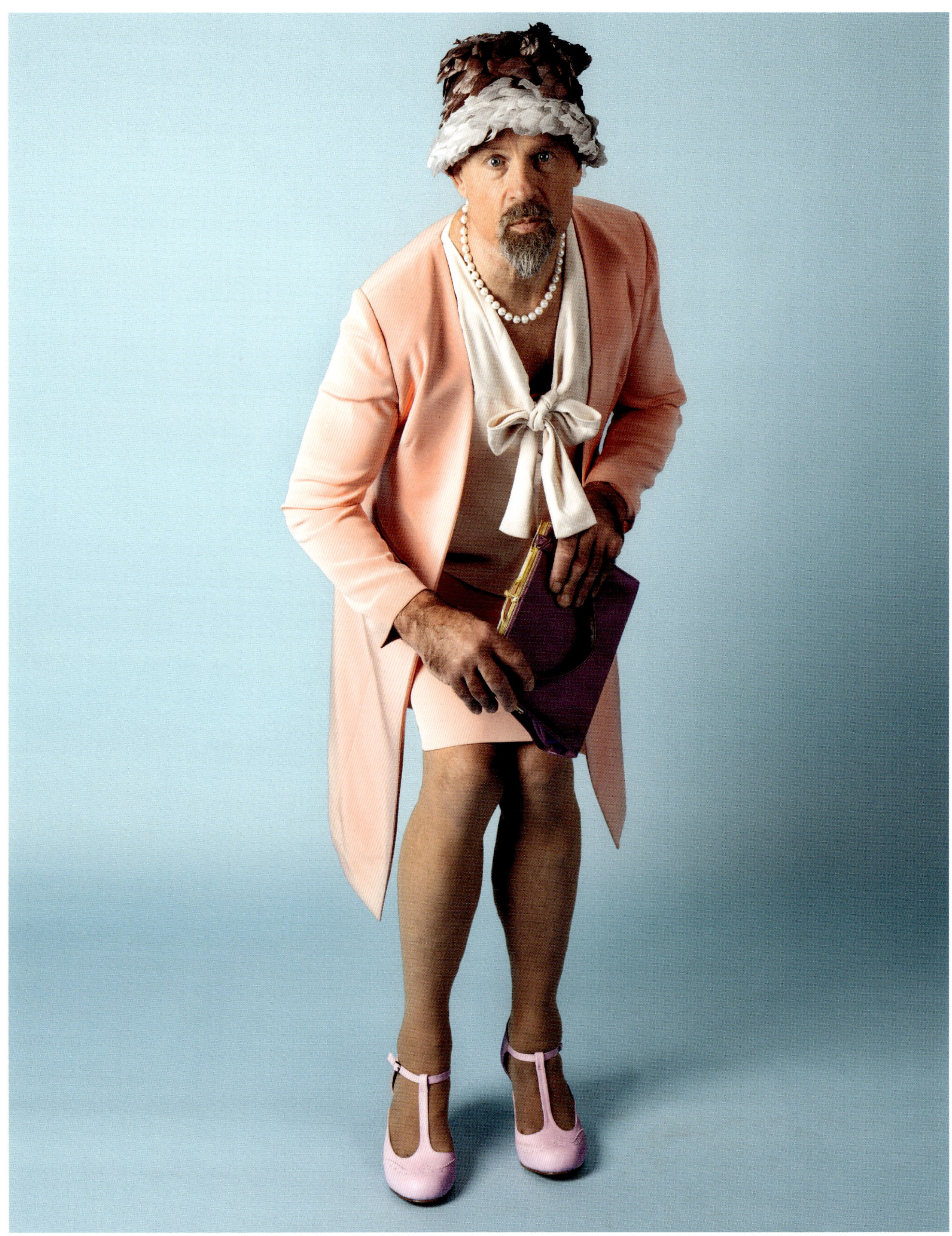

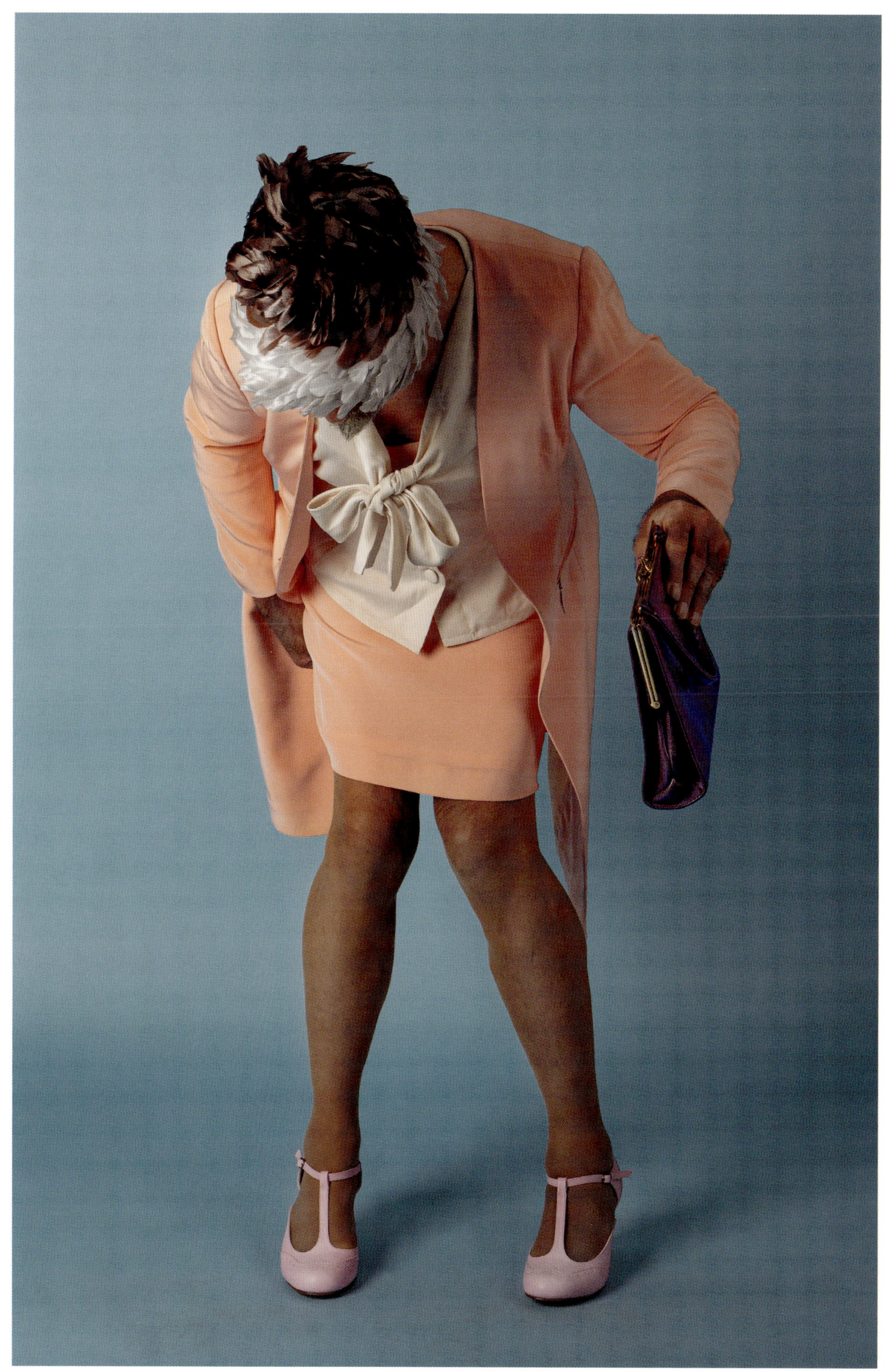

Opposite
MOTHER OF THE BRIDE, 2022

Right
ADJUSTMENTS NECESSARY, 2022

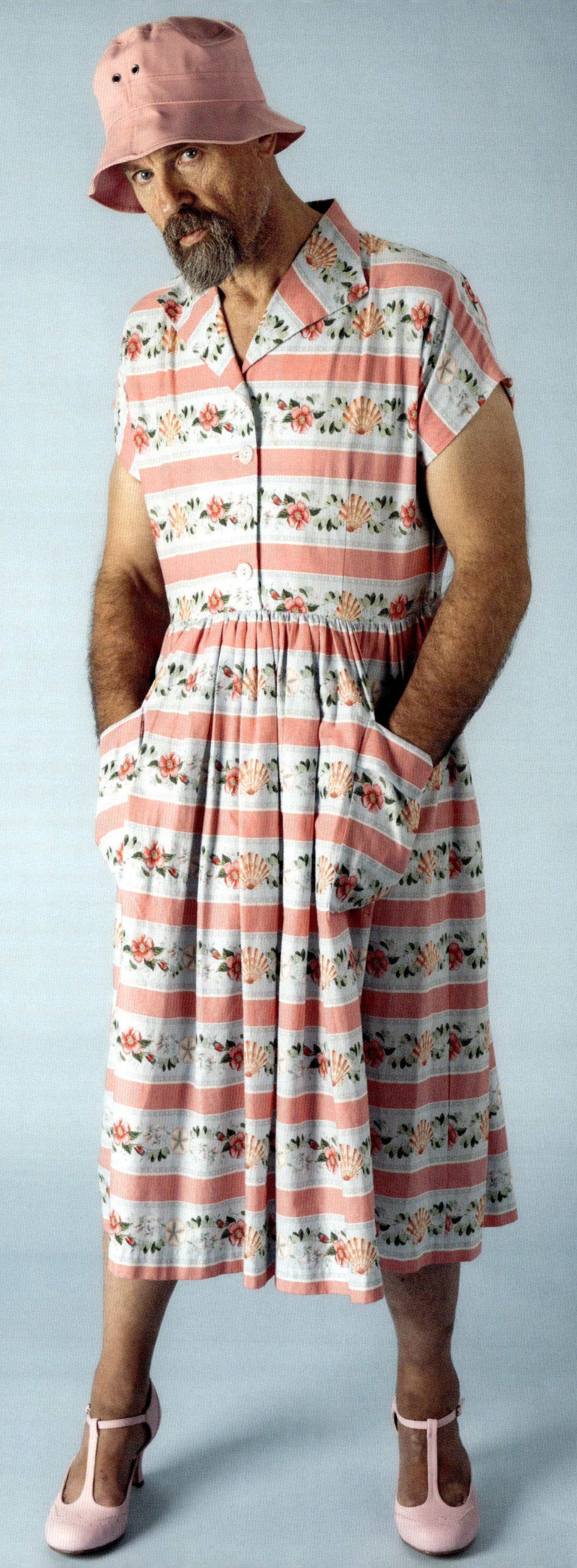

SUNDAY IN THE SUN,
2022

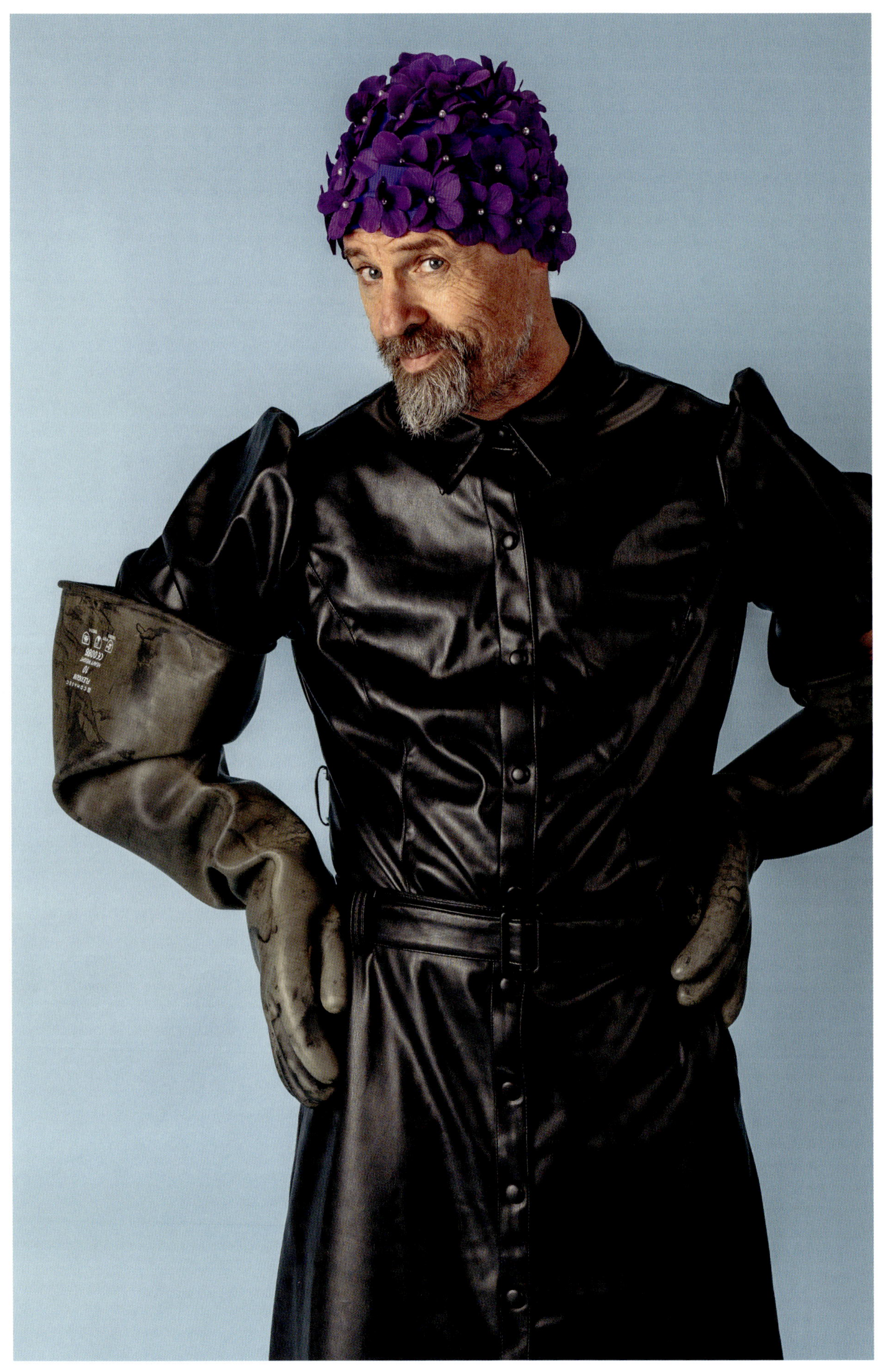

Left
SWIMWARE, 2022

Opposite
PANTO VILLAIN, 2022

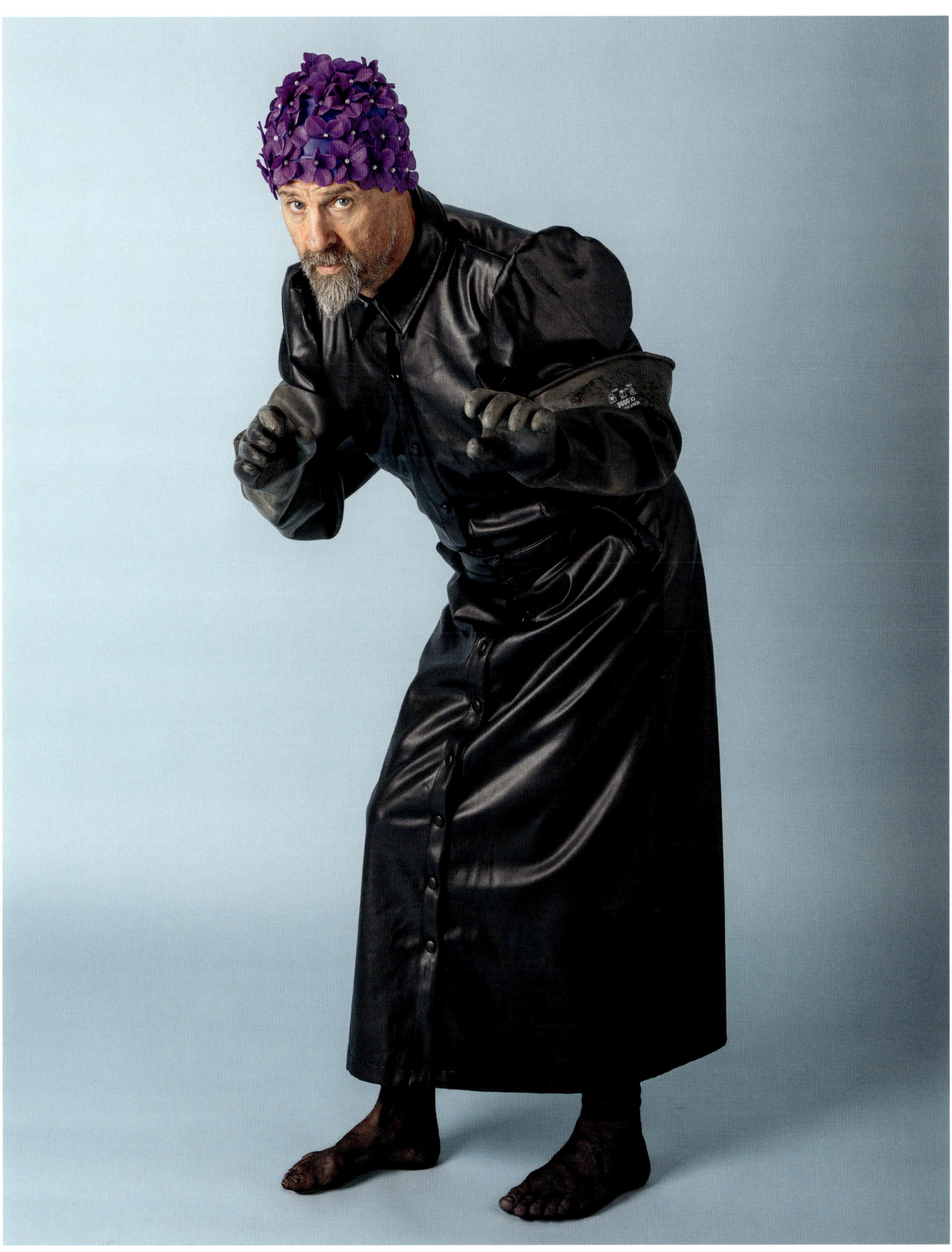

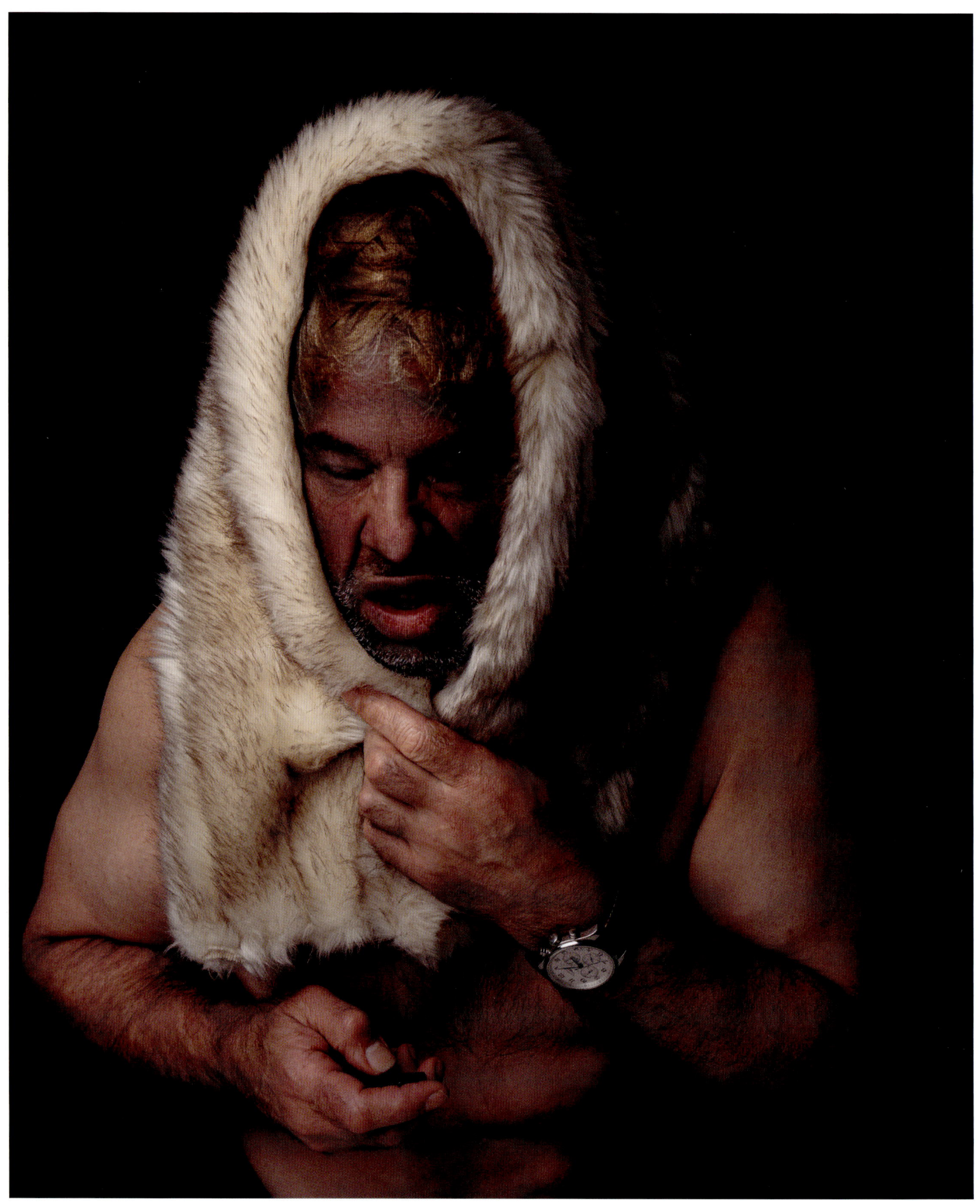

FUR BLONDE, 2020

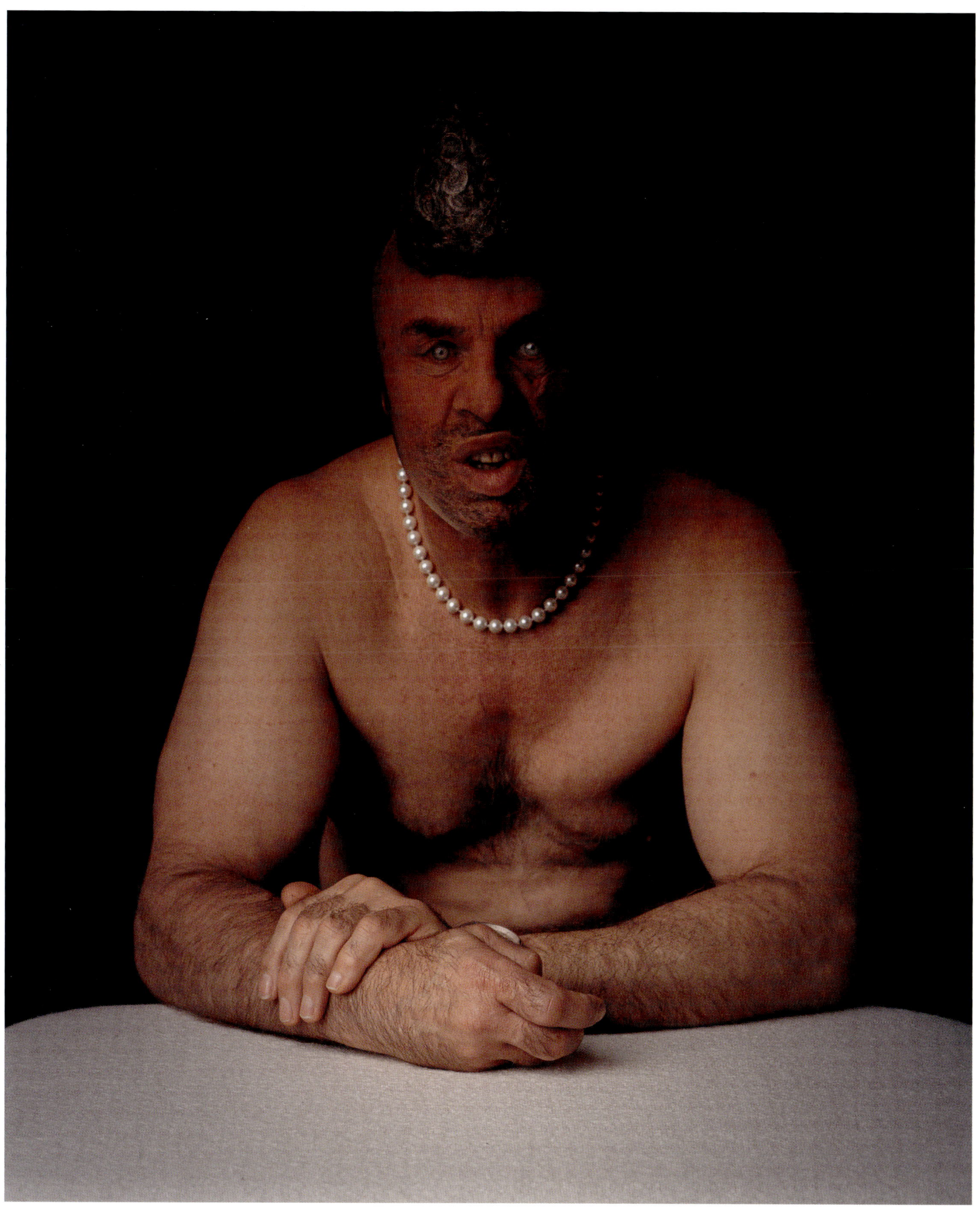

A' TEAM WANNABE, 2020

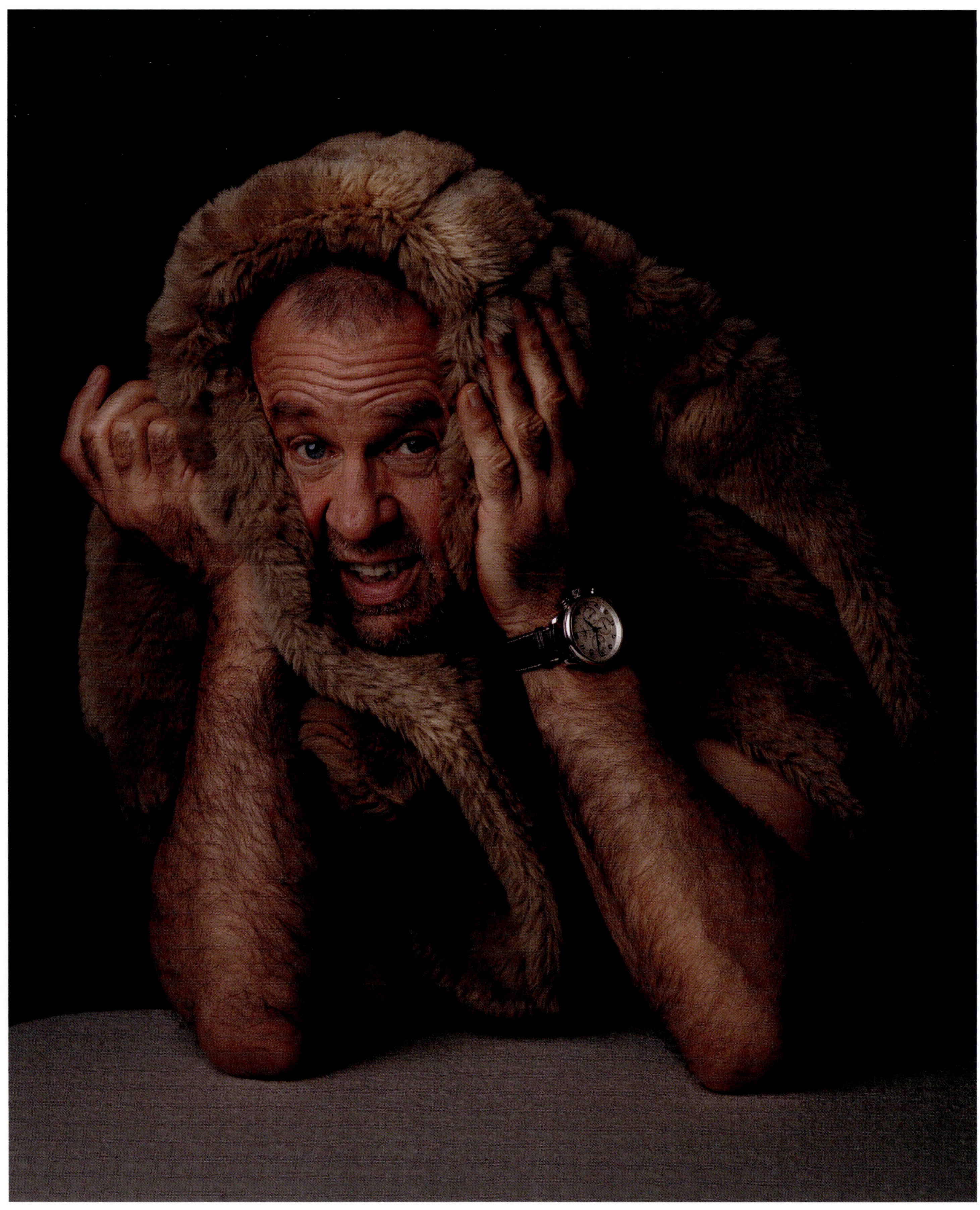

FUR HEADSHOT, 2020

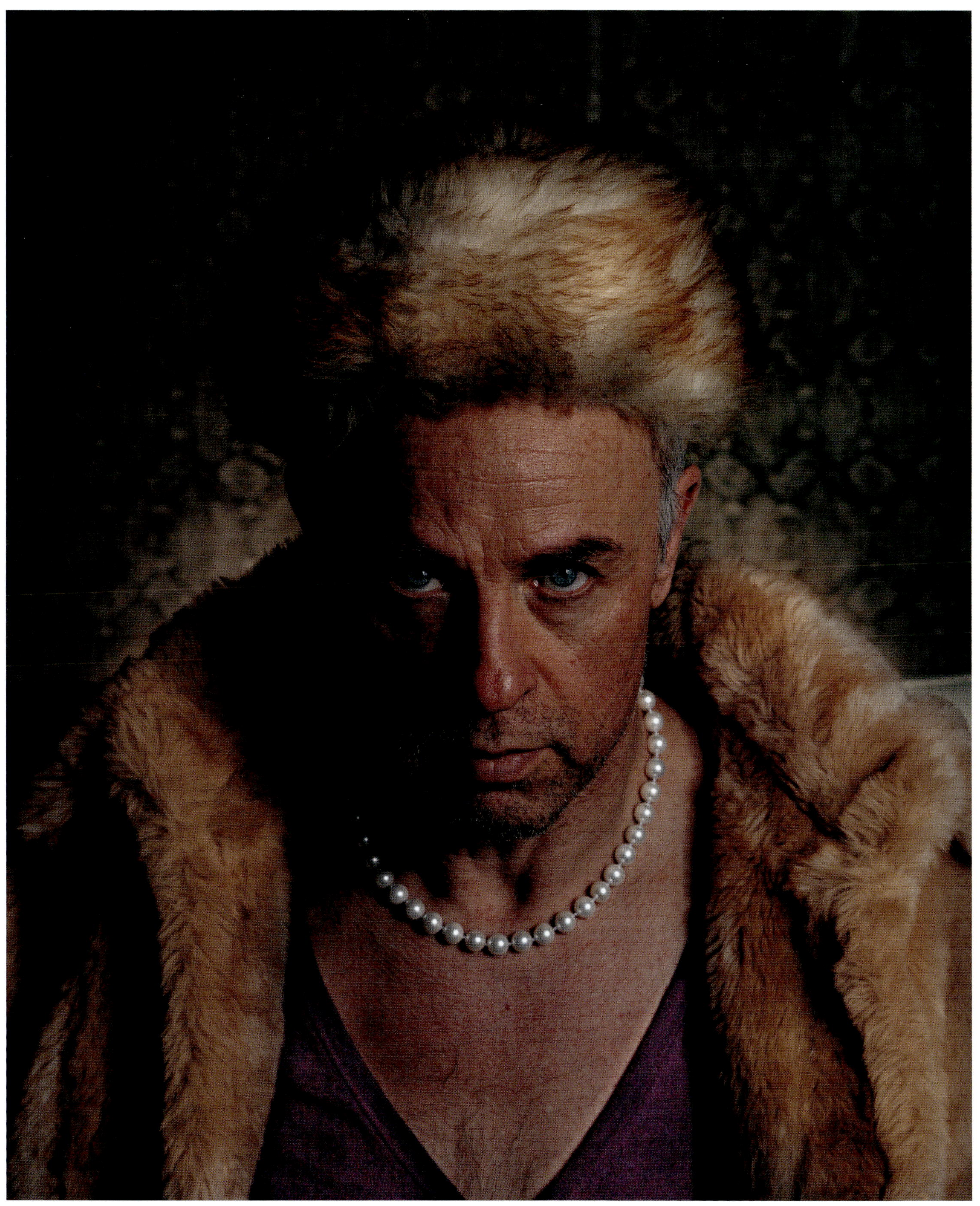

FUR HOOKER, 2020

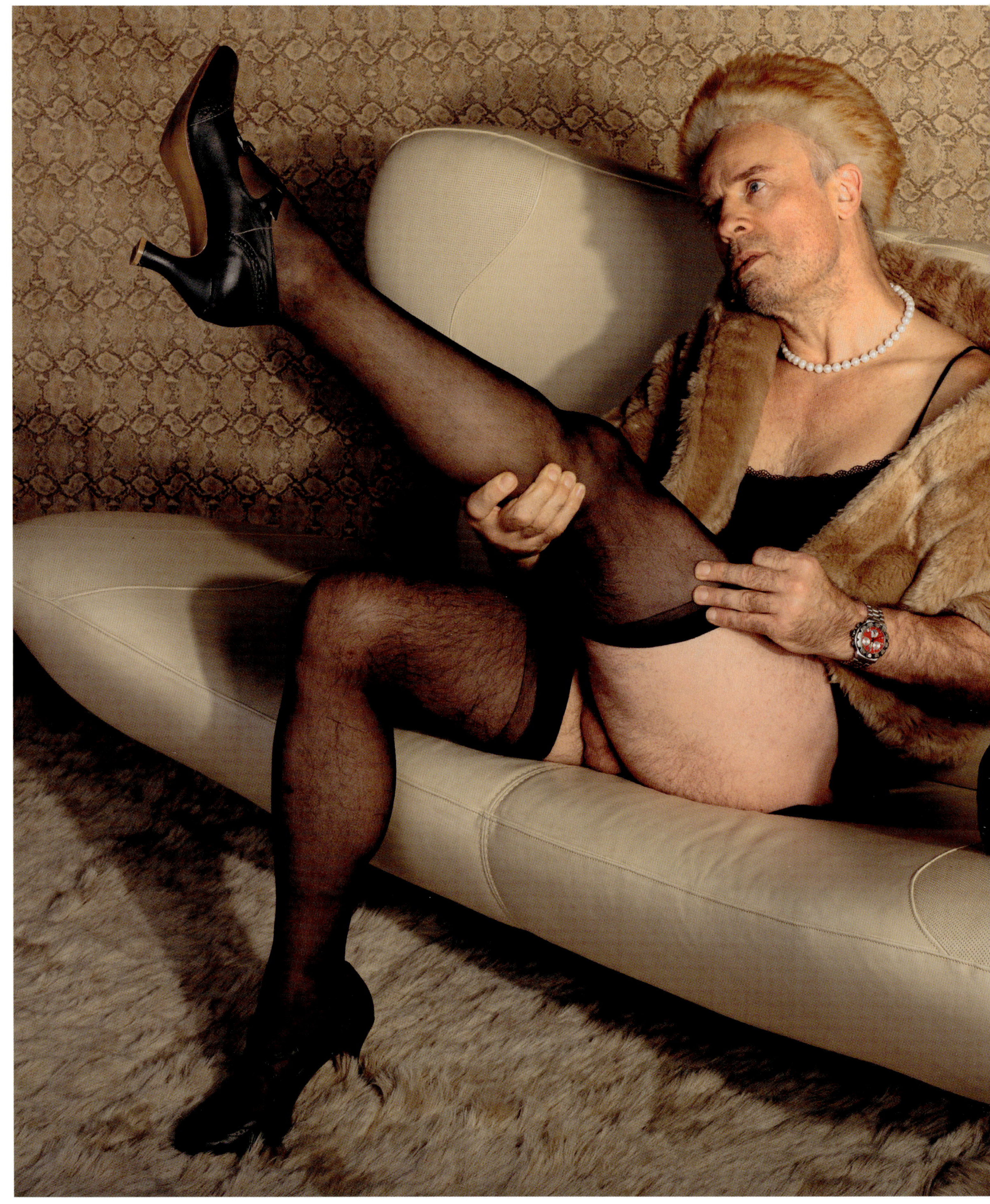

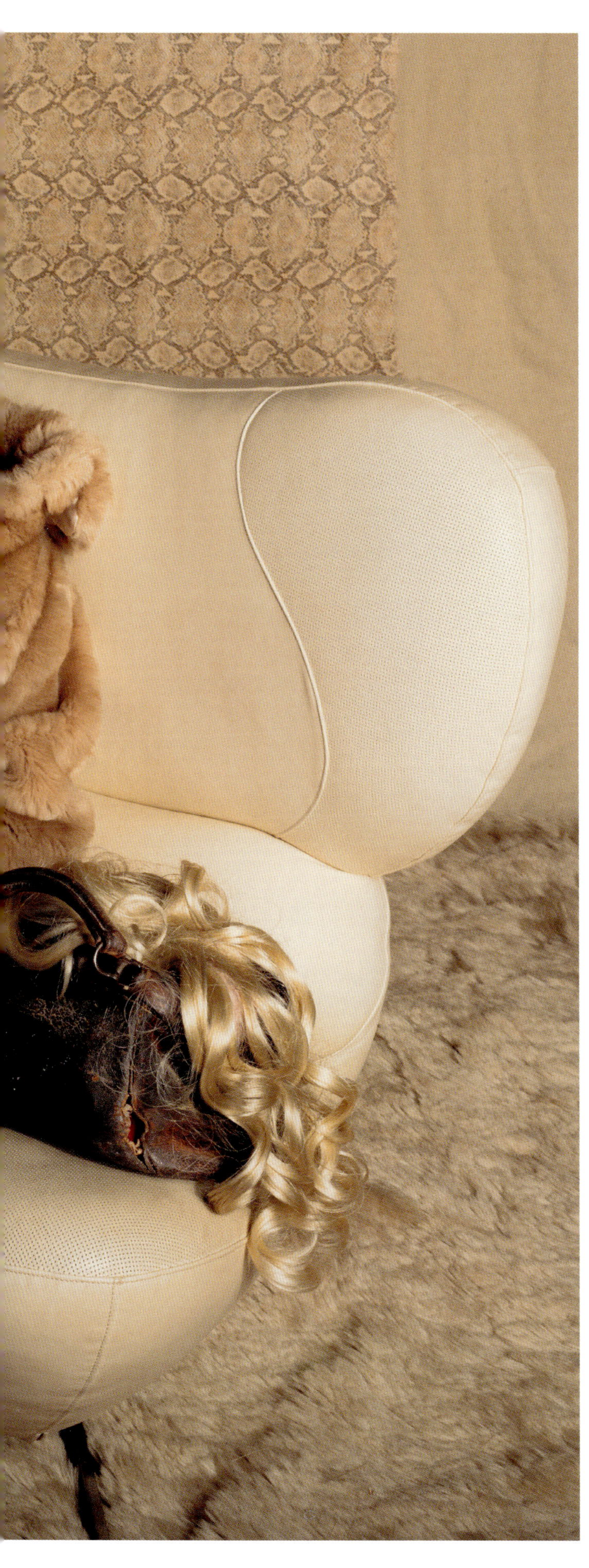

PORTRAIT BOURDIN, 2020

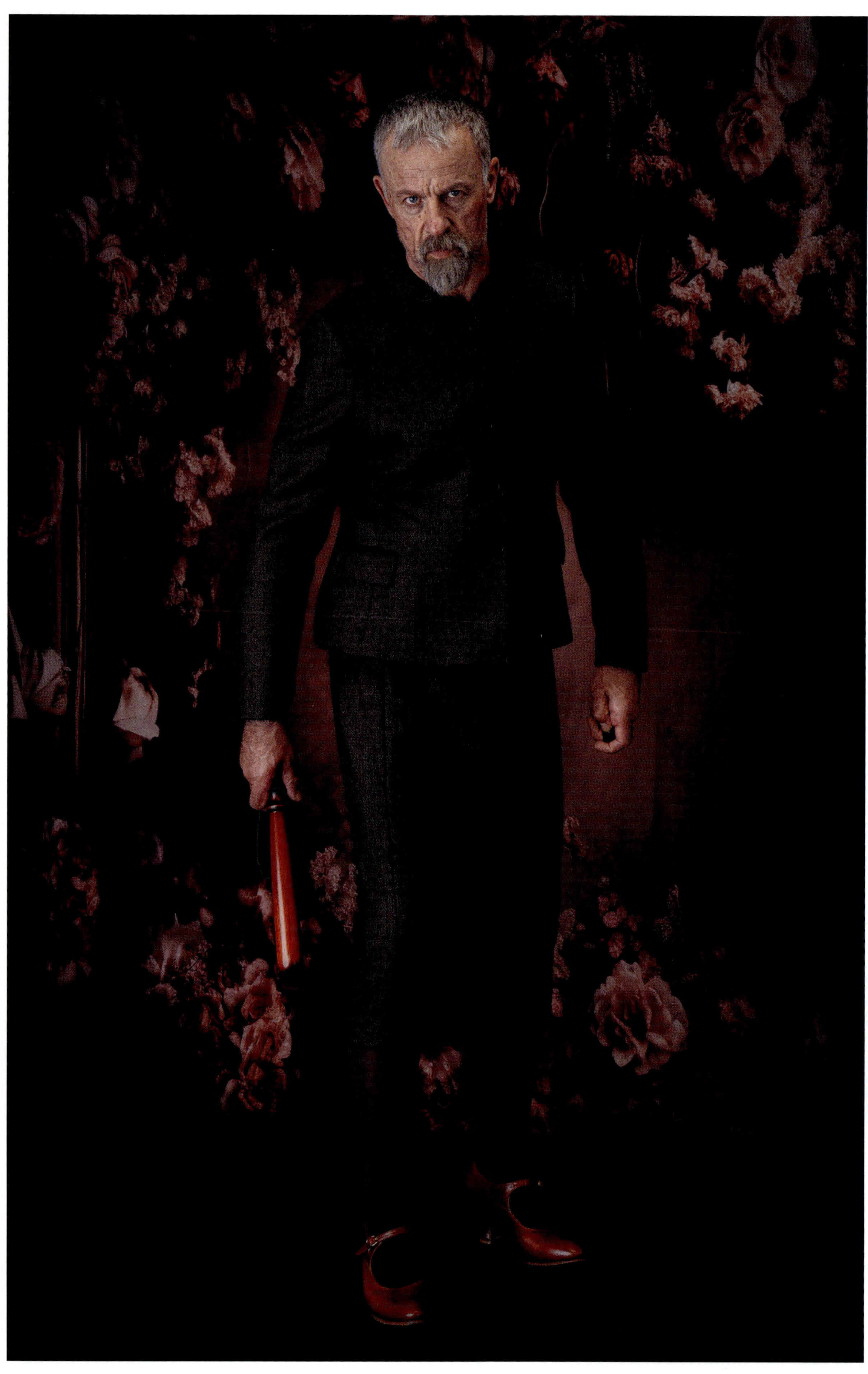

GUARDIAN, 2024

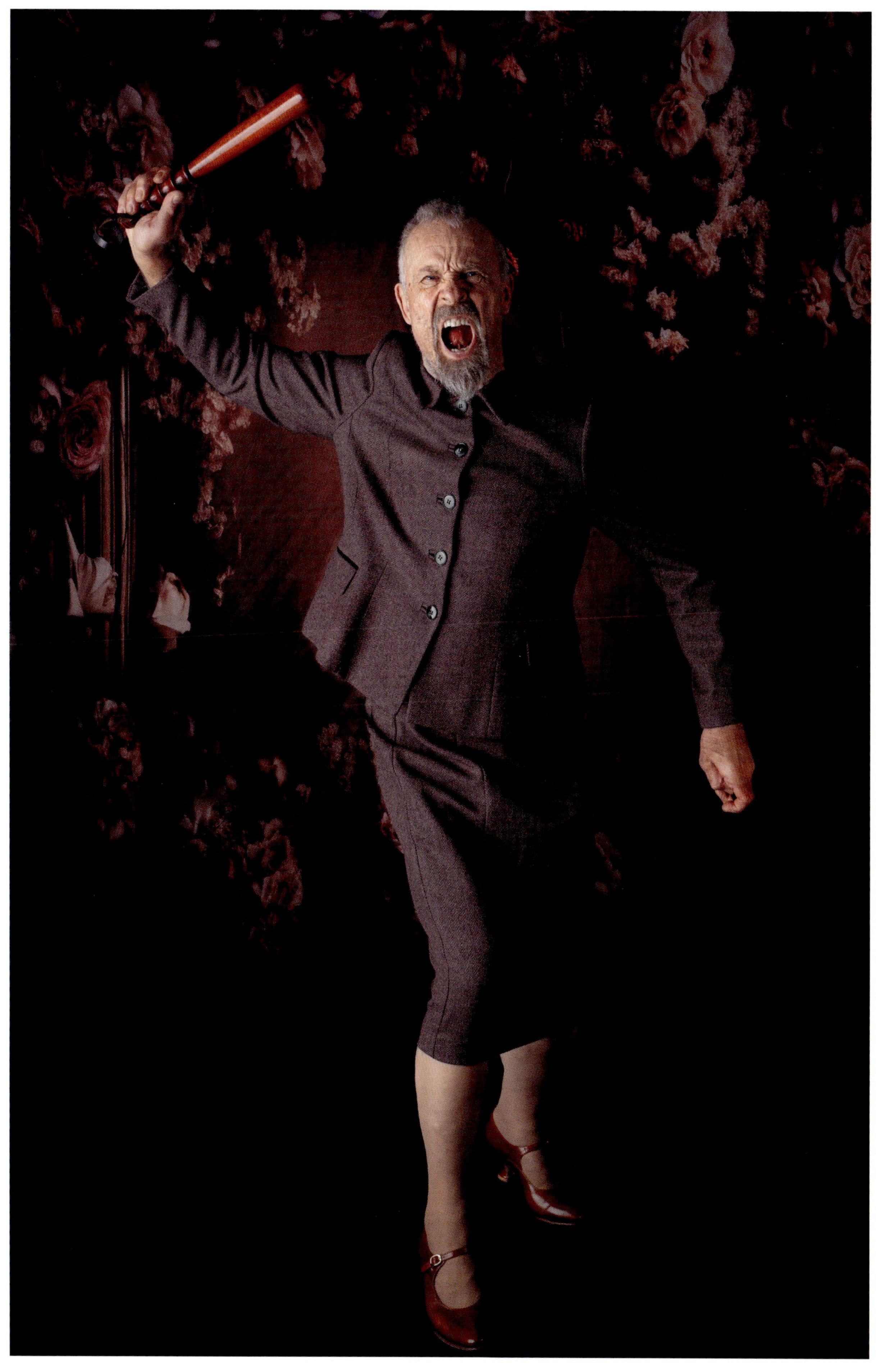

ROSE GARDEN GUARD,
2024

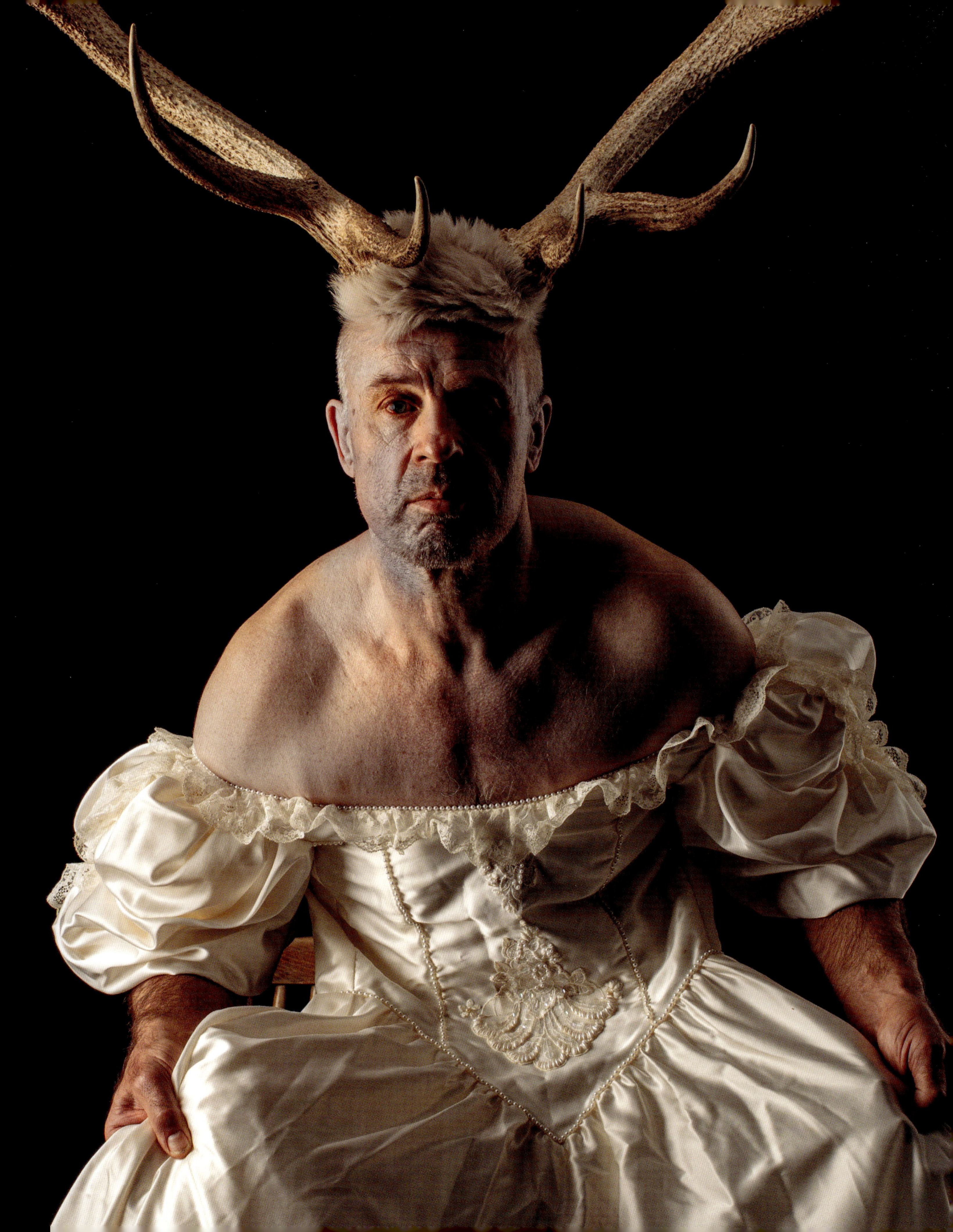

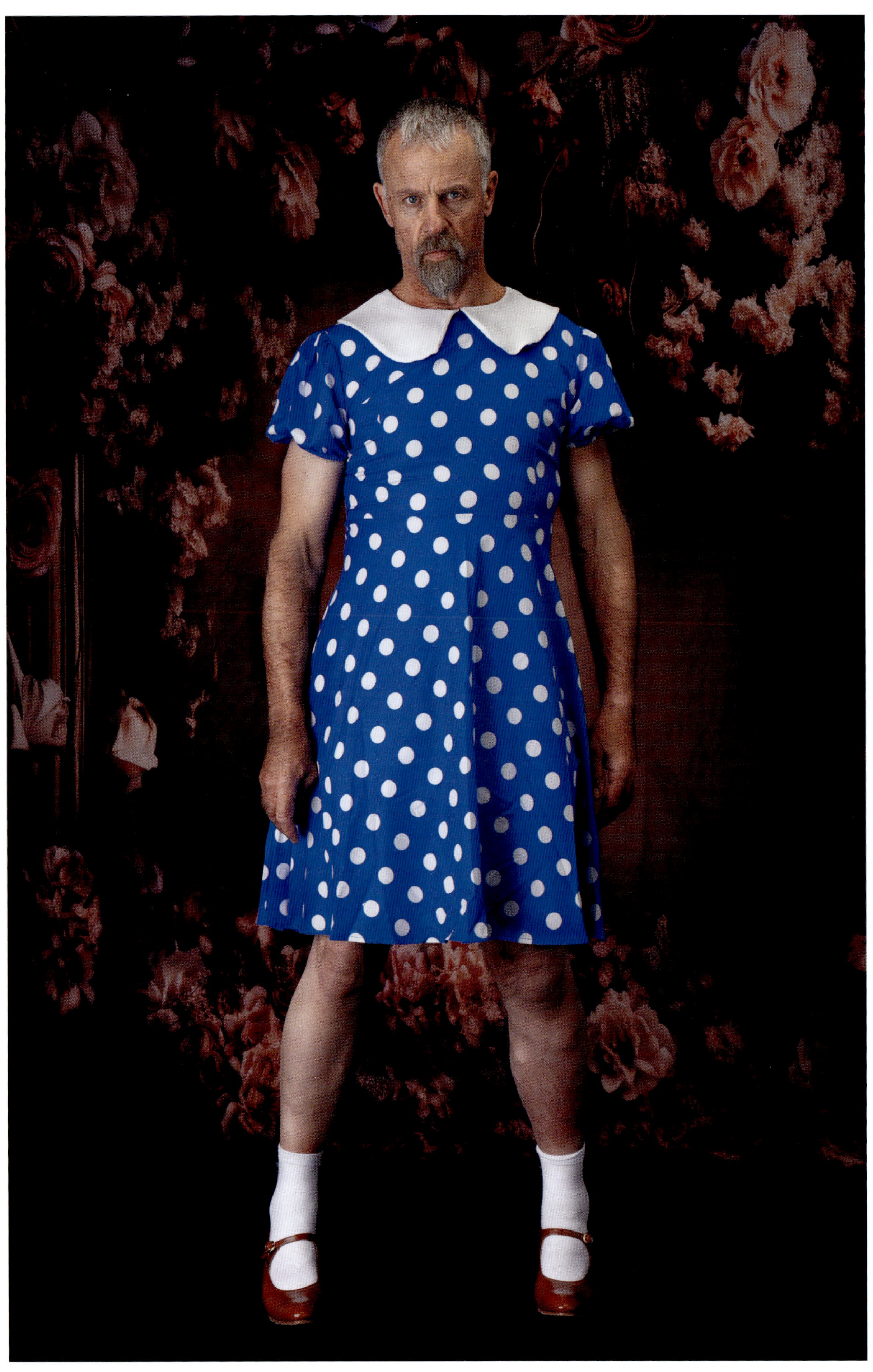

MINNIE, 2024

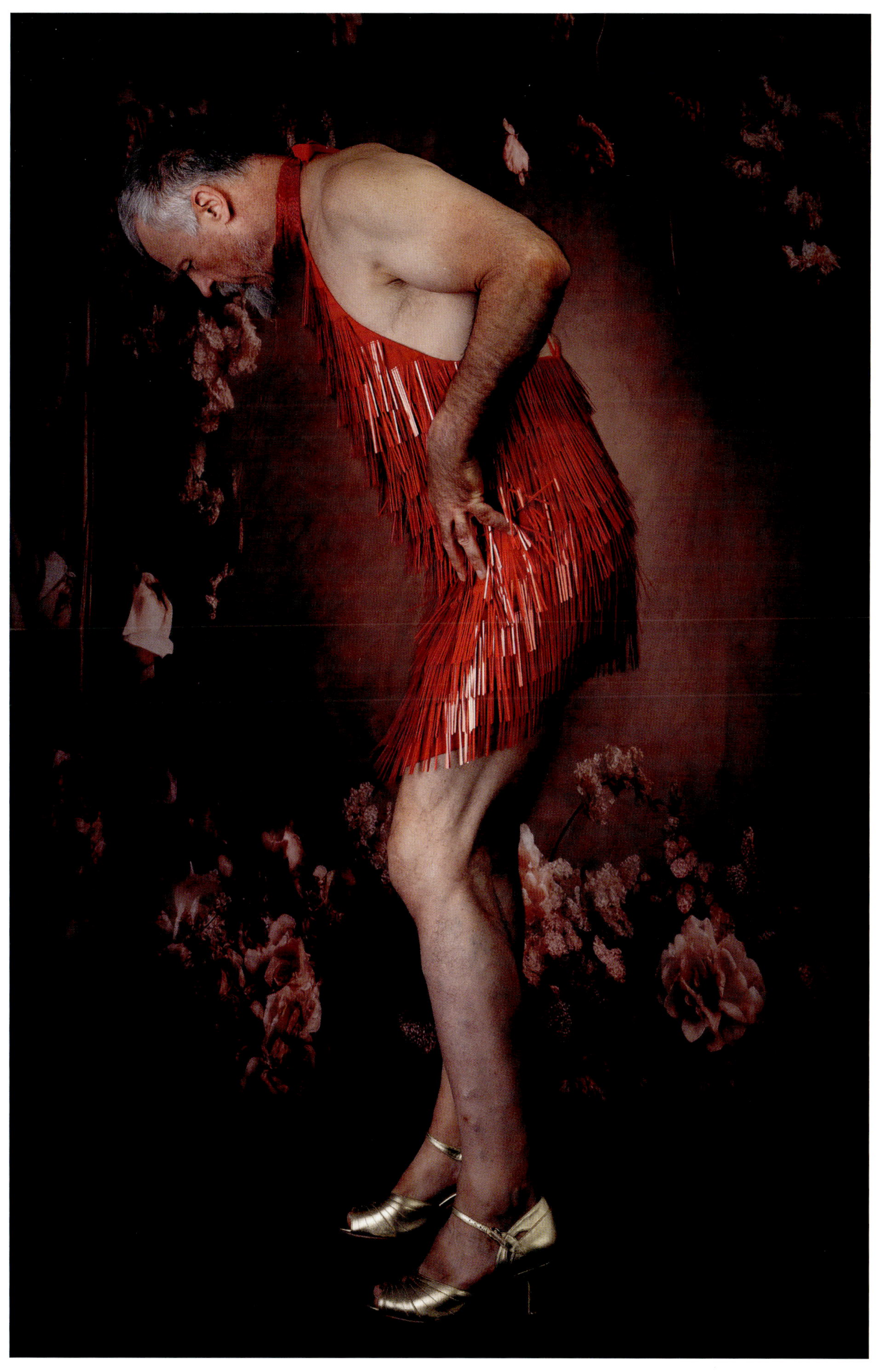

PARTY GIRL, 2024

191

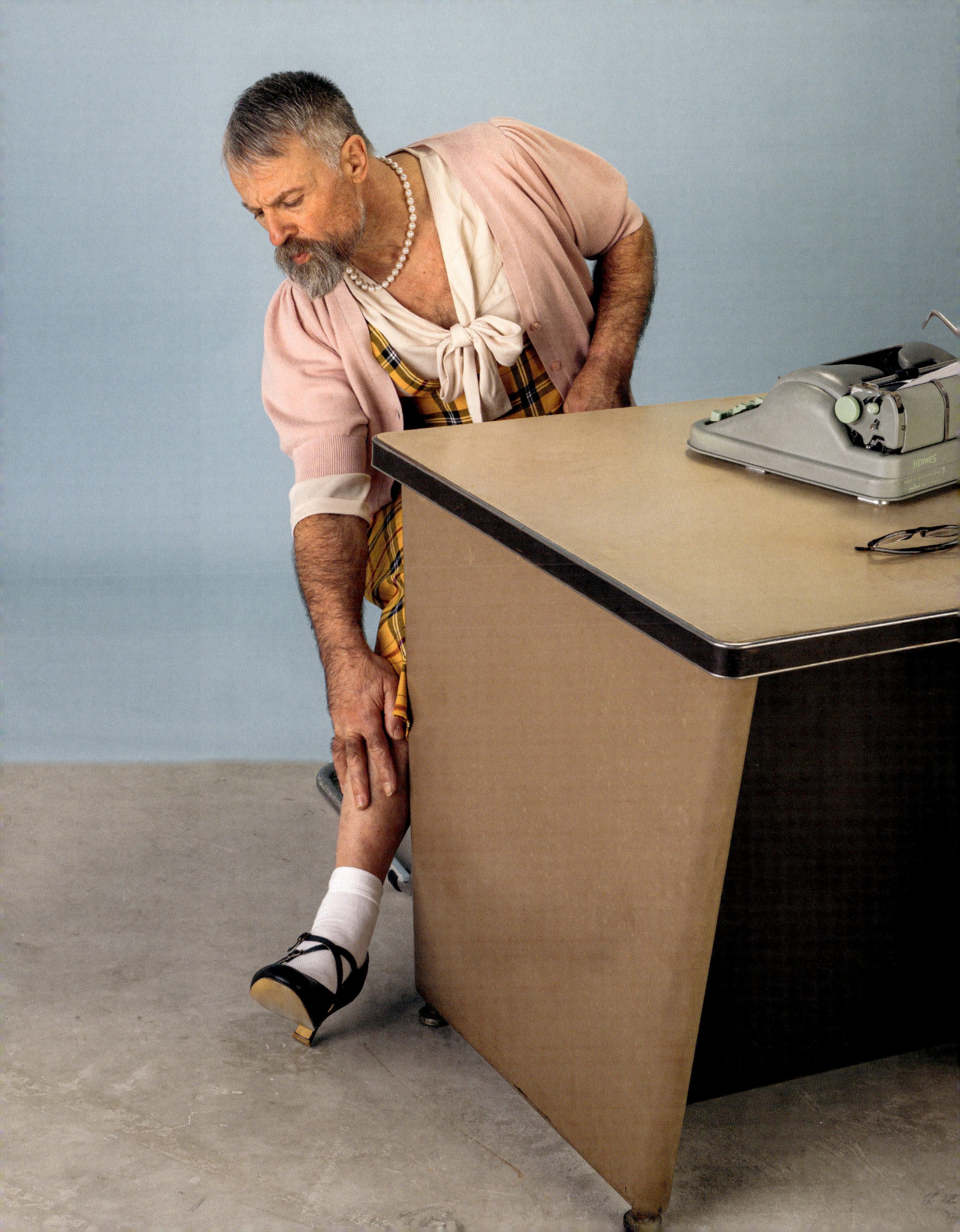

HERMES

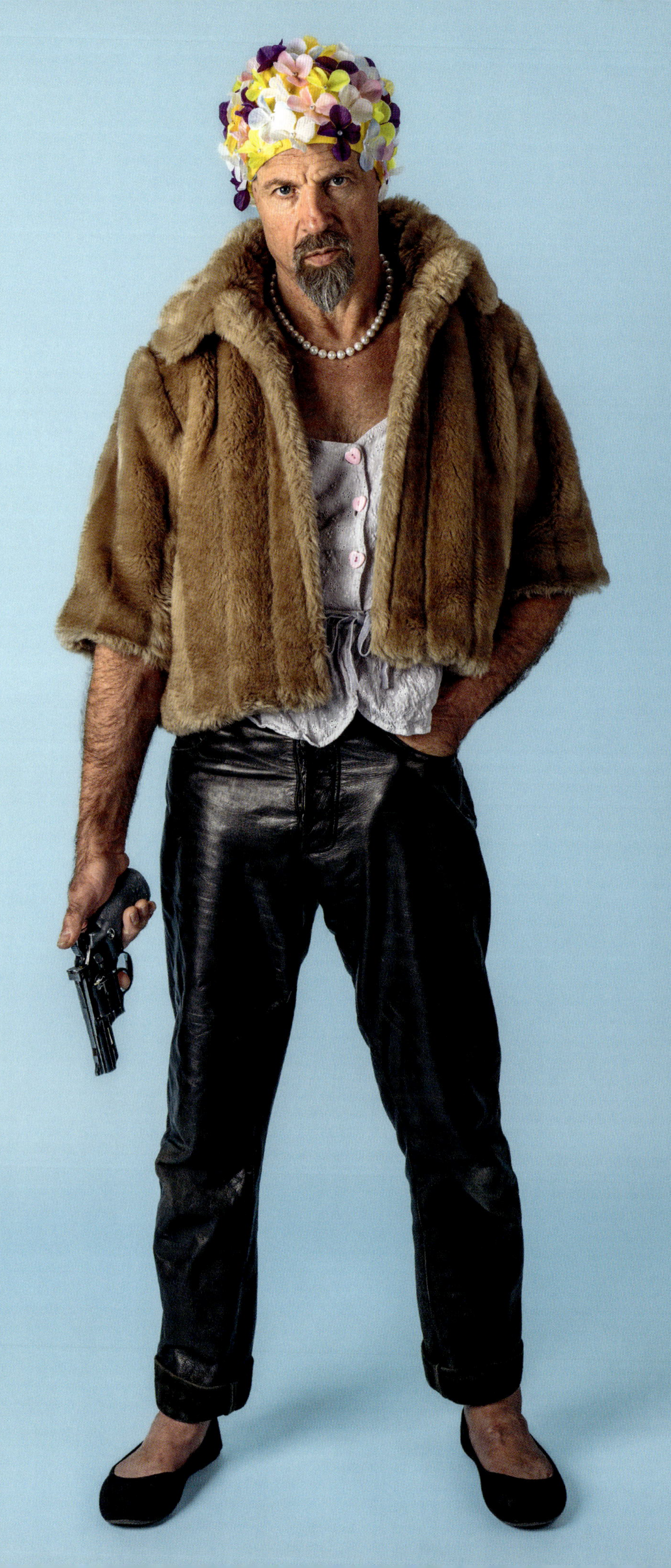

GANGSTA FAIRY, 2022

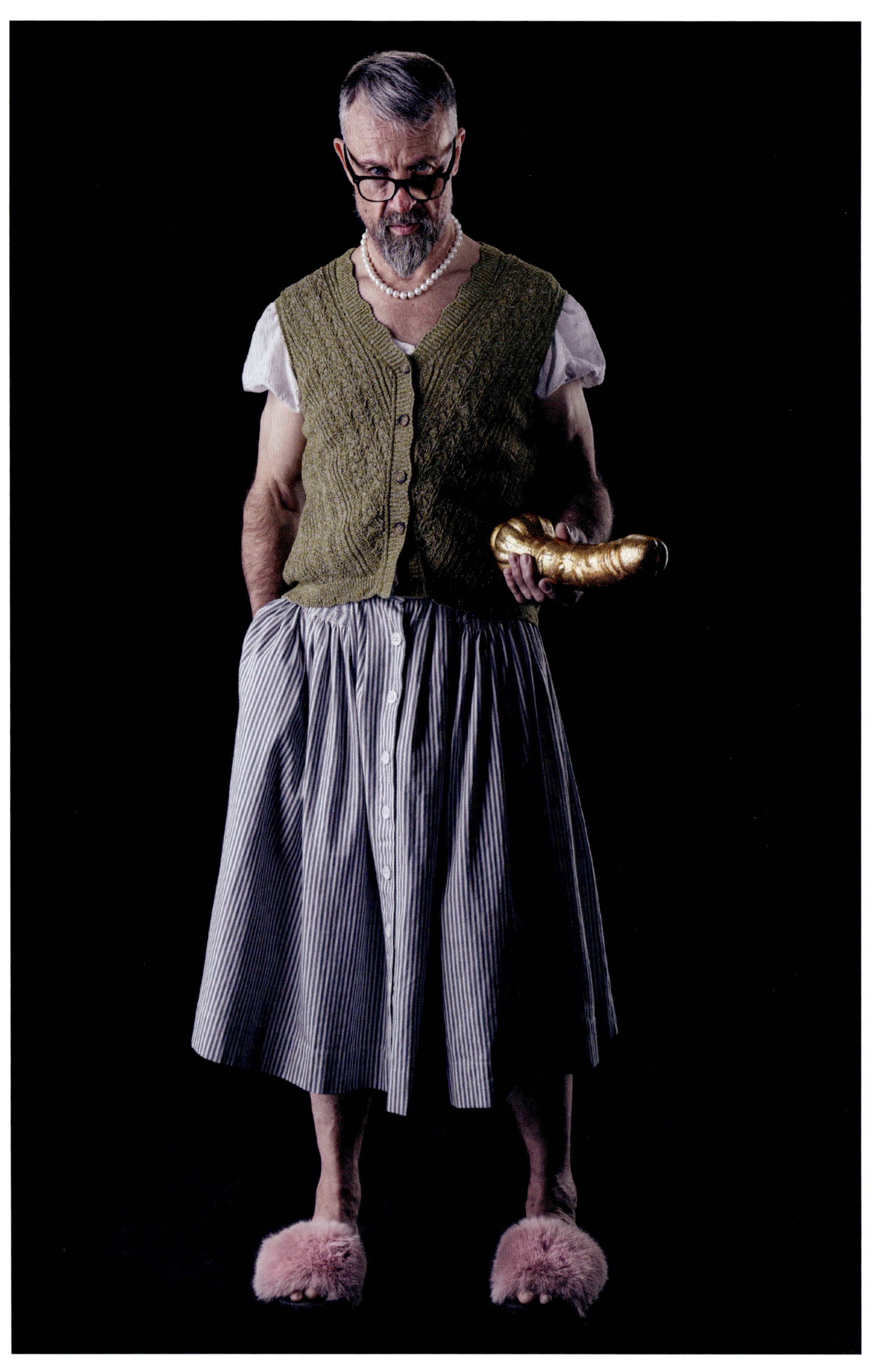

Left
PEDAGOGUE PERVERT,
2023

Opposite
BUSINESS BABE, 2020

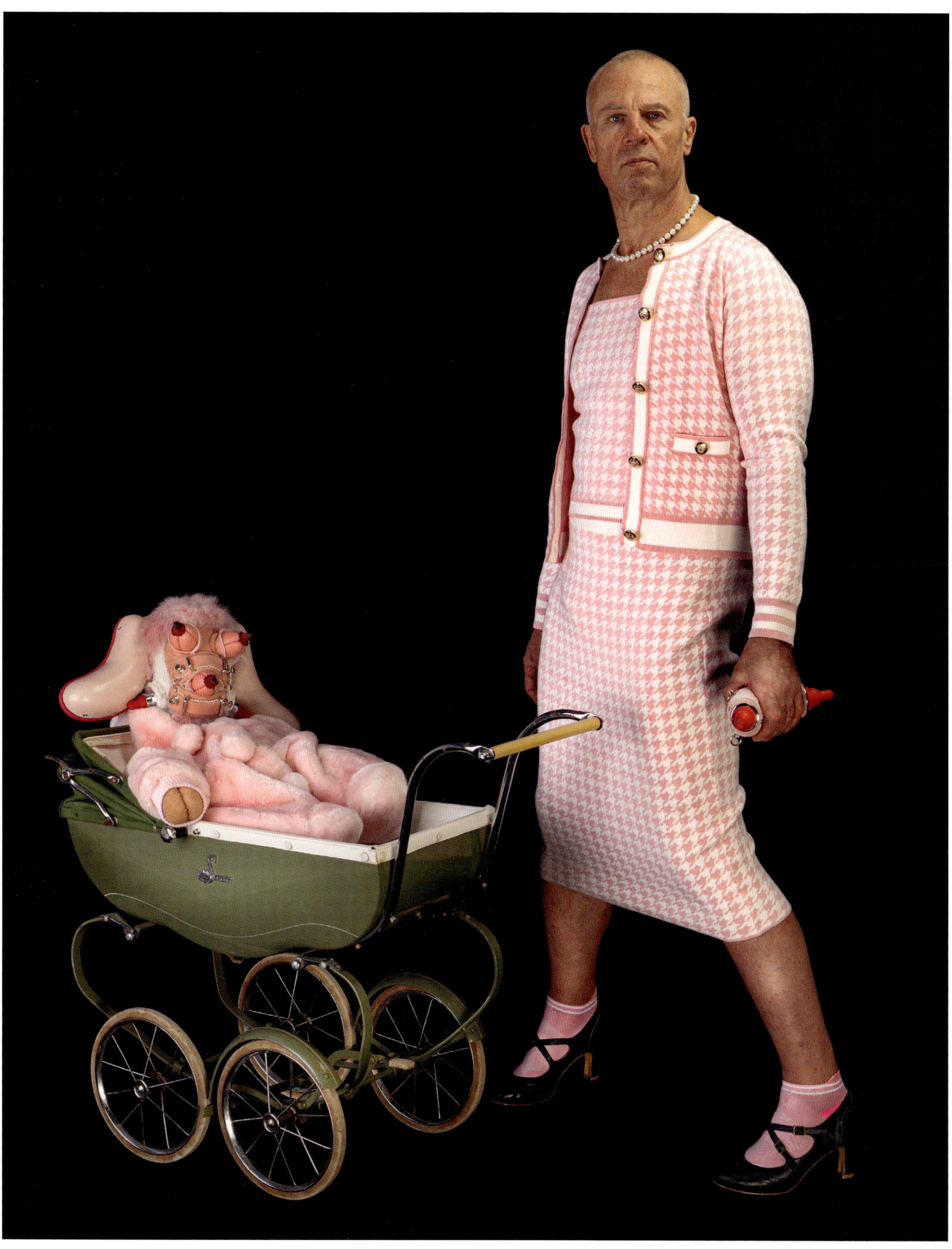

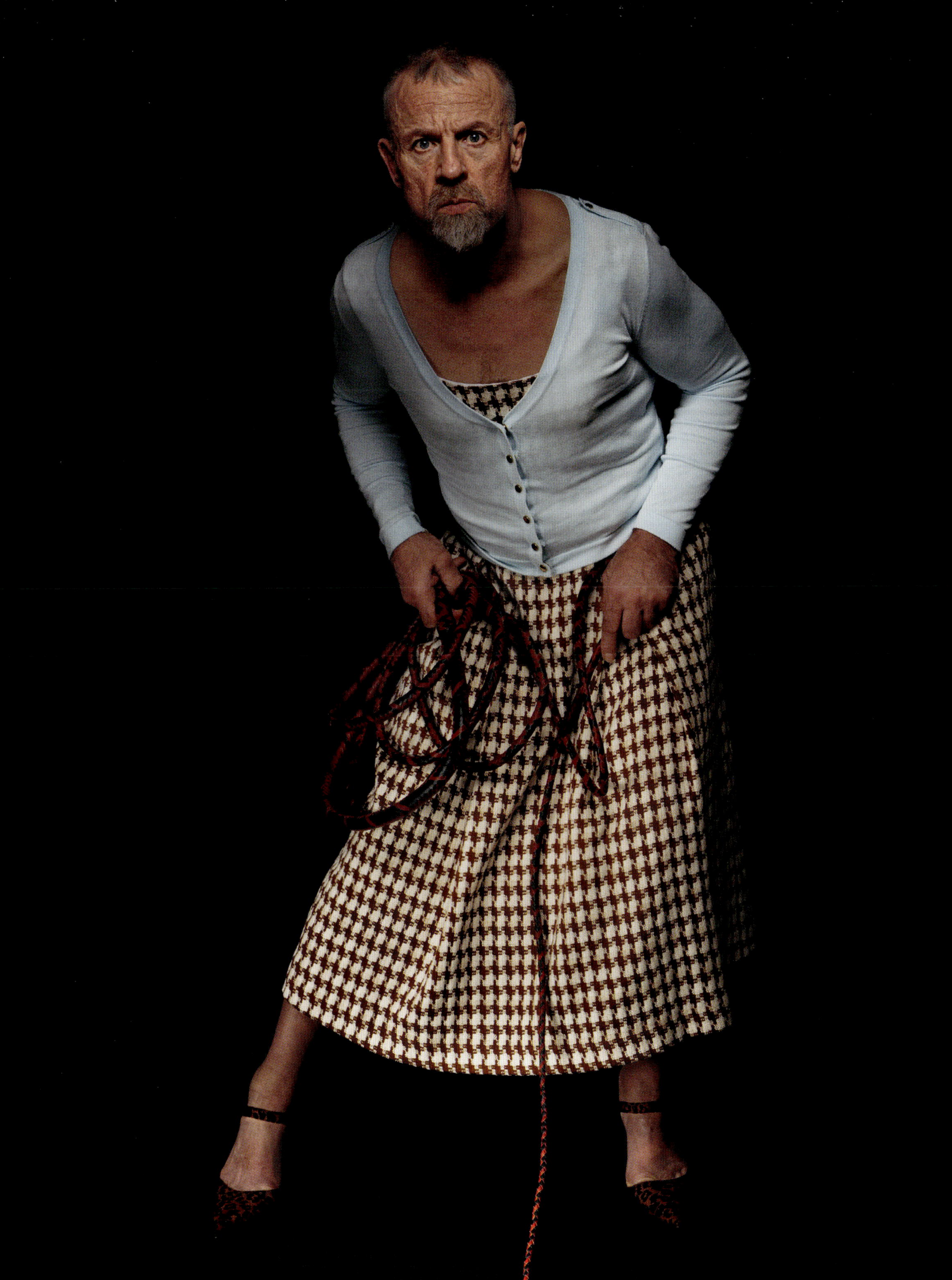

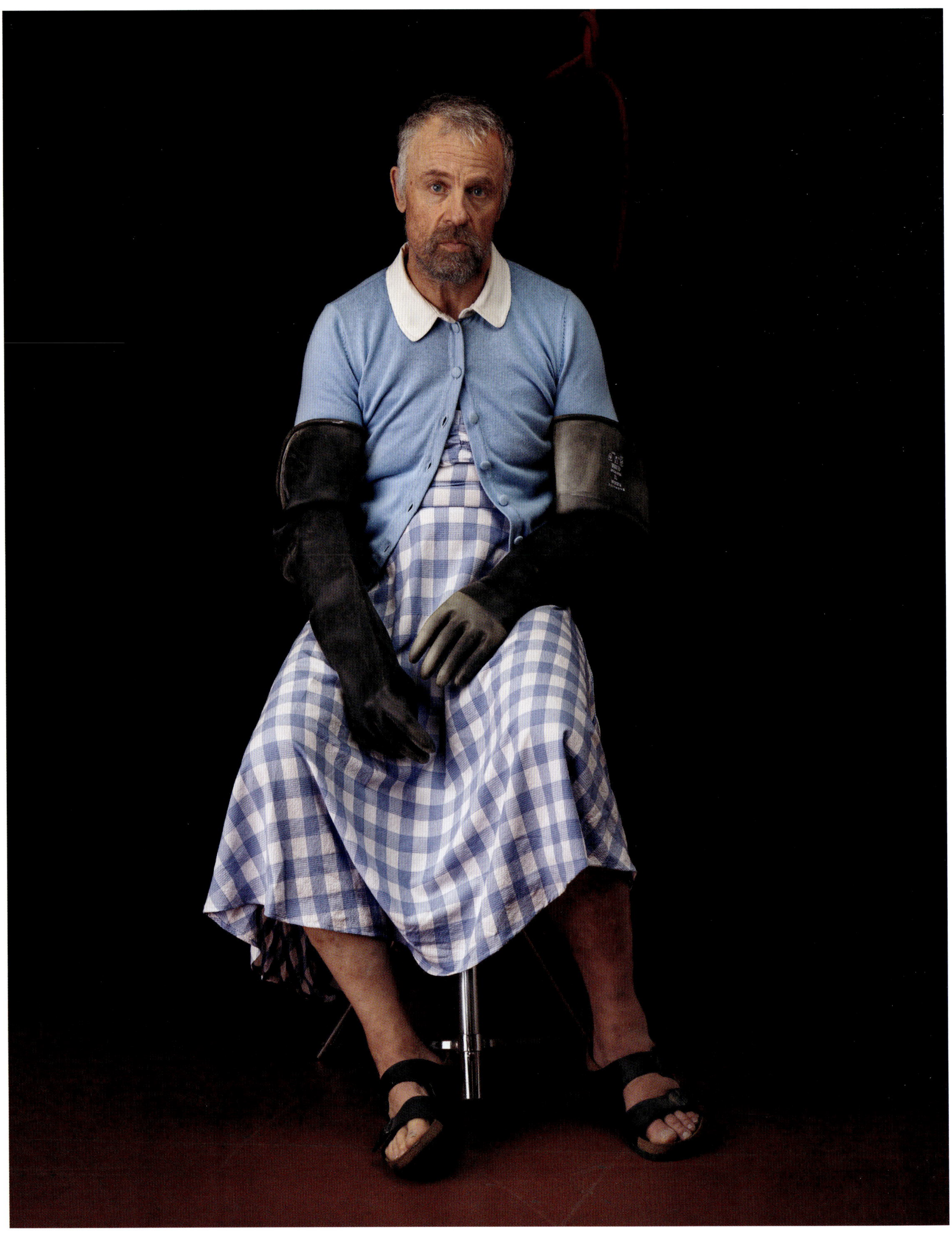

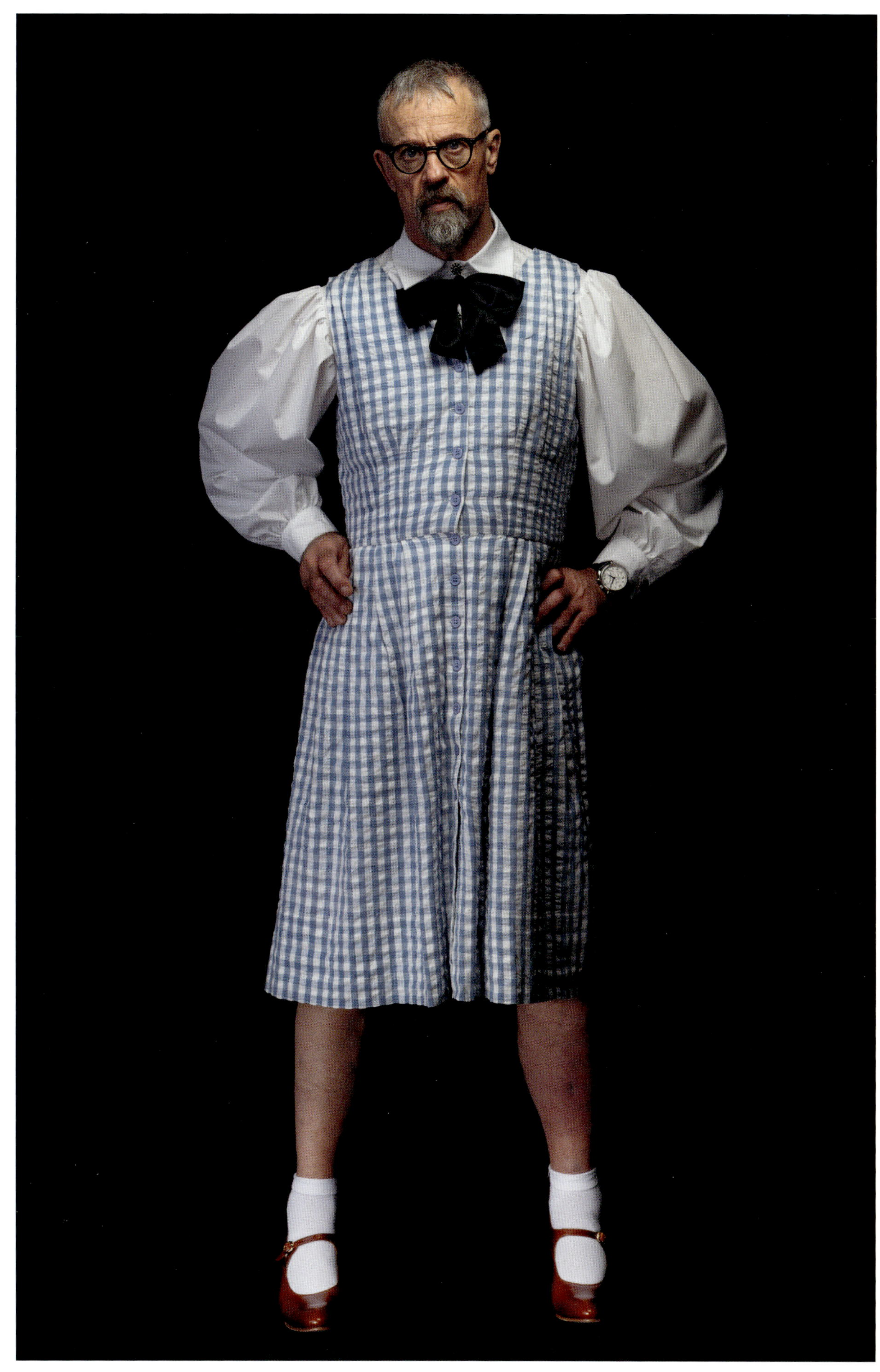

Opposite
TROUBLE WITH THE DRAINS, 2019

Right
WANNA BE IN MY TICK-TOCK?, 2024

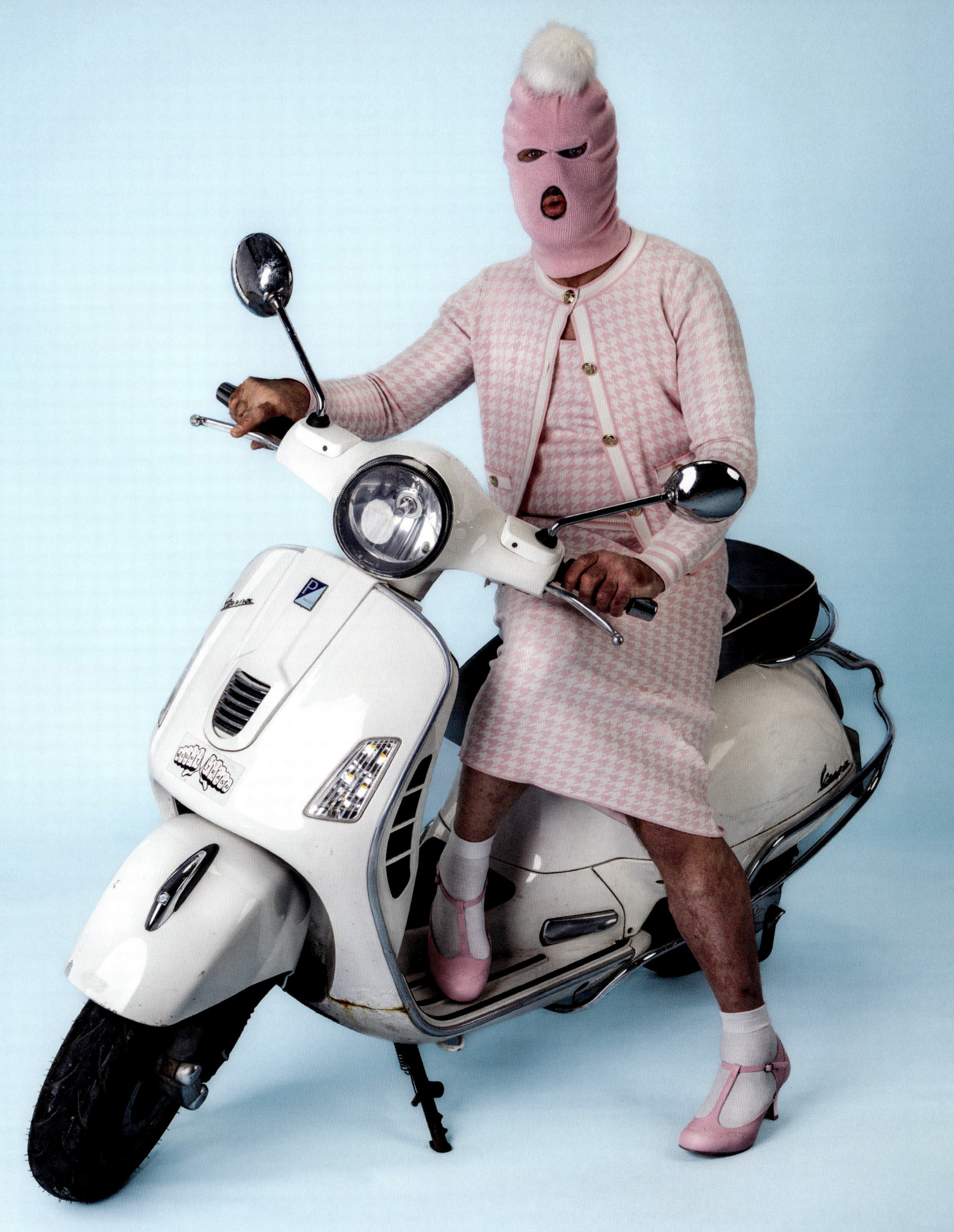

EXHIBITIONS

SOLO EXHIBITIONS

2022

"Mal-content", Cable Depot, London.
Curated by Iavor Lobomirov

2021

"Absorption", Cross Lane Projects, Kendal,
Cumbria. Curated by Vanya Balogh

2019

"No Mirror", open studio for Lakes Alive,
Cross Lane Projects, Kendal, Cumbria

2017

"A Return to Old Certainties", Lobomirov/
Angus Hughes Gallery, London

2012

"Saturnia", Brussels, Belgium

2010

"To Have and to Hold", The Wapping
Project, London

1999

"Lost Cherries", Electrum Gallery, London

1996

"The Story So Far", 2–4 Southgate Road,
London Liberty, London

1993

Liberty, London
Southbank Centre, London

1992

Southbank Centre, London

1988

Cobra and Bellamy Jewellery, London

SELECTED GROUP EXHIBITIONS

2024

"Drop it", BCMA Gallery, Berlin, Germany.
Curated by Pascal Rousson and Cedric
Christie
"Drop it", Finch Gallery, London. Curated by
Pascal Rousson and Cedric Christie
"AS SELF AS SELF AS". Curated by David
Cooper, Asylum Studios, Suffolk

2023

"The Gift", Cross Lane Projects: Vestry St,
London. Curated by Vanya Balogh

"No Comment", OHSH Gallery, London.
Curated by David Cooper

2022

"Zero Gravity", Sussex. Curated by Sara Pager
"A Modern Capricho", Cross Lane Projects:
Vestry St, London. Curated by Rebecca
Scott and Simon Marsh
"Dirty Pictures", St Leonards-on-Sea.
Curated by Jude Montague

2021

Cross Lane Projects at London Art Fair:
Edit 2021, 20–31 January

2020

"Made With..." Curated by John Stephens,
Cross Lane Projects, Kendal, Cumbria
"Imperfectum". Curated by Vanya Balogh,
Cello Factory, Waterloo, London
"Amsterdam, my blue heaven, my red hell",
London. Curated by Vanya Balogh and
Mario Varas Sanchez

2019

"Miniscule 2". Curated by Vanya Balogh,
Cross Lane Projects, Kendal, Cumbria
"Flugblätter". Curated by Birgit Jensen,
Maebashi, Japan
"Flugblätter". Curated by Birgit Jensen,
Cross Lane Projects, Kendal, Cumbria
"Miniscule Venice". Curated by Vanya
Balogh, Venice, Italy
"Collecting Craft", Charmian Adams
Collection, Holburne Museum, Bath,
England
"Empire II". Curated by Vanya Balogh,
Venice, Italy
"Flugblätter". Curated by Birgit Jensen,
Schloss Plüschow Mecklenburgisches
Künstlerhaus, Upahl, Germany
"Flugblätter". Curated by Birgit Jensen and
Mark Patsfall, Clay Street Press, Cincinnati, US
EMPIRE II in Oaxaca, in Association with
the Museo de Arte Contemporáneo de
Oaxaca, Mexico

2018

"Violence silence", Cello Factory, Waterloo,
London
"Empire II", Tallin Art week, Haus Gallery,
Tallin, Estonia
"Chinese open-embracing the underdog",
Q Park, Soho, London

"Protocol", Q-Park, Cavendish Square,
London
Cross Lane Projects – Lakes Alive open
weekend, Kendal
"Empire II", Paris FIAC
"Flugblätter". Curated by Birgit Jensen,
Dordrecht, Holland

2017

"EMPIRE II", Venice Biennale, Italy
"EMPIRE II" at Brussels Art Week in
association with Frédéric de Goldschmidt
and John Adams, Brussels, Belgium
"EMPIRE II", White Post, in association
with Corridor Gallery, London
"EMPIRE II", in association with Provincial
Project Space, Kendal, Cumbria
"EMPIRE II", SPEKTRUM | art science
community, Berlin, Germany
"EMPIRE II", in association with Unit 1
Gallery | Workshop, London
"Crash", Q Park, Cavendish Square, London
"Fit the Slit", Lido, Venice, Italy
"Flugblätter". Curated by Birgit Jensen,
Loitz, Germany
"Chinese Open", Q Park, Newport Place,
London

2016

"Big Deal No. 7", Q Park, Leicester Square,
London
"The Kick Inside", Florentin 45 Art Space, Tel
Aviv, Israel
"Drive Thru", Q Park, Cavendish Square,
London
"Curious Bodies", Clerkenwell, London
"Nirvana. Les étranges formes du plaisir",
Gewerbemuseum Winterthur,
Switzerland

2015

"Big Deal No. 666", London
"Fall of the Rebel Angels", Venice 56th
Biennale, Italy
"Silent Movies", Q Park, Cavendish Square,
London
"Fit the Slit", Lido, Venice, Italy
"Chinese open", Q Park, Soho, London
"Cutlog", Paris, France
"Office Sessions", Beak St. London
"Sunday in the Park with Ed", Display
Gallery, London
"Bazaar", Lubomirov/Hughes Gallery,
London

2014

"Nirvana. Les étranges formes du plaisir", mudac (Musée de design et d'arts appliqués contemporains), Lausanne, Switzerland

"Unlikely Union", National Rugby Stadium Gallery, Twickenham, London

"We could not agree", Q Park, Cavendish Square, London

"Subito Carceris", 100 Years Gallery, London

"Fete worse than Death", Red Gallery, London

"Big Deal, "Marvelous Mix-ups!", Loud & Western Building, London

"Day Job", Samia Gallery, London

"Sexism", Samia Gallery, London

"Chinese Open", Q Park, Chinatown, London

2013

"What's going on?", The Usher Gallery, Lincoln Museum

"Vitis Vinifera", London

"The Aesthetics of Ruin", Ozone Galerie, Belgrade, Serbia

"Final Cut", Wapping Project, London

"Beyond Precious", Galerie 19 Paul Fort, Paris

"Unlikely Union", Stringer Gallery, London

"Big Deal No. 5", Q Park, London

Directional Forces "Colony 55", Venice, Italy

"Degrading", Studio 1.1 Gallery, London

"Chinese Open", Q Park, Chinatown, London

"Summer Show", CUL DE SAC Gallery, London

2012

"On the Road", CUL DE SAC Gallery, London

"Big Deal No. 4" (virtual)

"Vroom", NW8, London

"End of the World", Papier Fabrik, Graz, Austria

"Cabinet Exhibition", Islington Arts Factory, London

"Baculum", Anderson Pertwee & Gold Gallery, London

"Plate", Alice Herrick Gallery, London

"Queen of Diamonds", Electrum Gallery, London

"Widely Absurd", The Hundred Years Gallery, London

"Target the Heart", Electrum Gallery, London

"Exterritorial", Studio 1.4 Vienna, Austria.

2011

"Sexy 100", London

"Big Deal No. 3", Camden Collective, London

2010

"Miniscule", Oblong Gallery, London

Electrum Gallery, London

"The Moment of Privacy Has Passed", The Usher Gallery, Lincoln

2009

"V22 Presents: The Sculpture Show", The Biscuit Factory, London

2000

"Sofa", Lesley Craze Gallery, Chicago

"La Renaissance Du Bijou", part 2, Galerie Piltzer, Paris

1999

"La Renaissance Du Bijou", part 1, Galerie Piltzer, Paris

1998

"Very British", Galerie D'or, Oldenburg, Germany

1995

The Blue Gallery, Walton Street, London

1994

"Artists & Artisans of De Beauvoir", Bowater House, London

Victoria & Albert Museum, London

1993

"Today's Jewels, From Paper to Platinum", Lesley Craze Gallery, London

1992

The Economist Building, London

1991

Smiths Gallery, London

COLLECTIONS

Charmian Adams Collection

Swiss National Museum, Switzerland

The Collection, Lincoln Museum, 2013–15

PUBLICATIONS

Vanya Balogh, *Fall of the Rebel Angels*, University of Bath in conjunction with Venice Biennale, 2015

Vanya Balogh, *Empire II*, Victor Hotz Publishing, published in conjunction with Venice Biennale, 2017

Beatriz Chadour-Sampson and Janice Hosegood, *Barbara Cartlidge and Electrum Gallery: A Passion for Jewellery*, Arnoldsche Art Publishers, 2016

Beatriz Chadour-Sampson, *Rings of the 20th and 21st Centuries: The Alice and Louis Koch Collection*, Arnoldsche Art Publishers, 2019

Marco Costantini, *Nirvana, les étranges formes du plaisir*, Infolio, 2014

Cross Lane Projects, *Absorption*, Cross Lane Publishing, 2021

Cross Lane Projects, *Made With*, Cross Lane Publishing, 2020

Cross Lane Projects, *Miniscule II*, Cross Lane Publishing, 2019

Imogen Eveson and Jules Wright, *Wapping Project on Paper*, Black Dog Publishing, 2014

Derren Gilhooley and Simon Costin, *Unclasped: Contemporary British Jewellery*, Black Dog Publishing Ltd., 2001

Mike Healey, ed., *Quotes – Inspirational Quotations | Creative Responses*, Strawlitter Productions, 2019

Birgit Jensen, *Flugblätter | Flying Letters: Ein Projekt von Jensen*, Clay Street Press, Cincinnati, US, 2019

Lisa Z. Morgan, *Design Behind Desire*, Farameh Media, 2011

Michael Petry, *MirrorMirror: The Reflective Surface in Contemporary Art*, Thames & Hudson, 2024

Louise Salter and Nigel Daly, "Desire", *Laboratory Arts Collective Magazine*, 2015

BIOGRAPHIES

MARK WOODS

Mark Woods (b 1961, Surrey) is a British artist with a background in contemporary jewellery production and in boat-building. He produces highly elaborate artefacts that blur the boundaries between jewellery, fine art, fetish objects and items from a cabinet of curiosities.

He co-directs Cross Lane Projects with his wife, Rebecca Scott, in Kendal, Cumbria, and the couple have also opened a salon space in Shoreditch, London: Cross Lane Projects: Vestry Street. His recent solo exhibitions include "Mal-content" at the Cable Depot, London; "Absorption" at Cross Lane Projects; and "No Mirror" at the open studio for Lakes Alive, Cross Lane Projects, 2019. Woods' recent group exhibitions include "Zero Gravity" in Sussex, 2022; "A Modern Capricho", Cross Lane Projects: Vestry Street, London, 2022; "Dirty Pictures", St Leonards-on-Sea, 2022; Cross Lane Projects at London Art Fair, 2021; "Made With…", Cross Lane Projects, 2020; "Imperfectum", Cello Factory, Waterloo, London, 2020.

PAUL CAREY-KENT

Paul Carey-Kent is a freelance art writer and curator, and a member of the International Association of Art Critics. He is Visual Fine Arts Editor of *Seisma Magazine* and writes regularly for *Art Monthly*, *STATE* and the Canadian magazine *Border Crossings*. He has a weekly column online for *FAD Magazine* and a monthly interview online for *Artlyst*. He is active on Instagram and co-runs a project on early works by famous artists. Paul has curated more than 50 exhibitions: examples from 2024 include "Say It With Flowers", White Conduit Projects, Islington; "St Leonards Meets the World", Electro Studios, St Leonards; and "Seismic: Art Meets Science", GIANT, Bournemouth. He recently published *The Book of Ladders* in Mexico, in collaboration with Mexico-based sculptor Adeline de Monseignat.

PETER SUCHIN

Peter Suchin is an artist, critic and curator. He has published over 350 essays and reviews in a wide range of books and publications, including *Art & Design*, *Art Monthly*, *Frieze*, *The Guardian*, *Here and Now*, *Variant* and *Mute*. His catalogue essays include writings for the London galleries Annely Juda, Standpoint, Danielle Arnaud and Domo Baal. Among Suchin's solo displays of paintings and installations are "Memory Objects", ETSU, Johnson City, US, 2002; "Compendiums and Palimpsests", T1+2 Artspace, London, 2003; "A Critical Contagion in the Quiet of the Night", &Model, Leeds, 2014; and "Optimum State", Gaunston Studios, London, 2024. Group shows include "Lost in Translation", HAU, Athens, Greece, 2004; "Merz=", Bregenz Kunstverein, Austria, 2006; "Climbing the Underside of the Ladder", Durden & Ray, Los Angeles, US, 2022; and "Forces of the Small", Filet, London, 2023.

MICHAEL PETRY

Michael Petry is an artist and author, and is Director of the Museum of Contemporary Art (MOCA), London. Petry co-founded the Museum of Installation, was Guest Curator at the Kunstakademiet, Oslo, and was Curator of the Royal Academy Schools Gallery. Petry co-authored *Installation Art* (1994) and *Installation in the New Millennium* (2003), and authored *Abstract Eroticism* (1996), *A Thing of Beauty Is…* (1997) and *The Trouble with Michael* (a monograph of his practice, 2001). His book *Hidden Histories: 20th Century Male Same Sex Lovers in the Visual Arts* (2004) accompanied the exhibition "Hidden Histories" that he curated for The New Art Gallery Walsall. *Golden Rain* (2008) accompanied his installation for the "On the Edge" exhibition for Stavanger 2008, European Capital of Culture. Petry's book *The Art of Not Making: The New Artist Artisan Relationship* was published in 2011. More recent books accompanying exhibitions include *Nature Morte: Contemporary Artists Reinvigorate the Still-Life Tradition* (2013) and *The Word is ART* (2018) for Thames & Hudson. Petry's latest book *In League With Devils* (2023), which includes a foreword by Stephen Fry, was published for his solo show of the same name at the Dadian Gallery, Henry Luce III Centre for the Arts and Religion, Washington DC; The Parsonage, Searsport, Maine; and Vane, Newcastle. Petry's new book *MirrorMirror: The Reflective Surface in Contemporary Art*, published by Thames & Hudson (2024 UK/2025 US), includes Woods' work.

ACKNOWLEDGEMENTS

IMAGE CREDITS

Mark Woods would like to thank the many advisors, supporters and friends who have been supporting his practice over the years.

Special thanks to: Rebecca Scott and Clayton for their ongoing support. Michael Petry, Paul Carey-Kent and Peter Suchin for their contributions to this book. The team at Cross Lane Projects and Vestry Street: Emma Benyon and Rebecca Larkin. Vanya Balogh, Cedric Christie and Chris (Spag) Mayson; Black Dog Press for their support for this project and professional advice.

Marcel Duchamp 20, Étant donnés, 1946–66 (mixed media assemblage), English: Given: 1. The Waterfall, 2. The Illuminating Gas, French: Étant donnés: 1° la chute d'eau / 2° le gaz d'éclairage, Philadelphia Museum of Art / Gift of the Cassandra Foundation, 1969 / Bridgeman Images. © Association Marcel Duchamp / ADAGP, Paris and DACS, London 2025. Pierre Molinier 145 © Pierre Molinier, Adagp, Paris, 2024. Courtesy the artist and Mennour, Paris

Dennis Pedersen 112, 113, 116, 117, 120–121

Paul Tucker 8, 9, 18, 19, 21, 22–23, 28, 29, 32, 38, 39, 40–41, 42–43, 44, 45, 46–47, 50–51, 52, 53, 64, 65, 66–67, 70–71, 72, 73, 74, 75, 76–77, 79, 80, 81, 84–85, 86–87, 89, 90–91, 92, 93, 94, 95, 98–99, 100–101, 103, 104–105, 106, 109, 114, 115, 118–119, 122, 123, 125, 126–127, 128–129, 130, 131, 132, 133, 135, 136, 137, 138, 139

Mark Woods 6–7, 10–11, 12, 14, 15, 17, 31, 33, 34, 35, 37, 49, 54–55, 56, 57, 58, 59, 60, 61, 62, 69, 82–83, 96–97, 107, 141–144, 146–203

This book is published by Black Dog Press Limited, a company registered in England and Wales with company number 11182259. Black Dog Press is an imprint within the SJH Group. Copyright is owned by the SJH Group Limited. All rights reserved.

Black Dog Press
The Maple Building
39–51 Highgate Road
London NW5 1RT
United Kingdom

+44 (0)20 8371 4047
office@blackdogonline.com
www.blackdogonline.com

Creative direction and design by Anton Jacques
Editor: Miranda Harrison
Printed in Lithuania by Kopa

ISBN 978-1-912165-62-9

British Library Cataloguing in Publication data:
A CIP record for this book is available from the British Library.

black dog press